Stanley Rothman   **Charles Mosmann**

Computers and Society

THE TECHNOLOGY AND ITS SOCIAL IMPLICATIONS

Second Edition

SCIENCE RESEARCH ASSOCIATES, INC.
Chicago, Palo Alto, Toronto, Henley-on-Thames, Sydney, Paris, Stuttgart
A Subsidiary of IBM

Library of Congress Cataloging in Publication Data

Rothman, Stanley, 1927–
    Computers and society.

    Includes bibliographical references and index.
    1. Computers and civilization. I. Mosmann,
Charles John, 1929–   joint author. II. Title.
QA76.9.C66R67 1976   301.24'3   75-31622
ISBN 0–574–21055–5

Printed in the United States of America

Contents

iii

v
Contents

Acknowledgements

We wish to acknowledge the following for permission to reprint or adapt material:

Control Data Corporation, Minneapolis, Minn., for Figures 1-1, 3-4, 3-6, and 3-7.

Computerworld, Norton, Mass., for Figure 1-2.

Novosti Press Agency, Moscow, U.S.S.R., for Figure 1-3.

Reilly & Lee, Inc., for Figure 1-4.

Compix (UPI) for Figure 1-5. A United Press International photograph.

The *Los Angeles Free Press,* for Figure 1-6.

Brandon Communications, New York, N.Y., for the cartoon on p. 19.

Digital Equipment Corporation, Maynard, Mass., for Figure 1-7.

Data Management, Park Ridge, Ill., for Figure 1-8.

Science Research Associates, Inc., Chicago, Ill., for Figures 2-1, 3-1, and 5-1 from M. Bohl, *Information Processing* (1971); Figures 2-7 and 5-6 from *Computer Concepts Transparency Masters;* and Figure 4-6 from *Principles of Business Data Processing Transparency Masters.*

Keuffel & Esser Company, Morristown, N.J., for Figure 2-2.

A. S. Barnes & Company, Inc., Cranbury, N.J., for Figure 2-3.

Monroe, The Calculator Company, Orange, N.J., for Figures 2-4 and 2-6.

International Business Machines Corporation, Armonk, N.Y., for Figures 2-9, 2-12, 3-5, 3-8, 3-11, 3-12, 3-13, 3-14, 3-15, 6-3, 11-1, 11-2, 11-3, 11-4, 11-6, 20-3, and the cartoons by Charles Eames on pages 44, 64, 102, 129, and 254.

Datamation, for Figure 3-9. Reprinted with permission of Datamation © copyright, Technical Publishing Company, Barrington, Ill., 60010, 1970.

General Automation, for Figures 3-16 and 6-4.

Hewlett-Packard, Palo Alto, Ca., for Figures 3-17 and 6-1.

MITS, Inc., Albuquerque, N.M., for Figure 3-19.

Magnavox Research Laboratories, Torrance, Ca., for Figure 3-20.

Univac, a division of Sperry Rand Corporation, Blue Bell, Pa., for Figures 4-1, 4-4, 5-7, and 10-7.

Tektronix, Inc., Irvine, Ca., for Figure 4-2.

Digi-Log Systems, Inc., Willow Grove, Pa., for Figure 4-3.

Ira W. Cotton, Network Management Survey, U.S. Department of Commerce, for Figure 4-6.

TRW Systems, Inc., Redondo Beach, Ca., for Figures 5-10 and 15-1.

The Department of the Army, San Francisco District Corps of Engineers, for Figure 6-2.

G & C Merriam Co., Springfield, Mass., for Figure 7-1.

Patrick H. Winston, The Artificial Intelligence Laboratory, Cambridge, Mass., for Figures 7-2 and 7-3.

The Register, Santa Clara, Ca., for Figure 7-4.

Stanford Research Institute, Menlo Park, Ca., for Figure 7-6.

Stanford Research Institute, L. D. Erman, and Charles C. Tappert, for Figure 7-7.

IEEE Computer Society, Long Beach, Ca., for Figure 7-8. Copyright 1975 by The Institute of Electrical and Electronics Engineers, Inc. Reprinted by permission, from COMPUTER, May 1975.

The M.I.T. Press, Cambridge, Mass., for Figure 7-9.

Stewart Burgess of Computer Exchange Ltd., London, England, for the cartoon on p. 162.

John Gram, for Figure 8-3.

Jane Mosmann, for Figures 8-4, 9-2, 9-3, and 20-2.

EDUCOM, for Figure 9-1, from "The Times Information Bank on Campus" by John Rothman, in *Educom Bulletin,* Fall 1973.

The Burroughs Corporation, Detroit, Mich., for Figure 10-3.

Continental Airlines, for Figure 10-5.

Scientific American and Ralph Morse, for Figure 10-6, from the February 1975 issue of *Scientific American.*

The University of California at Irvine, for Figures 12-1 and 12-3.

Stanford University News Service, Stanford, Ca., for Figure 12-2.

Harper & Row, Inc., for Figure 12-4. Copyright 1975 by Wayne Holtzman. Reprinted by permission of Harper & Row Publishers, Inc.

The National Center for Higher Education Management Systems, Boulder, Colo., for Figure 12-5.

THE Journal and Jeanne I. Leone, for Figure 12-7.

The Washington Convention and Visitors Bureau, Washington, D.C., for Figure 13-1.

Computers and Automation for Figure 13-3 (reprinted with permission from "Computers and Automation" April 1963) and the cartoon on p. 304 reprinted with permission from "Computers and Automation" January 1970) copyright 1963, 1970 by and published by Berkeley Enterprises, Inc., 815 Washington St., Newtonville, Mass. 02160.

The Federal Bureau of Investigation, Washington, D.C., for Figure 14-1.

GTE Sylvania, Mountain View, Ca., for Figure 14-3. Reprinted by permission from General Telephone and Electronics.

Charles Saxon, for the series of cartoons beginning on p. 296.

The Newspaper Enterprise Association (NEA) for the cartoon on p. 317. Reprinted by permission of the Newspaper Enterprise Association (NEA).

Roger Marshutz, for the photograph on p. 319.

The Stoelting Company, Chicago, Ill., for Figure 17-1.

The *Los Angeles Times,* for Figures 17-3 and 17-4.

Prentice-Hall, Inc., Englewood Cliffs, N.J., for Figure 18-3.

Martin Secker & Warburg Limited, London, England, and Harper & Row Publishers, Inc., New York, New York, for the table "Methods of Prediction" from SCIENCE PROPHECY AND PREDICTION by Richard Lewinsohn. Copyright © 1961, by Harper & Row, Publishers, Inc. By permission of the publishers.

Harper & Row, Publishers, Inc., for the chart "The Past—Now—The Future" from PROPHETS OF THE FUTURE by Arthur C. Clarke. Copyright © 1962 by Arthur C. Clarke. Reprinted by permission of Harper & Row, Publishers, Inc.

The Twentieth Century Fund, New York, N.Y., for Figure 20-1, "GROSS NATIONAL PRODUCT: The Flow of Income and Expenditures in the United States, 1969 (in billions)." Source: *Survey of Current Business,* July 1970. © 1970 by The Twentieth Century Fund.

Material on pp. 308–09 from *The Making of a Counter Culture* by Theodore Roszak. Reprinted by permission of Doubleday & Company, Inc. Also reprinted by permission of Faber & Faber Ltd.

Preface to the Second Edition

In the years that have passed since this book was first conceived, computer technology and its public image have changed. In the 1960s, when the first edition was written, the computer appeared a major threat to human liberty, a symbol of all that was wrong with our technology-based society. Students were protesting what they saw to be the failures of our society; computer centers were attacked, even bombed, as part of this protest. The computer was seen by major writers to be the center of the threat to privacy and an important weapon in the abuse of political power.

Many of the most disturbing events of the past decade have at least demonstrated that we do not need a computer to threaten privacy or to abuse power. The issues of secret dossiers, misuse of presidential authority, struggles between Congress and the Administration, massive unemployment,

illegal campaign funds, inflation—all assumed such significance in the press and in our daily lives that the computer was no longer needed as a symbol of what *might* happen.

In all the plots and counterplots, attacks, and cover-ups associated with the name Watergate, the computer played absolutely no role whatsoever: not because it wasn't possible but because it wasn't necessary. All of the power of computer-based analysis and modelling and information manipulation neither helped nor hindered the economic crises of the early 1970s. The large-scale unemployment of 1974 and 1975 had nothing to do with automation, and concerns about how we would use our leisure seemed somehow premature.

Still, the computer is real and its potential effects on our lives remain as great as ever. The computer places tremendous amounts of information in the hands of anyone with the money and desire (and intelligence) to use it. The threat to privacy and the realities of computer fraud and larceny still exist. But so do the positive effects. Computers may have played no role in Watergate, but computer-based files made it possible for investigators and prosecutors to sift through the mammoth amounts of contradictory evidence. Computers may not tell us how to cure inflation or recession, but they help economists examine the evidence as they attempt to find a solution.

The technology itself continues to change. We now have minicomputers and microcomputers of astoundingly little cost and great power. Progress has been made in the field of artificial intelligence. New applications in many diverse fields have appeared and have proved themselves economically effective.

The basic structure of this edition remains the same as the first, working its way from the technology through applications, to social impact and the future. A new chapter has been added on artificial intelligence. Descriptions of applications have been expanded, too. Students, we discover, are more interested in how computers will affect their own futures, their jobs and educations, and their credit transactions than in more abstract considerations.

When the first edition was written, there were few courses that dealt with computers and society. Now there are hundreds of schools in the United States and elsewhere that offer such courses. It is now accepted that computer literacy, like music appreciation, is a legitimate and even a necessary part of a person's education. We persist in our judgment that this appreciation can be gained without having programmed a computer. However, since the text has come to be used by students of computer science as well as the general student body, we have added more technical depth.

As in the first edition, we are in debt to many who have commented on the drafts and to the many teachers who have used the text and offered ideas for its improvement. In particular, we wish to express our gratitude to those who read and criticized an earlier draft of this second edition: Sharon Sickle, Susan Finch, Carl Grame, Daniel O'Donnell, Denbeigh Starkey, William Lane, Martin Greenberger, Berry Bateman, Don Mann, Doug Haden, and Eric Weiss.

Preface to the First Edition

To write a textbook implies that there is something to teach. The social implication of computers is not a discipline. It has neither algebra nor body of controlled experimental evidence. There has been a great deal said on the subject, which in itself is data. Congress has investigated, the press have viewed with alarm, and social scientists have forecast doom. Professionals in the computer industry have, with few exceptions, ignored the subject; the few who have given it their attention have tended to view it as a technical problem to be solved by more refined engineering techniques. But what is the subject and how is its data to be organized?

Any text which falls between traditional academic disciplines is likely to be seen as something of an anomaly. This book starts out in the guise of a text on technology and, halfway through, adopts the methods and data of a social science. It seems incontrovertible to the authors that this is the only way it is possible to present the subject at all. A course on the social consequences of computers in which students are given no technical facts about computers is bound to leave them with little they can use. A course that teaches the technology but not the social impact is of no value to the majority of students who will have no professional contact with computers. Thus we are left with the need for a course that presents the basic facts of the technology and then constructs an analysis of the social issues on this technological foundation. This is what this book aims to do.

Who should teach this course? The authors hope that many interested teachers will try it. The computer or mathematics teacher may find the latter sections harder to teach than the earlier

3

ones; the social scientist may find the reverse to be the case. But we live in a world where it is essential that we all bridge this gap.

What department should offer it? This makes little difference, except in the matter of student expectations. No matter what the course is called or how it is described, many students will expect engineering from engineers and sociology from sociologists, facts from scientists and opinions from humanists. In some institutions, departments are emerging where this course fits naturally—departments dealing with the many interdisciplinary problems the world seems to face today. A good name being used for one of these departments is "social ecology." This book may perhaps be most fairly judged as a text in social ecology because it deals with the ways in which man's technology and social institutions interact.

What institutional resources are required? This is emphatically not a programming text and no computer is required for the students' use. However, if there is a computer nearby, it would be of value to have the students visit it, watch how it is used, and talk with the people who run it. The references and suggested ancillary readings assume at least a minimal technical library with the leading computer periodicals and some major books on computing. If the college library cannot supply these resources, the teacher should consider finding some way of making them available before the course begins. Our best hope is that some of the students will be curious, contrary, belligerent, or skeptical enough to go to the library to find the weapons to refute statements with which they take issue.

In writing a book about a subject where much of the data is of questionable objectivity, it is hard to be totally confident of one's lack of bias. The authors have lived and worked with computers

for many years and can hardly be expected to view the computer and its institutions as unquestionably evil. On the other hand, they have lived in the world, too, and know that no technology, accepted uncritically, is necessarily an unquestionable good. Part I of the book attempts to survey the ground that will be covered and to exhibit the point of view and the method the authors plan to use.

Discussion of the subject requires, as we suggested above, a basic minimum knowledge of what a computer is, what it does, and what it will some day be able to do. Part II provides the student with facts about the computer with which he can cut through some of the distortions that swell popular computer literature and which he can use to form his own opinions on how computers can best be used as tools of human progress.

Part III attempts to exhibit the ways in which technology affects human affairs. A range of computer applications is described, first presented in a value-free form and then analyzed in terms of social and ethical issues.

Part IV deals with the ways in which technology can be controlled for man to reap its benefits without suffering the threatened curse of unplanned and uncontrolled technological progress. Finally, Part V talks about the future and the student's possible post-college world.

A textbook, rather than inundating a student with facts and opinions, should give him some examples to work, questions for research, or some way of testing his newly acquired knowledge. In any area, but particularly in one so new and subject to such radical change, the goal must be to teach the student how to arrive at his own judgments about questions not yet evident, unasked in his text or by his teacher. Thus the examples will ask the student to think about new computer applications, to seek precedents in non-computer systems, to develop techniques for dealing with new questions, or to predict the influence of systems on their users or subjects (which in itself will involve him in understanding how fundamental human characteristics are involved with automated systems).

The genesis and motivation for this book is a serious concern for a situation that, in the face of uninformed citizens and a naive press, may turn in either of two unacceptable directions. A powerful threat to freedom may go uncontrolled; a major tool of progress may be needlessly suppressed. The only means of steering a path between these alternative dangers is by having, in voting booths as well as in government, in readers as well as in writers of the news, men and women who understand technical, political, and moral issues.

The basic conflict is between the ideal of individual freedom and the pressing need for planning, order, and security. The public debate over computers in society will be dominated by this issue. The debate is bound to fall under the shadow of unethical practices, unfair computer uses, and disastrous failures that may occur. Just as labor legislation and civil rights legislation had to wait until the subconscious response to unfairness became conscious to a group large enough to be heard, so the average response of awe and suspicion toward computers will have to crystallize before laws are enacted. When this crystallization takes place, will it be to thwart the useful as well as the dangerous? Will it stop the petty infractions and allow the grand conspiracies to act freely? We do not know the answers to these questions; we do know that no good can come from a situation in which everyone relies on someone else to understand the problem.

The authors wish to make a general acknowledgement to all of those who read and commented on the text, providing advice and counsel that we did not always have the good sense to take. Janet Rothman and Jane Mosmann contributed in numberless ways, not least by their patience. Janet also contributed significantly to the research by gathering materials from obscure sources. Miss Christine Sorrentino patiently typed and retyped. Special thanks are due to Paul Armer, the Harvard Program on Technology and Society; Marilyn Bohl, IBM; Carl Grame, DeAnza College; Frank Holden, San Francisco City College; William Lane, Chico State College; Dan O'Donnell, DeAnza College; Eric A. Weiss, Sun Oil Company; William Viavant, University of Utah; and Michael Duggan, University of Texas. Parts of this book are based on a course given at the University of California at Irvine; we also want to express our gratitude to the students who sat through some rather imperfect drafts and whose insights and enthusiasm helped improve and enlighten the text.

. . . the sole end for which mankind are warranted, individually or collectively, in interfering with the liberty of action of any of their number is self-protection. That the only purpose for which power can be rightfully exercised over any member of a civilized community, against his will, is to prevent harm to others. His own good, either physical or moral, is not a sufficient warrant. He cannot rightfu ly be compelled to do or forbear because it will be better for him to do so, because it will make him happier, because, in the opinions of others, to do so would be wise or even right. . . . Over himself, over his own body and mind, the individual is sovereign.

JOHN STUART MILL
On Liberty (1859)

PART ONE

Why Study Computers?

A Point of View

1

Our society is in the midst of a debate. We are trying to determine whether technology can be controlled and directed toward the betterment of humankind or whether it will lead to the restriction of human liberty. This choice has been made most alarming by the modern electronic digital computer.

The computer is one of the most revolutionary inventions of this century. Although it has been in use for about thirty years, we still cannot foresee its full impact. In the next few years, we as citizens will be called on to resolve some very new and very complex issues about this invention. This book has brought together some of the materials needed to start answering these new questions.

"Computers are complicated machines for scientists and engineers. I don't have the background to worry about them and couldn't care less." Many people have used this argument to avoid the subject. Unfortunately, ignorance makes the misuse of computers possible. Consider the off-the-record remark of an aide to the mayor of a large city: "If I had access to the computers that keep police records, voting records, tax and property information, I could keep my boss in office forever." So some technical facts do have social consequences. If what he said is true, what goes on in computers should concern many people who now consider them no more than technical curiosities.

Computers have complex effects on our world. They have become important and powerful tools for collecting, recording, analyzing, and distributing tremendous masses of information. And such power and information can be misused in ways that demand social rather than technical judgment.

Figure 1-1 A typical computer center

The computer has further social impact. It saves countless years of tedious work by clerks, administrators, technicians, and scientists. But some of us view this as a threat to our jobs. The computer makes it unnecessary for us to monitor tedious, repetitive processes. But some interpret this as a loss of human control. The computer allows us to do things that were impossible without it. But by doing them, we come to depend on the computer. Each technical fact about the computer seems to have advantages *and* disadvantages. How can we tell which is which? How can we reap the value and control the danger? These are the questions that should concern all of us. They are not solely the responsibility of the technicians and the scientists in our society. They are what this book is about.

Today, computers are nearly everywhere. They recorded your birth and hospital records. When you started school, they recorded your grades and assigned you to classes. When you got a job, they calculated your salary and wrote your paycheck. They compute your taxes and issue your bank statement. Your bills—from utilities and oil companies, from doctors and department stores, insurance companies, credit and loan agencies—are compiled by a computer. Your name is on file already in computers in several bureaus of your national government, in state and county offices, and (unless you live in a very small town) in your city hall. If you have ever borrowed money or opened a charge account, bank and credit reference agencies will have your name and number in their files.

Computers have created a new industry that

employs hundreds of thousands of people. Walk past office buildings late at night and you will find lights from the computer centers reflected in the dark streets. The 12-to-8 shift is working. Or drive past a new commercial development in almost any large city and see the mini-skyscrapers with the word *computer* over their doors. Or glance at the ads in the Sunday paper and note the space devoted to computer schools, programmers wanted, and computer dating services. Look at the number of companies in this fast-growing field (figure 1-2). Only a handful existed ten years ago.

The computer revolution was originally an American phenomenon. It is no longer. The conditions that make computers attractive in America apply in any industrially advanced country. International computer conferences are held in Scotland and Yugoslavia, in Jerusalem and Moscow. The Japanese computer industry is beginning to challenge American companies for markets around the world. The U.S.S.R. is also a large producer of computers (see figure 1-3). America's present lead in the technology gives it a head start in some of the social problems of computers as well, but other nations are seeing the symptoms too.

Computer Attitudes

Indeed, computers are nearly everywhere. Yet, back in the computer dark ages—say twenty-five years ago—someone called them *mechanical brains*. This human analogy, although a distortion, has persisted and makes us think of ultimate control by a superbrain. Orwell's 1984 is here, now!

Or is it?

Granted, ours is now a highly automated world that will become even more deeply involved with computers as industrialization and urbanization reach more nations and more people. The compu-

ter's opponents have a full storehouse of negative social prophecy (from Mary Shelley and Samuel Butler to Kurt Vonnegut and Theodore Roszak) to draw on to support their arguments. Its proponents, on the other hand, can only fall back on technology and its real but complex contributions. Since these are abstract and rarely personal, they can never be adequate answers to emotional predictions of disaster.

You may ask, "Why be so concerned with what the public thinks about computers?" One of the principal limits on the use of computers is the attitudes of their potential users. If they are irrational and hostile, this potentially valuable tool can never be used fully. On the other hand, rational hostility demands action. Distinguishing between rational and irrational attitudes is one of the aims of this book.

Let us review society's current reaction to computers to see whether we can isolate some of the reasons for these attitudes. We will cover three major concerns—power, automation, and morality—themes that will recur many times in this book. Then we will explore the control of computers, our future with them, and the question of responsibility.

The Power of Computers

Certain aspects of computer use concern many technologists. As information systems grow larger and become more interconnected, our institutions seem to become increasingly dependent on them. We all become vulnerable to the kinds of accidents (and deliberate subversions) to which such systems are subject. For example, some major cities have experienced large-scale power failures resulting in blackouts that have continued for hours or days. In 1969 a single power failure in the New York

Computerworld Stock Trading Summary

TRADE*QUOTES

All statistics compiled, computed and formatted by TRADE★QUOTES, INC. Cambridge, Mass. 02139

EXCH		PRICE 1974 RANGE (1)	CLOSE MAR 12 1975	WEEK NET CHNGE	WEEK PCT CHNGE
	COMPUTER SYSTEMS				
N	BURROUGHS CORP	62-109	89 3/8	-2	-2.1
O	COMPUTER AUTOMATION	2- 14	5 1/8	- 1/8	-2.3
N	CONTROL DATA CORP	10- 38	17	- 3/4	-4.2
N	DATA GENERAL CORP	10- 38	21 3/4	+2 3/8	+12.2
O	DATAPOINT CORP	5- 15	10 1/4	+ 1/2	+5.1
O	DIGITAL COMP CONTROL	1- 5	1 1/4	0	0.0
N	DIGITAL EQUIPMENT	46-121	79 3/4	-3 1/4	-3.9
N	ELECTRONIC ASSOC.	1- 3	2 3/8	- 1/8	-5.0
A	ELECTRONIC ENGINEER.	4- 11	6 7/8	+ 1/8	+1.8
N	FOXBORO	19- 48	29 1/8	+ 1/4	+0.8
O	GENERAL AUTOMATION	6- 40	7 3/4	+ 1/4	+3.3
O	GRI COMPUTER CORP	1- 2	1/4	0	0.0
N	HEWLETT-PACKARD CO	54- 90	87 3/4	+ 1/8	+0.1
N	HONEYWELL INC	18- 86	31 3/8	+1	+3.2
N	IBM	152-251	213	-6 1/4	-2.8
O	INTERDATA INC	8- 22	22 1/8	+2 1/8	+10.6
O	MEMOREX	2- 5	4 1/2	+ 7/8	+24.1
O	MICRODATA CORP	1- 5	2 1/4	- 1/4	-10.0
N	NCR	14- 40	23	-1 1/2	-6.1
N	RAYTHEON CO	21- 39	32 5/8	+1 3/8	+4.3
N	SPERRY RAND	24- 44	34 1/2	- 1/8	-0.3
A	SYSTEMS ENG. LABS	1- 3	2	0	0.0
O	ULTIMACC SYSTEMS INC	1- 2	3 3/4	+ 1/2	+15.3
N	VARIAN ASSOCIATES	6- 13	9 1/8	+ 1/4	+2.8
N	WANG LABS.	7- 20	9 3/4	- 3/4	-7.1
N	XEROX CORP	50-127	75 3/4	-2 5/8	-3.3
	LEASING COMPANIES				
O	COMDISCO INC	1- 7	2	+ 1/4	+14.2
A	COMMERCE GROUP CORP	2- 6	3 3/8	- 1/8	-3.5
A	COMPUTER INVSTRS GRP	0- 4	1	0	0.0
M	DATRONIC RENTAL	1- 1	5/8	0	0.0
A	DCL INC	0- 1	3/8	0	0.0
N	DPF INC	2- 5	4 1/2	+ 1/2	+12.5
O	EDP RESOURCES	2- 3	2	0	0.0
A	GRANITE MGT	1- 3	2 3/4	+ 3/8	+15.7
A	GREYHOUND COMPUTER	2- 6	2 1/2	+ 3/8	+17.6
A	ITEL	3- 6	5 5/8	+ 3/8	+7.1
N	LEASCO CORP	5- 12	6 3/4	- 3/4	-10.0
O	LEASPAC CORP	0- 0	3/4	0	0.0
O	LECTRO MGT INC	1- 1	1/8	0	0.0
O	NRG INC	1- 5	2 1/4	- 1/8	-5.2
A	PIONEER TEX CORP	2- 10	2 3/8	0	0.0
A	ROCKWOOD COMPUTER	0- 1	1/2	- 1/8	-18.1
N	U.S. LEASING	5- 24	11 5/8	- 3/8	-3.1
	SOFTWARE & EDP SERVICES				
O	ADVANCED COMP TECH	1- 2	3/4	0	0.0
A	APPLIED DATA RES.	1- 3	1 5/8	- 1/8	-7.1
N	AUTOMATIC DATA PROC	21- 57	43 5/8	-2 3/4	-5.9
O	BRANDON APPLIED SYST	1- 1	1/4	0	0.0
O	CENTRAL DATA SYSTEMS	4- 6	3	0	0.0
O	COMPUTER DIMENSIONS	1- 3	2	0	0.0
O	COMP ELECTION SYSTMS	3- 4	3 3/4	- 1/4	-6.2
O	COMPUTER HORIZONS	1- 5	3/4	0	0.0
O	COMPUTER NETWORK	1- 2	1 1/4	0	0.0
N	COMPUTER SCIENCES	2- 4	3 3/4	+ 1/4	+7.1
O	COMPUTER TASK GROUP	1- 1	1/2	0	0.0
O	COMPUTER USAGE	2- 4	3 3/8	+ 1/2	+17.3
O	COMSHARE	2- 4	2 7/8	+ 1/8	+4.5
O	DATATAB	1- 3	1 1/8	0	0.0
A	ELECT COMP PROG	1- 1	1/4	0	0.0
N	ELECTRONIC DATA SYS.	11- 25	13 1/2	- 7/8	-6.0
O	INFONATIONAL INC	1- 2	1/8	0	0.0
O	IPS COMPUTER MARKET.	1- 1	3/8	0	0.0
O	KEANE ASSOCIATES	2- 4	1 3/4	0	0.0
O	KEYDATA CORP	1- 6	2 5/8	+ 1/4	+10.5
O	LOGICON	2- 5	3 3/4	0	0.0
A	MANAGEMENT DATA	1- 2	1 3/4	- 1/8	-6.6
O	NATIONAL CSS INC	5- 37	8	- 1/2	-5.8
O	NATIONAL COMPUTER CO	1- 1	1/4	0	0.0
A	ON LINE SYSTEMS INC	9- 30	9 1/4	- 1/8	-1.3
N	PLANNING RESEARCH	2- 4	3 7/8	+1	+34.7
O	PROGRAMMING & SYS	1- 1	5/8	0	0.0
O	RAPIDATA INC	1- 5	1 5/8	- 1/4	-13.3
O	SCIENTIFIC COMPUTERS	1- 1	1 1/8	0	0.0
O	SIMPLICITY COMPUTER	1- 1	1/4	0	0.0
O	TYMSHARE INC	6- 12	11 3/4	+ 5/8	+5.6
O	UNITED DATA CENTER	2- 4	2 7/8	0	0.0
A	URS SYSTEMS	2- 4	2 1/2	- 1/8	-4.7
N	WYLY CORP	1- 5	3 1/4	+ 1/2	+18.1
	PERIPHERALS & SUBSYSTEMS				
N	ADDRESSOGRAPH-MULT	3- 11	7 1/2	+1 1/4	+20.0
O	ADVANCED MEMORY SYS	1- 7	3 1/2	+ 3/4	+27.2
N	AMPEX CORP	2- 5	4 5/8	+ 1/2	+12.1
O	ANDERSON JACOBSON	1- 4	1 3/4	- 1/8	-6.6
O	BEEHIVE MEDICAL ELEC	1- 7	2 1/4	+ 1/4	+12.5
A	BOLT,BERANEK & NEW	5- 9	5 7/8	+ 1/4	+4.4
N	BUNKER-RAMO	3- 8	6 3/4	+ 5/8	+10.2
A	CALCOMP	4- 11	6 3/4	+2 1/4	+50.0
O	CAMBRIDGE MEMORIES	3- 16	4	+ 3/4	+23.0
N	CENTRONICS DATA COMP	7- 23	13 3/8	- 1/4	-1.8
O	CODEX CORP	8- 27	25 3/4	+2	+8.4
O	COGNITRONICS	1- 2	1/2	+ 1/8	+33.3
O	COMPUTER COMMUN.	1- 2	3/8	- 1/8	-25.0
O	COMPUTER CONSOLES	2- 3	3	0	0.0
A	COMPUTER EQUIPMENT	1- 2	1 3/8	0	0.0
O	COMPUTER MACHINERY	1- 5	1 1/2	0	0.0
O	COMPUTER TRANSCEIVER	1- 2	1 1/8	- 1/8	-10.0
O	COMTEN	1- 5	3 1/8	+ 3/8	+13.6
N	CONRAC CORP	10- 22	17 1/8	-1 5/8	-8.6
O	DATA ACCESS SYSTEMS	2- 3	1 1/8	0	0.0
O	DATA 100	4- 13	10 3/8	+1 5/8	+18.5
A	DATA PRODUCTS CORP	2- 4	3 7/8	+ 7/8	+29.1
O	DATA TECHNOLOGY	1- 4	1 7/8	+ 1/4	+15.3
O	DATUM INC	1- 4	1 1/4	- 1/8	-9.0
O	DECISION DATA COMPUT	3- 13	5 3/4	+ 7/8	+17.9
O	DELTA DATA SYSTEMS	1- 2	1/2	+ 1/8	+33.3
O	DI/AN CONTROLS	1- 2	5/8	0	0.0
N	ELECTRONIC M & M	1- 4	2	+ 1/4	+14.2
O	FABRI-TEK	1- 3	7/8	0	0.0
O	GENERAL COMPUTER SYS	1- 4	1	- 1/4	-20.0
N	HAZELTINE CORP	2- 7	3 1/2	+ 1/4	+7.6
N	HARRIS CORP	13- 34	20 3/8	+ 5/8	+3.1
A	INCOTERM CORP	1- 6	2 7/8	- 1/8	-4.1
O	INFOREX INC	1- 5	3	+ 1/4	+9.0
O	INFORMATION INTL INC	6- 14	11 1/4	+ 1/4	+2.2
A	LUNDY ELECTRONICS	3- 3	2 7/8	0	0.0
O	MANAGEMENT ASSIST	1- 1	3/8	0	0.0
A	MILGO ELECTRONICS	6- 18	11 3/8	-1	-8.0
N	MOHAWK DATA SCI	1- 4	2	+ 1/4	+14.2
O	ODEC COMPUTER SYST.	1- 3	3/4	0	0.0
O	OPTICAL SCANNING	2- 6	2	0	0.0
O	PERTEC CORP	1- 6	4	+ 1/2	+14.2
A	POTTER INSTRUMENT	1- 5	1 3/4	0	0.0
O	PRECISION INST.	1- 3	1	0	0.0
O	QUANTOR CORP	2- 8	4 1/4	+ 1/4	+6.2
O	RECOGNITION EQUIP	2- 5	3 3/4	- 1/4	-6.2
N	SANDERS ASSOCIATES	2- 8	4 7/8	+ 1/4	+5.4
O	SCAN DATA	1- 2	1	0	0.0
O	STORAGE TECHNOLOGY	6- 15	9 1/8	-1	-9.8
O	SYCOR INC	4- 13	7 1/4	0	0.0
O	TALLY CORP.	1- 4	1 1/2	0	0.0
O	TEC INC	1- 7	3 1/4	0	0.0
N	TEKTRONIX INC	18- 48	30 3/4	- 3/4	-2.3
N	TELEX	1- 4	2	+ 1/4	+14.2
O	WANGCO INC	3- 13	3 3/4	- 1/8	-3.2
O	WILTEK INC	1- 8	2 1/2	- 1/4	-9.0
	SUPPLIES & ACCESSORIES				
O	BALTIMORE BUS FORMS	4- 6	5	+ 1/2	+11.1
A	BARRY WRIGHT	4- 7	5 3/4	+ 1/8	+2.2
O	CYBERMATICS INC	1- 2	5/8	0	0.0
A	DATA DOCUMENTS	23- 54	38	+ 1/2	+1.3
O	DUPLEX PRODUCTS INC	6- 22	20 1/8	+ 1/8	+0.6
N	ENNIS BUS. FORMS	4- 7	6	+ 1/4	+4.3
O	GRAHAM MAGNETICS	5- 11	7 1/2	- 1/4	-3.2
O	GRAPHIC CONTROLS	6- 14	13 1/4	+1 3/4	+15.2
N	3M COMPANY	43- 79	53 1/8	-3	-5.3
O	MOORE CORP LTD	33- 57	48	+1 1/2	+3.2
N	NASHUA CORP	15- 45	15 1/2	- 1/8	-0.7
O	REYNOLDS & REYNOLD	6- 35	14 1/2	+ 1/2	+3.5
O	STANDARD REGISTER	10- 17	16 1/4	0	0.0
O	TAB PRODUCTS CO	4- 11	6	0	0.0
N	UARCO	13- 23	19 3/4	+ 1/2	+2.5
O	VANIER GRAPHICS CORP	3- 4	4	0	0.0
A	WABASH MAGNETICS	3- 7	4 1/8	+ 1/8	+3.1
N	WALLACE BUS FORMS	14- 24	19 3/4	- 1/2	-2.4

EXCH: N=NEW YORK; A=AMERICAN; P=PHIL-BALT-WASH
L=NATIONAL; M=MIDWEST; O=OVER-THE-COUNTER
O-T-C PRICES ARE BID PRICES AS OF 3 P.M. OR LAST BID
(1) TO NEAREST DOLLAR

Figure 1-2 A listing of the major computer systems and service companies

Figure 1-3 A computer factory at Kiev in the U.S.S.R.

state system eventually spread over a large segment of the East Coast. The network of power stations that was designed to shift capacity as the needs arose had not been designed to prevent a local blackout from spreading. This incident didn't involve a computer, but by analogy, people are concerned about single errors in a national network of computers being amplified and spread. For example, consider a national network of computers communicating with each other by a communications satellite. If human operators became so confident of their systems that they abandoned their manual files and teletypes, a failure of the satellite could seriously cripple the system throughout the entire country. Thus the more we

rely on computer systems, the more reliable they must become.

The more powerful computer-based systems become and the more information they contain, the more tempting they appear to those who might misuse them. As the mayor's assistant indicated in the earlier example, having masses of information available that could be used to forward one's own interests can be a powerful temptation. Dishonest politicians, embezzling clerks, blackmailers, and others who might misuse information systems represent serious threats to the public, threats that grow with the size and flexibility of such systems.

In the traditions of Western democracy, social or political power is always suspect. It was Lord Acton who noted that "power tends to corrupt; absolute power corrupts absolutely." There are few historians or politicians today who would dare to disagree with him. If it is true that knowledge is power, then the computer by its very nature contributes to the concentration of power.

One might then argue this way:

☐ Information is essential to control and is therefore a chief component of political and social power.

☐ Computers cause information to become available and centralized.

☐ Centralized information therefore means centralized power.

☐ Power that can be put to use will someday be put to misuse.

☐ Therefore computers are bound to be put to evil purposes.

Does such power really exist? Can the computer be used to manipulate individuals and groups of people? Is it possible for someone in the public trust to use public records in this way? Although the argument is somewhat overdramatized, the answer to all these questions is basically *yes*—unless we institute controls, checks, and laws to govern the limits of use and access to computer-based systems. Is it possible to do this? Yes. Our form of government is designed to prevent excesses of power. We are the best-informed society in the history of humankind. All that is required for adequate control is *informed involvement*.

The Omnipresent Computer. Some people acquainted with the methods of computer system development and with bureaucratic procedures foresee another danger. When computers are used to help predict the consequences of various decisions, the management of business and gov-

ernment will tend to depend on them increasingly. But to use computers in this way involves assumptions about economics, human behavior, international relations, racial tensions, and war that are far from perfect and sometimes in fact are not justified. Furthermore, the more such assumptions involve human behavior, the more difficult they are to confirm. Yet busy administrators and decision makers in many fields base the future of their enterprises on these devices with the prayerful faith that they are better than nothing. Thus they may be misled by a device whose only authority is complexity.

These problems are real but they are not insoluble. We hope to show that better trained executives and officials, better informed citizens, carefully designed procedures, and legislation can control them and harness the "awesome power" of computers for the general good.

Some of the anxiety that people feel about these problems is real and is based on knowledge of what can happen. Another sort of anxiety, equally real, is based on ignorance or only on a belief in computer mythology. Consider the image of the computer in many minds today: it is all-knowing, all-powerful, infinitely fast, completely reliable, totally rational; it uses hundreds of servants who are kept busy "feeding" it information and "listening" to what it tells them to do. It is no wonder that people feel of lesser importance in its presence. Copernicus, Darwin, and Freud successively denied our claims to the center of the universe, divine creation, and total rationality. They lowered our self-confidence as rulers of the universe; now it appears as though technology may have produced a better ruler. The technologist or scientist who understands the computer's limitations as well as its capabilities may wonder at the insecure person who feels inferior to a few cabinets of

Figure 1-4 Tiktok, the "patent double-action, extra responsive, thought-creating, perfect talking mechanical man," was introduced in Frank L. Baum's *OZ* series in 1907

electronic gear; but more often than not, the technologist has neither the time nor the persuasive ability to explain the computer myth.

A general fear of progress further distorts our understanding of the computer's proper role in our society. Every new technological advance has its

Figure 1-5 A destroyed computer center

detractors who argue that it must be bad because it is different. The automobile was decried because it was dirty and scared the horses; the telephone was an invasion of privacy; Edison's electric light was a useless frivolity. Yet we have come to accept all these devices and even to depend upon them. We have realized, tacitly if not overtly, that their advantages and conveniences outweigh their disadvantages. However, in some cases, it now appears necessary to reevaluate some of these dependencies. Electric power, for example, has become an absolute necessity and cheap power a prime source of economic growth, but the environmental effects of massive power-generating plants are a considerable price to pay. You must attempt, in this relatively early stage in the computer era, to exercise more foresight than our ancestors did in the introduction of other technologies; you must control their effects on the quality of life—your lives and those of your children.

Automation

When a technological invention is first put to limited use, it often replaces work formerly done by hand. People whose jobs disappear because of a technological improvement are bound to be skeptical of its advantages. For example, the telephone sharply reduced the need for telegraphers; these workers must have seen it as a socially disruptive and evil device. The news that a new machine will employ many people in new ways is good news only if you are one of those people.

The process of replacing human labor with automatic, machine-directed processes is called

Figure 1-6 A headline from the Los Angeles *Free Press*

automation. The computer, as a machine that can replace people in a wide range of occupations, is seen by many to be the ultimate symbol of automation and a threat to many workers and their jobs. A new generation will have to be educated to supply a job market that technology in general—and computer technology in particular—has made distinctly different.

People Versus the Computer. For those who feel that their jobs are threatened by new computer-based techniques, it is difficult to think of the computer in unemotional terms. It must appear to them as indeed very much like a mechanical brain, coldly and relentlessly replacing men and women in all aspects of life.

Others, whose applications for loans or jobs or credit cards have been rejected on the basis of information about them stored in computer-based files, are likely to feel the same impotent hopelessness. The computer becomes a monster; it coldly and ruthlessly removes all human aspects of person-to-person relationships and makes it difficult, if not impossible, for an individual to be treated with respect and individuality.

Much of what has been said and published about the social effects of computers really has to do with a set of beliefs about what people are and what they are not. Inevitably, comparisons are drawn between our abilities and the machine's, between the human brain and the computer. The brain can store 100,000,000,000 times more information than the computer; the computer can perform more arithmetic in one second than a person can do by working forty hours a week for four years. If one starts with the foregone conclusion that machines are replacing humans and doing human-like things, one is bound to discover that people and computers have much in common. But such an analysis is dangerously oversimplified. Invariably, such comparisons of memory size, speed, and so forth miss the point of what a human being can do.

A human being can use both feelings and rational knowledge to arrive at judgments in a fashion that cannot be programmed into a computer. Computer specialists have struggled unsuccessfully for many years to imitate some of the simplest things a three-year-old child can do, such as interpret the meaning of a spoken sentence. Beyond literal meaning lies the impossible challenge of subtleties of intent. The judgments that a human being can form even as a small child—about whether a person is to be trusted, whether he or she is hostile, whether a statement is to be taken literally or as a joke—are impressive and complex processes. Those who accuse computer technologists of being immoral because they have created an artificial being overestimate the capabilities of computer intelligence and underestimate the magnificence of the human mind.

It can be argued, however, that the computer will be the beneficiary of unlimited technical progress while the brain will not. Each decade brings the computer closer to the sophisticated symbol-processing abilities of humans. Who can say what the limit of its ability is? We will elaborate on this point later in the text; however, the fact remains that computer and human capabilities appear to be basically different and, for the foreseeable future, no human-like robot is likely to emerge.

The fear that the computer will control people is independent of this comparison of capabilities. Computer-based systems aready exert some control over people: your plane cannot take off because the air traffic-control computer is overloaded; you cannot register for a class because you slipped up in typing your student identification number; you are delayed in renewing your car registration because you lost the punched card. The real question is how far this control must extend before it becomes threatening. The first sign of the threat will be a weakening of our right to make choices. For example, if people want to use a computer to pick their mates, they should certainly be allowed to do so. If they *must* use such a service, their freedom is lessened. If they want to use a computer service to prepare their tax returns, fine; if they *have* to, that is bad. If an automated student registration system places constraints on the student's freedom simply to accommodate the new system, the net effect is bad. The question to be aware of is this: are your choices being limited for the convenience of a machine?

The Moral Questions

Behind and at the heart of these fears, anxieties, risks, and opportunities lie two basic issues that are related to the question of our responsibility and our right to limit the application of scientific knowledge and control technological developments:

☐ Is there something basically immoral about the computer?
☐ Will it affect our morality?

The first question can only be meaningful in a very limited sense, because objects have no morality. Moral questions can be asked only about the people who invent, create, and use these objects.

The development of the atomic bomb during the 1940s led to the first real need to meet the issue of moral responsibility in science. After the bomb had been developed, tested, and used in the final phases of World War II, some of the scientists who took part in this massive effort felt obliged to ask whether their actions had been totally responsible and whether or not they had acted morally in helping create such an instrument of death. The history of this discussion is fascinating but is only partly relevant to our subject. What matters here is the general form of the question posed: If the consequence of a discovery or invention can be foreseen as dangerous to society, is the discovery itself evil? Should it be suppressed? If so, how far ahead must a scientist predict the consequences

of his research? The atomic bomb rests on a history of theoretical ideas going back beyond Newton (1642–1727). At what point, then, does responsibility begin? An even more difficult question is this: If an invention or discovery has both good and evil consequences, who is in a position to weigh them fairly against one another? There are no facts and few objects that are totally evil, from which no good can come. Splitting the atom produced important new sources of energy that can be applied to peaceful purposes as well as war; explosives are used in breaking rock for all kinds of construction activities; poisons are used to control harmful insects. Similarly, there are few beneficial ideas that cannot be seen to have the potential to produce some harmful consequence. For example, the development of morphine led to heroin and heroin addiction; air transportation increased the deadliness of war. Examples could be cited of advantages and disadvantages that will (or may) stem

from the development of the computer. It, however, is a tool with no purposes or goals of its own. The people who understand it and use it must decide the purposes to which it will be applied. In fact, we will see that one of the computer's drawbacks is the difficulty that people have in specifying precisely the purposes for which their machines are to be used.

Morality. Now, turning to the second question, morality may be viewed as the body of rules defining the individual's relations with the social group. A judgment about the effect of the computer on morality (as contrasted with whether the computer is inherently immoral) then has to be concerned with how it can affect the relations among people. If, as some suppose, we become a society in which public and private institutions know a great deal about individuals because of dossiers (files on private lives) in computers, it is conceivable that our traditional public morality will be reinforced by fear. People will feel that their personal secrets are not safe with a computer.

On the other hand, if the standards of what is considered an acceptable public image change because we come to realize that the lives of most people contain regrettable incidents, then the computer could contribute to the demise of a useless facade. While it is this use of computers for counterintelligence and credit checking that is the most worrisome, the authors' interviews with men and women who have access to these massive personnel files show the shallowness of this facade. The sheer weight of social mishaps (arrests without convictions, minor criminal records, divorces, financial embarrassments, bouts of alcoholism and so forth) in so many of the files make such persons much more tolerant and willing to accept the kinds of errors in judgment that people make. The facts of the matter are even more obvious. Consider the following well-accepted statements.

a. Nearly fifty percent of marriages in the United States end in divorce.
b. There are over six million alcoholics in the United States.
c. The President's Crime Commission of 1967 concluded that forty percent of all male children will be arrested for a non-traffic offense during their lives.

Blackmail and blackballing for these matters, with or without a computer, may eventually cease to be even interesting.

In terms of this understanding of morality, it is not yet possible to predict what influence the computer will have, but these are the issues at stake.

Now, having taken our preliminary look at the disturbing questions of power, automation and morality, let us examine the area of computer control and its future.

Who Is in Control?

Basically, no one! However, if this is to change, what responsibilities must we face as consequences of using computers? For example, there are computer-based systems that can provide information about people's preferences, attitudes, and interests. A manufacturer of soap or cigarettes can use computers to help decide how best to advertise those products and thus maximize sales. This is no more than good business, we may think. But if the same techniques are used to maximize the number of votes a political candidate receives, we are no longer sure that this is simply good business.

However, if we look at the situation closely, it is clear that the basic question need not involve the computer at all. Questions of truth in advertising—and politics—existed before the computer was dreamed of. Like television, although to a lesser extent, the computer's power and flexibility allow its users to influence people for both good and evil.

In the future, the computer will be everywhere. More and more of our affairs will come to depend on it: transportation, education, health services, merchandising, finances, communications, and the necessities of life as well as the luxuries. Computers will assist the organizations of people who control and carry out these activities. Some of these people will use the organizations—and the computers—for immoral purposes. In the minds of many there will be a transference of responsibility from the people who control the system to the system and the computer itself. An aviation disaster may be blamed on the computer rather than on the managers and developers of the air traffic control system. The fact that disasters, injustices, and catastrophes occurred before the computer was invented will not make the public less critical of its roles in our society and economy.

Such misassignment of responsibility occurs in many cases: we blame movies for deteriorating moral standards and guns for crime. The fallacy is particularly hard to overcome in the case of computers. The peculiarly human-like image that surrounds the computer is probably at the root of the confusion. Even sensible people talk as though a computer *caused* an accident, *made* a mistake, *committed* an injustice, or *broke* a law. This is as illogical as blaming a knife for what it cuts or a movie screen for what it displays. There have been few criminal prosecutions for the misuse of computer files to date. (There have been prosecutions for stealing computer time and data, and in the Equity Funding case, which we will discuss later, people were convicted of using a computer to commit fraud.) In part, this absence of prosecutions may be due to the fact that there are few laws governing the use of computer files. Further, the development and use of large information files in computers is in its early stages. This statement may seem odd after nearly thirty years of computer use, but, as we will see later, the computer has some predictable future developments that will revolutionize it and make its impact even more strongly felt.

The Potential for Control. If the potential for both good and evil is so great in computer applications, it is reasonable to expect society to exert some controls. Let us look at how society has used and controlled other technologies to shed some light on the control of computers. Many products have significantly influenced society in ways that their inventors could not have predicted. Television and the automobile are two good examples. Television has probably had the most dramatic impact of all technological innovations in the last twenty-five years. Every day, at the flick of a switch, we can see news in the making, entertainment ranging from baseball to Shakespeare, and even some educational programs. Simultaneously, there are side effects: the power of the press and responsible, in-depth journalism has diminished; many once-important magazines have failed; participatory sports have declined in favor of watching television; reading and the art of conversation have declined; inoffensive but mediocre shows have increased, and programs that are intellectually challenging have virtually disappeared; sex and violence have been emphasized; potentially socially disruptive news events such as riots and bombings have been amplified. The sum of these negatives is so impressive that it profoundly concerns many psychologists and sociologists. In a few decades the habits and interests of virtually the entire nation have been changed, but change is not necessarily the same as improvement. Some of these effects (such as the abundance of violence and sex) are so important that government agencies are working on them; industry associations are working on others.

The amplification effect of television is so great that key events can modify public opinion in a matter of hours, and this impact can affect government with equal swiftness. When President Nixon fired Watergate prosecutor Archibald Cox in 1973, public reaction was swift and unmistakable. When Martin Luther King was assassinated in 1968, TV stations were asked to exercise restraint in covering small incidents lest they develop into major riots.

In the field of computers, however, the grievances are not as obvious to the average citizen and there is no experience or precedent for government control of computers. We may be warned, for instance, that television coverage of some news event or personality is biased; we need only observe it to draw our own conclusions. However, a comparable harm to a large number of people caused by a computer might be extremely difficult to detect. It might, in fact, require the services of another computer to reveal the conspiracy.

The automobile, mobilizing both the law abiding and the law breaker alike, has also significantly affected society in general and law enforcement in particular. It has spawned a gasoline and road-building industry and countless small businesses. Automobile manufacturing is one of the largest components of the American economy. Sociologists point out that it has even affected our morals by providing lovers with privacy they never before enjoyed.

If someone had predicted at the birth of the automobile industry that cars would be responsible for more deaths than suicide, homicide, and tuberculosis combined, would we have hesitated to produce automobiles? Would the pioneer manufacturers have sought other products to engage their talents? Would the government have intervened and prohibited production? These are hypothetical questions, and the most we can say is that it seems unlikely. We would probably have gone ahead and built cars anyway. The sad facts of the case are that before the event, we did not know what the consequences might be and we could not control them. The automobile with its good and bad effects has become so important to our society that we cannot seem to change it.

A democratic society is not well constituted to predict and prevent technical catastrophes. Unless a danger is immediate and presented in simple and dramatic terms, it is difficult for the issue to gain

attention in a society that seems to be driven only by crises. For example, in the late 1950s, Senator Kefauver explored the narcotics problem and accurately predicted its consequences. It was ignored as strictly a ghetto matter. Now, over twenty years later, addiction is epidemic. The problem of the responsible social forecaster in the computer field is to predict the future without resorting to the easy oversimplifications and exaggerations that seem to be the only means of gaining attention in the news media and in the government.

Today, and the Future

Now, some thirty years after the invention of the computer, we can take some comfort from studies made of its social impact during the last fifteen years of extensive use. These fifteen years have seen an amazing growth in every aspect of national life. The computer helped facilitate this growth and thus in a small way caused it. As we look at the major public and private uses of computers during this period, the important matters to observe are the effects on the individual's rights to privacy, confidentiality, and legal due process. In the United States, the introduction of computers into organizations that process personal information has not noticeably changed these rights and in some cases has strengthened them.

Unfortunately, it is not possible to generalize from the experience of the United States to the entire world. We must distinguish between countries of differing traditions. The Anglo-Saxon countries resist the "resident's registry" that is normal in France and Germany. Sweden and Italy will not let the police coordinate data banks, while France and Germany raise no objection. Sweden

Figure 1-7 A small, self-contained computer used in schools

and Israel have national citizen numbers and identification cards whereas Britain, Canada, and the United States have never accepted such. Thus although the concepts of privacy, confidentiality, and due process differ, there is world-wide concern.

This is where we are today, but how about the future? Every major enterprise of science, government, education, and industry in the late twentieth century will rely on computers. The computer will enable us to manage larger and larger organizations and solve more and more complex problems.

It thus will assist in making possible more and larger schools and colleges, more successful medical and agricultural research, more economical industry and cheaper products. Its use has already helped bring about major changes of tax structure, legal statutes, and government budgeting that are not obvious but are widespread positive influences in our society. There will be more.

However, the world of the future has been described as inhuman, automated, and plastic. It is easy to see this future world as a forbidding place where people are healthy and well-fed but lack gaiety or true happiness. But it is equally possible to portray the future world as warmer, better educated, and emotionally fuller. Consider a world where everyone could have, for the price of a telephone call, direct and rapid access to any information in any library. Such simple access to information could improve the process of education, to say nothing of its substance. Having simple and rapid access to your own financial transactions could equalize a battle with government tax agencies, a bank, a department store, or an insurance company. A person could effectively plan his or her own finances. A manager could do more than simply react to daily crises. We would have fewer tedious jobs and more challenging opportunities to lead fuller lives.

The Computer in our Service. It is possible today to build a device that could completely manage most bookkeeping problems. It could be used to write all checks, compare a budget against actual expenditures, balance the checkbook, process cancelled checks returned by the bank, verify the statement balance, and keep track of tax-deductible expenditures and list them by category for preparation of your tax return. It could be used to write checks regularly for fixed expenditures like rent and car payments. This could take the guesswork out of most checking accounts and remove any doubt about what bills have been paid. It could put disagreements over who is spending how much for what on a factual basis (if not settle the argument) and even do away with the possibility of overdrafts.

In another field, the success with which an automobile is used today depends greatly on the knowledge and conscientiousness of its owner. He or she must change the filters and oil and have the car lubricated according to a time or mileage schedule. The oil, battery, radiator water, and tire pressure must be checked when gas is bought. Seasonally, anti-freeze must be put in. Most owners don't do all these things regularly, which reduces their cars' effective lives, economy of operation, and their own safety. They run their cars with a vague knowledge of the mileage they are getting and a painful awareness of the size of the repair bills. Automobile designers have generally avoided the use of electronics as unreliable and expensive, but when the cost of small computers begins to rival the cost of auto parts, we will see them installed in cars. Such small computers can take care of many of the routine problems that owners cope with now. In addition, they can monitor cylinder, tire, and radiator pressure; radiator and transmission temperatures; alternator charging rates, fuel flows, brake fluid pressure and level; power steering and brake controls, and many other matters. They can warn the owner of impending failures before conditions arise that cause expensive bills or accidents. This warning system should prolong the life of both the owner and the car.

Still looking at future uses of computers, suppose that all known literature, knowledge, history, and science were automatically available. If students learned how to gain access to this body of knowledge, the only limits to their ability to answer questions would be their own intelligence and the answerability of the question. This is not to suggest that computer analysis will become an alternative to true scholarship; it is only to predict that computers will someday remove the drudgery of acquiring information. Curiosity requires success to flourish. Such a computer system, well designed, could do much to encourage curiosity on the part of society in general.

Communications and computers will make

NAN GOLUB

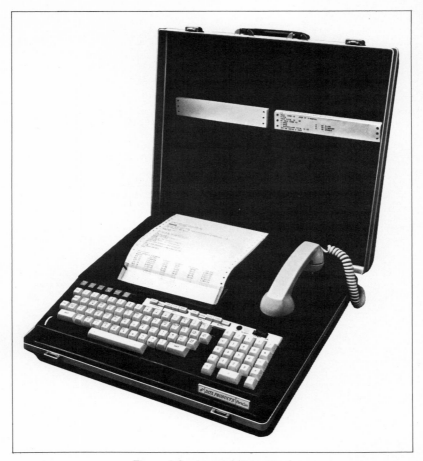

Figure 1-8 A portable terminal

information and services of all kinds as convenient as the telephone makes conversation. This will affect transportation needs (fewer workers will crowd the highways between city and suburb), styles of life (there will be a less sharp distinction between working and non-working hours), the structure of the family will change (working parents will be more accessible during the day), and thus interpersonal relationships will change also. Computers and communications can help bring about this radical shift in our working and living habits and make daily life less anxiety-prone,

leaving people with more emotional energy to invest in each other, in the work they do, and in the pleasures they seek.

Ultimately, we must ask whether the most is being made of the opportunity to use computers in our service rather than the opposite. The answer to this question (like most questions) is yes *and* no. Any potentially profitable computer service is bound to be pursued avidly by a number of small and large computer-related companies. Therefore the answer is *yes*. As to services of great benefit but questionable profitability, like services for the poor, the answer is more often *no*. There are few institutions or businesses chartered to identify or provide such services.

Thus while it is easy to foresee the computer contributing directly to a less troublesome, more predictable, easier existence for those already reasonably healthy, employed, and educated, it is not so clear that it will help the poor, the sick, or the ignorant as directly. The computer's contribution to general social progress must be viewed as indirect although no less important. Computer-assisted research in the social and behavioral sciences, educational and medical advances, and improvements in the processes of government will contribute to social progress. Whether in fact any such progress contributes to our general spiritual or emotional condition is determined by what we do with it as individuals. The opportunity is there.

Technology and Social Responsibility

The computer is here to stay. It is part of our society. Its very existence raises issues of morality, rights and responsibilities, and control that are made difficult by the technical intricacies of the computer itself. Networks of business-owned data banks will spread and unite and endanger privacy. There is a mounting impersonality between individuals and large enterprises. The opportunity for sabotage, embezzlement, and the mishandling of information grows as fast as the systems using computers grow. For example, if we make the mistake of exercising good sense only a little bit at a time and look ahead only a year or two into the future, the use of population surveillance and control measures could increase without our being aware of it. We might be caught in such a web before we realized what was happening. Legally,

we can and we must limit and control computer misuse in order to retain our rights and liberties as individuals, for this is the very soul of our political heritage.

Technically, it is possible to design computer systems so that they are much less vulnerable to theft or sabotage than manual systems. Computer-based systems can be designed to provide more individual and personal service than manual systems. The computer industry has a major responsibility. The individual engineer, programmer, or scientist within the industry must consider the human meaning of the system he or she is engaged to create. However, neither of these assertions of responsibility is a statement about morals any more than a statement of good business practice. The rest of us have a responsibility too. The United States must, as a healthy society, provide its people with the opportunity to choose their form of life, not conform to what is comfortable to a bureaucracy or a machine.

If you want to live in a world in which the computer is a panacea rather than a plague, there are a few crucial things that must be done. Do not leave the responsibility for the social impact of computer applications in the hands of technicians. Insist on individual, government, and corporate responsibility and liability for the computer's effects on people. Recognize the computer as an inanimate tool with enormous potential for either good or evil, the choice of which is in the hands of men and women, not inanimate systems. Our government is designed so that you are neither dependent on the excellence of your leaders nor vulnerable to their failings; so too should you be free of the men and women who make and run your computers.

Can you have this freedom within your current system of government and laws? In our opinion, yes. The mechanisms to control technology and its employers are there. In the past offended people have used these mechanisms so belatedly that technology has caused changes with which you are still struggling. You must use these mechanisms faster if only because of the rate at which this technology is getting more powerful. The speed with which you can act is only limited by how well you understand the problems and how well you understand the options you have.

Exercises

1. List the positive and negative social consequences of computers that are mentioned in this chapter. Can you add any others?

2. Defend or criticize the statement that "inanimate objects have no morality."

3. In what ways are the histories of the atomic bomb, television, and the automobile relevant to the present and future development of the computer?

4. Start a collection of newspaper, magazine, and television items about computers. Analyze their content carefully and try to distinguish the emotional from the factual aspects of what they are saying. Maintain the collection throughout the course; note how it grows and changes.

5. Cartoons and jokes are good indications of how people feel about things. Start a collection of cartoons and jokes about computers that reveal a general attitude toward them.

6. How important is the computer in your community? Check the yellow pages of the telephone directory for computers and computer-related products and services.

7. For the purpose of comparison, write an essay on your present set of attitudes toward the computer. At the end of the course we will ask you to rewrite it. As you think about the issues we raised in this chapter, try to discover what your values are. For example, on privacy, do you believe anyone seeking privacy has something to hide? There is no right or wrong answer to this question. The only point is for you to recognize what your personal values are.

For Further Information

At the end of each chapter, we will suggest some additional readings that will assist you in finding more detailed information on topics we have covered. These are not intended to be definitive or complete bibliographies but are small selections of information sources that may be available in libraries to which you have access.

Most of the topics touched on in chapter one will be dealt with in more detail later in the book, so no further references will be given here. However, there was some discussion of attitudes toward computers and automatic machinery. These are revealed most clearly in some works of fiction. *Frankenstein* (1), *Erewhon* (2), *Brave New World* (3), and *1984* (4) are classics. They precede the advent of the computer but prophesy the coming supremacy of technology over human ends. There are many others that could be cited. Capek's play (5) is the work that introduced the word *robot* into the English language.

Modern science fiction has utilized the computer extensively. An interesting article by Ascher (6) deals with the way in which these representations of computers reflect facts and attitudes about them. A few science-fiction works are included in this list: *Player Piano* (7), an unforgettable vision of the ultimate automation, and *The Moon is a Harsh Mistress* (8), which is one of the few works that present the computer as a loyal friend to man and not as an enemy. *2001* (9), both as a book and as a movie, presented an unforgettable (if fanciful) portrait of a computer called Hal.

Of Men and Machines (10) is an anthology of poems, essays, and short stories dealing with machines and their creators. It is available in paperback and is a valuable book to have in your personal library.

The question of the moral responsibility of scientists for their creations was an important issue, as the text indicates, in the case of the development of the atomic bomb. *Brighter Than a Thousand Suns* (11) is an absorbing account of this development. In addition, the *Bulletin of the Atomic Scientists* (12) is a periodical that has concerned itself with moral issues in science. It has been in publication since 1945 and contains a great deal of interesting and valuable material.

References

1. Mary Shelley, *Frankenstein* (1817) (New York: Macmillan, 1970).

2. Samuel Butler, *Erewhon* (1871) (Baltimore: Penguin Books, Inc., 1970).

3. Aldous Huxley, *Brave New World* (New York: Harper & Brothers Publishers, 1932).

4. George Orwell, *1984* (1949) (New York: Harcourt Brace Jovanovich, 1949).

5. Karel Capek, *R.U.R.* (1921) (New York: Oxford University Press, Inc., 1961).

6. Marcia Ascher, "Computers in Science Fiction." Harvard Business Review *41* (November-December 1963).

7. Kurt Vonnegut, Jr., *Player Piano* (New York: Holt, Rinehart and Winston, Inc., 1952).

8. Robert A. Heinlein, *The Moon is a Harsh Mistress* (New York: G. P. Putnam's Sons, 1966).

9. Arthur C. Clark, *2001: A Space Odyssey* (New York: New American Library, 1968).

10. Arthur O. Lewis, Jr., *Of Men and Machines* (New York: E. P. Dutton & Co., Inc., 1963).

11. Robert Junck, *Brighter Than a Thousand Suns* (New York: Grove Press, Inc., 1958).

12. *Bulletin of the Atomic Scientists*, 1945-present.

It is desirable to guard against the
possibility of exaggerated ideas that
might arise as to the powers of the
Analytical Engine. In considering any
new subject, there is frequently a
tendency first to overrate what we
find to be already interesting or
remarkable; and, secondly, to be
a sort of natural reaction, to under-
value the true state of the case. . . .
The Analytical Engine has no pre-
tensions whatever to originate
anything. It can do whatever we
know how to order it to perform.
It can follow analysis; but it has no
power of anticipating any analytical
relations or truths. Its province is
to assist us in making available what
we are already acquainted with.

ADA AUGUSTA, COUNTESS LOVELACE
*Notes to T. F. Menabra's
Memoir* (1842)

PART TWO

What Are Computers?

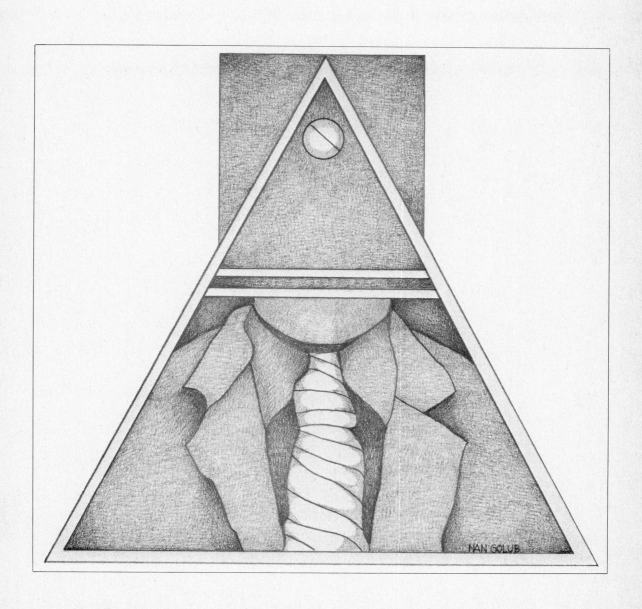

Computer Concepts

2

To understand the role that computers play in the modern world and to make some reasonable judgments about the future, we must begin by trying to separate emotional arguments from statements of fact. In order to do this, we really must understand something of what the computer is and what it does. Without some technical background in computing, one has little basis for evaluating any statement of what computers will one day be doing.

However, the computer by itself is not the whole story. An analysis of the machines, what their components are, and how they fit together is not enough. Could we adequately understand the impact of television by analyzing electronics and high-frequency radiation? Certainly not! We would know only a small part of the story if we did not also consider the programs presented and the

people whose responsibility it is to make the system work as a whole. The same is true of the computer. "What are computers?" can only be fully answered if we extend the subject to include how the machine is made to perform its functions.

This will seem reasonable to most readers. However, we must also extend the subject in the other direction and explore to some depth the scientific and technical bases of computing. Many other technologies can be understood well enough by a non-technical reader without much attention to the actual technical details. For example, most of us know as much as we need about the telephone without considering the subject of electronics. However, the computer is a relatively new device and one of unusually wide applicability. We can come to grips with what it does and what it can ultimately do only by considering the question of how it does it. The next few chapters may seem highly technical to some of you. However, bear with us. Their content is profoundly important to understanding the basic human issues that arise from computer applications.

The Computer

There are many ways to explain what a computer is. It can be described in terms of its powers and limitations, how it developed from its earliest crude form, how it is designed, or what it looks like. All of these approaches are used in this text because you, the reader, may understand things more easily in one form than another. The purpose of this book is neither to equip you to use the modern computer nor to teach you how to manage a computer installation. The principal things it attempts to teach are how the computer has come to be such a powerful tool and what its limitations are.

Powers and Limitations. The powers and limitations of the computer can be summarized in terms of a few brief generalizations.

POWERS

1. *Speed:* The computer can perform elementary arithmetical or logical operations in billionths of a second.
2. *Accuracy:* It can solve complex problems with virtually unlimited accuracy.
3. *Reliability:* It can work for thousands of hours, error-free.
4. *Universality:* A computer theoretically can solve any problem whose solution method can be stated precisely. "Theoretically" omits limitations of cost or time. There are still problems, like weather forecasting, that are well defined and yet strain the largest and fastest computers.
5. *Faithful servant:* It does exactly what it is told for as long as is required, no matter how boring or distasteful the task might seem to you.
6. *Memory capacity:* It can store immense files of information to which it can gain access in fractions of a second, seconds, or, at worst, in a few minutes. The information in this memory doesn't fade, change, or get lost.

LIMITATIONS

1. *Complexity:* The computer is so complex that setting it up to solve a new and substantial problem involves high costs and long delays.
2. *No innate intelligence:* While a computer has great capabilities, it can only be used to solve well-structured problems. It cannot discover new ways of solving problems.
3. *Cost:* While costs of computation have been going down steadily, high cost is still a limiting factor in many potential computer applications.
4. *Faithful servant:* It performs as instructed and if the instructions are in error, it will commit those errors tirelessly, too.

So far what we have told you is that a computer is a complex, expensive, rather literal machine for processing information with great accuracy, speed, and reliability. This much is simple enough. It might even seem reasonable that a machine that does exactly what it is told will do just that even if it is told to do something stupid. As you read this very general listing of powers and limitations, you may have noticed that we used the word *information* to describe what was stored in the machine's memory, not the word *number* which is implied when we talk of arithmetic and mathematics.

Figure 2-1 Communications symbols

Indeed, initially the computer was designed as a tool to manipulate numbers and thus solve arithmetic problems. The most important fact about its development was the discovery that a machine that can store numbers can store any symbols that can be assigned an identifying number.

What this means is that one can store symbols (language, mathematics, music, and so on) by establishing some correspondence between a number and the symbol, just like a code in which we substitute the number 1 for the letter A, 2 for B, and so on. The simple ability to store these symbols does not necessarily imply that the computer can manipulate them, of course. In order to do that, we must be able to describe each process we want it to perform on these symbols. People manufacture, use, and manipulate many symbols that represent facts about the world as it is, as it was, or as we would like it to be. We call these symbols and the facts they represent *information.*

Since the invention of the wheel, machines have come to replace muscles; in many areas of work, we are now basically concerned with working with information to control our machines and our future. A computer is a machine to help us with this remaining work, work that has always been regarded as essentially and finally human: it is an information machine, reading, sorting, comparing, and altering our symbols.

This description may seem very general and broad, and it is. But the power and the potential of the computer rest precisely on this breadth and generality. A general-purpose computer is not merely a machine for performing a specialized task; it can be applied as generally as our systems of symbols—in discourse, mathematics, science, logic, or models. Its limitation is that the process the user wishes it to perform must be described in detail in terms of the basic operations the machine is capable of. For example, imagine that you had to explain to an illiterate person how to look up a word in the dictionary. You would have to tell him or her, in terms he could understand, on the basis of his prior experience and abilities, (1) what the possible letters of the alphabet are, (2) the order in which they occur, and (3) how, by comparing the string of letters in the word he is looking for with those in the dictionary, the definition could be located. The level of detail of this task roughly corresponds to computer programming.

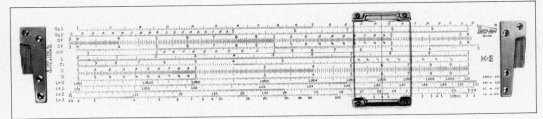

Figure 2-2 A slide rule

Now perhaps you can see why more technical detail is required before you will be prepared to form your own judgment about the threat and opportunities presented by the computer. You now know the computer's basic limitations, capabilities, and the general power it has as a symbol manipulator, but you are still in no position to consider for yourself whether any particular computer application is technically or economically feasible, potentially error-prone, or subject to control. (Note that economic feasibility is mentioned and will be returned to many times in this book. Computer applications must pay for themselves; unlike art, they cannot exist for their own beauty.)

How it evolved. The progress of many sciences has been limited by the ability to measure and record. The ability to analyze physical problems has always been limited by the ability to compute. For example, Karl Gauss, a brilliant German mathematician of the 1800s, spent twenty years of his life calculating orbits by hand that the computer could have done in a few hours.

We need only look at the accounting profession or at astronomy to see why such tools as the slide rule, the table of logarithms, the hand-operated adding machine, and the multiplying and dividing desk calculator could not cope with masses of numbers without certain problems. First, their use is limited by the rate at which a person can combine two or three numbers in a simple fashion and copy down the results. Further, their accuracy is limited by the tendency of people to make errors when doing repetitive operations. Finally, their

precision is limited to three digits in the case of the slide rule and generally ten digits in the case of the desk calculators and adding machines. Scientific calculations often require far more accuracy than this. The modern computer was developed out of this need to process numbers and do arithmetic more quickly, more accurately, and less expensively.

The Evolution of the Computer

To understand how the computer evolved, let us consider, by analogy, a sequence of musical devices that increase in complexity.

Music-making Machines. A cymbal has one action; it plays one note. A piano is a device that has eighty-eight notes, or actions, and the keys can be played in any arbitrary order. Like the piano, a music box has many actions or notes, but it is an automatic device: the sequence in which the sounds are struck is fixed. It plays only one tune. The player piano is more complex: it is a music box that can play many tunes. It has all the available actions of a piano, yet every roll of paper music that is placed in it causes it to produce a different tune. In a player piano (shown in figure 2-3), the roll of paper contains the information about what notes are to be struck and in what sequence. The sequence of actions (striking the keys) is controlled automatically by holes in the roll of paper as they pass sensors; the sequence is changeable because the roll is changeable.

Figure 2-3 The player piano, whose action is similar to the computer's

Arithmetic Machines. The evolution of the computer can be understood by comparing it to this sequence of musical devices. An adding machine, like a cymbal, has one action. You enter the number into the keyboard, depress a button, and it adds that number to whatever number was already registered on the counter.

The early counters, shown diagrammatically in figure 2-5, were series of wheels. There was one wheel for each position in the sum being accumulated. Each wheel had ten positions to represent the digits: 0, 1, 2, 3, 4, 5, 6, 7, 8, 9. When a wheel had already been advanced to the "9" position and was about to go to the "0" position, it caused the wheel on its left (representing the next higher position in the number) to advance one position—the *carry* operation.

Although modern desk calculators are almost all electronic, we will continue the explanation in terms of the old-fashioned mechanical calculators. A desk calculator of this kind has a counter, but its actions are *add, subtract, multiply,* and *divide.* Its counter wheels can subtract (roll backwards) as well as add. It performs multiplication as

over-and-over addition and division as over-and-over subtraction. Like the piano, there is no fixed sequence in which these operations are performed. Just as the music determines the sequence of notes played on the piano, the sequence of arithmetic operations (actions a person takes at a desk calculator) is determined by the problem. The set of instructions the person follows is sometimes called a *procedure.*

Card Machines. The next step in the evolution was to find a way to set up procedures and supply data automatically and repetitively in a way that corresponds to the way a music box plays a tune. The technique for doing arithmetic with counters was already available. What was needed was a way of storing numbers and reading them into a machine.

In 1890 Herman Hollerith designed a type of card in which numbers and letters could be represented as combinations of holes. A Hollerith card is shown in figure 2-7.

The modern card has eighty columns. Each column has a position for the ten digits and three

Figure 2-4 An early adding machine

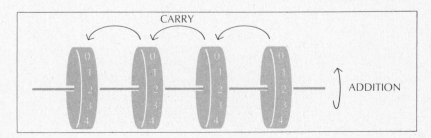

Figure 2-5 Counter wheels

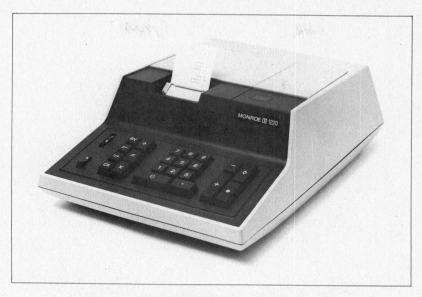

Figure 2-6 A desk calculator

zone punches above the one. As you can see from figure 2-7, the letters of the alphabet are represented by combinations of the three zone punches and the digits 1 through 9.

The card reader, the device originally designed to read the information from the card, is dia-grammed in figure 2-8. Cards are fed past the reader at a constant rate. The reader consists of eighty wire brushes, one positioned over each column of the card. The card passes between the brushes and a roller, and an electrical circuit is completed when a hole allows the brush to touch the roller.

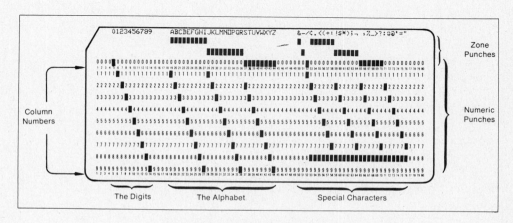

Figure 2-7 A Hollerith card

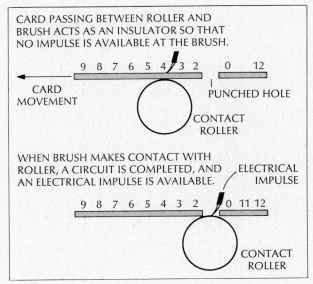

CARD PASSING BETWEEN ROLLER AND
BRUSH ACTS AS AN INSULATOR SO THAT
NO IMPULSE IS AVAILABLE AT THE BRUSH.

9 8 7 6 5 4 3 2   0   12

CARD
MOVEMENT   PUNCHED HOLE

CONTACT
ROLLER

WHEN BRUSH MAKES CONTACT WITH
ROLLER, A CIRCUIT IS COMPLETED, AND   ELECTRICAL
AN ELECTRICAL IMPULSE IS AVAILABLE.   IMPULSE

9 8 7 6 5 4 3 2   0 11 12

CONTACT
ROLLER

Figure 2-8   Diagram of a card reader

Otherwise the card serves as an insulator. Since the card is passing through the read station at a constant rate, the machine can identify which digit is punched in the column by the time the electrical circuit is completed.

These early machines were on the level of the music box. They performed a fixed sequence of actions for each card. They read the number from each card and added it to the counter. When the last card was read, the operator could get the sum by reading the visible counter.

The next stage in the evolution was to provide for a number of different actions (multiply, divide, subtract) and a fixed number of sequence steps between the reading of successive cards in which these actions could take place. This was done by a wired control panel called a *patch board*.

Thus our music box could play a more complex tune on the numbers that it read from each card. For example, one might feed such a machine a deck of cards, each of which had three numbers on it. The patch board could instruct the machine

to calculate the sum of the squares of the numbers and accumulate the sum over all the cards of the deck, as well as count the number of cards in the deck. On the last card, the procedure might be to divide the sum of the squares by the number of cards. However, every time the machine was used for a new problem, the patch board had to be torn down and rebuilt. This took time and introduced the possibility of errors if the procedure was complicated. Therefore the plug board shown in figure 2-9 was invented. It allowed one to wire up a given problem on a board that could be inserted and removed from the machine and saved for later use. Thus one could build a library of plug boards that could solve many problems, like the rolls of music for the player piano that make it play many tunes.

This added flexibility only created a greater appetite for better machines to solve more complex problems. These problems required more constants, intermediate results, and tables than could be stored in the few counters that early machines

Figure 2-9 A plug board

had. Thus the number of counters was increased and special registers that just stored numbers were added. These were called *memory units*.

Automatic Sequence Computing. The flexibility afforded by more memory was also soon inadequate to the need. The machines still allowed only a short sequence of steps. Further, they required that essentially the same sequence of steps be performed on each card. Scientists wanted to perform different calculations on different cards in a deck, depending on events that took place during the computation. Accountants calculating a payroll needed to be able to vary the deductions from a salary check according to the base rate of pay of the individual employee. They wanted instruction sequences that allowed for this kind of decision making.

There were simple facilities on the early machines that could be used to alter the course of a calculation and thus in effect make a decision. They could indicate when a counter developing a running total overflowed (that is, passed the highest possible value and returned to zero) or when it turned negative. These indicators could be used to change the course of the calculations.

It was crude, but here is an example of how such decision making worked. Suppose each card in a deck to be processed contained two numbers. The problem is to find the smaller number on each card. Finding the smaller of two numbers—call them a and b—can be done by subtracting b from a. If the difference is negative, then a is the smaller number.

But once again the machine's resources were being strained beyond their limits. More sequence steps were required for making these decisions. And arithmetic had to be done for determining the course of the calculations as well as the calculations themselves.

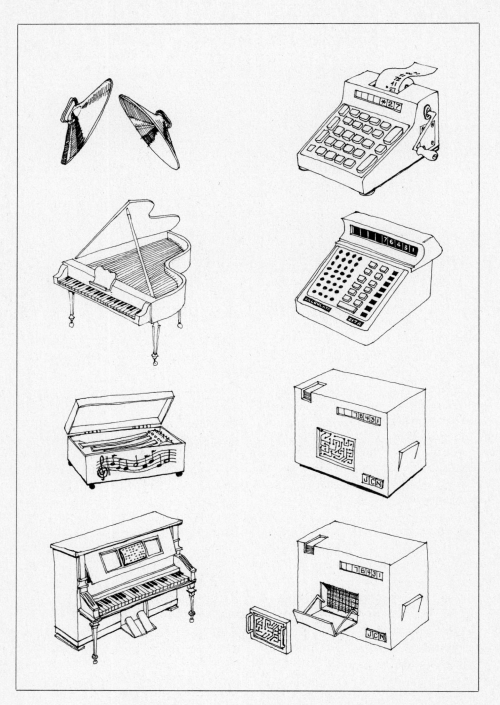

Figure 2-10 Music machines and computing machines

Step 1: Make sure the "sum" is zero to start with.

Step 2: Add the number on line number ① of the list of 1000 numbers to the "sum."

Step 3: Add 1 to the number in the circle in step 2.

Step 4: If the number in the circle is less than 1001, go to step 2.

Step 5: Otherwise, stop.

Figure 2-11 Procedure for adding numbers

It became clear to John von Neumann in 1946 that if the data and sequence instructions could be put into some different kind of a machine *all at once* at the beginning of the problem, the machine could be free of the requirement to do its computations on one card at a time, in the time between card readings. Then a computation could take as much time as was required, and its course could be determined by the results of the calculations rather than by something external like a plug board. This led to the concept of the *internally programmed machine.*

The Internally Programmed Machine. In this machine, the instructions to control the computer's operation are stored as numbers in its memory and can be manipulated and changed just like the data to be processed.

To explain this power, let us take a simple example. Suppose we have a sequence of operations we wish to perform, say, 107 times. Each time the sequence is performed, it is counted; when 107 is reached, the required number of steps has been completed. The ability to alter its operations on the basis of the results of a computation (in this case, comparing the count with 107) permits the computer to decide to stop.

Suppose we want a computer to add a list of 1000 numbers. We could instruct the machine to add the second to the first, then add the third. . . . But this would take 999 instructions. If our instructions can change in accordance with the results of a calculation, our task becomes much simpler. Figure 2-11 is a sequence of instructions showing this idea: the program modifies itself (by changing step 2), makes a decision (in step 4), and modifies the sequence in which the steps are done.

At this point we must pause in our explanation of what a computer is to introduce a related concept. It is sometimes easier to understand procedures—especially the complex procedures that some computer programs consist of—by presenting them graphically in the form known as a *flowchart.* A flowchart illustrates the order in which actions are performed and what decisions are to be made during the process. By convention, rectangular boxes represent actions to be performed; diamond-shaped boxes represent decisions. Arrows connect the boxes to illustrate the flow of the process. To illustrate what we mean, look at the flowchart of Oscar's day in figure 2-12.

Oscar has many actions. He sleeps, shaves, dresses, eats, kisses his wife, and goes to work. The flowchart shows the order in which he does these things and the decisions he faces: get up (what time is it?), eat (how much does he weigh?), kiss his wife (how long has he been married?), go to work (does the car start?). The flowchart describes the order in which Oscar does these things and answers these questions.

Now, to return to the main line of our explanation of computers, the program to add 1000 numbers can be represented in flowchart form, as shown in figure 2-13.

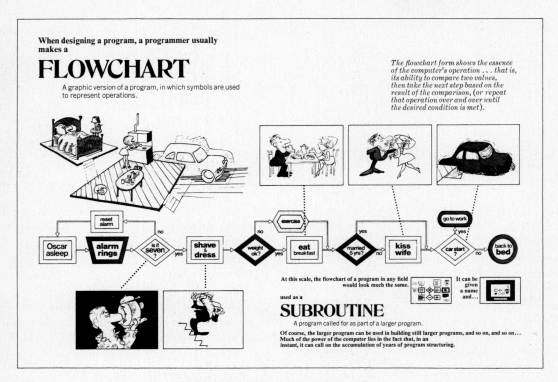

Figure 2-12 A flowchart of Oscar's day

We will leave this example for a short while to begin the explanation of the structure of a computer. Then we will return to it to illustrate how the computer works.

The Computer. In order to explain how a computer uses numbers for instructions and modifies them, it will be helpful to have a schematic diagram of a computer to work with:

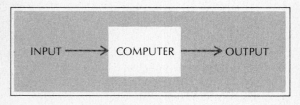

In simplest terms, some information goes into

the machine and is called *input;* other information comes out and is called *output.* This still does not explain what happens inside the computer; so we need a somewhat more elaborate diagram. (In this chapter we are focussing strictly on what goes on inside the computer. We will cover how the information gets in and out later.)

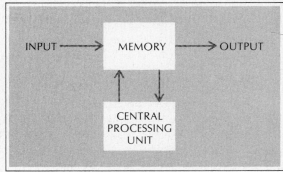

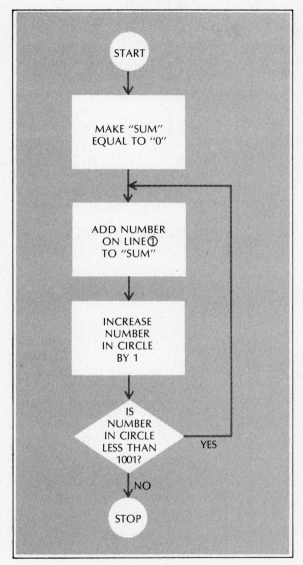

Figure 2-13 Flowchart for the problem

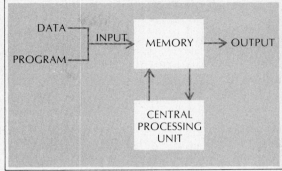

The information that goes in is of two kinds: the data that is to be manipulated and modified to produce results and the instructions that tell the machine what is to be done (the *program*).

To clarify the way in which instructions and data are used, we must make the schematic distinguish the two different functions of what is called the *central processing unit*—the control function and the arithmetic and logic function.

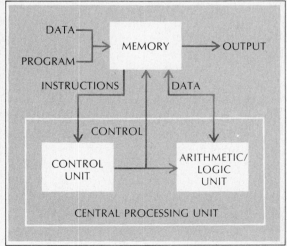

The information that goes into the machine is stored in a device or set of devices called a *memory*. The information can then be directed to the central processing unit as it is needed. However, this diagram is still too simple. A distinction about the input to the computer must be made.

The instructions of the program are sent, one at a time, in order, to the control unit. It then interprets them and does two things: it directs what data should be sent to the arithmetic/logic unit and tells the arithmetic/logic unit to perform certain operations (add, subtract, compare, and so on) on the data. The location within the arithmetic/logic unit in which calculations are performed and where partial results are saved is called the *accumulator*. (The schematic diagram is now almost complex enough. It is not clear yet how information gets into and out of the memory, but we will take that up in chapter three.)

The computer's memory consists of a series of cells (usually called *words*) that can each store a number or an instruction. These words are organized and numbered so that each instruction or other piece of information in the memory can be referenced by its location. It is sometimes helpful to think of the memory in terms of a set of post office boxes or pigeonholes: as a serially numbered set of storage locations.

Each instruction that is sent from the memory to the control unit usually consists of two parts—the *operation code* and the *address*. The operation code indicates what operation is to be performed (add, subtract, and so on); the address tells what memory location is involved.

Computer Instructions

Some examples of computer instructions will make this clearer. Figure 2-14 presents a simple set of instructions for a hypothetical computer.

If the operation code is "01", the instruction means that the content of the specified location in memory, "L", is to be added to the accumulator and the sum left there. If it is "02", then the content of the specified location is to be moved into the accumulator, replacing whatever was there before and thus erasing it. All the arithmetic operations are basically like this.

Thus if we have numbers stored in memory locations "1024" and "1025" and we want their sum to be put in memory location "1026", we proceed as shown at the bottom of the page.

The memory locations of these instructions (3702, 3703, 3704) were chosen arbitrarily. However, when such instructions are executed, it is assumed that the computer is told where to start and that the next instruction is to be taken from the next sequential location in memory. For example, if the instruction being executed is an "01 1024" that was taken from location 3703, then the next instruction to be executed will be the one at 3704, whatever it happens to be. Operation codes 07, 08, and 09 can be used to modify this sequence. They allow the program to jump to another set of instructions, somewhere else in memory, either unconditionally (09) or depending on the contents of the accumulator (07 and 08). They are therefore called the *unconditional branch* and the *conditional branch*

MEMORY LOCATION	INSTRUCTION	MEANING
3702	02 1025	Erase the previous contents of the accumulator and move the contents of "1025" to the accumulator.
3703	01 1024	Add the contents of "1024" to the accumulator.
3704	06 1026	Move the contents of the accumulator to "1026", replacing the previous contents.

OPERATION CODE		
01	ADD L	Add the contents of location L to the accumulator.
02	MOVE L TO ACC	Erase the previous contents of the accumulator and move the contents of location L to the accumulator.
03	SUB L	Subtract the contents of location L from the accumulator.
04	MULT L	Multiply the contents of location L by the accumulator. Find the product in the accumulator.
05	DIVIDE L	Divide the contents of location L by the accumulator. Find the quotient in the accumulator.
06	MOVE ACC TO L	Move the contents of the accumulator to memory location L, replacing the previous contents.
07	IF NEG L	If the contents of the accumulator are positive or zero, proceed to the next instruction; if negative, the next instruction to be executed is the one at location L.
08	IF ZERO L	If the content of the accumulator is zero, the next instruction to be executed is the one at location L.
09	GO TO L	Take the next instruction from location L.
10	STOP	Do not perform any further operations.

Figure 2-14 List of instructions

instructions. Branch instructions enable us to change the order of performing a set of instructions. We can skip some or jump from one set to another. We can set up a group of instructions (a *subroutine*) and then reuse it rather than write the same group of instructions for each usage, and we can modify a sequence of instructions to reflect the requirements of a particular situation. Thus a program can modify its own instructions (by performing arithmetic operations on them) and can make decisions (by selecting alternative sets of instructions depending on some result of the calculations or the data).

Let us now return to our program to compute the sum of 1000 numbers—a program that modified itself and made a simple decision—and rewrite it in the language of the computer as we have just defined it. The program itself will begin in memory location 0000; the list of numbers to be added is assumed to begin at memory location 0020 and to extend through 1019. We specify the starting point of the program because the machine can start at any point and the programmer must choose the location of the 1000 numbers so that his or her program can find them. In addition to the program and the numbers, a "1" is needed so that it can be added to the address of the next number—like adding "1" to the number in the circle—and an empty cell to keep the "sum" in. These will be stored immediately after the program itself. The computer program, together with its earlier description, is shown in figure 2-15.

Notice that this code consists of fifteen numbers, and if any are wrong or in the wrong place, the program will not work. For example, if in 0013 we had a "2" rather than a "1", the program would have added every other number from the list of 1000.

The modern computer has many elaborations of the basic capabilities represented so far, but its power rests in the fact that such a simple set of instructions as shown in figure 2-14 can calculate the solution of any problem that can be stated and solved mathematically or procedurally. This is not to say that it is economically feasible to program any given problem. However, the unit cost of computation has decreased by more than a thousandfold in the last thirty years. This in itself has been a tremendous contribution to the computer's use.

A file search. We will now illustrate some of the power of this simple set of instructions with a more realistic example than the problem given above. We will analyze a problem in just enough detail to show the feasibility and cost of this small list of instructions in solving it and to illustrate the level of detail to which a problem must be reduced before it can be solved with a computer.

Imagine yourself to be a detective searching the files for suspects in a strong-arm robbery. An eyewitness described the criminal as male, about forty years old (thus born in the 1930s), with a New England accent (thus he probably grew up in New England). The criminal was heard to say that he was a native of New York (thus he was born in New York) and he was seen driving away from the scene of the crime in a red Pontiac. Your computer file has the following information on each suspect:

- ☐ Name
- ☐ Sex
- ☐ Date of birth
- ☐ Place of birth
- ☐ Known addresses
- ☐ Criminal convictions

The file contains records on 10,000 individuals. For the sake of simplicity, we will assume that there are no aliases or misspelled names in the file. This assumption removes two of the most difficult problems in maintaining a "people" file. Smith, Smyth, Smithe, Smits, and Schmidt may be five people or one person. The other problem in maintaining such a file is that there may be several hundred people with the same name. There may be several hundred Juan Rodriguezs in Los Angeles, in which case the home address or wife's first name has to be used to distinguish among them. (You can begin to see why a unique social security number is not only a convenience in organizing certain kinds of files—it also helps to prevent misidentification.)

The motor vehicle registration file is a separate file that we will use and it has, in addition to the

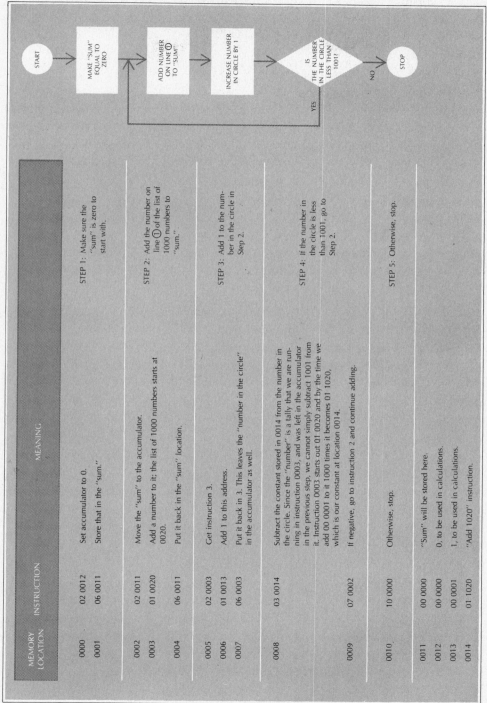

Figure 2-15 Program for adding numbers

vehicle registration and license numbers, the following information for each owner:

☐ Name of owner
☐ Make of car
☐ Color of car

This file contains records on ten million cars and owners.

We will begin with the criminal history file because it has fewer items and thus less searching is required. It is in alphabetical order by subject's name. This will be of no help in this case, since we are looking for the name. Further, since there may be many men who fit the description given, we will have to search all the records and then find those who own red Pontiacs.

Let us see what the program is like for checking whether an individual's record fits the description of the suspect. To find out whether a person was born in the 1930s we must compare the date of birth in the record with the numbers 1930, 1931, . . . 1939. To do this we test whether the date of birth simultaneously satisfies two tests: whether it is less than or equal to 1939 and greater than or equal to 1930. We do this rather than conduct ten tests to see if the date of birth is equal to 1930, 1931, . . . , 1939. Figure 2-16 is the flowchart of this process.

We will now code the program corresponding to this flowchart, but first we must make some assumptions about where various records and constants are stored in the numbered locations of memory. Let us assume the constant "1930" is stored in location 0020, the constant "1939" is stored in location 0021, and the dates of birth are stored in locations 101 to 10,100. Figure 2-17 shows the coding. We must now test to determine whether the man was born in New York City (NYC).

For the sake of simplicity, we will assume that all cities in the country have a serial number. Let us say NYC is represented by the serial number 35001, and the computation is simply to check whether the place of birth equals 35001. The flowchart for this test is shown in figure 2-18.

The coding of the birthplace check is shown in figure 2-19. It assumes the place of birth data is located in 20,001, . . . , 20,000, and assumes that the number 35001 is stored in location 0022.

To find whether the subject grew up in New England, we have the same problem as we had finding out whether he was born in New York City, except that we test his previous addresses during the years before he was twenty-one years old against a file of the names of the New England states. This is more complex, because we have to subtract date of birth from date of residence in New England and see whether the difference is less than 21. Similarly we compare the list of criminal convictions against the code number for strong-arm robbery. We will not code these tests.

There is one last matter that we must illustrate, and that is what happens at location 0050 when we go on to consider the next person. We must modify all of the instructions in the code that get date of birth and place of birth and add one to them so that the next person is considered. This involves adding a constant "1" to the address portion of those instructions. The instructions that do this are in locations 0001, 0005, and 0009. This is like adding "1" to the circled number in the previous example.

The coding of the block on the flowchart

GET THE NEXT
MAN'S RECORD

follows in figure 2-20. Assume the constant 00 0001 is stored in location 0023.

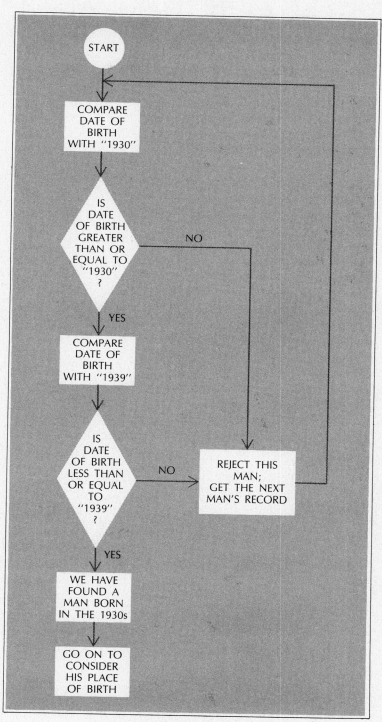

Figure 2-16 Date of birth check

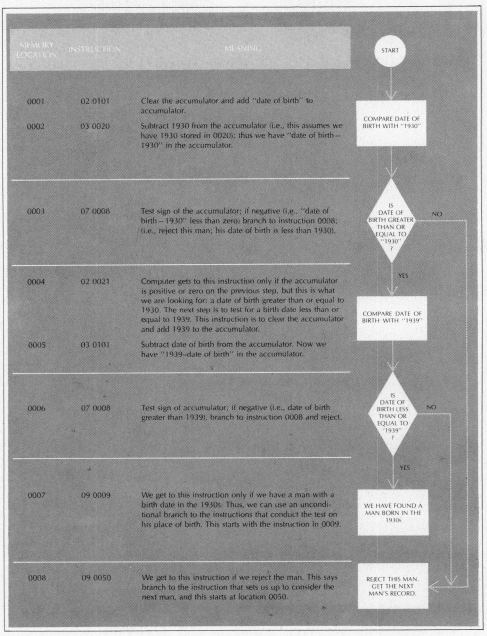

MEMORY LOCATION	INSTRUCTION	MEANING
		START
0001	02 0101	Clear the accumulator and add "date of birth" to accumulator.
0002	03 0020	Subtract 1930 from the accumulator (i.e., this assumes we have 1930 stored in 0020); thus we have "date of birth – 1930" in the accumulator.
		COMPARE DATE OF BIRTH WITH "1930"
0003	07 0008	Test sign of the accumulator; if negative (i.e., "date of birth – 1930" less than zero) branch to instruction 0008; (i.e., reject this man; his date of birth is less than 1930).
		IS DATE OF BIRTH GREATER THAN OR EQUAL TO "1930"?
0004	02 0021	Computer gets to this instruction only if the accumulator is positive or zero on the previous step, but this is what we are looking for: a date of birth greater than or equal to 1930. The next step is to test for a birth date less than or equal to 1939. This instruction is to clear the accumulator and add 1939 to the accumulator.
0005	03 0101	Subtract date of birth from the accumulator. Now we have "1939 – date of birth" in the accumulator.
		COMPARE DATE OF BIRTH WITH "1939"
0006	07 0008	Test sign of accumulator; if negative (i.e., date of birth greater than 1939), branch to instruction 0008 and reject.
		IS DATE OF BIRTH LESS THAN OR EQUAL TO "1939"?
0007	09 0009	We get to this instruction only if we have a man with a birth date in the 1930s. Thus, we can use an unconditional branch to the instructions that conduct the test on his place of birth. This starts with the instruction in 0009.
		WE HAVE FOUND A MAN BORN IN THE 1930s
0008	09 0050	We get to this instruction if we reject the man. This says branch to the instruction that sets us up to consider the next man, and this starts at location 0050.
		REJECT THIS MAN. GET THE NEXT MAN'S RECORD.

Figure 2-17 Date of birth check—coding

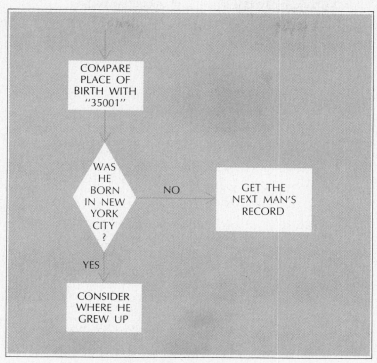

Figure 2-18   Birthplace check

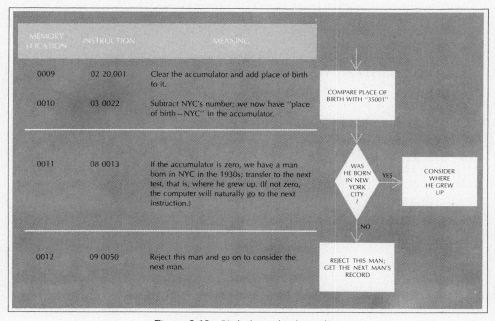

MEMORY LOCATION	INSTRUCTION	MEANING
0009	02 20,001	Clear the accumulator and add place of birth to it.
0010	03 0022	Subtract NYC's number; we now have "place of birth – NYC" in the accumulator.
0011	08 0013	If the accumulator is zero, we have a man born in NYC in the 1930s; transfer to the next test, that is, where he grew up. (If not zero, the computer will naturally go to the next instruction.)
0012	09 0050	Reject this man and go on to consider the next man.

Figure 2-19   Birthplace check—coding

MEMORY LOCATION	INSTRUC-TION	MEANING
0050	02 0001	Clear the accumulator and add instruction 0001 to the accumulator.
0051	01 0023	Add 00 0001 to it.
0052	06 0001	Move the modified instruction back to location 0001.
0053	02 0005	Clear the accumulator and add instruction 0005 to accumulator.
0054	01 0023	Add 00 0001 to accumulator.
0055	06 0005	Move the modified instruction back to location 0005.
0056	02 0009	Clear the accumulator and add instruction 0009 to accumulator.
0057	01 0023	Add 00 0001 to accumulator.
0058	06 0009	Move the modified instruction back to location 0009.
0059	09 0001	Branch back to the start of the program.

Figure 2-20 See the next record—coding

This process finally produces a list of names of suspects who fit the description. We can then proceed with this list to the motor vehicle registration file, where we must find whether any of these suspects owns a red Pontiac by searching for the vehicles registered under these names.

There are some artificial things about this example. Why a criminal in the course of a strong-arm robbery would mention his birthplace or even drive his own car on a job, we don't know. There are also some oversimplifications of file organization and handling of alphabetic information. However, you can still see some of the computer's limitations and scope, and that was the point of subjecting you, the reader, to all that detail.

Depending on how many strong-arm robbers this police file had, this search could still take a couple of hours of computer time and cost over $1000 in a modern computer system. The point is

that we cannot search arbitrarily large files at negligible cost.

Let us reexamine what we really did in this example. We took the search process and broke it down into very elementary steps—many more than you would have to do if you were instructing a clerk to perform this task. When you have to specify every step of a computation, you end up with many instructions. The more instructions you write, the more errors you are likely to make. The machine does precisely what it is told to do, errors and all, so a programmer must spend considerable time and effort checking out his or her program.

The earliest computers had little more than the capabilities just described—a few thousand words of memory and an arithmetic unit that required as much as several milliseconds (thousandths of a second) to add two numbers. (At this point you will just have to suppress your curiosity about how a computer with only a few thousand words of memory searched files with millions of entries. Take our word for it. They did.)

Summary

As we indicated at the beginning of the chapter, the point of this detailed description was not to teach you to become a computer programmer but to allow you to see the powers and limitations of the computer and how its characteristics influence the way it is used. On the basis of what you have now read, several things should be clear.

First, we can see how the computer has become a widespread, general-purpose machine. While much of the discussion so far has been about numbers and arithmetic, the holes in the punched card and the numbers in the computer memory can represent the letters of the alphabet and thus can communicate English-language information. They can also represent locations on a two-dimensional surface; therefore a diagram or a map can be stored on a computer. They can stand for notes on the scale and represent music. The solution to any problem can be implemented on a computer if the procedure for solving it can be stated completely and explicitly and if all the data can be represented in code by numbers.

Many of the powers of the computer came about simply because it is a machine. As the components of the machine (vacuum tubes at first, then transistors and more advanced circuits) became faster and more reliable, the whole machine did also. As the machine could process longer numbers, the computations became more accurate. As better and cheaper devices became available to build memories from, the memories became larger to accommodate more information. Although the computer has evolved into a more elaborate device, it still contains no innate intelligence. All that even the largest and most complex computer is capable of doing is arithmetic, storing numbers, making simple decisions on the basis of arithmetic, and performing the sequences of operations given to it by humans. However, even in this simple example of the search for criminal suspects, we have seen the power of simple arithmetic. Recall that our order list has the ability only to determine whether a number is zero or negative and to make a decision on that basis. But we used that ability to determine whether two numbers were equal and whether one number was smaller than the other. This allowed us to search for names and compare dates of birth with a range of dates—in short, to store and retrieve information. You will see later that a computer can be programmed to do far more complex things, like playing chess and checkers.

We can also see some of the computer's limitations. The amount of instruction and the level of detail it requires is much greater than would be required to tell a human being how to do a comparable task. In order to cause the computer to do some of the more complex things that seem worthwhile and possible, very large sets of instructions have to be written. Programmers must often work for days, weeks, and even months to create useful systems.

Finally, because of the level of detail and the large size of computer programs, people make mistakes in writing them. It is, in fact, very unusual to see a program of more than a hundred steps that does what it is supposed to do the first time it is run on a machine. Roughly fifty percent of the cost of a program is the testing and error correction that must follow its writing. Thus if you read a newspaper article that states that a computer made a mistake, it is most likely that a computer programmer actually made it.

Exercises

1. A system of symbols is sometimes called a *code*. Give some examples of codes that you know of.

2. In the sense in which we described machines as single-action, multiple-action, or fixed-sequence, classify these machines: a milling machine, a sewing machine, a record player, a washing machine, a toaster, a dishwasher, a loom, a hammer, a lathe.

3. What are the major components of a computer? How are they related?

4. What is a program?

5. Try your hand at doing a simple programming task. Modify the flowchart on page 45 so that it will add only those numbers greater than "0", ignoring the negative numbers. Now make the corresponding modifications to the program in figure 2-13.

6. What are the limitations of a machine that will only do exactly as it is told?

7. Now that you have found out that the computer is really simple conceptually and it is the program that is complex, review the threats and dangers discussed in chapter one and see if you view any of them differently.

8. What is the significance of being able to write a sequence of instructions that can make a decision and modify itself?

9. As programs become terribly complex, the programmer's ability to check out all of the possibilities diminishes. Can you conceive of a problem in which the unforeseen logical consequences of its program could become dangerous?

For Further Information

The history of the development of computers has never been written at length. However, many introductory books about computers (see below) contain brief historical surveys, some of them lavishly illustrated with pictures of the old machines. An article by Saul Rosen (1) provides a useful summary of facts about early computers. Thomas M. Smith's paper (2) is really an essay on the problem of writing a history of computers in terms of issues and ideas. Goldstine (3) presents the view of someone who participated in the early developments himself. The Eames book (4) is a fascinating collection of pictures of all kinds of things in the history of computers.

A book by Jeremy Bernstein (5) contains some fascinating historical details, particularly about Charles Babbage, who developed a nineteenth-century precursor of the digital computer. Further, it is about the best armchair introduction to computers and computing ever written. D. S. Halacy's book (6) is another good non-technical introduction to computers. *Computers and Computation* (7) is somewhat more technical and detailed: it is written for a scientific audience but not for computer specialists. All three of these books are available in paperback editions, by the way. The *National Geographic* article (8) is another good introduction, largely because of its excellent pictures; it is available in almost any library.

If you want to know more about how computers work, you will have to turn to one of the more technical introductions to computers. A large number of such books, generally of very high quality, are in print. By and large, they are how-to-do-it books designed as programming textbooks. However, even the armchair reader will find them helpful in some areas. The references that follow contain a selection of them (9–15).

References

1. Saul Rosen, "Electronic Computers: A Historical Survey," *Computing Surveys* **1:**1 (March 1969).

2. Thomas M. Smith, "Some Perspectives on the Early History of Computers," in Zenon W. Pylyshym, ed., *Perspectives on the Computer Revolution* (Englewood Cliffs, N.J.: Prentice-Hall, Inc., 1970).

3. H. H. Goldstine, *The Computer from Pascal to von Neumann* (Princeton, N.J.: Princeton University Press, 1973).

4. Charles and Ray Eames, *A Computer Perspective* (Cambridge: Harvard University Press, 1973).

5. Jeremy Bernstein, *The Analytical Engine: Computers Past, Present, and Future* (New York: Random House, Inc., 1966).

6. D. S. Halacy, Jr., *Computers, the Machines We Think With* (New York: Dell Publishing Co., Inc., 1964).

7. *Computers and Computation, A Scientific American Book* (San Francisco: W. H. Freeman, 1971).

8. Peter E. White, "Behold the Computer Revolution," *National Geographic Magazine,* **138:**5 (November 1970), pp. 593–633.

9. Eric Weiss, *Computer Usage Fundamentals* (New York: McGraw-Hill Book Company, 1975).

10. William Desmonde, *Computers and their Uses* (Englewood Cliffs, N.J.: Prentice-Hall, Inc., 1965).

11. Fred M. Tonge and Julian Feldman, *Computing: An Introduction to Procedures and Procedure Following* (New York: McGraw-Hill Book Company, 1975).

12. Thomas C. Bartree, *Introduction to Computer Science* (McGraw-Hill Book Company, 1975).

13. C. W. Gear, *Introduction to Computer Science* (Chicago: Science Research Associates, Inc., 1973).

14. Robert and Nancy Stern, *Principles of Data Processing* (New York: John Wiley & Sons, Inc., 1973).

15. G. B. Davis, *Introduction to Electronic Computers* (New York: McGraw-Hill Book Company, 1971).

Computer Hardware

3

The preceding chapter has presented an account of how computers work in terms of some of the basic concepts developed with the first computing machines that were built. The present chapter will consider how these concepts are realized in actual computer hardware and what capabilities a modern computer actually has.

The concepts have changed very little. However, the size, speed, and cost of computer resources have been altered so drastically that they differ in kind as well as degree. In the earliest machines a few thousand cells of memory for the storage of programs and data were all that economy and technology would allow. A modern computer with a few *million* cells of memory is by no means unusual. Thirty years ago, additions performed in two milliseconds were a technological achievement;

today, additions performed at a thousand times that rate are comparatively slow. We have grown accustomed to large numbers and they no longer impress us. Richard Hamming has pointed out that a comparable improvement in other technologies would mean houses costing twenty to sixty dollars and cars hardly worth the price of a parking fee.

Describing *the* modern computer is no easy task. There are many different computer manufacturers in the United States and each produces a range of different models—different sizes at different prices for different markets. Computers that are used in offices and laboratories today were designed anywhere from two to ten years ago; they represent—since the pace of technological improvement has hardly slackened—a wide range of different circuit techniques, memory storage methods, and speeds. And, of course, they stand in the shadow of new developments that will make them obsolete and ready for retirement, in some cases, only a few years after they are installed.

However, independent from these considerations, most modern machines function in the same basic way, so that we will be able to describe the central processing unit, memory devices, and input and output units in sufficient detail to give a picture of a *typical* modern computer. We will conclude this chapter with a summary of different types of computer installations, their complements of equipment, their costs, and their approximate abilities for solving key problems.

However, before we can discuss the capacity of computers, communications systems, and the errors they make, we must talk about how information is actually represented in modern machines. Thus the next topic is encoding systems.

Encoding Systems

In written communication we use the letters of the alphabet, the ten digits, and a handful of special characters such as punctuation marks. It is not surprising that these symbols, designed for ease of production and interpretation by people, are inappropriate for other systems—particularly for electronic systems and computers. You will see why.

Morse code was the first system that used electrical patterns to represent written language. It used a combination of long and short electrical signals—easy to create, to send long distances over wires, and to interpret—to perform the same functions of letters and digits. It was, in fact, an *encoding system.*

A .-	1 .---
B -...	2 ..---
C -.-.	
D -..	etc.

In this simple system, the basic symbols are a short signal, a long signal, and no signal at all, which indicates the spacing between the other symbols.

The encoding system of digital computers is very similar to this. In fact, it is simpler still, since the two basic elements are the presence or absence of an electrical pulse at a given time or place.

The binary nature of the coding—that is, the presence or absence of a state or condition—makes it convenient to represent the elements of this coding scheme as digits 1 (presence) and 0 (absence). We can use these zeros and ones in series, treat them as numbers, and perform arithmetic on them. In order to explain how it is possible to perform arithmetic operations with numbers that use only zeros and ones, it will be necessary to discuss the binary number system first.

Binary Numbers. How can large numbers be represented by a system with only two digits, 0 and 1? It is very simple, although its strangeness may make it seem complicated at first. Actually, the binary number system works in a way that is exactly analogous to the method used in decimal arithmetic. In decimal arithmetic, we have only ten digits (0 through 9). We represent larger numbers by making their relative positions significant. To count, we run through the series we have available, 0 through 9, and then begin using two columns—10. When we add 1 to 9, we put down a 0 and add 1 to the next column to the left.

In binary arithmetic, we do the same thing, but the number of digits we have is very limited, so we are forced to use more columns almost immediately. In counting, numbers grow very long very quickly; in adding, carrying soon makes the numbers longer. Here are the first few numbers in binary, with their decimal equivalents:

BINARY	DECIMAL EQUIVALENT
0001	1
0010	2
0011	3
0100	4
0101	5
0110	6
0111	7
1000	8

But how is arithmetic performed on these numbers? In addition, the rules are very simple:

$$0 + 0 = 0$$
$$1 + 0 = 1$$
$$1 + 1 = 0 \text{ (with a one to carry) or } 10$$

To add two numbers involves only using these rules. Consider this simple problem:

```
a b c d e f
1 0 0 1 0 0
+   1 1 0 1
=         ?
```

Starting with column f, we add 0 and 1 and put down a 1; in e, 0 and 0 make 0. So far so good. In column d, 1 and 1 make 10, so we put down a 0 and carry the 1. In c, we add 1 and the 1 we carried; again, we put down a 0 and carry the 1. In b, the sum is 1; in a, also 1. We have the answer:

BINARY	DECIMAL EQUIVALENT
1 0 0 1 0 0	36
+ 1 1 0 1	+13
=1 1 0 0 0 1	49

For multiplication, the rules are equally simple. Here is the multiplication table in binary:

$$0 \times 0 = 0$$
$$0 \times 1 = 0$$
$$1 \times 0 = 0$$
$$1 \times 1 = 1$$

Learning the multiplication table in binary would certainly make arithmetic in elementary school much easier, but using it would be very tedious. Here is what we would have to do to multiply 5 times 5, for instance:

```
        1 0 1
      × 1 0 1
        1 0 1
        0 0 0
    1 0 1
  1 1 0 0 1
```

The basic operations in this process are very simple, but they appear cumbersome because they must be applied many times, even to perform arithmetic on relatively small quantities. It is much easier for us to add in the decimal system. But for computers, the binary system of arithmetic is ideal. These fast and tireless machines are perfectly adapted to performing large numbers of very simple operations.

Another important advantage of the binary system for computer use has to do with the basic technology involved. Many electronic devices have only two states (*on* and *off*) and can thus be used to represent (or store) a one-digit binary number—or a *bit*, as it is called (from *bi*nary dig*it*). Thus any number can be represented by a series of ones and zeros, and any such series can be represented by a series of on-off pulses, relays in one position or another, or spots magnetized with one polarity or the other. In this way, any number can be communicated from one part of a computer to another or from one computer to another (see figure 3-1). However, this would be a highly inconvenient way for a person to have to communicate with a com-

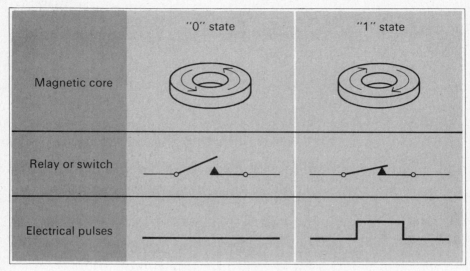

	"0" state	"1" state
Magnetic core		
Relay or switch		
Electrical pulses		

Figure 3-1 Binary components

puter, which is why the next section considers the representation of the symbols people use.

Representing Symbols. Besides using numbers to represent quantities for arithmetic purposes, we can also use them as symbols. Football players have numbers, for instance, and so do houses and streets. We use a number as a symbol to stand for these things and not as an arithmetic quantity: for example, you cannot add Fourteenth Street to Fourth Avenue and get eighteen of anything. So, in the computer, we use strings of binary digits to represent letters and punctuation marks.

How we assign numbers to represent other symbols usually does not matter, although for some purposes it will be convenient to have them in some order. For example, for the purpose of sorting names it is convenient to have *B* represented by a larger number than *A*. It is not surprising that several different methods are used in computers despite the fact that there is a national standard called ASCII (American Standard Code Information Interchange). The most common is called EBCDIC (for Extended Binary Coded Decimal Interchange Code). Each symbol is represented by a string of precisely eight bits. To be able to talk about these

eight-bit units, a name had to be invented: they are called *bytes*. Figure 3-2 shows some of the characters and their representations, or codes.

Within the computer, bytes are sometimes further grouped into units called *words*. This is probably an unfortunate nomenclature, since it can be misleading. It does not refer to a group of symbols containing a word of human language; rather, it is a name used for an element larger than a byte (usually sixteen to sixty-four bits) suitable for containing an instruction to the computer or a complete arithmetic quantity upon which some operation is to be performed.

Now that we have some concept of how the machine stores information, let us look in a little more detail at the parts of the computer that were described in very general terms in the previous chapter: central processing unit, memory, and input/output.

Central Processing Unit. The *central processing unit* (CPU), as we learned in chapter two, is the part of the computer that does the work, making the calculations and decisions that are required. Among the many computers available the differences in size, capability, and cost are very great;

SYMBOL	BINARY REPRESENTATION	SYMBOL	BINARY REPRESENTATION	SYMBOL	BINARY REPRESENTATION	SYMBOL	BINARY REPRESENTATION
1	11110001	A	11000001	a	10000001	$	01011011
2	11110010	B	11000010	b	10000010	?	01100000
3	11110011	C	11000011	c	10000011	×	11111010
4	11110100	D	11000100	+	01001110	÷	11111011
5	11110101						

Figure 3-2 Some EBCDIC characters

but the most important consequence of these differences is speed. In general, we can say that a small inexpensive computer can do everything a large one can do, but the large one will be able to perform a process in a fraction of a second that would take the small one hours, and in hours what would take the small one days or weeks.

Differences in the design of the circuitry in the CPU can account for great differences in speed. The time required to perform an addition may range from three hundred microseconds to a thousandth of that. But there are other ways of improving the speed of a computing system. Some computers, for example, can do several things at once: for example, perform a calculation and begin the interpretation of the next instruction. CPUs with many accumulators do not need to store partial results in memory and get them out again, which saves time.

In addition to the speed feature and thus the amount of work a system can perform in a given time, several other aspects are important. CPUs

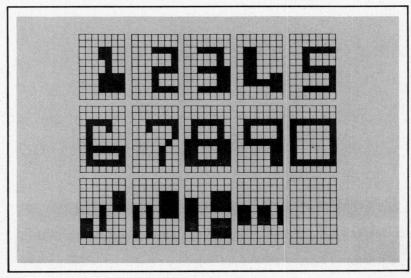

Figure 3-3 MICR characters

In the computer, the basic operations can be done within the order of a

NANOSECOND

One thousandth of a millionth of a second.

Within the half second it takes this spilled coffee to reach the floor, a fairly large computer could—

(given the information) (in magnetic form)

Debit 2000 checks to 300 different bank accounts,

and *examine the electro-cardiograms of 100 patients and alert a physician to possible trouble,*

and *score 150,000 answers on 3000 examinations and evaluate the effectiveness of the questions,*

and *figure the payroll for a company with a thousand employees.*

and a few other chores.

with a small word length may be able to easily handle only a small amount of memory because they cannot address more. This affects the complexity of the programs that can conveniently be operated. Some CPUs may be able to handle only a small number of input-output devices, which will affect their versatility. Finally, some computers can operate several processes simultaneously without their interfering with one another. This is important because it permits a mode of operation called *time sharing,* which allows many individuals to communicate with a computer at the same time. More will be said about time sharing in the chapter on software.

Memory Systems

There are three classes of memory devices used in computers; high-speed memory, which is directly associated with the CPU, a slower memory that can be accessed very quickly and at random, and an even slower memory that is accessed serially. *Random access* is the ability to select any element with equal ease and speed, like books from a shelf. With a serial device, not all items are equally accessible; the physical position of the element determines how fast it can be selected. This is exactly like locating a particular musical selection on a long tape recording.

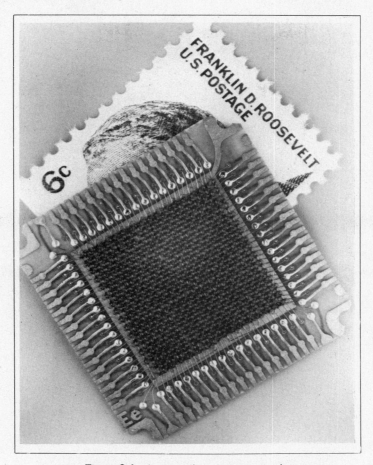

Figure 3-4 A magnetic core memory plane

The memory systems that we will discuss in the next section are all erasable. This means that numbers can be written in the memory, read from it, and erased by writing over an existing number with a new number or zeros. (There are also non-erasable computer memories that use photographic techniques.)

High-Speed Memory. The circuitry of the modern computer can now work in billionths of a second. In fact, although the speed with which electronic devices can change state (from zero to one) still limits a computer's effective operating speed, there are circumstances in which the speed electricity can travel in a wire limits the design of the system.

This has resulted in much redesign and repackaging of computer components.

Many modern high-speed memories can be read in 275 nanoseconds (billionths of a second). This is the time (called *access time*) required to transfer a word of information from the memory to the control or arithmetic unit. This rate controls the speed at which the central processing unit operates. We are now at the stage in which the more advanced computers can perform hundreds of millions of instructions per second.

Random-access Memory. Although there are many devices for constructing memories, the most common physical unit for storing information in

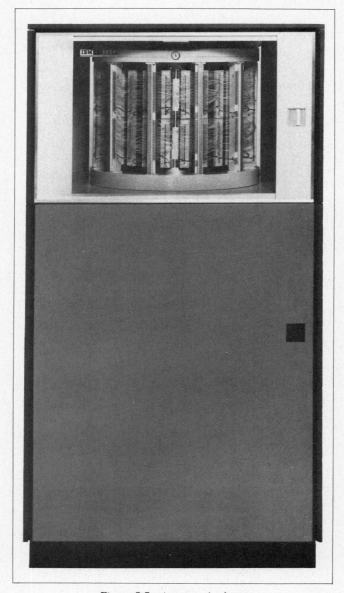

Figure 3-5 A magnetic drum

high-speed memories is a magnetizable ring of metal called a *magnetic core*. One magnetic core is required for each bit of information to be stored.

The cost of a magnetic core memory is on the order of a few cents per bit, and therefore 100-million-bit core memories are prohibitively expensive. Yet fairly rapid access to that much information and more is often needed. The solution to this problem has been to compromise the speed of access for some of the information. The data that may be needed is stored in high-speed core memory; information that is less frequently

Figure 3-6 A disk pack

needed is stored in slower memory. *Magnetic drums* and *magnetic disks* have near random-access memories that give access to information in thousandths of a second (milliseconds).

Both of these devices are based on the same principles. They use rotating surfaces covered with a material that can be magnetically polarized in one direction or the other by a writing head and later sensed by a reading head. The polarized spots are arranged in many tracks.

In the case of the magnetic disks, like the long-playing record, the information is on concentric tracks. The read/write heads move in and out to access information on one disk. If there is a stack of them, the head moves up and down the stack of disks, rather like the player arm on phonograph records in a jukebox. More expensive devices have one read/write arm per disk.

There are also disk pack units (smaller disk-like units) in which the stack of magnetic plates is removable. By simply inserting the disk pack, a tremendous block of information can be installed

in the machine. A large library of data or programs can be kept on these relatively inexpensive disk packs.

In the magnetic drum (used less frequently now), tracks form rings around the entire periphery of the drum. There is one read/write head for each track. The heads are usually not movable.

In all of these devices, the computer must wait until the information it wants comes under the read heads. The average time this takes is called the *average access time*. Once the information is properly positioned, it can be transferred to the central processing unit much more quickly. The speed at which this is done is called the *transfer rate*. In a modern disk system, an access time of forty milliseconds is average; the transfer rate for the system should be about a million bytes per second. Disks or disk packs of this quality come in units that store at least thirty million bytes. Since a great number of them can be connected to the same computer, there is no effective maximum; systems that store several hundred million bytes are

Figure 3-7 A disk pack unit

by no means uncommon. The cost of this storage is (compared to core memory) very cheap. Hardware rental and maintenance costs will be about eight dollars per million bytes per month.

To put these quantities into some perspective, let us consider the information content of a newspaper, a dictionary, and an industrial personnel file of a medium-sized company. Storing these files on disk could cost $8 per month for the newspaper, $80 for the dictionary, and $96 for the

personnel file. This is, of course, only the cost for the hardware on which the data are to be stored. It does not include the costs of the computer used to put the data there, the space and personnel needed to support the system, or the cost of getting at the information once it is on the disk. The monthly cost at a typical commercial service center would be about $400 for the newspaper and about $4000 for the dictionary or the personnel file.

Let us consider the significance of the transfer

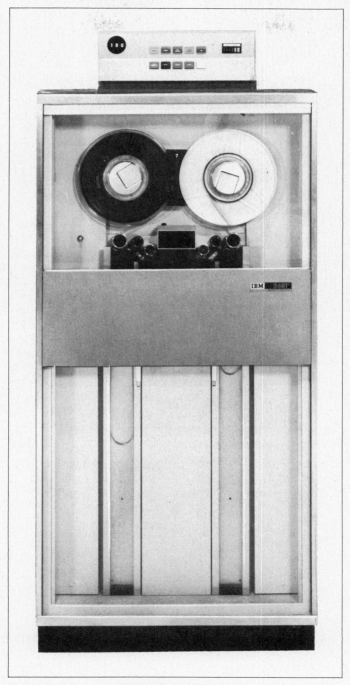

Figure 3-8 A tape drive

Figure 3-9 A typical tape library

rates and the average access times. If we have a disk containing, for example, a million five-digit numbers, the computer could add them all up and produce the sum in something under a second. But the transfer of the five million bytes (one byte per digit) of information from the disk to the computer's core memory would take five to ten seconds. The reason this can be done so rapidly is that when the computer calculates a sum, it can just add the numbers in the order they are stored.

If our problem is a little more complex and the computer cannot just take the numbers off in the order they are stored, we must then wait, on the average, forty milliseconds for each number. Under these circumstances it would take eleven hours to access and read them.

Serial Memory. The magnetic-tape system consists of a tape drive and a replaceable reel of half-inch magnetic tape. It provides slow but cheap and all-but-infinite auxiliary memory for computer systems. The surface of the tape can be magnetized and then sensed as the tape passes across the read/write heads. If the search for information on tape is for a specific piece of information of unknown location, then, on the average, each search has to go halfway through the tape. This can take on the order of a minute to a minute and a half. Therefore tapes are not used for random searches, but are primarily used for serial access to bulk data.

Typically, two million bytes of information can be stored on a tape. Once the right place is found on it, the rate at which information can be transferred from it to the computer varies from 15,000 to 120,000 characters per second. The cost of a reel of computer tape is $30.00 or about .0002 cents per bit, which is considerably cheaper than drum or disk.

Input/Output Devices. Input/output devices are quite slow in relation to the speed of the computers with which they are used. In many systems, one or more smaller computers are used to control input/output operations. In such an arrangement, the smaller computers take their commands from

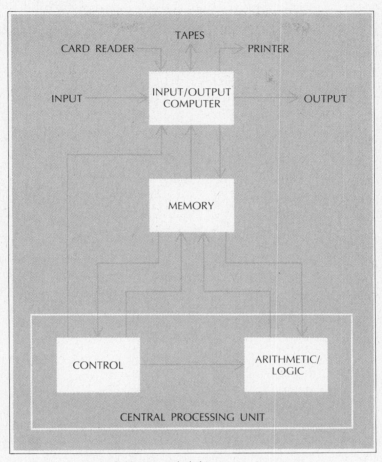

Figure 3-10 Expanded data-processing system

the large computer, which directs what information is to be transferred and at what time. The schematic of a computer that was presented in chapter two can now be expanded as shown in figure 3-10.

The devices we will discuss here are for large-scale input and output of data. The devices used for communication between computers and people will be discussed in chapter four.

Data Input. First of all, before information can get into the computer, it must be transferred from its original form—usually a handwritten, typed, or printed document—into a form that the computer's input device can accept. One means of accomplishing this is a *keypunch,* which an operator uses much like a typewriter to punch holes in cards. This operation currently costs about five to twenty cents per eighty-column card, punched and verified (checked for accuracy). The reason that the range of costs is so wide is that the source documents vary greatly in quality and the cost of manual labor is high. In fact keypunching costs can in some cases dominate the creation of a new system. For example, the development of a law-enforcement computer system for a large state can require five to ten million dollars worth of keypunching to put the records into a form that can be input to

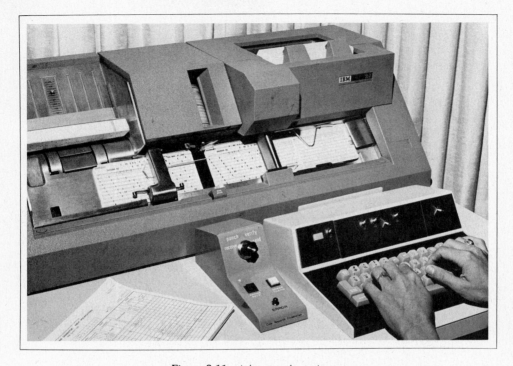

Figure 3-11 A keypunch station

the computer. Automation of many library systems has been hampered by the prohibitive cost of converting millions of catalog cards into machine-readable form.

Punched cards have always been the predominant input medium. However, they are bulky, cumbersome, and slow to process. Other means have therefore been invented. Some of these, like the keypunch that produces punched cards, consist of a keyboard on which an operator must type the information. However, instead of on a punched card, the data may be stored on a punched paper tape, a magnetic tape, or a disk. *Punched paper tape* is similar to magnetic tape. Holes are punched in it to store information, and certain other devices read it. In other cases, the information may be fed directly from the input terminal into the computer. These terminal devices will be discussed in chapter five.

But all of these methods require a human operator to recopy the information before it can be input to the computer. Three other kinds of input devices are now frequently used that do not have

this disadvantage: mark sensing readers, magnetic ink character recognition equipment, and optical character recognition equipment.

Mark-sense devices detect the presence or absence of graphite marks on paper, just as a card or paper-tape reader detects the presence or absence of holes. The page or card that serves as the input medium has certain designated areas that can be blackened with a pencil. The reader detects whether the mark is present by measuring the light reflected from the spot. Mark sensing sheets are particularly useful when many people must prepare the input, since no special equipment other than a pencil is required. Thus these sheets are frequently used for questionnaires (such as a census, a survey, or college registration, for instance) and for multiple-choice tests and examinations.

In some cases, such as bank checks, it is important to have all or part of the information on a document in a form that can be read both by people and by machines. The most frequently used

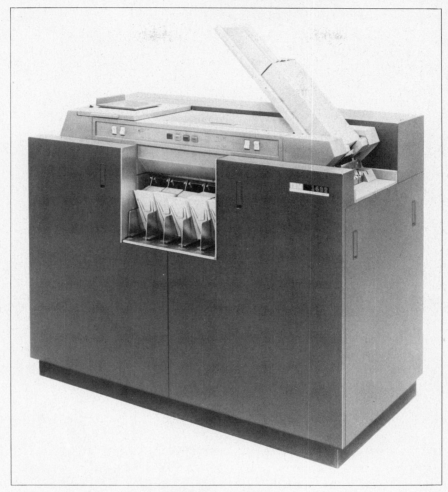

Figure 3-12 A card reader

system for this purpose is *magnetic ink character recognition* (MICR). The special characters (see figure) are most familiar from their appearance on checks and other bank documents. They are printed in an ink that contains a magnetic substance. MICR machines check for the presence or absence of magnetism on seventy locations within each character's area and identify the character by this pattern.

More sophisticated are *optical character recognition devices,* which rely on reflected light instead of magnetic ink. Some of the simpler equipment of this kind recognizes characters by matrix matching (like the MICR, by checking a matrix of points within the character area). An optical character reader can read all the information on a typed page in less than one second. More versatile and complex machines recognize characters by the presence of curved lines, horizontal or vertical straight lines, closed loops, and so on. Some of them are even able to recognize carefully handwritten block characters. These more versatile machines are naturally more error-prone and more expensive. They range in price from $100,000 to $1 million.

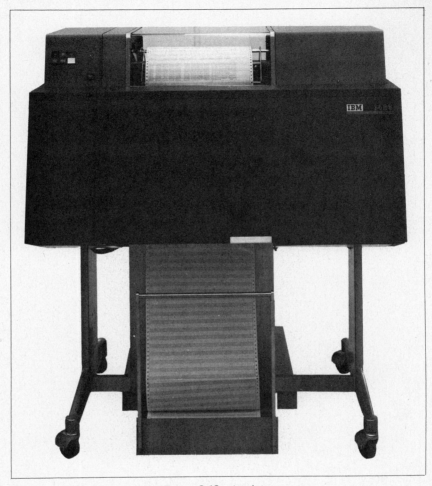

Figure 3-13 A printer

Input Devices. Keypunch machines record the information on cards. Other key entry devices store information on tapes or disks. Optical or magnetic interpretation equipment also usually produces output material that can be carried to a computer and serve as input. In order to read these cards and tapes, the computer must have special equipment called *input devices.*

The *card reader* is found on almost all computers today except the very smallest, since the card is almost a universal form for transmitting and storing data. Modern card readers can process from 100 to 2000 cards per minute, which is a relatively slow process as far as computers are concerned.

Magnetic tape—which we have already discussed as a memory device—also serves as input when the information from key-entry stations or optical or magnetic character readers is stored on tape. Some computers also accept punched paper tape and magnetic tape cassettes as input media. This method of input has a few particular advantages: it is low in cost and also is available as a communications medium between computers and some laboratory devices and teletype machines.

Output Devices. The *printer,* as the principal output mechanism for the computer, makes its marks on paper in a variety of ways. It may use

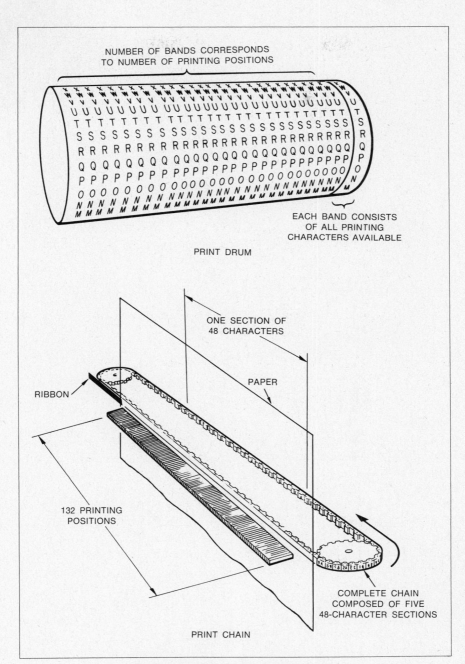

Figure 3-14 Printing mechanisms

Figure 3-15   A plotter, which produces two-dimensional output

hammers (one for each position that can be printed), rotating drums with raised characters for impact printing, or travelling print chains. It essentially creates an entire line of print at once. Printing speeds vary between 500 to 2000 lines per minute. Other printers spray ink in the pattern of the letters and numbers. A *card punch,* which is often part of the same unit that reads cards, operates somewhat the way a card reader does. There is one punch station for each column of the card. Thus when the row that corresponds to the number to be punched passes by, a device is activated that pushes the punch die through the card. Cards can be punched at speeds of 100 to 200 cards per minute.

Specialized output devices are sometimes used. Very often, these are not connected directly to the computer. In such cases, for example, the computer writes the output information on magnetic tape, which is later read by another machine that produces the desired output. Another very valuable output device is the *plotter.* It consists of a pen held over a large sheet of paper (see figure 3-15). The information from the computer controls the pen's movement and straight or curved lines can be drawn. This allows the computer to produce output in the form of charts and diagrams, as well as architectural plans and engineering drawings. Some striking artistic experiments have also been attempted.

Some applications produce such voluminous records that microfilm rather than paper is used for output. In these cases an image of a page of output is produced on a cathode ray tube or tele-

Figure 3-16 Minicomputers

vision screen and then is photographed. Other machines can, under computer control, produce typography suitable for publication.

Minicomputers

Minicomputers are not fundamentally different from their older and larger cousins. Their main significance is their small size, low cost, and the wide range of applications that these advantages encourage.

There is no accepted standard definition of minicomputers—other than that they are no more than a few cubic feet in size and cost less than $10,000. These limits may have changed by the time you read this. The design and low cost of minicomputers depends upon the availability of such low-cost units as shown in figure 3-16. Predictors of the future envisage entire central processing

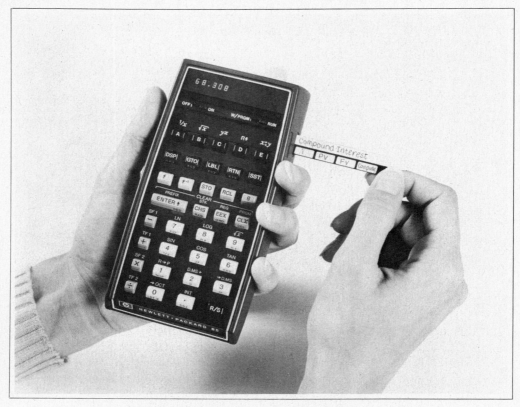

Figure 3-17 A programmable calculator

units on a single semiconductor chip that costs less than $10.00. The present effect of this trend toward miniaturization can be seen in the hand-held calculator, which is sold over the counter at $50 to $200, and in programmable calculators that cost less than $1000. The type of applications for which minicomputers have been used does not require, in general, highly accurate (20 significant digits) scientific computation. Thus they usually have a short word length: 16 bits. Some have 65,000 words of high-speed memory and perform millions of operations per second. Since many of their applications involve real-time control and the use of numerous peripheral devices, their input/output structure is elaborate. They have good communica-

tions capability; some can handle 500,000 16-bit words per second.

Because of the short word lengths, a minicomputer's basic set of instructions available to the programmer is generally less elaborate than those of the large-scale computer, and some are not much more elaborate than the sample order list shown on page 47. Consequently they are harder to program.

Much of the economic justification of the really large-scale computers depends on an "economy of scale" argument—that is, whether one is able to accumulate a sufficiently large load of computing to be done. Thus a computer that rents for $40,000 per month has to be justified by a requirement for

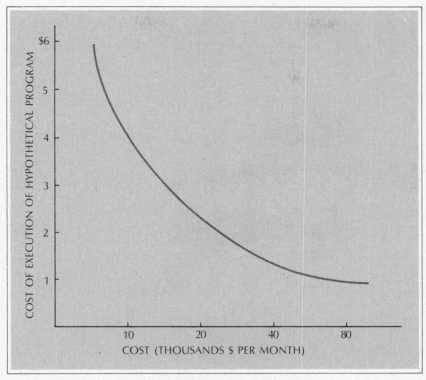

Figure 3-18 Economy of scale

millions of computations per second. Minicomputers are economically justifiable if the problems they are required to solve are simple and a minimal computer is adequate for those problems. However, the application has to be very well understood because badly understood applications have a way of growing in size and complexity before the system is finished.

Another development that has already begun to overshadow the minicomputer is the availability of *microcomponents*. A separate memory, an eight-bit register, and a four-bit arithmetic unit are now available for a few cents a bit. They operate at speeds faster than a microsecond. They are being assembled into computers and are being used in engineering applications. Computers are being used as components in engineering design, which

will change the nature of the field. Even now we find these micro-components in everyday devices like power drills, where they are used to control speed.

Summary of Capabilities

Up to this point, we have discussed the capabilities of parts of a computer. Now it is time to put it all together and to give some thought to cost. This has been done in table 3.1; it shows the equipment configuration of four computer installations and their approximate costs in terms of monthly rental. The systems represent the very small to the moderately large.

The first, a Century 101 computer manufactured by the National Cash Register company, is a

Table 3.1 Machine capabilities

MACHINE NAME	CORE STORAGE (BYTES)	DISK STORAGE (MILLION BYTES)	DISK TRANSFER RATE (BYTES/ SECOND)	CPU OPERATIONS PER SECOND	MAGNETIC TAPE DRIVES	PRINTER SPEED (LINES/ MINUTE)	CARD READER (CARDS MINUTE)	CARD PUNCH (CARDS MINUTE)	TYPICAL MONTHLY RENTAL
1. NCR Century 101	32,000	10	312,000	40,000	0	300	300	0	$2225
2. Burroughs B2771	120,000	110	325,000	25,000	4	1100	475	150	9000
3. CDC Cyber 70-74	1,300,000	472	806,000	100,000	4	1200	1000	300	40,000
4. IBM 370/158	1,000,000	400	1,130,000	100,000	6	1200	1200	250	75,000

popular small computer. It is intended essentially as a business system for a small- or medium-sized company. Input is cards; output is printed reports. It has a relatively small core memory because the applications such a system might support do not require more. It has a good disk system for file storage, but no tapes. Systems like this have been installed in many business offices, in hospitals, and in government offices. A system almost identical to the one described can be found in the city hall of one city the authors know of with a population of 50,000. The cost of this system, including some of the support requirements, is equivalent to the cost of a staff of an accountant and one or two clerks.

The second system in the table, a Burroughs B2771, is a more ambitious system. It has ten times the storage of the first and four tape units for file backup. It would support a fairly extensive range of applications. It would most typically provide the computation required for the business data processing of a medium-sized corporation as well as supporting the needs of the company's engineering and research departments.

The Cyber 70, Model 74, produced by Control Data Corporation, would support a considerably greater load of work. One might expect to see such a system in a very large corporation with a considerable volume of engineering problems as well as business systems to run. It would be appropriate for a large university, where it would support administrative work, instruction, and research. In these environments, it would be expected to provide both batch and interactive service from fifty or more simultaneous users.

The IBM 370/158 is a big system, although by no means the largest we could expect to find. It is larger than most businesses would require and

would probably be installed at a scientific research facility. A service bureau for a state government, a major research institute, or a large university would be appropriate sites for such a system.

Many other computers, produced by many other manufacturers, could have been selected. For each of these, various sizes of memory might be specified. In selecting a computer, the options are very great. Components of different sizes and speeds can be selected, depending on what the buyer expects to use the system for. If the purchaser will have a great deal of printed output, for instance, very fast printers (and probably more than one) will be wanted. If, on the other hand, there will be little printing but very large storage requirements, the buyer will spend money on fast disks and be satisfied with a slower and more economical printer. The buyer may well modify the configuration after it is installed, adding, deleting, or changing components. To further complicate matters, the buyer may select different parts from different vendors, buying the central processing unit here, the disks there, and the card reader from a third vendor.

Because of this complexity, it is misleading to try to compare four such different systems in detail. The very small system will be able to perform economically the applications for which it was designed, but it will not be able to perform the very large and complex mathematical functions that the two largest systems are designed for. With regard to the CPUs' cost of operation, it is generally true that the cost of performing a task is cheaper on larger computers (see figure 3-19). However, as the cost of peripheral input/output units and the size and cost of storage grow, the overall price of systems may no longer obey this very general rule of thumb.

Figure 3-19 A do-it-yourself computer kit

A Million-Dollar File

We can look at the costs of computer services in another way. Maintaining a file of 100,000 names with records of 1000 characters per name (that is, a system with random access to a 100-million-character file) will cost about $38,000 per month. Assuming that operation costs such as space, rental, air conditioning, insurance, personnel, and so forth are approximately equal to machine costs, the bill will approach the impressive annual cost of one million dollars. Moreover, if such a system is to be connected to a nationwide network of inquiry stations, the communications will (as we

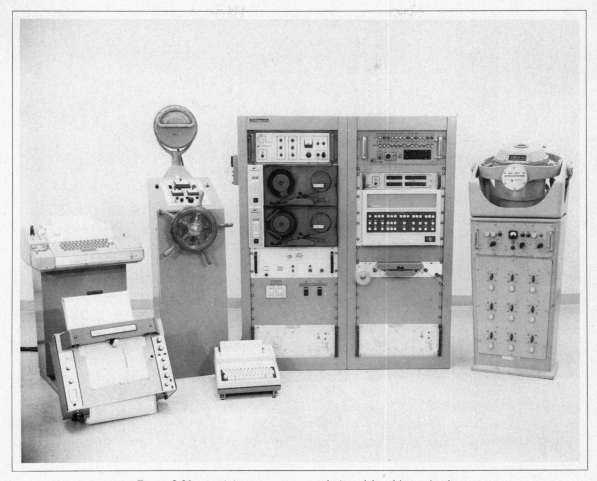

Figure 3-20 A minicomputer system designed for ship navigation

shall see in the next chapter) add still greater costs. Let us look at these figures another way. A million dollars a year will support a file of records for 100,000 names. One might argue that ten dollars a name is not a bad price for information on a group of very interesting people. On the other hand, for such a system to be of great value, 100,000 is far too small a number. A file of that many scientists or credit risks or criminals would have

limited social or financial value because it wouldn't be used frequently enough.

There are cases in which such a file is an economically sound investment. An airline reservation system is one of these. Each flight listed is referred to frequently and from many locations; one million characters is about big enough; and the need for fast and accurate record keeping is a good financial justification for the system's cost. The point that we are making (and we said we would return to it many times), is that the large-scale, online, rapid-access systems are expensive and this use requires good financial justification.

The Future. The history of progress in the computer industry has shown that about every five or six years there is a fifty percent decrease in the unit cost of computation. Thus we might expect to see the costs of maintaining, sorting and searching files, and performing arithmetic halved again in five years.

Progress in electronics—that is, in the circuitry of the CPU itself—has been more rapid than that in electromechanical devices such as tape and card readers, printers, and random-access storage units. In chapter twenty we will consider possible future improvements.

The effect on the world at large of minicomputers will first of all be to make computers more commonplace. As pieces of educational training equipment, they will become as inexpensive and thus as common as film projectors. Secondly, their costs will rival those of such products as home sound equipment and we will find hobbyists using them. Figure 3-20 shows a kit for assembling a minicomputer at home for less than $400. These two effects, combined with the American love of gadgets, will produce new computer applications around the home. We can expect to find homes in which everything between the garage doors and the fuse box is connected to a computer. Minicomputers have become the subjects of *Popular Mechanics* articles as well as professional journals. As for engineering applications, minicomputers are now being built to fit standard engineering equipment racks and compete in cost with power supplies. Much of electrical engineering design will use digital techniques, microcomponents, and minicomputers.

In total, as of this writing, somewhere between twenty-five and thirty-five thousand minicomputers are being shipped each year, and market studies optimistically predict continued growth. The value of 1975 shipments is expected to be $300 million, and the value of minicomputers in use at that time is roughly estimated to be over $2 billion. This is the newest and most vital development in the computer industry, but it still constitutes less than one percent of the industry's gross sales.

Exercises

1. Why is binary arithmetic used in digital computers?

2. The word *code* has been used in two different senses in this chapter and the last—one having to do with programming and one with the use of symbols to represent other things. Define and distinguish these two senses.

3. Translate the following binary numbers into decimal numbers.
   a. 1011
   b. 1111
   c. 11

4. Estimate the number of bits required to store any book of your choosing in a computer.

How many books are there in your college library (roughly)? How many bits of storage would it take to store the whole library in a computer? Using the cheapest storage medium mentioned in this chapter, what would it cost?

5. Research any computer application described in the literature in which the computer has been used to replace clerical personnel. How much faster is the computer than the people? How much less expensive is the computer? Is cost the only reason the computer was installed?

6. You have now gone from the very general statement of powers and limitations of a computer to a rather explicit set of sizes, speeds, and capabilities of some modern computers. You haven't had the complete story yet, but from your present vantage point, how do you view the omnipotent computer?

7. Why is a machine with a sixteen-bit word length adequate for controlling most natural processes?

9. If you were able to buy a programmable minicomputer for $100, would you? For $10? What would you do with it? Suppose for the same prices, you could get one with attachments that could pick off a number of electrical signals, measure them, and input them to the machine. What could you do with that?

For Further Information

The best sources of information about what computers are doing now will be in books and periodicals published more recently than the book you are now reading. The *Computer Yearbook* (1) is available in some scientific and engineering libraries. *Advances in Computers* (2) is an annual publication that catalogs and describes the development of the technology. It is intended for specialists in the field, and a beginner may find much of the material too difficult; however, he or she may be rewarded by leafing through a few volumes to see what is being discussed. Another good publication is the *Annual Review of Information Science and Technology* (3), although this deals more with applications than the computer hardware itself.

If these works are too detailed and too technical, you may find some of the magazines in the field easier reading. In particular, the ads represent the marketplace graphically and authoritatively. A selection of magazines is included among the references. (4-9). *Computerworld* is a weekly, published in newspaper-like format, and contains a great deal of topical information. *Datamation* is published monthly and is probably the most widely read periodical among computer people. *Computers and People* (formerly called *Computers and Automation*) appears monthly and publishes a number of articles on the social impact of computers as well as the technical aspects of the subject. Each year one of the issues contains a "Computer Directory and Buyer's Guide" that includes directories of companies, products, and services, lists of computer organizations, a census of computers, and an extensive (2600 at last count) list of applications.

Although these magazines and annuals will give the latest information, there are several books dealing with computer hardware that can be recommended highly (10–15). Bartee (12) is the best place to start. William Sharpe, an economist who is also a computer expert, has written a book on the economics of computation (16). The authors have relied on it in this chapter and elsewhere; you may want to look into it also.

(17), (18), and (19) provide a good introduction to minicomputers and some discussion of why they are chosen over the large-scale computers.

References

1. *Computer Yearbook and Directory* (annual)

2. Franz Alt and Morris Rubinoff, eds., *Advances in Computers* (New York: Academic Press, Inc.) (annual).

3. Carles Cuadra, ed., *Annual Review of Information Science and Technology* (Encyclopedia Brittanica Press) (annual).

4. *Computerworld* (weekly)

5. *Datamation* (monthly)

6. *Computers and People* (monthly)

7. *Infosystems* (monthly)

8. *Computer Decisions* (monthly)

9. *Data Processing* (monthly)

10. C. Gordon Bell and Allen Newell, *Computer Structures* (New York: McGraw-Hill Book Company, 1971).

11. Herbert Sobel, *Introduction to Digital Computer Design* (Reading, Mass.: Addison-Wesley Publishing Co., Inc., 1971).

12. Thomas Bartee, *Digital Computer Fundamentals* (New York: McGraw-Hill Book Company, 1966).

13. William Gear, *Computer Organization and Programming,* 2d ed. (New York: McGraw-Hill Book Company, 1974).

14. Ivan Flores, *Computer Organization* (Englewood Cliffs, N.J.: Prentice-Hall, 1969).

15. Yaohan Chu, *Computer Organization* (Englewood Cliffs, N.J.: Prentice-Hall, Inc., 1970).

16. William Sharpe, *The Economics of Computers* (New York: Columbia University Press, 1969).

17. John A. Murphy "Plug-Compatible Miniperipherals", *Modern Data* (December 1973), pp. 30–39.

18. Staff of *Computer Decisions,* "Succeeding with Minicomputers", *Computer Decisions* (November 1973), pp. 36–48.

19. Fred Gruenberger and David Babcock, "Speaking of Minis", *Datamation* (July 1973), pp. 57–59.

Communications and Terminals

4

As long as computers were simply super-calculators, getting data from card readers and printing out results, they were necessarily bulk processors of payrolls or instruments of large-scale scientific analysis. When techniques were developed to allow individuals to interact with computers inexpensively and more directly—in terms of their own problems rather than through complex technology—the use of computers exploded. That explosion continues today. The devices with which people communicate with the computer and with which it answers are called *terminals, displays,* or *consoles,* and they are the first topic of this chapter.

Early computer users had a serious limitation: they had to be in the same building with the computer. The development of techniques that allowed data to be reliably transmitted over high-

speed communications lines enabled computers to communicate with people and each other at great distances. This development has caused another explosion of applications. Organizations are now able to share data and computing power through a communications network. For example, the remote branches of a multi-national company, the members of a world-wide police cooperative, or the partners in a sharing consortium of universities can now be in instant contact. Such communications technology is the second subject of this chapter.

Terminals and Displays

The devices we have discussed so far for getting data in and out of a computer are punched cards, card readers, magnetic tape, disk packs, and high-

Figure 4-1 A typical terminal

speed printers. These operations usually take place at speeds of thousands of characters per second. Therefore they do not match well with the slower rates at which a person can type (150 words per minute, maximum), read (2000 words per minute, maximum), or listen. However, there are many situations in which it is appropriate for a person, even with this slow input/output capability, to communicate directly with a computer. For example, airline clerks use small terminals to check reservations for customers waiting at reservation desks. A bank clerk at a similar console can check the status of a checking account balance before cashing a check. A stockbroker can answer a client's question about the latest price quotations of stocks and bonds with a terminal like the one shown in figure 4-1.

Although it seems that a great deal of computer time would be wasted by this process, such is not the case. Because of the tremendous difference in data rate between people and computers, one computer can serve many terminals simultaneously. While one person is talking, thinking, or searching for the next key to press, the computer can be serving several other terminal users.

Thus terminals permit us to use the computer in a totally different way from that possible with the more cumbersome batch input/output devices discussed earlier. The method is conversational: the user types a line and the computer reacts immediately, which may affect what the user may decide to type next. For this reason, this mode of use is called *interactive* and the devices that make it possible are called *interactive terminals* (see figure 4-2).

At an interactive terminal, a programmer can write computer programs, an intelligence analyst can ask questions of a data base, or a typist can enter information for a new data base. The device most often used for input is a typewriter keyboard,

Figure 4-2 A graphic terminal that will print a copy of what appears on the screen

modified to put out coded electrical signals representing the keys struck. The coded computer output is transmitted to the terminal and decoded there so that the appropriate characters appear on the paper.

Some of these terminals can be attached to any telephone line (see figure 4-3). The user dials a number that connects him or her directly to an input line of a computer and sets the telephone handset into a pair of recessed holes on the terminal. When he or she depresses a key at the terminal, an electrical signal is created, converted into an audible code (by an acoustic coupler), and fed into the telephone mouthpiece. The telephone system obligingly transmits the sound of the data to the other end, where it is converted

Figure 4-3 A portable terminal

into another electrical pattern and sent to the computer. The computer decodes the signal by means of a special device called a *modem* (for modulator/demodulator) and makes the appropriate reaction. Messages are returned in more or less the same way. This great flexibility allows the user to gain access to the computer from any place he or she can use the telephone—which today is almost anywhere in the world.

The message returned from the computer can be printed on paper one character at a time (like a typewriter), or displayed on a cathode ray tube (CRT), the same tube that forms the basis of a television set. In fact, some terminals can be coupled to any television set for computer output, as in figure 4-3.

There are several other options available for data input and output at a terminal. Tape casettes like those used for sound recording are used at some terminals to store data or programs temporarily. For example, the user can instruct the computer to output all of the working data and write it on a casette for use when he or she returns to this (or some other) terminal. Such a casette can store approximately 200,000 characters of information.

Microfiche readers are coupled to microfilm storage systems so that the computer can select any of thousands of color pictures to display to the person seated at the reader. This has proven to be extremely useful in cases where the terminal operator must have access to a data base that is too large to be stored in the computer.

However, there is a special class of problem in which the user of the computer must be able not only to see a picture of the problem but also be able to work with it. A military command and control system is an example of this situation. For example, a weapons allocation officer in an automated air defense system must be able to see the location of enemy bombers as sensed by radar and projected on a map of the terrain. The officer can then direct interceptors or instruct new planes to take off. Further, under some circumstances the officer must be able to point to parts of the picture and have the computer sense what has been pointed to. For example, if an electronic surveillance officer sees radar clutter on the display scope and believes it to be the enemy jamming the radar, he or she must be able to point to this area so that the computer can process these data

Figure 4-4   A light pen

in a special way. Such terminals are called *graphic* terminals.

The Graphic Terminal.   The principal mechanism in the display console is the cathode ray tube. This tube is, in principle, the same device that is used in the television set. A specially coated surface inside the face of the tube lights up when a stream of electrons hits it. At the neck of the tube is a device that can direct this stream of electrons very precisely. Output can be displayed by controlling the path that the stream draws over the face of the tube. Letters, numbers, curves, and lines can be drawn this way.

A light pen (see figure 4-4) is often used to interact with the computer. It is a light-sensitive device that can be placed against the face of the tube to flag a certain area to the computer for further action, as in the case of the radar officer instructing the computer to consider certain clutter as potential jamming. Here is how it works: The computer systematically and constantly scans the surface of the tube. The light-sensitive pen puts out a signal when the scanning beam hits it, alerting the computer to the area where the pen is pointing. In addition, the display console may include either a specially designed keyboard or a typewriter for digital input to the computer.

There are also other graphic techniques in use, such as the Plato terminal manufactured by Magnavox using a panel made by Owens-Illinois. It consists of two thin sheets of glass encapsulating a matrix of 256 by 256 wires. The panel holds a small amount of gas at each intersection of the matrix, which lights up when both wires receive current. This panel (8½ inches by 8½ inches) is less expensive than the CRT display, and doesn't have to be rewritten periodically as a CRT does. Furthermore, it can be used in a fully lighted room.

Architects, among others, benefit from interactive graphic displays. Building stress and load calculations can be computed and displayed graphically for inspection and modification. More unusual applications will enable an architect to lay out a building completely in a computer and then display any view of it on the display scope. The architect will be able to see it in any perspective, as if he or she were flying around the building in a helicopter, walking around the grounds, walking through the halls and rooms, looking at any angle, or even opening a section of the floor to see how easy or difficult it would be for a plumber to reach some pipes. This will help the architect design, estimate costs, realize implications of proposed modifications, and prevent major mistakes.

Intelligent terminals. In some cases, it has proven helpful to give some terminals a small amount of computational capability. They are then able to satisfy some of the demands of the user locally and thus make fewer demands on the remote computer, thereby reducing communications costs. Because of their greater flexibility, they are sometimes called "intelligent" or "smart" terminals. Such a terminal may help the user format a page of input, spacing the data appropriately and backing up to help correct typographical errors, before the entire page is communicated to the computer. Other terminals may have some memory, so that the user can select any of several "pages" of output to examine. The terminal may be able to enlarge or decrease the size of a graphic image or generate different type fonts, including Russian or Greek. In fact, the capabilities of the most elaborate intelligent terminals are equivalent to those of a small computer. These devices allow the user to do a considerable amount of programming and computing independently, communicating with a larger computer only when a problem's size or complexity demands it.

Why Use an Interactive Terminal? There are many reasons for using interactive terminals. In the case of the military officer in a command and control center, time is the justification. The speed of modern airborne weapons has made the use of plotting boards and telephones obsolete.

But interactive computing has broader applications than those for military systems. Many people, such as engineers, who can use computational assistance must use diagrams, plots of data, maps, and plans as well. For the computer to be applied to their problems, it must be able to interact with them in the pictorial language they use. Thus if a statistician is studying a curve and wants to eliminate some data, he must be able to point to the data to be removed rather than go keypunch a card.

Engineers, mathematicians, and scientists use interactive computing as an aid to creativity. Some problems are so difficult that the problem solver needs a picture of the problem. He or she needs to be able to change the picture, rapidly try out a

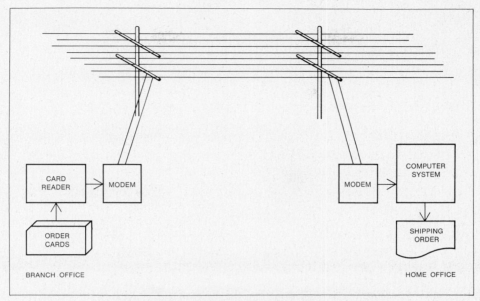

Figure 4-5   An online communications system

new idea, and see the results displayed. This must all be done within the limits of human patience and ability to maintain a line of thought. The person is being creative, not the machine; the machine's power simply facilitates the person's creativity. Since it is difficult to put a dollar value on creativity, and these consoles can be relatively costly, they are found more frequently in scientific research facilities than in engineering shops.

Interactive displays are also used in information retrieval systems. The user may be a graduate student searching an automated library index, a manager inspecting a data base of operating costs, or an intelligence analyst checking an inference about enemy activity. Such processes require the ability to browse through data. An interactive display allows the user to skim through general data rapidly and call for more limited displays to refine the search.

Digital Communications Systems

In recent years, the area of digital communications—the transmission of digital data—has grown dramatically. This development has been supported by the use of terminals, which we discussed earlier in this chapter, and by the growing importance of computer-to-computer communication.

Digital communications is the fastest growing part of the communications industry today; American Telephone and Telegraph expects that by 1980 the volume of digital messages will rival that of voice traffic. At the same time, more and more computers are being designed to communicate with other machines. In 1965, about one percent of the computers installed were linked directly to some sort of data communications system. Now, a decade later, the figure is estimated to be above fifty percent. The reasons for this tremendous growth are easy to determine. Industrial firms have found that they can use digital communications to collect data from remote offices. Brokerage firms, airlines, and hotels, for example, have found that prompt servicing of customer inquiries justifies the costs of what have come to be called real-time systems (see figure 4-5).

Real-Time Systems. *Real-time* is a generic term that is used to cover a fairly wide range of applications: any system that operates between the speed of light and the U.S. mail can be a real-time system. When a computer can receive information about a process, perform its calculations, and output facts in time to affect the process while it is still going on, we say that the computer acts in real time. The information the computer deals with reflects a current situation. More will be said about real-time control systems in chapter six.

Many large corporations have a number of computer installations linked to one another to distribute the computer workload equally and thus make use of any idle time. Another technique used at some multi-campus colleges and universities as well as in business and industry is to use several conveniently placed computers connected to a centrally located large one. The small computer handles problems of communication with the users and small computations; major computations and large jobs are sent over digital communications lines to the large computer. This is economical because the large computer's time is not wasted on problems that can be easily handled by a small computer.

Computer Networks. When one or more computers (plus any number of remote terminals and input/output stations) are connected by communications circuits, the entire system is com-

monly called a *computer network*. When the purpose of the network is to support a single purpose or group of activities (such as the information processing needs of a single company or government organization), the system usually consists of a single large central computer with smaller computers and terminals located as required. The small computers' primary function is to manage the communications traffic, as we will discuss in chapter six. They concentrate messages (combining the input from several terminals, for instance), and locate and assign message routes.

Some networks, however, are much more complex than this. They include many major computers, not just one at the center. A system with multiple computers has some special advantages. It allows users to minimize communications costs by making use of the closest computer. Under unusually heavy loads, work can be shifted back and forth among the computers automatically. In other systems, some specialization is encouraged: some kinds of work will gravitate to the centers that perform it best or more economically.

TYMNET, for instance, is a commercial network to which more than forty computers are connected. The communications are managed by some ninety minicomputers. The network is centered in the United States but has some stations in Europe. The General Electric network has centers in 300 cities from Japan to Europe. The ARPA network (sponsored by the Advanced Research Projects Agency of the U.S. Defense Department) is the most ambitious network so far constructed. Although sponsored by the U.S. Department of Defense, its primary function is not military. It connects more than forty computers at universities and research centers throughout the United States and in England and Norway as well. The Pacific network, centered at the University of

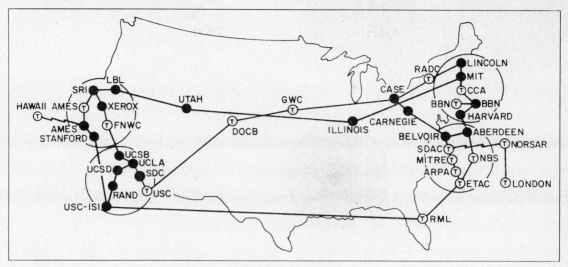

Figure 4-6 ARPANET

Hawaii, is now under development and will link more computers, from Alaska to New Zealand, and tie them into ARPANET.

These large networks are designed to serve users with many different requirements and purposes who need a wide variety of computing capabilities. ARPANET provides access to many different computers, including the ILIAC IV, as of this writing the fastest and largest computer ever built. Associated with the ILIAC is a unique "archival" memory with a capacity for a trillion bits.

One important fact about the communications costs of some of these networks (including ARPA-NET and TYMNET, for instance) must be pointed out. The user is assessed for the amount of information transmitted, not for the distance it must travel. Thus a user is not penalized for selecting a distant computer. All the network's computing capability is as near as any part of the network.

Data transmission capabilities vary considerably. For slow terminals like Teletypes, which have a limiting speed of five to ten characters per second, lines with a capacity of 110 baud are considered

sufficient. (A 110-baud line is a line that is capable of transmitting 110 bits per second.) Ordinary telephone lines, usually called voice-grade lines, can carry 2000 baud and more. This is ample for any individual terminal. However, concentrating several users and including computer-to-computer communication makes higher transmission rates desirable. One service (called TELPAK in the United States) with a 500,000-baud rate is commercially available. Such lines are the equivalent of 240 voice-grade lines, and the costs are naturally high.

In chapter five we will discuss the concept of time sharing, which is the programming approach used in these networks.

A Massive Communications System. Some of the current fear of computers is related to the notion of a massive system with an all-inclusive data base and a complex communication network that can make information instantly available to many widely dispersed stations. However, there are limitations on such a system, and a major one of these is cost. In the United States, digital com-

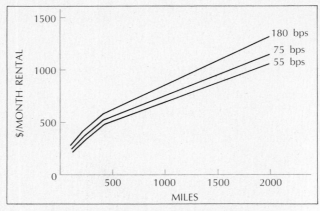

Figure 4-7 Low-speed communications costs

munications rates are determined by the FCC, public utility commissions, and the telephone companies. Figure 4-7 represents the monthly rental cost for a two-way line with terminals at both ends for distances of up to 2000 miles. A nationwide network with one hundred 180-bps lines, each of approximately 2000 miles, would cost roughly $1,500,000 a year in communications alone. Communications bills of this size are by no means uncommon among large companies with many branch offices.

Higher-speed services (1600 and 2400 bps) are available. Greater speeds naturally mean more expensive communications. For example, a large computer network using five hundred 400-mile 2400-bps two-way data links would cost roughly $5 million per year (as of this writing) for communications alone. We have already seen that a large-scale computer with 100 million characters of random-access memory (and this size is necessary for such a real-time application) can rent for as much as $85,000 per month; the operating costs will amount to that much again. If this computer were connected to the 500 two-way lines of 2400 bps capacity, the total price tag would be close to $6 million per year. For this, the user buys a system that will gather, process, and report what is going on at 500 places at 2400 bps and will store 100 million characters.

Let us translate this mass of equipment and costs into a frightening hypothetical situation. Say we are keeping track of one million people and storing 100 characters of information about each of them. If we assume that each of the 500 locations has an equal share of the workload, it will be involved with roughly 2000 people. Let us assume that each station is willing to select its 2000 people and report continuously on their complete doings, through their phone calls, movements, mail, financial transactions, and so forth (recognizing that there are severe legal restrictions on this sort of thing).

But: in order to produce the information to supply this system, we will need four million policemen working three shifts per day simply to keep track of one million people. This by itself would cost more than the entire United States spends on law enforcement in one year.

Social Implications. The point is this: while the example is deliberately exaggerated, extensive surveillance requires such a great quantity of money that it cannot be spent without attracting considerable public attention. Such a system could not come into being secretly. If private or corporate funds were used to develop such a system, it could hardly be kept secret from the thousands of people involved who work for the large corporations that sell and lease the computers, terminals, and lines. Later we will consider the responsibilities these firms have in such matters. The sad lesson of our recent political history is that political surveillance doesn't require millions of people or even a computer to be threatening.

The good effects of the development of terminals and digital communications have been to translate highly technical computer capabilities into terms relevant to a wider range of problems, to speed up the availability of data, and to increase the sharing of knowledge and computing power. Chapters five and six will help to complete your understanding of these areas by discussing the programs that make computer use possible.

Exercises

1. Study a special-purpose display keyboard like an airline terminal or a stock market quotation terminal and list the kinds of questions you can ask with it.

2. Assume you are designing a computer system that provides information on call to racetrack fans. These fans will phone your central office and be free to ask any questions they wish about the horses, jockeys, tracks, or past races. Tabulate all possible types of questions that bettors might ask and decide whether they could be put in a standard format. If they can be standardized, what buttons would you need on your keyboard? Are the questions so varied that a full typewriter keyboard would be necessary to enter the question into the computer?

3. Assume that you are in Redondo Beach, California, and need some particular information that is only in one library in San Francisco. You ask three minutes worth of questions, which costs $2.15. The librarian listens to your questions and calls back with the answers

later. The answers also take three minutes and cost another $2.15. Two-way digital communications would cost $470 per month and both you and the librarian would have to type rather than talk. How many minutes worth of questions would you have to ask in order for it to be cheaper to use digital communications?

4. What can you communicate by voice that you cannot communicate by teletype?

5. Find out what facsimile transmission is, who uses it, and why.

6. In chapter 3, we saw that the cost of operation of a range of computer systems varied from $1 to $10 per minute. Human skills, over a range of occupations, cost from $2.50 per hour to $150,000 per year—from 4¢ to $100 per minute. Thus in some circumstances when a person's time is cheaper than the computer's, it is worthwhile to attach a terminal to the computer to let the less expensive person save expensive computer time. Similarly, where the less expensive computer can save a person's

valuable time, it is done by terminal as well. Give one example of each case.

7. Find and describe a real-time computer system that uses communication lines and displays.

8. The possibilities for computer use will become even greater as the costs of terminals and communications decrease. One of the possibilities is to use home television with the extensive communications network the cable TV companies are setting up. If a computer became available in the home by a mere attachment to the TV set, what do you think would be done with it? You can either imagine the answer to this question or research the considerable literature that has already grown up around it.

9. A continuation of question 8. The prospect of such a communications network being tied to a computer system has also aroused some fears. Similarly, you can either imagine them or research them.

For Further Information

As with chapter three, up-to-date information on the content of this chapter is in the annuals and other periodicals that have been recommended. However, a few more extensive surveys and background studies can be recommended if you want more detail.

One of James Martin's books (1-3) will be a good and thorough introduction to the subject of communications for the purposes of computing. Another good book is by Abramson and Kuo (4). There are a number of other excellent texts on communications, but the average reader will probably find them too detailed and with little direct relevance to computing. Books on displays are also likely to be concerned with engineering details. However, the three references given (5, 6, and 7) will supply any additional information you may want. The *Computer Display Review* (8) is a loose-leaf publication with up-to-date information on available systems. If your library has a copy, it might be interesting for you to leaf through it.

Among briefer works, there are papers on communications and displays in the *Computers and Computation* book we have cited (9, 10). The June 1970 issue of *Datamation* was devoted entirely to "Keyboard Data Entry" and provides a good survey of that subject (11). An article by Lyle Smith (12) presents a good survey of available systems.

References

1. James Martin, *Telecommunications and the Computer* (Englewood Cliffs, N.J.: Prentice-Hall, Inc., 1968).

2. James Martin, *Teleprocessing Network Organization* (Englewood Cliffs, N.J.: Prentice-Hall, Inc., 1970).

3. James Martin, *Introduction to Teleprocessing* (Englewood Cliffs, N.J.: Prentice-Hall, Inc., 1972).

4. Norman Abramson and Franklin F. Kuo, *Computer-Communication Networks* (Englewood Cliffs, N.J.: Prentice-Hall, Inc., 1973).

5. Harry Poole, *Fundamentals of Display Systems* (New York: Spartan Books, 1966).

6. H. R. Luxenberg and Rudolph L. Kuehn, eds. *Display Systems Engineering* (New York: McGraw-Hill Book Company, 1968).

7. Sol Sherr, *Fundamentals of Display System Design* (New York: John Wiley & Sons, Inc., 1970).

8. *The Computer Display Review,* Keydata Corporation.

9. John Pierce, "The Transmission of Computer Data," *Computers and Computation* (San Francisco: W. H. Freeman, 1971).

10. Ivan Sutherland, "Computer Inputs and Outputs," *Computers and Computation* (San Francisco: W. H. Freeman, 1971).

11. *Datamation,* June 1970.

12. Lyle B. Smith, "A Survey of Interactive Graphical Systems for Mathematics," *Computing Surveys 2 no. 4* (December 1970), pp. 262–301.

System Software

5

Computers can make rapid calculations, search large files, compare numbers and make decisions, and send messages via telephone lines to distantly placed terminals and displays. But organizing these capabilities into a coherent system capable of solving problems and realizing goals depends on computer programs. Programs have been given the somewhat facetious name *software* to indicate that they are distinct from but parallel to the "hardware." More exactly, software includes not only the program itself but also documentation of the program (analogous to hardware blueprints) and the training required for people to use the total system and operate and maintain the programs. One might expect that each program is designed to solve a specific problem and therefore that all programs are different. In part, this is true. But there are also some problems that are very

general, and thus the programs that solve them are also very general in their applicability. This chapter will begin the discussion of software by describing a class of programs that solve a very particular and general problem: to help programmers and computer users make better use of computers. These programs are called *system software*.

System Software

One of the intentions of chapter two was to give you a feeling for the complexity of computer programming. The reasons for such complexity are partly the nature of the computer, partly the nature of the problems being programmed, and partly the nature of the human thinking process.

The computer requires absolute specific detail.

the devices themselves, the electronics and mechanics are referred to as hardware, but...

the directions that make the hardware perform operations are known as

SOFTWARE

A computer's programs, plus the procedure for their use.

(**PROGRAM**)
A set of instructions for performing computer operations.

Every operation it is to perform and the location of every element of information it is to use must be in the program, and the program must be perfect. People are well adapted to dealing with broad concepts, but they are less adept at converting these general plans into details. In such activities, people are error-prone, slow, and expensive—especially in comparison with computers.

In addition, some of the details of a computer program cannot be determined until it is to be run. For example, the assignment of the specific addresses in memory where instructions and data are to be located may depend on what else is in the machine at the same time.

Finally, to operate a computer as an efficient productive machine requires assistance. Detailed scheduling of work is too difficult to do in advance. Balancing workloads among the computer's various parts—taking into account its users' rapidly shifting priorities and making sure that the next job is always ready when the present one is done—can save large amounts of computer time and money.

We will first discuss those programs that assist the computer programmer and then those whose purpose is to operate the machine efficiently. They are both called *system programs.*

Programming Languages

Computer programmers must specify clearly and precisely what the computer is to do. Ideally, they should be able to do this in a language comfortable to them and in which they will make few mistakes. This language can then be converted into machine language by a computer program called a compiler.

A programming language must meet some very special requirements; its design is an intricate task. Natural languages, like English, will not do. They are too ambiguous and much too complex for easy conversion into machine instructions. The language of mathematics is concise and precise, but it is not well adapted for describing the wide range of procedures that computer programs may include. It is also better adapted (as is English) to declarative statements (announcements); a computer program since it describes what the computer is to do, is essentially imperative (commands).

A programming language should, in fact, have all these characteristics:

☐ It should be primarily imperative rather than declarative (although some declarative statements are needed).

☐ It should be unambiguous. Every statement should have only one meaning.
☐ There should be a verb in the language for each operation the computer can do.
☐ The user or programmer should be able to choose the nouns, which name the information to be processed.
☐ It should require only those symbols normally available on a typewriter: capital letters, digits, and some special characters like , . () * / + − $. (See figure 5-1).

A number of languages have been developed that satisfy these criteria. Some of the most widely used are described in figure 5-2. All are fairly general and can be used to solve the same simple problems, but each is primarily designed to accommodate a particular class of problems.

It is not necessary for you to learn to read or write programs in these languages, but you may be interested to see what they look like and how much more suitable they are to human use than the machine language that was shown in chapter two. Because it is a widely known and used language, FORTRAN is used in the first set of examples that follow.

FORTRAN. Here is a complex mathematical statement and its equivalent in the FORTRAN character set:

Common mathematics

$$R = \frac{(A + B) \cdot (C - D)^2}{B}$$

FORTRAN

$$R = (A + B) * (C - D) ** 2/B$$

At first glance, the FORTRAN statement may

Figure 5-1 Symbols the computer is usually required to reproduce

look peculiar indeed. However, a few explanations will make it easier to understand. First, the equal sign does not mean (as it does in mathematics) that an equality exists; rather, it is an imperative statement meaning that the variable cited on the left, R, is to take on the value described on the right side of the equation. We might also explain it by saying that the results of the computation specified on the right of the equation are to be stored in the memory cell identified by the name on the left. Thus, while the statement "N = N + 1" is nonsense in mathematics, in FORTRAN, it means "add one to N."

Second, the small number of special characters makes it necessary to use what is available. "*" is used to represent multiplication and "/" to represent division. In our example, $(C - D)^2$—the raising of a number $(C - D)$ to a power, 2—is indicated by the double asterisks, $(C - D)**2$. If you are acquainted with the conventions of mathematical symbols, the expression on the right seems awkward and even ugly; but its meaning is unique and its form is ideal for computer processing.

Here is a program in FORTRAN to add a list of 1000 numbers and output the answer, corresponding to what we did in chapter two.

```
1   DIMENSION LIST (1000)
2   ISUM = 0
3   DO 4  I = 1, 1000
4   ISUM = ISUM + LIST (I)
5   WRITE (6,6) ISUM
6   FORMAT (4HSUM = , I5)
7   END
```

The first statement is declarative: it defines LIST as a series of 1000 numbers and reserves a block of 1000 cells in memory. The second statement declares a variable called ISUM to have an initial value of zero. The third statement means "DO statement number '4' 1000 times, giving the variable I the values 1, 2, 3, and so on, up to 1000." Statement (4) means "ADD LIST (I) to ISUM and store it back into

FORTRAN: (FORmula TRANslation). An early (1955) language designed for solving mathematical problems in the sciences. Widely used since then, it has undergone a series of revisions known as FORTRAN II, FORTRAN III, and FORTRAN IV.

COBOL: (COmmon Business Oriented Language). Designed by a committee made up of representatives of manufacturers and users, this language is now very commonly used in accounting and business applications.

ALGOL: (ALGOrithmic Language). A language primarily designed for the description and exchange of scientific and mathematical procedures rather than machine implementation. However, it has been implemented on a number of machines.

APT: (Automatic Programmed Tool). A special-purpose language for describing functions of numerically-controlled machinery, such as milling machines, and so forth.

BASIC: (Beginners All-purpose Symbolic Instruction Code). A simple language developed at Dartmouth College specifically for use in instruction. It allows the user direct interaction with the computer.

APL: A very concise language for interactive programming.

PL/1: A general-purpose language, combining some of the features of the special languages developed for scientific, business, simulation, and command-control applications.

SNOBOL: A language that can be used to manipulate information in the form of natural language; it stresses an ability to handle symbolic rather than numeric data and is used in such applications as language translation, question answering, and automatic abstracting programs.

Figure 5-2 Computer languages

ISUM." Thus as I goes from 1 to 1000, every number in the table called LIST is added to ISUM.

Statement (5) says, "Write the quantity sum out on unit 6 (a terminal) according to statement (6)." Statement (6), the format statement, controls the output. It gives the label for the output "SUM =" to be printed before the answer, which it describes as a five-digit integer (I5). Statement (7) tells the machine it is finished.

This should give you an indication of the relative ease of programming in FORTRAN versus the machine-language work shown in chapter two. Notice that it is not necessary to specify machine addresses for the instructions and the constants, zero and one.

However, the problem that was perfectly adequate to demonstrate the power of the computer (to modify its own instructions and thus make decisions) is not adequate to show the power of the programming language. Therefore let us consider a more complex example:

A program to compute the silver required for a cash payroll will analyze the individual amounts to be paid to each person in order to determine how many coins of each denomination the paymaster needs. For each sum to be paid, the program will check the "cents" part of the net amount and determine how many half-dollars, quarters, dimes, nickels, and pennies will be needed.

Figure 5-3 flowcharts one way that this problem may be solved. It is a method that comes up with the smallest number of coins by always using the largest coin possible. Furthermore, the flowchart considers only what is to be done for one individual payment. It doesn't take us through all of the payments to be considered.

Figure 5-4 is a FORTRAN program corresponding to the flowchart in figure 5-3. The program is listed on the left, with some explanatory comments on the right. You will need some definitions. AMOUNT is the name of the storage location where the number of cents to be paid to the employee is stored. This is the number the program analyzes to determine the coins required. C50 is the location for the number of half dollars; C25 for the number of quarters; C10 for dimes; C5 for nickels; and C1 for pennies. The numbers down the left-hand column correspond to the numbers on the blocks in the flowchart in figure 5-3. They are also part of the program logic. "100" is the location of the routine to take care of errors; to limit the detail, we have not included the error routine itself in this example.

One last observation can be made here. For the first time you have examined enough detail to understand the problem of flexibility in the design of an information system. For example, suppose we insisted that the employee be paid only in pennies, nickels, dimes, and quarters because it was too complicated to include half dollars in the program. Or we could, at the expense of a little more programming, allow employees to choose whether they want half dollars in their pay envelopes or not. It is at this level that the convenience of *the programmer versus the user* is balanced. Also, it is standard practice in programs like these to have the machine edit the data before using it. For example, the machine could reject any payment that showed more than 100 cents. This would probably be a mistake in keypunching, but it might be true. However, as soon as general sensibility tests are contrived, unusual occurrences run afoul of them. A billing system that rejects a payment that isn't exactly correct will reject the check of a person who rounds off to the nearest dollar. Thus reasonable design must anticipate the handling of exceptions. It is precisely this kind of flexibility (or the

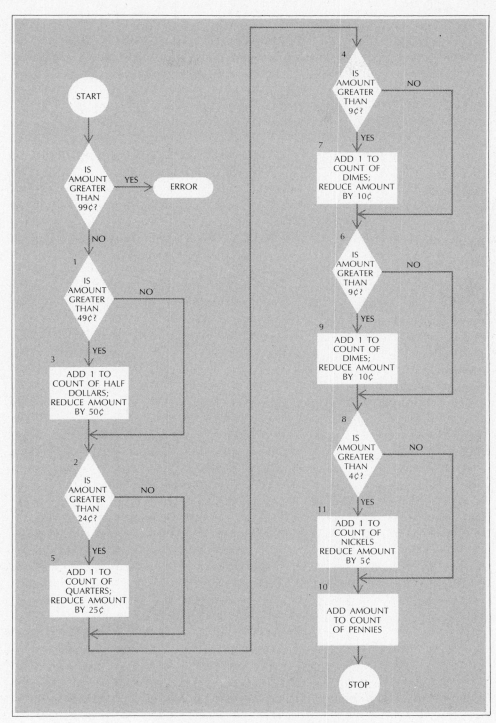

Figure 5-3 A flowchart for the problem

FORTRAN CODE	EXPLANATION
IF (AMOUNT-99) 1,1,100	If the quantity obtained by subtracting 99 from AMOUNT is negative or zero, go to the statement labelled "1"; if it is positive, go to "100."
1 IF (AMOUNT-49) 2,2,3	If AMOUNT minus 49 is negative or zero, go to statement "2"; if it is positive, go to "3."
3 C50 = C50 + 1	Add one to C50, the number of half-dollars, and put the sum back in the C50 location.
AMOUNT = AMOUNT-50	Reduce AMOUNT by 50 cents.
2 IF (AMOUNT-24) 4,4,5	If AMOUNT minus 24 is negative or zero, go to "4"; otherwise, go to "5."
5 C25 = C25 + 1	Increase C25 (the number of quarters) by one.
AMOUNT = AMOUNT-25	Decrease AMOUNT by 25 cents.
4 IF (AMOUNT-9) 6,6,7	If AMOUNT minus 9 is less than or equal to zero, go to "6"; otherwise, go to "7."
7 C10 = C10 + 1	Add one to count of number of dimes.
AMOUNT = AMOUNT-10	Decrease AMOUNT by ten cents.
6 IF (AMOUNT-9) 8,8,9	If AMOUNT minus 9 is less than or equal to zero, go to "8"; otherwise, go to "9."
9 C10 = C10 + 1	Add one to count of number of dimes.
AMOUNT = AMOUNT-10	Reduce AMOUNT by ten cents.
8 IF (AMOUNT-4) 10,10,11	If AMOUNT minus 4 is less than or equal to zero, go to "10"; otherwise go to "11."
11 C5 = C5 + 1	Add one to count of number of nickels.
AMOUNT = AMOUNT-5	Reduce AMOUNT by five cents.
10 C1 = C1 + AMOUNT	Add what is left to the count of number of pennies.
STOP	The end of the program.

Figure 5-4. A FORTRAN program for the cash payroll problem. With some practice, programmers are able to read the FORTRAN code as well as English, and for a simple problem like this, one might not even construct a flowchart.

lack of it) that accounts for a satisfactory or unsatisfactory program.

Compilers. The program that converts other programs written in FORTRAN and other such procedure-oriented languages into machine instructions that can be run on the computer is called a *compiler*. The compiler program's input is a string of statements in (say) FORTRAN—on cards, on tape, or typed at a terminal. It produces various sets of information printed out for the user, such as listings of the instructions as they were compiled, error messages, and so forth. To avoid confusion, the symbolic program (the FORTRAN statements) that is input to the compiler is called the *source program;* the output in binary machine language is called the *object program.* Figure 5-5 shows the process of compiling and then running a program originally written in FORTRAN.

Figure 5-6 shows the output of a typical FORTRAN compiler. This one produces machine instructions for the XDS Sigma-7 computer. This output of that compiler shows the original FORTRAN statements together with the machine instructions actually generated by the computer for this FORTRAN statement. The instructions are

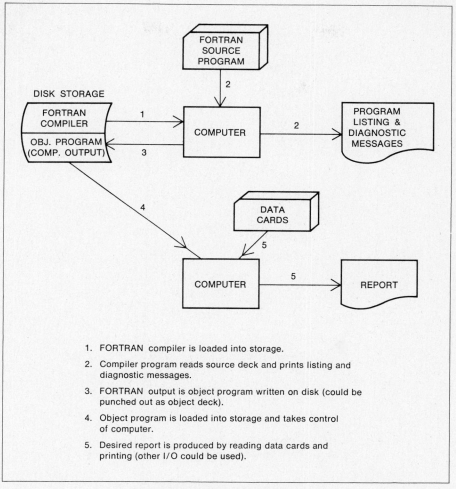

Figure 5-5 FORTRAN compile steps

presented in several forms, and various additional pieces of information about them are presented for the programmer's use. There is no listing, you will notice, of the actual binary form of the instructions since normally it is of use only to computers.

All of the languages cited in Figure 5-2 are *machine-independent*. This means that they allow the programmer to specify the functions to be performed in a general way, independent of the word length and type of instructions available on a particular computer. A FORTRAN program can be run on almost any medium- to large-scale computer on the market today. A compiler can produce the object program in the language of only one computer model. Thus every new computer must have a new compiler for each language the manufacturer wants to make available with the machine. While the interchangeability of standard language programs is an ideal all manufacturers strive for, in reality, FORTRAN programs written for one machine or compiler usually require some modification before they can be run on a different machine.

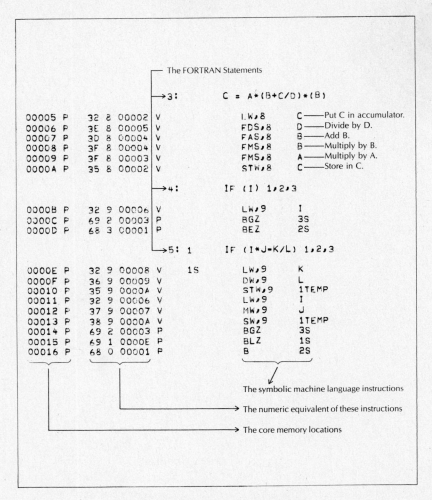

The FORTRAN Statements

```
                                    ┌─ The FORTRAN Statements

                                    ├──→3:        C = A*(B+C/D)*(B)

00005 P    32 8 00002 V                    LW,8      C ────Put C in accumulator.
00006 P    3E 8 00005 V                    FDS,8     D ────Divide by D.
00007 P    3D 8 00004 V                    FAS,8     B ────Add B.
00008 P    3F 8 00004 V                    FMS,8     B ────Multiply by B.
00009 P    3F 8 00003 V                    FMS,8     A ────Multiply by A.
0000A P    35 8 00002 V                    STW,8     C ────Store in C.

                                    ├──→4:        IF (I) 1,2,3

0000B P    32 9 00006 V                    LW,9      I
0000C P    69 2 00003 P                    BGZ       3S
0000D P    68 3 00001 P                    BEZ       2S

                                    └──→5: 1      IF (I*J-K/L) 1,2,3

0000E P    32 9 00008 V     1S            LW,9      K
0000F P    36 9 00009 V                    DW,9      L
00010 P    35 9 0000A V                    STW,9     1TEMP
00011 P    32 9 00006 V                    LW,9      I
00012 P    37 9 00007 V                    MW,9      J
00013 P    38 9 0000A V                    SW,9      1TEMP
00014 P    69 2 00003 P                    BGZ       3S
00015 P    69 1 0000E P                    BLZ       1S
00016 P    68 0 00001 P                    B         2S
```

The symbolic machine language instructions

The numeric equivalent of these instructions

The core memory locations

Figure 5-6   FORTRAN compiler output

One requirement of a programming language, you will recall, was that it must be unambiguous. A consequence of this is that the compiler can do a considerable amount of error checking. Of course, a meaningful and grammatical statement may still be wrong, but a compiler can sift out a number of obvious errors, like branching to numbered statements that don't exist, performing arithmetic on non-numeric variables, or adding inches to minutes. FORTRAN programs have to be just as exact as machine-language programs, and they can easily consist of several thousand statements. Thus locating errors is still a major problem. If there are obvious errors in code, the program will not compile. Instead, the computer will print out an indication of what kind of error was made.

Each particular computer has its own method of addressing bytes, words, and "pages" (large groups of words) in its memory. Data has to be packed so that memory requirements are minimized. These problems complicate programming, but compilers and their supporting systems programs simplify many such problems for the programmer.

Most programming languages also give the programmer collections ("libraries") of subroutines to perform functions common to his particular type of problem area, such as routines for frequently used mathematical functions, for sorting files, or for converting coding systems from one form to another. The programmer need only refer to a subroutine and the compiler will transfer a copy of it from the library to his program.

The net effect of compilers is to make programs less expensive and time-consuming to produce and to reduce the amount of training programmers need.

Other Systems Programs. Besides compilers, there are other programs that are primarily for the use of programmers. A few examples will clarify their functions. If the object program is taken away from the computer in the form of cards or tape, there must be a program to read it into the computer when the user decides to run it. Such a program is called a *loader*.

If files of programs or data are maintained on disks or on tape, a number of different programs are useful for their maintenance. File-maintenance functions include:

☐ Producing a catalog of the files currently in storage

☐ Deleting old or inserting new files

☐ Copying files

☐ Changing information within files (editing)

☐ Locating a file of a given name and moving it (perhaps to merge with another file)

Finally, there are programs to help programmers test their programs since, as we have indicated, new programs frequently have mistakes in them. A programmer may know what the content of some specific words in memory should be at given points in his program. He or she can use a *trap program* to check those words as the program is being tested. The programmer may also want to be able to follow the decisions made at each branch instruction and therefore will use a *trace program*. Or, if the contents of memory is required, *dump* can be used.

Operating Systems

Once a number of such programs exist, managing them becomes a problem in itself. They are therefore assembled into a system and given some control mechanism and a means for communicating with the user or computer operator. This systematic collection of programs is called an *operating system*.

The main part of the operating system that controls the other programs and communicates with the computer operator is called the *executive* or the *monitor*. Its function is to maintain an efficient and continual flow of work through the machine, locating from secondary storage (disk or tapes) the systems programs that are required and transferring them to the memory when they are needed. Its major function can be described as follows:

1. *System control.* The executive communicates

Figure 5-7 A computer operator at a main console

with the equipment operator about work to be performed, changes in scheduling, and available resources, such as equipment that may or may not be available or loading tapes and disk packs as they are needed.

2. *Job scheduling.* The executive reads (from cards or tape) the string of jobs that are to be performed. As part of each job description, the various systems programs and files that are required are listed. The executive brings all of these resources together and then allows the job to be run.

3. *Supervising.* The executive's major function is to supervise the operation of the various programs, their use or input and output equipment, and the overall flow of work through the machine.

The operating system also expedites a number of other functions. Not the least of these is keeping track of how much time is used on each job so that appropriate billing is possible. Figure 5-8 shows a schematic of a typical operating system for a large computer.

Thus the objective of the operating system is to make a computer center run efficiently and smoothly.

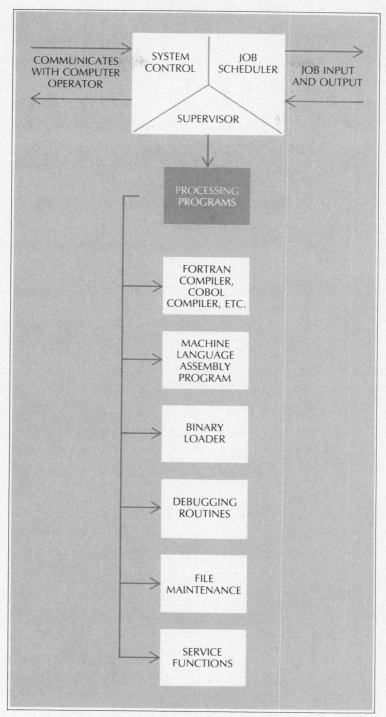

Figure 5-8 The functions of a typical operating system

Making Computing Available

The cost of computing can be, as we have seen, extremely high. Since the cost-effectiveness of computers increases with size, there has been a tendency to make them bigger and bigger. Yet many potential computer users cannot justify spending tens of thousands of dollars per month for a computer installation and a technical staff.

Several developments have helped make computing power available at modest costs. One of these is the computer service bureau. This type of company generally accepts prepared data from a customer, runs the customer's programs, and provides standardized reports. Service bureaus have as clients many small companies without computers of their own. They are also used heavily by larger companies whose own computing facilities are overloaded. Service bureaus often specialize in particular needs like technical computing, accounting, or payroll.

Another type of company that brings computing power to organizations that do not want to become involved with the details of data processing is the facilities management corporation. These corporations operate computer centers, complete with staff, often on their clients' premises.

A third alternative is the minicomputer. It costs less than $10,000 as of this writing and has a considerable range of capabilities.

Time Sharing. A totally different approach, and perhaps the most innovative method of distributing computer power to many small users, is time sharing. Time sharing is based on the computer's ability to execute many different programs in a way that makes it appear they are being executed simultaneously. Each program can be working on a different problem for a different user. In general,

this technique is called *multiprogramming*. When each of the concurrently operating programs is communicating directly with a user by means of communications lines and terminals, the technique is called *time sharing*.

Although a time-sharing system seems to execute a number of programs simultaneously, in fact only one of the programs is actually operating at a given time. The method commonly used is for the central computer to spend a small amount of time (perhaps 0.01 to 0.1 second) on each user's program in turn. After each has had its turn, the cycle is repeated. Since the entire cycle takes only a few seconds, it appears that the users are in fact getting simultaneous service from the computer. Figure 5-9 illustrates this "round-robin" system. Even though the computer is slowed down by having to attend to many users, it is usually able to keep up with the demands of each, since each user must often think or look something up between his inputs to the time-sharing terminal. Also, as we have seen, terminals are very slow compared to the computer. Figure 5-10 shows a time-sharing system in use. Figure 5-11 gives a schematic diagram of a typical time-sharing system.

The primary advantages of time sharing for the user are convenience and accessibility. Work does not have to be sent to a distant center. The terminal can be at the user's desk and he or she can get immediate responses. Furthermore, if the user's computer is part of one of the networks described in chapter four, a whole variety of computers can be accessed from the terminal.

The cost the user must pay for such a convenience is surprisingly small. Computers can operate this way with considerable efficiency; the increase in computerized bookkeeping (overhead) required

Figure 5-9 The round-robin system of time sharing

to keep track of many simultaneous users is largely compensated for by the fact that each user pays only for the machine capabilities he or she uses, plus some share of the overhead. The actual charge depends on how much time the user's terminal is connected to the computer, how much actual time the central computer spends processing the user's programs and, in some systems, the amount of disk storage required to store the user's files over long periods of time. A reasonable cost for many applications is about $6.00 per hour of terminal use plus telephone charges.

Table 5.1 gives a list of commercial, scientific, and engineering time-sharing applications, indicating the kinds of specialized services that are now being offered. Over fifty percent of time sharers are manufacturing establishments such as elec-

Table 5.1 Typical engineering time-sharing applications

SCIENTIFIC	COMMERCIAL
Circuit analysis	Investment
Antenna design	Capital programming
Logic design	Inventory analysis
Mechanical design	Market forecasting
Lens design	Educational data processing
Chemical simulation	Actuarial studies
Stress analysis	Text composition and editing
Test data reduction	

Figure 5-10   An actual time-shared system in use

trical, aerospace, chemical, and automotive companies. The remainder of the users are research organizations, schools, public utilities, the financial community, and the government.

As of 1971, there were more than 150 companies using the public telephone system to bring time-sharing services to businesses, educational institutions, the financial community, doctors and hospitals, engineers, and even football coaches. These organizations have developed into a seventy-million-dollar annual business in their first four years of operation. Estimates for 1975 indicate over one million terminals in operation. In addition, many companies provide time-sharing services for their own internal users.

The suppliers of time-sharing services will feel the effects of minicomputers most strongly and painfully. The costs of their operations, as of this writing, are so high that they have to earn $1000 a month per rental terminal to be profitable. This means that over a five-year period, their customer will have spent $60,000. That sum can buy a number of mini-computers. Thus, the time-sharing service companies are likely to lose those customers who don't have huge data bases to manipulate or highly accurate scientific calculations to perform.

It is impossible at this time to predict the relative dominance of large computer systems versus minicomputers versus time sharing. Only a weak generalization can be made: the market is so abundant and varied that there is probably room for all three to thrive. However, time sharing has

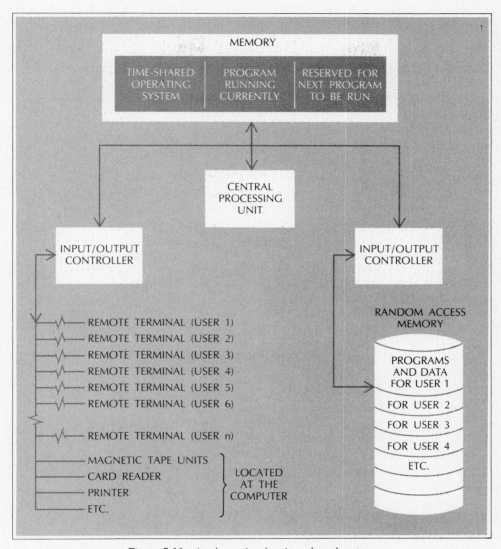

Figure 5-11   A schematic of a time-shared system

had a most dynamic impact on the computer market. It has introduced many individuals to the computer who might otherwise never have used it to solve their problems. The terminal's convenient location and its rapid response has led to its application in many new areas.

Summary

In chapter two we showed you the elemental level of computer programming. When computers were first developed, this kind of programming, called machine-language programming, was all that was available. It was difficult, costly, and error-prone. The programming languages we have shown you in this chapter have brought about tremendous changes. Now, anyone with a high-school education and patience can program. The power of a FORTRAN compiler to explode a single statement into ten or twenty lines of accurate machine-level code is a big aid to programmers. Also, programs written in standard languages like FORTRAN can, to some extent, be transferred from machine to machine. The net effect of all of this has been to make programming less expensive, quicker, and

more certain. The operating systems that manufacturers supply with their machines have made it possible for technically unsophisticated organizations to use computers efficiently. They now have only to know when to call the manufacturer's maintenance representative. Thus while it is the general nature of the computer that has caused its wide applicability, it is the development of programming languages and operating systems that has promoted the computer's use in every aspect of human affairs.

Exercises

1. Can you think of any other technology or development that has created essentially separate and different sets of practitioners? Computer technology affects engineers, who design and build computers and develop new components; users, who come from a wide variety of backgrounds; and programmers, who may be mathematicians, scientists, or of almost any profession. Each of these groups is largely disinterested in the professional concerns of the others. Yet each is, of course, dependent on the others. It is a rare person who is competent in all fields. What kinds of trouble do you imagine this has led to in the field?

2. Later in this book you will encounter an argument to the effect that the very process of formulating a problem so that it can be programmed for a computer has a number of interesting effects on the solution. Comment on one of the following effects:

    a. Formulating a program for a computer makes one understand a problem so thoroughly that in itself it is a benefit.
    b. Formulating a program for a computer is essentially dehumanizing.

3. Attempts have been made to construct artificial languages that people who speak different languages could use. What would you think of a spoken language that had the characteristics of a programming language?

4. Invent a time-sharing service that you think would make a good business.

5. What kinds of computer services are available in your community? (Check the ads in the newspapers and the yellow pages of the telephone book.)

6. Let us return to the general statement of powers and limitations of the computer that we discussed in chapter two. When you first read that list, probably the vaguest power

was "universality." Now that you have seen how the power of the computer is facilitated by programming languages, explain "universality."

7. Similarly, you should now have a better understanding of how complex a computer program can be. Invent a program whose design contains a hidden fault that the programmer didn't test and later causes a lot of trouble.

For Further Information

Systems programming has a literature of its own. Some of the major works in this field are cited among the references (1–9). None of these books can be recommended to the novice; they all require greater background in computer programming than this book has attempted to provide. The technique of time sharing, however, has attracted more general interest and a number of works have been published that are suitable for the non-specialist. In particular, *Conversational*

Computing (10) contains a collection of papers on different aspects of the subject. Several important historical papers are included, as well as others that discuss present concepts and issues for the future. Wilkes' book (11) is more technical but is extremely well written. Other books on time sharing (12–14) do not attempt to cover the subject so generally but are good introductions to the techniques involved.

References

1. Ivan Flores, *Computer Software* (Englewood Cliffs, N.J.: Prentice-Hall, Inc., 1965).

2. Donald Knuth, *The Art of Computer Programming*, vols. 1, 2, 3 (Reading, Mass.: Addison-Wesley Publishing Co., Inc. 1968–73).

3. Hopcroft and Ullman, *Formal Languages* (Reading, Mass.: Addison-Wesley Publishing Co., Inc., 1970).

4. Jean Sammet, *Programming Languages: History and Fundamentals* (Englewood Cliffs, N.J.: Prentice-Hall, Inc., 1969).

5. Saul Rosen, *Programming Systems and Languages* (New York: McGraw-Hill Book Company, 1967).

6. Peter Wegner, *Programming Languages, Information Structures, and Machine Organization* (New York: McGraw-Hill Book Company, 1968).

7. Mark Elson, *Concepts of Programming Languages* (Chicago: Science Research Associates, Inc., 1973).

8. Fred W. Weingarten, *Translation of Computer Languages* (San Francisco: Holden-Day, Inc., 1973).

9. Dionysios C. Tsichritzis and Philip A. Bernstein, *Operating Systems* (New York: Academic Press, 1974).

10. William Orr, *Conversational Computing* (New York: John Wiley & Sons, Inc., 1968).

11. M. V. Wilkes, *Time-Sharing Computer Systems* (New York: American Elsevier Publishing Co., Inc., 1972).

12. James Martin, *Design of Real-Time Computer Systems* (Englewood Cliffs, N.J.: Prentice-Hall, Inc., 1967).

13. D. F. Parkhill, *The Challenge of the Computer Utility* (Reading, Mass.: Addison-Wesley Publishing Co., Inc., 1966).

14. Greenberger, Martin, et al., *Networks for Research and Education* (Cambridge, Mass.: The M.I.T. Press, 1974).

Application Software

6

System software must be closely related to the hardware. From the user's point of view, software is an extension of the hardware that makes it more accessible and easier to use. One class of software may be called application software. It consists of programs that perform specific tasks of direct benefit to the user.

The types of software we shall present in this chapter perform functions of interest and value in a considerable range of human activities. *Information management systems* are sets of programs designed to help people deal with large collections of facts, maintain them and modify them, and get answers to questions about these collections quickly and easily. *Simulation models* are programs that help people understand and predict the behavior of large and complex systems, systems that may have nothing at all to do with computers. *Control sys-*

tems, the third type of programs to be presented here, represent the direct application of computers to the control of other kinds of machines, sometimes without direct human intervention.

Information Management

The accumulated working files of any enterprise constitute a tremendous resource of information. They could be analyzed, for instance, to indicate how the enterprise is changing, or to reveal in detail consequences of changes in policy. However, in most instances the files are so vast and unmanageable that such analyses are too expensive and time-consuming.

Often in very large organizations, even current data cannot be analyzed in the way the management might wish. In a major corporation or large government agency with hundreds or thousands of branches and offices across the world, information about what happened last week may have the same unmanageable characteristics as historical files. In some cases, for example, it would be extremely valuable to analyze data on last week's sales in order to plan this week's ordering of raw materials and next week's manufacturing operations—thus keeping inventory relatively steady without either over-supplied or out-of-stock items. But if the analysis of a week's sales takes more than seven days to perform, it is literally impossible to keep up; the analysis becomes irrelevant.

This problem is not confined to the large corporation. The scientist who has so much experimental data that he or she is unable to find out what the experiment proved and the census bureau that can barely process one decade's data before the next decade arrives face an identical problem: all such situations are crises in information management. In each case, there is a coherent but very large collection of information, or data base, that may require relatively simple calculations to be performed on it. However, it is not always possible to predict beforehand what kinds of information will be wanted, or in what form.

The kinds of operations to be performed and the techniques used to perform them usually do not depend on the content of the information in the system. Thus a single information system design can be used for managing the historical files of a state university, for providing current information to the top management of a world-wide manufacturer of machine tools, or for supplying a government agency with details on its personnel.

Characteristics of an Information Management System. Such a system is an information management system, sometimes abbreviated IMS. Many of these systems are designed and built for a single application. However, a growing number of systems have been successfully applied to a wide range of tasks. Many IMS's have been produced by commercial organizations (either computer manufacturers or software companies) and sold or leased to users.

In order to warrant the use of an IMS, a task must have these characteristics:

☐ There must be a large volume of information to be stored and used.
☐ It must be possible to organize this information along lines foreseen and planned for by the developers of the software.
☐ The basic purpose must be to (1) answer questions on the basis of a summary of information in the data, or (2) provide reports including information from the data base or summaries of the data.

Before discussing the range of applications further, it will be useful to learn something about how such systems work and what they can do. Basically, the system must allow the user to perform these functions:

☐ Define data formats and file structures. (A flexible file structure, for example, would permit one to take a telephone book organized by name and change it into a city directory organized by street address).
☐ Insert, remove, and change data.
☐ Request information in the form of a brief statement or a report.

A Personnel File. We will describe a single typical (but imaginary) system. Instead of describing its general capabilities and limitations, let us see how it might be used, particularly in terms of the three functions listed above—data definition, data insertion, and information request.

Suppose an agency must have fast access to personnel information. The personnel file is so large—25,000 employees—that it is economically necessary to think in terms of a computer-based system. The agency has acquired a general-purpose IMS—call it GPIMS—that will give them the capabilities they think they need.

The first requirement is that they define and describe the data they will include in the system. They will have to specify the names of the various pieces of information, the type of information each will contain (numeric, alphabetic, or alphanumeric), and the size of each (number of characters).

The personnel file will consist, first of all, of a number of items of information for every person in the file. For example, for every personnel identification number (ID number), there must be one and only one name, one social security number, one home address, and so forth. The definition of the items of information presented to GPIMS might look like this:

NAME	TYPE	SIZE
IDNUMBER	NUMERIC	7
NAME	ALPHABETIC	VARIABLE (MAXIMUM 20)
HOMEADDRESS	ALPHANUM	VARIABLE (MAXIMUM 40)
HOMEPHONE	NUMERIC	7
OFFICEPHONE	NUMERIC	5
OFFICEADDRESS	ALPHANUM	7
JOBCODE	ALPHABETIC	VARIABLE (MAXIMUM 10)
DIVISION (OF THE COMPANY)	NUMERIC	2
SALARY	NUMERIC	6
SEX	ALPHABETIC	1

Once the personnel file is completely defined, GPIMS may allow us to describe its relationship to other files. For example, it may contain an indication of the division or department each employee works in. Another file may list the various divisions and departments and facts about the responsibilities, products, and budgets for each. One can therefore associate the personnel file and the department file, using information from the department file to fill out a query in relation to personnel, or vice versa. The result of arranging multiple files and their potential interrelationships is a complex network of data definitions. It is a vital stage of development because any relationship between files that is not thought of at this stage will be very difficult to arrange after the file is built.

Data Base Construction. The second function to be performed is the insertion of information into the data base. In building our hypothetical file, the data definition phase was a very critical one: someone had to decide what information would be preserved and in what form. Certain questions had to be answered. What was a "safe" maximum size for name? What would be done about names that exceeded that maximum? When an employee's name was changed (by marriage, for example), would the old name be saved? In contrast, the next stage—inserting information into this structure—is basically a clerical operation. From the existing personnel file, which was maintained manually, clerks at terminals (or keypunches) type the information in the order and format directed. GPIMS accepts this information and stores it on a disk file, ready for use. After the data base has thus been constructed, clerks will type additions, deletions, and changes on a regular basis—in the case of the personnel system, probably once a week or once a month.

The purpose of all our work so far is to make the third phase possible: requesting information from the assembled and formatted data base. GPIMS, our hypothetical information management system, allows for the generation of standard reports and answers to queries.

Reports and Queries. Standard reports include such things as salary lists, company telephone directories, and so forth. The *query* ability allows the user to ask questions within the limits of the query language provided and the information in the data base. Suppose that the personnel manager of our company wants to determine whether male and female programmers earn roughly comparable salaries. The manager does not want an extensive printout (as in report generation) that lists all of the programmers with their salaries. What is wanted, to begin with, is a simple average salary for programmers of both sexes: i.e., two numbers. This is the coding:

```
10 GET PERSONNEL FILE
20 IF SEX = M and JOBCODE = PROGRAMMER
30 AVERAGE SALARY
40 PRINT AVERAGE
50 IF SEX = F and JOBCODE = PROGRAMMER
60 AVERAGE SALARY
70 PRINT AVERAGE
```

After making this request and seeing the two numbers, the personnel manager may not be satisfied. He or she may realize that some deeper analysis is required. It may be necessary, for example, to see how the salary of both sexes increases with the number of years of experience. The manager will generate from the data base some more detailed numbers that will, perhaps, bring to mind some even more detailed questions.

This simple example shows something of the capabilities of an information management system and how one might go about using it. The same capabilities could be used to manage files of information on widely different subjects and for very different purposes. For example, genetic data in a biological laboratory might be stored in such a system. The experimental subjects could be described, the family relationships stored in detail, and questions asked about the comparative statistics. A company might keep its parts inventory in this system, modifying it whenever something was added to or removed from stock. A college might have files describing students, faculty, courses, and classrooms, and relate all of these to each other. The ability of these systems to manage structured data bases over a fairly wide range makes them very powerful.

Systems Costs. The cost of systems like these varies, of course, depending on their complexity, flexibility, and the features that have been built into them. A system like the one in the example, however, which operates online (directly attached and under control of the computer) and has a reasonably flexible language and file structure, will cost something on the order of $500,000 or more to develop, write, and document. Once installed, eliminating small errors and making improvements from time to time will cost an additional $50,000 to $100,000 per year. In addition, the system's users will require some training and assistance in getting it installed and getting their applications on it. Such a system developed by a commercial organization, will cost three to five thousand dollars a month. This seems expensive for a computer program, particularly if we consider that the user must also pay for the computer time the system will use, plus the charges for communications, personnel, and so forth. The potential users have to ask themselves whether the questions they want answered and the reports they want to see are worth that cost. Often they are.

Figure 6-1 A data-base system in use

Such systems as our GPIMS are implemented both offline and online. The offline requests are run like any other computer program in a batch with other jobs. The online systems make the data base continuously available through a time-sharing system to terminals in the user's office. Furthermore, query languages have been developed that are a good deal more like English than that of our simple example.

Information management systems are limited mostly by the amount of information they contain, how frequently it changes, and how much flexibility the user needs in asking questions of it. If a standard set of questions can be predicted

Figure 6-2   A working model of the tidal movements in San Francisco Bay

before the file is created (as in a stock quotation system or an airline reservation system), the service can be quite fast.

Much of the fear of computer-based systems (in the areas of invasion of privacy and the spread of incorrect information, for instance) is focused on the use of systems like this. In later chapters we shall consider how such systems can be protected from errors and how file security can be maintained against the accidental (or deliberate) leaking of information.

Simulation and Models

In order to analyze and understand certain aspects of the real world, people build models. The most common of these (other than those used for toys) are engineering models of structures that are being planned. For example, planning a dam or a break-water, the ways the water and structure may interact are so complex that engineers may build a small-scale version in order to see how it works. They can deduce something about how the real structure will behave on the basis of what they learn. When aircraft are planned, the designers may build a scale model to test in a wind tunnel; using this, they can learn something about the behavior of the real airplane when it is flying. If the data from the model indicated that the plane will not perform correctly, they can revise their design and build a new model. We shall call these models, which look like the systems after which they are designed (except for scale), *physical models.*

Mathematical Models.   In cases where the actions of a system are well understood, the system's behavior can be represented with mathematical equations rather than by building a physical model. For example, the way in which water pressure builds up as depth increases is well known; so is the effect of water pressure on structures of various shapes, materials, and thicknesses. Therefore instead of building a scale model of a dam, an engineer can work out a set of equations for what will happen to it under various conditions. These equations form a kind of model, too: not a physical model, because the list of equations will in no way resemble a dam, but a mathematical model of physical behavior.

The advantages of a mathematical model over a physical model are easy to understand. It is always easier to manipulate symbols than things. For example, if one chooses to try a slightly different design, a physical model must be sent back to the workmen who built it. To construct a new mathematical model, however, all one needs to do is erase a few symbols and replace them with new ones or change the value of some constants.

There are other reasons to prefer a mathematical model to a physical one. We simply cannot build physical models of some systems. For example, weather prediction depends on a simulation of the atmosphere. It can be modelled with equations, but there is no convenient physical substance that could be expected to behave like a model of the weather.

However, manipulating the equations of a mathematical model may involve so complex and so long a series of arithmetic operations that it would be impossible to accomplish without a computer. So, although mathematical models of many systems have been theoretically possible for many years, it is only since the advent of the computer that they have become practical and widely used. For example, the computer has made it possible to use far more complex mathematical models of the weather and thus has made weather forecasting more accurate.

Probabilistic Models. For mathematical models as described thus far, the relationships among their elements are completely understood and the data required for their use is available. The models are based on a theoretical understanding of the engineering and physical principles involved and are expected to be one hundred percent accurate. However, in many systems one would like to investigate, this is simply not the case. Mathematical models cannot be constructed for systems that involve people (whose individual actions cannot be accurately predicted), incomplete data, or relationships that are imperfectly or incompletely understood. However, in many of these cases we do know something. For example, we know how people act on the average (if not individually), or what relationships probably exist. In these cases, we can predict the consequences of events in terms of their probabilities. We can make statements about the probable relationship among events and their probable outcome. Such statements constitute a *probabilistic model.* Some physical situations, such as games of chance, are usually analyzed in terms of probabilistic models. Like mathematical models, these are liable to be rather complex and require much calculation. Generally they must be written in the form of computer programs to be analyzed.

Some models predict what will happen; others predict "what would happen if." Perhaps the most widely publicized example of the first kind are the computer-based models that predict the outcome of major elections on the basis of early returns. These have come to be a permanent part of major network news coverage of election nights. It is impossible, of course, to know how individuals will vote. But models can be used to predict how,

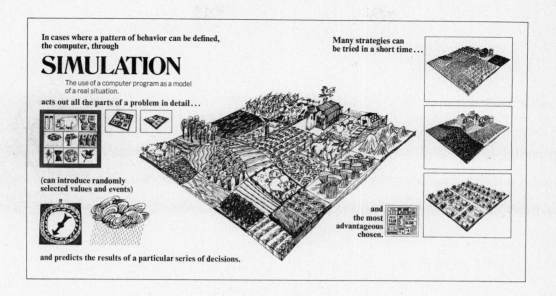

In cases where a pattern of behavior can be defined, the computer, through

SIMULATION

The use of a computer program as a model of a real situation.

acts out all the parts of a problem in detail...

(can introduce randomly selected values and events)

and predicts the results of a particular series of decisions.

Many strategies can be tried in a short time...

and the most advantageous chosen.

on the average, large blocks of people (religious, regional, age groups) will. There is no question of absolute accuracy, of course. Such predictions are based on the validity of the assumption that the future will resemble the past.

Other models of this type are used by colleges and universities to predict class sizes so that they can select classrooms of the right size, hire enough teachers, and so forth. These models use a profile of the student body: how many freshmen, sophomores, juniors, seniors, and graduate students there are; the percentage majoring in physics, chemistry, English, and so forth. On the basis of records of past classes, the model is used to predict the number of students who are likely to want to register for each of the courses offered.

What Would Happen If?   Other models are used to predict conditional futures: what would happen if some action were taken. Some large commercial organizations have models of the market for their products, including the probable effects of sea-

sonal variation, of weather, of style, of changes in taste, of competition, or of advertising. In planning a major campaign for a new product, they can use the model to predict what would happen to profit if the item sold for fifty-cents and if they spent $5,000,000 in television spot commercials. They can then ask such questions as: What happens to the profit if the price is increased to seventy-five cents and $6,000,000 is put into TV? In other words, what is the best combination of price and advertising cost to create maximum profits?

Highway and transportation planning make extensive use of computer-based simulation. When the old winding two-lane road from Town A to Town B cannot handle all the traffic, a wider road must be built. How big should it be? Four lanes? Six or eight? The prediction of who will want to use the road is a complex affair because roads not only move traffic, they generate it. For example, when a better road exists between A and B, more people in A will decide to do their shopping in B; people who live in A will take jobs in B. With this increase in traffic, more businesses will be built along the road itself. It is therefore difficult to predict what sort of traffic will exist and what kind of road will be required in five or ten years. Computer-based models are used to predict, for various possible roads, what the traffic patterns and the land-use patterns along the right-of-way are likely to be at various points in the future. Using this information, planners can propose a route that seems best to satisfy the complex and even contradictory requirements of the community at large.

Limitations of Modeling. All these models have definite limitations. First, they are built on assumptions. The election predictor assumes that ethnically and economically similar communities that have behaved similarly in past elections will behave alike in this election. This certainly will not be true in all cases; it is assumed only that it will be true in most. The school class-size predictor assumes that this year's students are like last year's and those of the year before. This will also usually be a good enough rule of thumb, but not always. The highway and land-use model assumes people will travel certain distances to accomplish their objectives and that their attitudes toward driving and highway construction will be as in the past. This may or may not be true, particularly if the prediction is made five or ten years into the future.

Thus there is an inherent limitation in the use of these models. This is by no means to downgrade their importance for the tasks to which they have been put; it is simply a reminder that any decisions based on such models are no better than their assumptions.

There is a second limitation to models. Since the model and the real world are not identical but only resemble one another, can we be certain that the differences are not critical to the characteristics we want to measure? The model plane in the wind tunnel, for instance, is useful for analyzing wing design, but it cannot be used to estimate passenger comfort. An election model can predict the attitudes of masses of people on some issues, but it cannot predict their attitudes on others, or the attitudes of individuals on any. The use of a model beyond the range of its assumptions is dangerous and misleading.

A third limitation is that while models can extrapolate known trends, they are powerless to predict novelty. For example, the manufacturer's market model cannot be used to predict things that are beyond the company's control, such as scientific discoveries proving the product dangerous to health, technological inventions rendering it obsolete, or a better, cheaper competitive product.

The purpose of each of the models we have described is prediction. Such models tell us simply the detailed consequences of assumptions the model builders have stated. In general, their output ought to be preceded by the following words: "If the relationships among the variables are as described and if the initial conditions are as described, then the consequences will probably be as follows . . ."

Models for Training. Another important use of models is in training. Some kinds of real-life activity are so costly and/or dangerous that people should not attempt to engage in them until they know how; but if they are to learn how, they have to practice safely. By building a model, one can simulate the environment in which trainees are expected to operate. This has been the long-standing approach to training pilots in the operation of large aircraft and in such specialized techniques as landing on aircraft carriers. It is also used to train people to deal with unlikely events. For example, air traffic controllers or astronauts can be exposed to simulated emergencies that train them and test their reactions to situations for which they must be prepared but which they may seldom experience.

Complex probabilistic models also provide the basis for "war games"—training exercises for military officers in which they are given a set of resources (weapons, men, supplies) and faced with battle problems. They are asked to decide how to use the resources to solve the field problems. On the basis of the answers they receive ("twenty percent of your forces have been wiped out"), they can evaluate their own actions.

The same technique is used in management games. The executives of a company (or of several competing companies) are given resources and the market is described to them. They decide how to spend their resources and keep the company in the black. The computer model determines the consequences of their decisions. The players can use their knowledge of business management to make the best decisions they can. If they prosper in the game, it is because they made wise decisions; if they go bankrupt, it is because they made mistakes or because something happened that was beyond their control. Either way, they learn something about how to solve problems in the business environment.

Models can thus be used for a wide range of purposes. It may seem surprising that so much use can be made of systems that do nothing in fact but tell us the logical consequences of our own assumptions. However, this is an important limitation of human thinking. We cannot always do this unaided. The other side of the coin is that the output of simulations can never be more accurate than the assumptions on which they are based. There is no way to get accurate information from a computer on the basis of inaccurate or false inputs.

We have emphasized the limitations of modeling in part because it is the use of modeling that causes the omnipotent image of the computer. Finally, the use of simulation is so widespread that special programming languages (SIMSCRIPT, for example,) have been developed to facilitate it.

Control Systems

Information management systems manipulate information. Simulation is the manipulation of symbolic representations of things and events. The final type of program to be discussed here is the control system that manipulates and controls events in the real world. The input to such a system is information about events that are taking place and situations that actually occur; its major output is not information for human use but rather decisions to be carried out, usually by other machines, in order to modify existing situations and to cause new events.

At one time in the history of computer science, some thinkers felt that the most important use of computers was for control purposes. Much thought was given to developing the theoretical basis of automatic control. This discipline was called *cybernetics*. In fact, however, the computer was so valuable simply for managing information for humans that computer science developed more broadly than cybernetics. Nevertheless, computers do control complex systems, some of which are of considerable importance and have interesting consequences.

A simple case is the mechanism that operates an elevator. It is a small special-purpose computer.

Figure 6-3 A process control system

Its input is information about situations in the real world: someone wants to get on at the third floor and go up; people want to get off at the second, seventh, and eighth floors; someone wants to get on at the fifth floor and go down. The information is communicated directly by people pressing buttons. On the basis of the information, decisions are made for events that another machine (the motor that operates the elevator) will cause to happen: pass floor four, stop at floor five, and so forth.

Communications Control. Data communications lines (telephone or teletype lines, for example)

are so expensive that it is usually worthwhile to use a minicomputer to handle message switching (choosing the right route to send a message) and save expensive line time. Data concentration is also often used to save communications costs. In this technique, data is "concentrated" by combining several slow-speed messages into a single higher-speed one by interleaving the messages before they are sent and then, at the receiving end, sorting them out again with another computer.

Minicomputers also handle parts of some applications, like airlines seat reservations systems, that are geographically spread all over the world. These systems deal with enormous amounts of communications traffic between remote offices and the central computer. The main computer could be overwhelmed by the tasks of handling communications lines, stopping every time a new message arrived, and consulting files, thus leaving no time for the basic task of assigning seats.

All communications applications must be able to convert from one code to another and from one transmission speed to another. They must also have techniques for error control, formatting of characters and messages, traffic accounting, and accumulating network statistics. These simple functions are all profitably performed by minicomputers rather than the main processors. This practice has become so common now that minicomputers are available for communications pre-processing for the large IBM 360/370, Univac 1108, Burroughs B-5500, and CDC-6600 computers.

Laboratory Control. Although many laboratory automation projects have in the past used time sharing or large digital computers, a number of minicomputers are now being sold for this purpose. In the laboratory, the computer is used first of all to control the experiment. If a large number of experimental conditions are to be tried, having a computer vary the controls is cheaper, faster, and more accurate than doing it by hand. This is particularly true when expensive facilities like nuclear equipment are being used. Second, transcribing experimental results from visual displays and strip charts by hand is slow and error-prone. With minicomputers, data is taken directly from the experimental equipment and processed, giving experimenters immediate results. This can shorten the research process itself and has made experimentation possible with more variables, faster measurement rates, and more data. As a result, phenomena are now being investigated

that were difficult to approach with classical laboratory techniques.

This approach has been put to work in such diverse fields as speech research, nuclear physics, oil exploration, and medical patient monitoring.

Industrial Control. In general, the industrial processes that justify such uses of computers are ones that are expensive, complex, and require a high degree of reliability. For example, in a chemical plant, concrete factory, power plant, or oil refinery, careful watch must be kept over various indicators and meters that monitor the events taking place. If certain limits are reached, immediate action, such as opening or closing valves, must be taken to change or correct the situation. Since such decisions are relatively simple and since detailed observation of the meters and indicators requires superhuman (or subhuman) patience, computers offer an ideal solution to the problem of control.

Minicomputers are also now being used for controlling machine tools that produce very intricate parts, for bonding processes, for photolithography, and for fabricating semiconductor devices. And computer-controlled test facilities are used for complex assemblies, such as jet engines, which cost thousands of dollars per hour to test. They find further use in materials handling and warehousing—for example, in controlling a fleet of forklift trucks.

Military Command and Control. In the early 1950s, scientists experimenting with the Whirlwind computer at the Massachusetts Institute of Technology considered a classic problem in control and wrote a program for their computer. The problem was to monitor and interpret radar information, scanning it for enemy aircraft, and to produce directions for other aircraft to intercept the enemy. The situation was more complex, in a way, than the situation in a chemical plant. It involved the kind of logical analysis and manipulation of symbols at which digital computers excel. It was also an area in which human beings were definitely limited. The scientists produced a program using all of the 128-word memory available to them and demonstrated it to the Air Force. The Air Force was so impressed by the performance of this very small program that it decided to build a large-scale air defense system using computer-based techniques. Called SAGE *(Semi-Automatic Ground Environment),* this system was the first use of computers to aid military command and control.

Most military control systems are highly classified and little can be read about them in available literature. In general, however, they have these characteristics:

☐ They operate in real time; that is, they make decisions and take action in direct response to information about what is happening now.
☐ They are usually combinations of control and information systems; that is, summary information is presented to humans who are part of the system and who make the major decisions.
☐ They use, in a sophisticated way, the computer for what it excels at (rapid calculation and storage and retrieval of masses of information) and the human being for the kinds of things computers cannot do (decision making in the face of vague or incomplete information).
☐ Because the range of military weapons and sensors (like radar) is so large, and the military reports to a distant civilian Commander In Chief (the president), communications and the

control of communication networks is usually an important part of these systems.

There are non-military command and control systems, of course. The control of space vehicles and air and surface traffic are examples of non-military systems that depend heavily on computer-based control.

Thus computers allow us to create systems that can control more accurately, safely, and economically than in the past.

Summary

Modeling and information-management activities have tended to produce computer programs that can be used by different people for different purposes. The activities in the control system area have produced elaborate collections of special-purpose equipment, communications systems, and computer programs that generally serve a specific purpose and cannot be used elsewhere. For example, one cannot take the American Airlines control system and use it for air defense.

These applications programs, many of which are supplied free of charge with the computer or are available through cooperative users' organizations, have increased the computer's usefulness for less sophisticated organizations. An organization without the in-house staff to develop an information system can still have and use one. A business without mathematicians on its staff can obtain and use modeling programs.

While later chapters will go into far more detail about the application of computers, we will at this point summarize the purposes that these three types of application areas serve.

Table 6.1 Computer applications

APPLICATION PROGRAM	PURPOSE
Control	Safety Conservation of resources Optimization of resources Improved response time
Information Management	Operations Management Research Planning Manufacturing Sales
Modeling	Planning Research Training Analysis Engineering Science Design

Exercises

1. Take an area you are familiar with that uses a machine but still remains under human control—like the operation of an automobile, a washer-drier, or a duplicating machine. If you want to put the machine under the control of a computer, what functions do you think you could turn over to the computer? A hint: you will probably have to assume some sensors that your machine doesn't have now.

2. What information would an IMS for the home have?

3. You are the director of a research team that is developing a simulation model of people's reactions to crisis. Two of your principal assistants have come to you to settle a difference between them. One assistant assumes that in crisis human beings come together to share and help each other. The other assistant assumes the law of the jungle—every man for himself. The purpose of the model is to help plan emergency relief stations in case of a nuclear attack. How do you resolve the difference and how do you predict that your decision will affect the outcome of the study?

4. What are the characteristics of a problem that makes it possible to use a general-purpose information management system? Give some

examples of cases where such systems would be inappropriate.

5. Specify the information contents of a student information system that could be used currently by student organizations and later be transferred to an alumni information system.

6. Investigate information management systems that may be used on your campus or in a nearby industry. Describe one.

7. Research and describe as many cases as you can of the use of simulation and control systems involving computers in manned space flights.

8. What is a probabilistic model? How does it differ from a mathematical model?

9. Research a modeling and simulation application. What are its limitations or dangers?

For Further Information

A good survey of management information systems is a book by Gordon Davis (1). Such systems are most generally described, however, in term of their application to specific fields. Ralph Brisco's book (2) is about their use in social sciences. The other references (3–8) are oriented toward either business management or libraries.

An excellent and easy-to-understand introduction to simulation is John Kemeny's essay "Games of Life and Death" (9). If you have read this and have some background in programming, you will find one of his examples worked out in more detail in a programming textbook of which Dr. Kemeny is co-author (10). Guetzkow's book (11) is a collection of papers on the application of simulation techniques in the social sciences. A few other good introductory texts on the subject of simulation are included in the references (12–17).

The first reference on command and control systems (18) is an article in an annual publication already recommended. It is a good general introduction to the subject. *The Bomb and the Computer* (19) is a history of war games and their influence. A few more general references are also included (20–22). The subject has rather broad engineering implications that are beyond the realm of this book. The word *cybernetics* has a curious history and is used to mean a number of different things to different people. The classic reference, however, is Norbert Wiener's book (23), first published in 1948.

The last three references (24–26) will give you a survey of the way minicomputers are used in control system applications.

References

1. Gordon B. Davis, *Management Information Systems: Conceptual Foundations, Structure, and Development* (New York: McGraw-Hill Book Company, 1974).

2. Ralph L. Brisco, *Data Bases, Computers, and the Social Sciences* (New York: John Wiley & Sons, 1970).

3. J. Kelly, *Computerized Management Information Systems* (New York: Macmillan, 1970).

4. S. S. Blumenthal, *Management Information Systems* (Englewood Cliffs, N.J.: Prentice-Hall, Inc., 1969).

5. John Dearden and F. Warren McFarlan, *Management Information Systems* (Homewood, Ill.: Richard D. Irwin, Inc., 1966).

6. Barton Hodge and Robert Hodgson, *Management and the Computer in Information and Control Systems* (New York: McGraw-Hill Book Company, 1969).

7. Allen Kent et al., *Electronic Information Handling* (New York: Spartan Books, 1967).

8. George Salton, *Automatic Information Organization and Retrieval* (New York: McGraw-Hill Book Company, 1968).

9. John G. Kemeny, "Games of Life and Death," in *Random Essays* (Englewood Cliffs, N.J.: Prentice-Hall, Inc., 1964).

10. John G. Kemeny and Thomas E. Kurtz, *Basic Programming*, 2d. ed. (New York: John Wiley & Sons, 1971).

11. H. Guetzkow, ed., *Simulation in Social Science* (Englewood Cliffs, N.J.: Prentice-Hall, Inc., 1972).

12. Geoffrey Gordon, *System Simulation* (Englewood Cliffs, N.J.: Prentice-Hall, Inc., 1969).

13. Francis Martin, *Computer Modelling and Simulation* (New York: John Wiley & Sons, Inc., 1968).

14. John McLeod, ed., *Simulation, the Dynamic Modelling of Ideas and Systems with Computers* (New York: McGraw-Hill Book Company, 1968).

15. Douglas E. Knight, Huntington W. Curtis, and Lawrence J. Foge, eds., *Cybernetics, Simulation, and Conflict Resolution* (New York: Spartan Books, 1971).

16. James R. Emshoff and Roger L. Sisson, *Design and Use of Computer Simulation Models.* (New York: Macmillan, 1970).

17. Julian Reitman, *Computer Simulation Applications* (New York: John Wiley & Sons, Inc., 1971).

18. Anthony Debons, "Command and Control: Technology and Social Impact," in *Advances in Computers,* vol. 11, by A.F.L. Alt and M. Rubinoff, eds., (New York: Academic Press, 1971).

19. Andrew Wilson, *The Bomb and the Computer* (New York: Delcorte Press, 1968).

20. Emanuel S. Savas, *Computer Control of*

Industrial Processes (New York: McGraw-Hill Book Company, 1965).

21. Someshaver Gupta and L. Hasdorff, *Fundamentals of Automatic Control* (New York: John Wiley & Sons, Inc., 1970).

22. Bruce Watkins, *Introduction to Control Systems* (New York: Macmillan, 1969).

23. Norbert Wiener, *Cybernetics, or Control and Communication in the Animal and the Machine* (Cambridge, Mass.: The M.I.T. Press, 1961).

24. Fred F. Coury, ed., *A Practical Guide to Minicomputer Applications* (New York: IEEE Press, 1972).

25. W. Daniel Gardner, "Those Omnipresent Minis," *Datamation* (July 1973) pp. 52–55.

26. James D. Schoeffler and Ronald H. Temple, eds., *Minicomputers: Hardware, Software and Applications* (New York: IEEE Press, 1972).

Artificial Intelligence

7

Researchers in computer science have made a major effort to develop machines for solving problems that are not as well structured as the ones we have been using as illustrations. Many of the information problems that people face cannot be solved with a carefully defined procedure. We say that we have to *think* about these problems, that they require *intelligence*. Countless examples can be given: making out someone's scribbled handwriting, understanding a joke, playing a game that requires strategy or deception, or recognizing a voice on the telephone. These are not (for us) difficult tasks; they are so natural that we learn many of them in the first years of our lives. But we do them by a process that—to the extent that we understand it at all—is totally different from the conscious, deliberate way we solve problems in mathematics or logic. We know how to transfer

our techniques for solving procedural problems to computers; we have talked about this quite a bit in previous chapters. But the question that continues to fascinate computer scientists is whether we can develop techniques for computers to solve problems that seem to require imagination, intuition, or intelligence when they are solved by humans.

This field has been called *artificial intelligence*. The name is unfortunate. It makes it appear that computers are, in some sense, in competition with us. If computers can think, perhaps they will some day think better than we do; perhaps they will "take over." Although this is unrealistic, the anxiety provoked by the name "artificial intelligence" deserves attention. One of the purposes of describing computer capabilities to you in such detail is to convince you that no parallel exists

ar·ti·fi·cial \ˌärt-ə-'fish-əl\ *adj* **1** : humanly contrived often on a natural model : MAN-MADE <an ~ limb> <~ diamonds> **2** : having existence in legal, economic, or political theory **3** *obs* : ARTFUL, CUNNING **4 a** : FEIGNED, ASSUMED **b** : lacking in natural quality : AFFECTED <the ~ smile of one who is not really enjoying himself> **c** : IMITATION, SHAM <~ flavor> **5** : based on differential morphological characters not necessarily indicative of natural relationships — **ar·ti·fi·cial·ly** \-'fish-(ə-)lē\ *adv* — **ar·ti·fi·cial·ness** \-'fish-əl-nəs\ *n*
syn ARTIFICIAL, FACTITIOUS, SYNTHETIC, ERSATZ *shared meaning element* : brought into being not by nature but by human art or effort *ant* natural

in·tel·li·gence \in-'tel-ə-jən(t)s\ *n* [ME, fr. MF, fr. L *intelligentia*, fr. *intelligent-, intelligens* intelligent] **1 a** (1) : the ability to learn or understand or to deal with new or trying situations : REASON; *also* : the skilled use of reason (2) : the ability to apply knowledge to manipulate one's environment or to think abstractly as measured by objective criteria (as tests) **b** *Christian Science* : the basic eternal quality of divine Mind **c** : mental acuteness : SHREWDNESS **2 a** : an intelligent entity; *esp* : ANGEL **b** : intelligent minds or mind <cosmic ~> **3** : the act of understanding : COMPREHENSION **4 a** : INFORMATION, NEWS **b** : information concerning an enemy or possible enemy or an area; *also* : an agency engaged in obtaining such information

By permission. From Webster's New Collegiate Dictionary © 1975 by G. & C. Merriam Co., Publishers of the Merriam-Webster Dictionaries.

Figure 7-1 Webster's definitions

between these machines and Frankenstein's monster. Although we give them human work to do, they are no more human than the steam shovel or the cotton gin. Although we call these machine techniques *intelligent,* remember that we add the word *artificial* in front of it. Artificial means made in imitation of something else; pretended. When you see an entertainer turn a rabbit into a silk handkerchief, you may call it "magic," but you know it is slight of hand. When you see a computer play chess or carry on a (typed) dialogue, you should have the same appreciation for the art (artifice, artificial) that created a computer program so capable of simulating human thought.

Artificial intelligence is today mostly a field of research, an attempt to develop and improve techniques. It includes elements of hardware and software design, psychology, electrical engineering, and mathematics. Its successes have been largely in solving abstract problems; however, there have been some practical applications as well, which we will also discuss. Some of the experimental efforts have been in recognizing handwritten characters, playing chess or checkers, analyzing grammar and translating one language into another, proving theorems in mathematics answer-

ing limited questions, and solving puzzles, particularly the kind that appear in "intelligence tests."

As to whether these kinds of accomplishments constitute intelligent behavior, it is difficult to give a straightforward answer. Many intelligent people are incapable of many of these things. Intelligence is itself only an intuitively defined concept. Although there are many IQ tests, there is no single definition of intelligence. One interesting test of intelligence was offered by A. M. Turing in 1950. His now-famous proposal was called the *imitation game.*

It is played with three people, a man (A), a woman (B), and an interrogator (C) who may be of either sex. The interrogator stays in a room apart from the other two. The object of the game for the interrogator is to determine which of the other two is the man and which is the woman. He knows them by labels X and Y, and at the end of the game he says either "X is A and Y is B" or "X is B and Y is A."

The interrogator (C) is allowed to put questions to A and B thus: C: "Will X please tell me the length of his or her hair?" Now suppose X is actually A, then A must answer. It is A's object in the game to try to cause C to make the wrong identification.

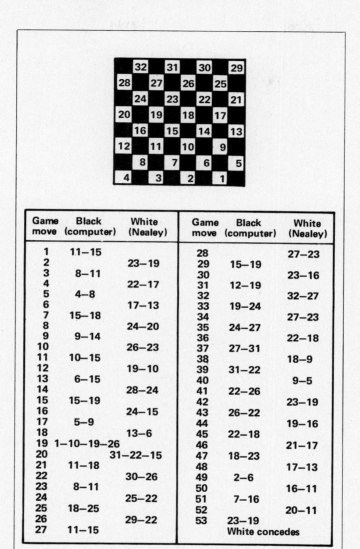

Game move	Black (computer)	White (Nealey)	Game move	Black (computer)	White (Nealey)
1	11—15		28		27—23
2		23—19	29	15—19	
3	8—11		30		23—16
4		22—17	31	12—19	
5	4—8		32		32—27
6		17—13	33	19—24	
7	15—18		34		27—23
8		24—20	35	24—27	
9	9—14		36		22—18
10		26—23	37	27—31	
11	10—15		38		18—9
12		19—10	39	31—22	
13	6—15		40		9—5
14		28—24	41	22—26	
15	15—19		42		23—19
16		24—15	43	26—22	
17	5—9		44		19—16
18		13—6	45	22—18	
19	1—10—19—26		46		21—17
20		31—22—15	47	18—23	
21	11—18		48		17—13
22		30—26	49	2—6	
23	8—11		50		16—11
24		25—22	51	7—16	
25	18—25		52		20—11
26		29—22	53	23—19	
27	11—15			**White concedes**	

Figure 7-2 A checker problem in a computer game

His answer might therefore be "My hair is shingled, and the longest strands are about nine inches long." In order that tones of voice may not help the interrogator the answers should be written or better still, typewritten. The ideal arrangement is to have a teleprinter communication between the two rooms. Alternatively, the question and answers can be repeated by an intermediary. The object of the game for the second player (B) is to help the interrogator. The best strategy for her is probably to give truthful answers. She can add such things as "I am the woman; don't listen to him" to

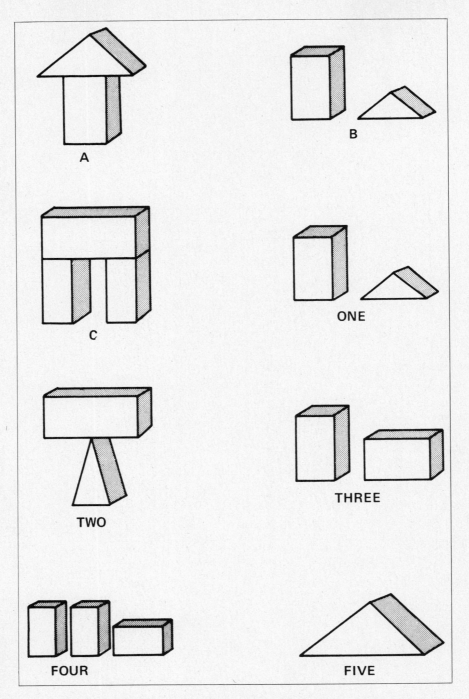

Figure 7-3 Sample test item used in artificial intelligence programs

her answers, but it will avail nothing as the man can make similar remarks.

We now ask the question, "What will happen when a machine takes the part of A in this game?" Will the interrogator decide wrongly as often when the game is played like this as he does when the game is played between a man and a woman? These questions replace our original, "Can machines think?"* Turing thus replaced a set of unsolved problems (the definition of intelligence and machine intelligence) with an easier problem—a test of behavior that we call *intelligent*.

If a computer is some day programmed to win at this game (and so far, no program has even approached this goal), what are the implications? Will it mean that computers can think as well as people can? Or only that an artful simulation of thinking has taken place, just as slight of hand simulates magic? For that matter, is it even theoretically possible that a program will be able to win at this game? Much philosophical discussion has taken place on these questions, and the fairest thing to say is that opinions differ.

To set this question aside, before we go into the actual accomplishments of artificial intelligence, we will describe *human* capabilities in information terms. We will then cover the accomplishments in the fields of heuristics, speech understanding, print and script reading, interactive pattern analysis and classification systems, and finally natural language processing. This leaves out the subject of humanoid robots, which we feel is beyond both the realm of this text and reasonable expectation.

------

*A. M. Turing, "Computing Machinery and Intelligence," reprinted in MINDS AND MACHINES, Alan Ross Anderson, ed. (Englewood Cliffs, N.J.: Prentice-Hall, 1964), p. 11.

Human Processing Capabilities

People are aware of their contexts and their needs. We make a total assessment of our time requirements, our physical needs, resources available, comforts and discomforts, pains and pleasures, rewards and punishments, threats and perils, *and we act*. We can vary our levels of awareness and shift contexts quickly. In short, we perceive our total situation and cope with it in the face of uncertain facts and outcomes. We deal easily with ambiguity of meaning and incomplete information. Our concerns and purposes need only be as specific as our situation demands, and it may change from instant to instant. We can undertake one set of actions and remain peripherally aware of other inputs, as when we notice a familiar face in a blur of people passing by, or a clock only when it stops ticking. We can simplify an apparently confusing problem by gaining insight into its structure. For example, when we deal with an obstructive person, we may discover the self-interest that the person is too devious to reveal.

We can, of course, solve problems and find means to ends. We recognize patterns (ranging from taking simple color blindness tests to resolving four conversations simultaneously over a noisy radio channel or even predicting our own futures). We can tolerate ambiguity of meaning (the basis for much humor) and resolve it when there is sufficient information. We can discriminate between essential and nonessential, relevant and irrelevant information. We learn consciously. Finally, we don't have to be formally instructed in how to do any of these things.

We view facts in the light of our present contexts and past experiences to give these facts meaning. We do not have to continually store an

Figure 7-4 Playing chess with a computer

abstract model of our world for reference; we have direct and continuous access to it through our senses. We also learn subconsciously and have access to our past experiences. Thus we do not have to live rigidly by a set of strictly defined rules.

These, then, are the abilities that the field of artificial intelligence imitates and—if you will—competes with.

Heuristics

Consider the following problem: you are designing a robot "bug" that is supposed to find the highest mountain wherever you place it. This bug, for simplicity of design, can only go forward or backward and turn to the left or the right. It has an eye that can see a limited distance and a computer to

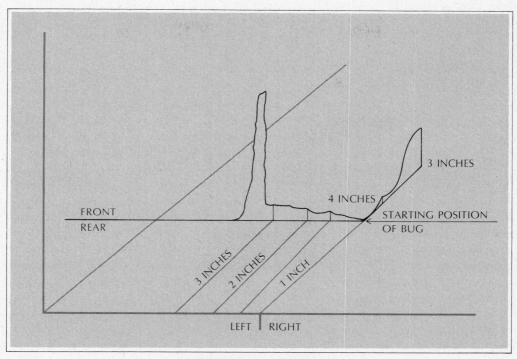

Figure 7-5 The bug problem

decide which way leads to the top. The design problem is to decide how far the eye should be able to see and how the computer shall determine which direction to go. Let us look at two designs of this bug.

Design One. The eye can see *one* inch to the front, back, left, and right of the bug. The computer determines whether one inch in each of these directions is higher than where the bug is now, and which is the highest. The bug then goes *one* inch in the direction of the highest point and stops to take another look. If none of the other points are higher than where it is, it stops. It has reached the top.

Design Two. This design is basically the same as the first, except that this bug can see *three* inches

in the distance and move *three* inches before it stops and takes another look around.

Now let's put these two bugs in the field and see which finds the highest peak. Figure 7-5 shows the field we have chosen to illustrate our point. The bug with one-inch vision looks around. It sees a flat plane behind it and to the right and ignores these points. However, there is a hill on the left and another in the front. At the one-inch range, the hill to the left is the higher, so the bug moves onto it. It stops, takes another look, and sees a higher hill on the left again. The bug goes on to it, and again moves one inch until it comes in range of the really high peak and climbs it. Starting from the same point, the bug with the three-inch vision sees a higher hill in front at the three-inch range and goes forward to the lesser peak.

We have deliberately chosen the shape of the

hills to contradict your expectation that the bug with the longest vision will find the highest peak. The criteria by which the bugs make their decisions are called *heuristics;* they are rules of operation that may or may not work every time. They have to be tested to see if they have value—if they save work, computation, or whatever. Heuristics are used in situations that do not yield to conventional mathematics. As it happens, we have chosen a problem for our example that mathematicians can analyze to some extent. If some assumptions about how sharply the mountains can rise are made, optimal search techniques can be determined for the bug, but in general *one* best rule cannot be found. This is the type of circumstance in which heuristics are used.

In general, their purpose is to provide "rule-of-thumb" solutions to problems that are too complex for mathematical analysis and too time-consuming to yield to a brute-force computer solution. For example, two people can play a game of chess in a few hours. But, if on the day of the creation of the earth, every atom had become what is today's most modern computer and each of these could make chess moves and decide who won, and if all of these computers had been set to work evaluating every possibility by trying them, that first game of chess would still be going on.

Some heuristics can help us estimate the right order in which to try solutions. Perhaps a good one for a jigsaw puzzle is *always try smaller pieces first.* The reason we say "perhaps" is that we would have to try the heuristic "start with the smallest piece" with a group of similar puzzles to see if it worked. A set of heuristics that helps in one type of puzzle may not help in another. A successful heuristic is the result of a practical test. Thus, heuristics are limited as problem-solving tools.

Early researchers in this field hoped to find general heuristics they could apply to many problems. For solving algebraic problems, they tended to try this heuristic: *use substitutions that reduce the length of the algebraic expressions you are working with.* Other researchers attempted to extract simple problems from the complex problem and then to try the way the simple problem could be solved on the larger, more complex one.

Little by little, it became apparent that even the most general set of heuristics wouldn't be useable without another set to tell when to use them. Eventually a cascade of rules would be required. And no one seemed to know whether human-like capability could ever be matched with a finite set of heuristics.

These kinds of considerations, plus the failure of many massively funded programs, caused artificial intelligence researchers to redefine their goals. They narrowed the scope of the problems they were trying to solve.

A practical and successful example of this is the DENDRAL program. It infers the structure of an organic compound from certain measurements. Specifically, it assists selection from among hundreds of thousands of possible structures. We will go into a little more detail on this problem to show you how a computer can make inferences in a very limited context.

This is a classical problem in organic chemistry. It is possible for two different molecules to have the same number of atoms of the same type and yet have different arrangements of these atoms. For example, ether and ethyl alcohol both have the same number of carbon, hydrogen, and oxygen atoms, but they are differently arranged. The problem is that any set of atoms can arrange themselves in hundreds of thousands of ways. No one person can consider all these to determine the structure of a molecule. Thus in the past such

Figure 7-6   Shakey, SRI's mobile robot

structures have been deduced intuitively. In the mid-sixties, the DENDRAL project was begun to use a computer to help make this judgment. The computer first produces a list of all possible structures (called isomers). Then it is given data about the mass spectrum of the chemical. A mass spectrometer analyzes a sample and measures the mass of the molecule's fragments. This process does not uniquely identify a molecule's structure, but it allows a computer to determine whether a structure being considered would produce a mass spectrum like the data it is given.

Thus we have a process with hundreds of thousands of possible answers and data that narrows the choices somewhat. However, even the fastest computers need heuristics to narrow down the search and save computation time. For example, the program must have a list of structures that have been considered and rejected in order to avoid reconsidering them. It has been estimated that heuristics improve the running time of such a program by a factor of 30,000.

The DENDRAL program took years to evolve and consists of about 40,000 instructions. It runs on a PDP-6 computer. We stressed the limited context in which inference was being assisted by a computer because of the easy extrapolations that are made. If a computer can be used to infer chemical structure, surely it can be used to infer anything. DENDRAL's use is limited to a specific class of organic compounds. The techniques of inference are the techniques of organic chemistry. New com-

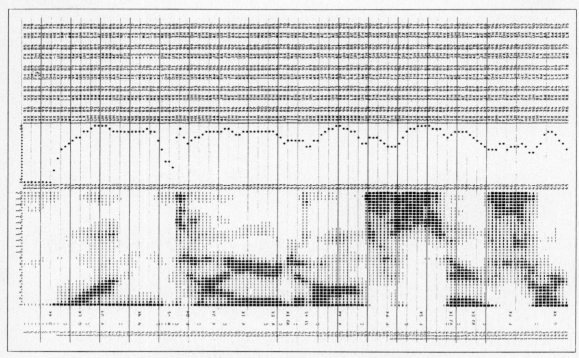

Figure 7-7   Digital sound spectrogram of a spoken sentence

puter programming techniques were developed for this problem that will no doubt be applied to other problems, but as of this writing, DENDRAL is the state of the art.

Speech Understanding

Automatic recognition of continuous spoken English (as opposed to the so-called "voice button" that recognizes a single spoken word) is a genuinely difficult problem. The reasons are many. There are no simple recognizable separations between basic sounds (phonemes) or words. Speakers' voices vary in intonation, pitch, and timbre due to age, sex, health, regional origin, and stress. Then there are pauses, errors, hesitations, incomplete words, false starts and mispronunciations. Furthermore, phonemes are pronounced differently, depending on the words that come before or after them. If all this weren't bad enough, background noise makes speech hard to understand.

Researchers at IBM, RCA, Bell Laboratories, and elsewhere have been attempting to solve this problem without a great deal of success for at least thirty years. You can understand why enormous sums of money have been spent on an apparently unmanageable problem when you consider what a partial solution could mean. For example, think how simple it would be to use a telephone if you could simply speak the number.

However, artificial-intelligence researchers are now attacking something less than the general problem with some success. This area is called *speech understanding* rather than speech recognition. The ways that the problem has been restricted are:

a) particular tasks are to be performed as a result of a spoken command, and

b) the vocabulary and sentence structure are severely limited.

These limitations will be made clear in the following examples. One system called "voice chess" accepts spoken orders to move chess pieces. The system has the best that speech recognition researchers have been able to produce in the way of phoneme identification. However, even trained researchers can identify oscillograms of sound waves only seventy-five percent of the time. A machine can do no better. But the program then uses this incomplete information in the limited context of chess. The vocabulary is limited to thirty-one words. A small number of action statements are available, like "move," "check," and "take." The computer has a record of where all the pieces are on the board and a knowledge of what is a legal move. Thus it can check whether a statement makes sense in terms of the positions of the pieces on the board. Let us emphasize that this program does not play or "understand" chess. It merely interprets spoken orders to move chess pieces. Unfortunately, this system's accuracy has not yet been completely reported.

Another system that indicates the state of the art is the Vicens-Reddy system. It accepts directions to a computer-controlled arm to pick up blocks. It uses a vocabulary of sixteen words and can cope with 192 sentences in a fixed format. If the acoustic processing part of the system is tuned to the particular speaker, the program selects the correct sentence eighty-five percent of the time. It can decipher the utterances of new speakers sixty-five percent of the time. Using a DEC PDP-10 computer with 500,000 bits of random-access memory, the Vicens-Reddy system operates in approximately ten times real time—that is, if it takes a speaker

two seconds to utter a command, it takes the computer about twenty seconds to decipher it.

The principal lesson of thirty years of research is that there isn't enough information in context-less and meaning-free language to be understood. However when the use of context and meaning are introduced, limited tasks become feasible.

Whether what is possible then becomes economically useful is a different question. It is not certain at this point that such systems will. First of all, they must be judged against standards of human performance, and they are very high. Second, it is not yet possible (and this too is an indication of the state of the art) to tell how much can be expressed in the limited language being used. Last, there are considerable problems of data-base management that get worse as the vocabulary increases.

In 1970 it was predicted that by 1976 systems using specific task-oriented contexts would be capable of handling vocabularies of 1000 words with a ten percent error rate. However, it seems doubtful that such a system would be of practical use.

Print and Script Readers

The reading of hand-produced script or print is subject to some of the same difficulties as the recognition of spoken language: incompleteness of letters and words, inaccuracies in spelling, differences among handwriting styles, and indistinct boundaries between letters (as between phonemes). In addition, there are variations in the size and slant of letters, spacing between lines, width of margins, and the angle the written line makes to the edge of the paper.

An early experimental system that recognized

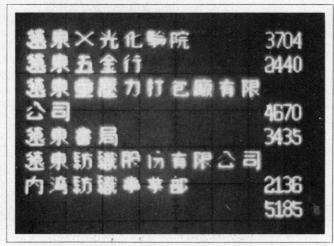

Figure 7-8 Chinese ideographs on a CRT

only the hand-printed letters AEILMNORST was eighty-five to ninety percent accurate on materials that a human control group was able to recognize with ninety-six percent accuracy. Another early system limited to reading hand-printed numerals searched the document for the numerals and traced them out. If the variation in their size was kept to less than 4:1 and slant was limited to plus or minus twenty degrees, the system could perform quite well. On numbers written by uninstructed writers, the system was ninety-two percent accurate. If the writers were given a half-hour of instruction, the numbers they produced could be read with ninety-nine percent accuracy.

Devices are commercially available that will accept machine-printed or carefully hand-printed numerals and the letters C, S, T, Z and X if they are written in precise locations.

As you might expect, this sort of capability is useful for handling mail, and indeed the USSR and Japan are using readers that process 20,000 pieces of mail an hour with ninety-three percent accuracy. This system requires the address code to be written in preprinted boxes on the envelope.

The Chinese are working on the problem also. There are, roughly, 40,000 ideographs (see figure 7-8) in Chinese, but a functional vocabulary need contain only 2000. A system has been built to recognize 1000 ideographs and it is ninety-nine percent accurate after it rejects seven percent of the input as unreadable. The designers of these machines hope to achieve processing rates of 3400 characters per minute.

Various techniques have been tried to read cursive script without a great deal of success. One technique measured the length of the word, counted closed loops and centerline crossings, and matched the results against a dictionary. This technique was about eighteen percent accurate. Another technique scored twenty-six percent by breaking each word into strings of connected line segments to deduce letters and then words. The users of this second approach expect that it could be made more sophisticated and possibly achieve sixty-eight percent accuracy.

As in the problem of speech understanding, it is expected that performance can be improved by the use of context. In this case we mean the use of redundancy in the English language. *Redundancy* is the presence of information not needed for understanding. If, for ex@mple, we were to re@ove a few let@ers from thi@ sente@ce, it wou@d s@ill be perfe@tly cl@@r. In normal English-language text, twenty-five percent of the print, on the average, can be obliterated without making it unreadable. Thus systems should be able to be built that miss identifying twenty-five percent of the letters and still get the meaning from the remaining correctly identified seventy-five percent.

In summary, the prospect of automatic reading of cursive script is bleak but not hopeless. However, as in the case of voice recognition, the problem will be pursued because of the enormous potential gains. Many records that people would like to incorporate in data-processing systems are handwritten and the costs of keypunching can seriously limit the creation of new information-processing systems.

Interactive Pattern Analysis and Classification Systems

It should be apparent by now that the best chance of success for an artificial intelligence project is to make its goals very specific and limited. Indeed, by incorporating a good deal of data about their problems' contexts, such programs have shown more promise in recent years. However, there has been another approach to pattern-analysis and classification problems of artificial intelligence which some believe is superior. This approach uses an interactive partnership between a person and a computer. The idea is to allow the person to use a console with graphic displays and facilities to do what he or she is best at (and better than a computer at) and let the computer do its part on what the person is worst at. The capabilities of such systems give us an indication of what people are worst at:

a) Cross-referencing massive sets of data
b) Accepting new processing routines once they have been experimentally tried
c) Presenting a highly precise graphic display and offering the ability to alter the picture experimentally to gain insight into the data. Systems with this capability can rotate, compress, or expand the graphic image. Some can even create a moving picture as if the camera were taking the viewer on a trip.
d) Focussing attention by changing scale, blinking selected portions of the displayed data, or providing a label on a displayed data point to make it easy to refer to
e) Facilitating the detection and location of clusters of data that identify the principal effects sought in research. Typically, difficult research problems are multi-dimensional. They involve measurements of many variables. For example, the classification of handprints requires some twenty-three different measurements. Most people aren't very good at visualizing more than three dimensions, yet visualizing a problem seems to be an important part of human problem solving. Such consoles can compress data and identify unusual data points.

As long as these kinds of facilities are rapid enough, often the human problem solver can provide what he or she is good at: insight into the structure of the problem.

Natural Language Processing

One of the most practical and useful things computers might do would be to process natural language. (English and other spoken languages are

Доклады Академии Наук СССР
1950. Том LXX, № 8

ЭЛЕКТРОТЕХНИКА

А. Г. ЛУНЦ

ПРИЛОЖЕНИЕ МАТРИЧНОЙ БУЛЕВСКОЙ АЛГЕБРЫ К АНАЛИЗУ И СИНТЕЗУ РЕЛЕЙНО-КОНТАКТНЫХ СХЕМ

(Представлено академиком А. Н. Колмогоровым 30 XI 1949)

В последнее время для анализа и синтеза релейно-контактных электрических схем параллельно-последовательного соединения с успехом используется аппарат булевской алгебры (¹⁻³). Но этого аппарата оказывается недостаточно для теории схем общего типа, а также для теории многополюсных схем. В настоящей статье предлагается для исследований такого рода использовать матричную булевскую алгебру и описывается ряд результатов, получаемых в этом направлении.

§ 1. Матричная булевская алгебра

Пусть $\mathfrak{U}$ есть некоторая булевская алгебра (¹). Будем рассматривать матрицы с элементами из $\mathfrak{U}$. Как и для обычных матриц (с элементами из поля), для матриц с элементами из $\mathfrak{U}$ можно ввести операции сложения и умножения, которые мы будем записывать: $A + B$, $A \times B$. При этом также будут иметь место ассоциативные, коммутативный (для сложения) и дистрибутивный законы.

Введем понятие «определителя» квадратной матрицы с элементами из $\mathfrak{U}$, как суммы $n!$ слагаемых, составленных таким же образом, как и в обычном определителе n-го порядка. Такие определители будут обладать рядом свойств, аналогичных обычным свойствам определителей.

Для пары матриц с элементами из $\mathfrak{U}$ мы введем еще операцию «булевского умножения», обозначив ее $A \cdot B = C$ и определив элементы матрицы C через элементы матриц A и B следующим образом:

$$c_{\alpha,\beta} = a_{\alpha,\beta} b_{\alpha,\beta}$$

для всех индексов α и β.

Квадратную матрицу с элементами из $\mathfrak{U}$, по главной диагонали которой стоят единицы, будем называть «булевской», а множество булевских матриц n-го порядка с элементами из $\mathfrak{U}$ обозначать $\mathfrak{U}_n$, и в самом деле является булевской алгеброй относительно операций сложения и булевского умножения. В дальнейшем только о матрицах из $\mathfrak{U}_n$ и будет идти речь.

§ 2. Многополюсники

Каждую релейно-контактную схему (или часть схемы) можно задать, указав непосредственную проводимость между ее узловыми точками. Поэтому на исследуемой электрической схеме выберем l точек (полюсов) $M_1, M_2, \ldots, M_l$ и будем изучать схему относительно этих точек. Обозначим непосредственную проводимость от полюса

(APPOSITION, Enclosure, Appendix, Application) MATRIX

BOOLEAN ALGEBRA (TO, Towards, By, For) ANALYSIS (AND, N)

SYNTHESIS RELAY-CONTACT (CIRCUIT, Diagram, Scheme).

(IN, At, Into, To, For, On, N) (LAST, letter, new, latest, lowest, worst) (TIME, tense) FOR ANALYSIS (AND, N)

SYNTHESIS RELAY-CONTACT ELECTRICAL (CIRCUIT, diagram, scheme)

PARALLEL- (SERIES, successive, consecutive, consistent) (CONNECTION, junction, combination) (WITH, from) (SUCCESS, luck)

(TO BE UTILIZE, to be take advantage of) APPARATUS BOOLEAN

ALGEBRA. BUT THIS APPARATUS (TO FIND X-SELF, to turn out, to be found, to prove) (INSUFFICIENT, inadequate, scanty) FOR

THEORY (CIRCUIT, diagram, scheme) (GENERAL, common) TYPE, (BUT, and, yet, if, while) ALSO FOR THEORY MULTIPOLAR (CIRCUIT, diagram, scheme). (IN, At, Into, To, For, On, N) (PRESENT, genuine) (ARTICLE, item, clause) (TO BE OFFER, to be propose, to be suggest) FOR (INVESTIGATION, research, analysis, exploration, paper, essay) (SUCH, so, a sort of) (SORT, kind, family, genus, gender) (TO UTILIZE, to take advantage of) MATRIX

BOOLEAN ALGEBRA (AND, N) TO BE DESCRIBE (ROW, series) RESULT, GOTTEN (IN, at, into, to, for, on, N) THIS (DIRECTION, trend, order, permit).

I. MATRIX BOOLEAN ALGEBRA

(LET, Though) a (TO BE, to eat, O.K.) SOME BOOLEAN

ALGEBRA. TO BE (TO CONSIDER, to examine, to discuss) MATRIX

Figure 7-9 Stages in Russian-English translation by a computer

DOKLADY AKADEMII NAUK SSSR
1950, Vol. 70, No. 3

A. G. Lunts

THE APPLICATION OF BOOLEAN MATRIX ALGEBRA TO THE ANALYSIS AND SYNTHESIS OF RELAY CONTACT NETWORKS

Communicated by Academician A. N. Kolmogorov, Nov. 30, 1949.

In recent times Boolean algebra has been successfully employed in the analysis of relay networks of the series-parallel type.(1-3) This algebra is inadequate, however, for a theory of more general networks and for a theory of multi-terminal networks. The purpose of the present paper is to employ a Boolean matrix algebra for investigations of this nature and to describe a series of results obtained along this line.

1. Boolean Matrix Algebra

Let a be a Boolean algebra.(1) We will examine matrices composed of elements from a. As in the case of ordinary matrices (made up of elements from a field) we may define for matrices composed of elements from a the operations of addition and multiplication, which we will write as: A + B, A × B. The associative, commutative (for addition) and distributive laws apply in this case.

We introduce the concept of the determinant of a square matrix containing elements from a, as the sum of the

---

Doklady Akademii Nauk SSSR
1950, Tom LXX, No. 3

A. G. Lunts

1   (Apposition, Enclosure, Appendix, Application) Matrix
    of
    Boolean Algebra (To, Towards, By, For) Analysis (And, #)
    the
    Synthesis Relay-Contact (Circuit; Diagram, Scheme).

    (In, At, Into, To, For, On, #) (last, latter,
    recent
5   new, latest, lowest, worst) (time; tense) for analysis
    of
  (and, #) synthesis relay-contact electrical (circuit;
    containing
    diagram, scheme) parallel-(series, successive, consecutive,
    of
  consistent) (connection, junction, combination) (with, from)
    has been
  (success, luck) (to be utilized, to be taken advantage of)
    the
10 apparatus Boolean algebra. But this apparatus (to find
  self, to turn out, to be found, to proved) (insufficient,
    the   of
  inadequate, scanty) for theory (circuit; diagram, scheme)
  of general, common) type, (sub, and, yet, if, while) also.
    the   of   probably O.K.
  for theory multipolar (circuit; diagram, scheme). (Any
    The
15 (At, Into, To, For, On, #) (present, genuine) (article,

Figure 7-9 (cont'd)

called *natural languages* to distinguish them from artificial languages like FORTRAN and COBOL.) We have seen that computers can be used to handle letters and words as easily as numbers, but only when the information is carefully structured and precisely defined, as in the information systems described in chapter six. A considerable research effort has been underway for two decades to develop techniques so that computers can deal with a sentence, a paragraph, or a book in ordinary English. For example, we might ask the computer to summarize a text or sift through it and answer some questions on the basis of what was found. Or we might ask that the entire text be translated into another language.

The uses that could be made of such capabilities are clear. Much of the work of libraries is involved in classifying and indexing books on the basis of what they are about—something that is hard to do without reading at least part of the book. Other library tasks involve helping people find the answers to questions of fact.

Computer users are also hampered by the fact that they must learn the strange languages computers understand before they can write a program. How much easier it would be if we could explain our problem in English! And programs to help students learn (we will explore this subject in more detail in chapter eleven) would be much more satisfactory if students could describe their problems in their own words.

Using computers to process natural language has turned out to be much more difficult than the early researchers anticipated. Although some of our sentences are very straightforward, surprisingly many of the statements we read, hear, and utter are highly ambiguous and depend on a thorough understanding not only of words and grammar but of the world we live in. Small children and even illiterate adults have no trouble with sentences that are beyond the most complex heuristics yet devised for computers. For example:

"We saw the Grand Canyon flying to California."
"The girl guides fish."

In each case, two interpretations are grammatically possible; one of them, however, is very unlikely and we would always choose the other.

So far, the computer's ability to deal even with simple sentences is severely limited; nevertheless, some progress has been made. Approximate translations of technical text (always more straightforward than general writing) from Russian to English are possible, although they require human editing to make them readable. Some programs for tutoring students make fairly clever analyses of student answers to questions. But, by and large, there have been few practical applications so far. Most of the work in natural-language processing, as in artificial intelligence generally, remains in the form of laboratory efforts. Some of these experimental systems analyze sentences grammatically and fit them into general categories for interpretation. Others build on this and attempt to develop related sentences, even to carry on conversations. One of the best known of these programs is called ELIZA and was developed by Joseph Weizenbaum at M.I.T. Here is a sample dialog between a person and ELIZA. (The computer output is printed in capital letters here).

Men are all alike.
IN WHAT WAY?
They're always bugging us about something or other.
CAN YOU THINK OF A SPECIFIC EXAMPLE?
Well, my boyfriend made me come here.
YOUR BOYFRIEND MADE YOU COME HERE?
He says I'm depressed much of the time.
I AM SORRY TO HEAR YOU ARE DEPRESSED.

It's true. I am unhappy.

DO YOU THINK COMING HERE WILL HELP YOU NOT
TO BE UNHAPPY?

I need some help, that much seems certain.

WHAT WOULD IT MEAN TO YOU IF YOU GOT SOME
HELP?

Perhaps I could learn to get along with my mother.

TELL ME MORE ABOUT YOUR FAMILY.

My mother takes care of me.

You can see that fairly simple techniques have been used to turn sentences around and make questions of them. The automated interviewer has nothing of its own to contribute to the conversation; the objective is simply to keep the person talking (or typing). However, many people who have conversed with ELIZA have been surprised to learn they had been talking to a computer.

This brings us back to the point from which we started our discussion of artificial intelligence—the Turing test. How far is ELIZA from passing the test? Quite a long way. ELIZA doesn't have any information and cannot make a straightforward answer to a question. ELIZA and other such programs have only scratched the surface in simulating the ways humans actually react to language. Robert Simmons, a computer scientist at the University of Texas, has used the sentence, "I went to three drugstores," to distinguish between three levels of language analysis. A system based on syntax alone (like ELIZA) can only turn the statement around and reply, "How did you go to three drugstores?" A more sophisticated system would be based on semantic analysis and would be able to draw on the fact that people go to drugstores for a purpose. It might reply, "What did you buy in three drugstores?" But the third level, which the computer will have to achieve to pass the Turing test, requires the further information that one does not normally go to one drugstore after another. An obvious human response would be, "Three! What did you want that the first two stores were out of?"

Linguists and computer scientists have learned how to build words and grammar into computer programs. But people structure concepts in a unique indefinable way. Language reflects this. It is by no means clear that all of these concepts can be formalized and that heuristics for processing language in a human way will ever be stated in a form useable by computers.

Summary

We have taken you on a very quick tour of some of the highlights of artificial-intelligence research and suggested some of the possibilities and limitations of this field. We started with the general question of whether computers can think, listen, or read, and showed that their general accomplishments to date in this area are minor. Then we saw that as the aims of such research programs become more specific (such as sorting mail or deducing organic structures), they become quite practical but less applicable to other areas. The most powerful systems of all are those in which computers do not totally replace human efforts but cooperate instead: in which computers do what they are best at and people do what they are best at. We hope in the chapters that follow to be able to convince you that a computer can become a partner rather than a rival of human beings trying to solve problems.

Exercises

1. What is the difference between an algorithm and a heuristic?

2. Find a defensive heuristic for the game of tic-tac-toe. That is, find a rule of play for the person who plays second and marks the squares with O's. (This always leads, at least, to a draw.) To help you get started, we will diagram most of the possible outcomes in a game in which two moves have already been made. The "F" means a move is forced. The "D" means a draw position. "W-O" means that you, the second player, have won. "W-X" means that the first player has won.

Before we start, note that the portion of the game shown here starts with a position that is one of seventy-two possible two-move combinations, and the second and third lines leave even more possibilities. So it should be clear that the simple game of tic-tac-toe explodes into many options.

Second, look at the positions in which wins occur. If you are searching for a defensive heuristic, you must look ahead and see if any move you are considering leaves a place where the opponent can move to create a winning position. One way to do this is to test out your proposed heuristics on a tree diagram of this sort. Another is to team up with another member of your class and play the game.

3. What uses can you imagine for an automatic script reader other than those mentioned in the text?

4. What prospects do you see for a computer that could search the contents of a book for key words, phrases, or proper nouns?

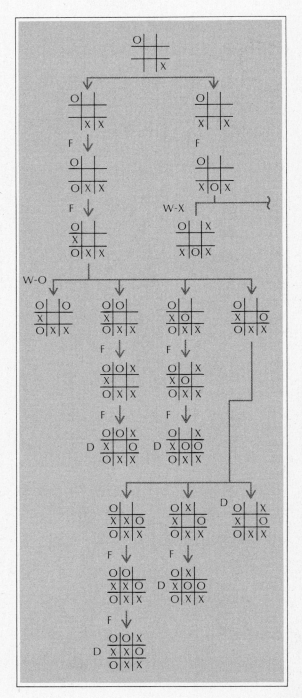

5. Do you see any potential impact of progress in artificial intelligence on employment or unemployment?

6. Construct a simple three-sentence syllogism and show what kind of knowledge a computer would have to have in order to conclude the syllogism. For example: All dogs howl at the moon. George is a dog. Therefore George howls at the moon.

For Further Information

In general, the literature of artificial intelligence is difficult and not to be recommended to the novice. Jackson's book (1) is an exception; it is carefully written, yet informal. It makes a good introduction. If you enjoy educated and witty sarcasm, you will want to look into the Dreyfus book (2), which is quite critical of the potentialities of artificial intelligence generally. In fairness, we should mention a reply to Dreyfus (3) which is, however, less likely to be found in your library. Most of the conference proceedings (4) are pretty heavy going unless you have a graduate degree in computer science, but one paper in it is recommended—the one by Furschein, Fischler, Coles, and Tenebaum, called "Forecasting and Assessing the Impact of Artificial Intelligence on Society." It represents what professionals in the field think of future possibilities. Allen Newell's report (5) is a very well written booklet and can be understood without a technical background. It presents the state of speech understanding backed up with good explanatory appendixes. Two of the references (6 and 7) are clearly written with extensive bibliographies. The Nilsson book (8) requires some calculus. *Machine Intelligence* (9) appears annually and has up-to-date reports on current research. For example, (10) has a good article on DENDRAL. If you would like to know more about it and have some background in chemistry try (11).

References

1. Philip Jackson, *Introduction to Artificial Intelligence* (New York: Petrocelli Books, 1974).

2. Hubert L. Dreyfus, *What Computers Can't Do: A Critique of Artificial Reason* (New York: Harper & Row, 1972).

3. Seymour Papert, *The Artificial Intelligence of Hubert L. Dreyfus: A Budget of Fallacies* (Cambridge: M.I.T. Project MAC, 1968).

4. *Proceedings of the Third International Joint Conference on Artificial Intelligence* 20–23 August 1973, Stanford University.

5. Allen Newell et al., *Speech Understanding Systems* (New York: American Elsevier Publishing Co., Inc., 1973).

6. Leon D. Harmon, "Automatic Recognition of Print and Script," *Proceedings of the IEEE,* **60:** 10 (Oct. 1972) pp. 1165–76.

7. Laveen N. Kanal, "Interactive Pattern Analysis and Classification Systems: A Survey and Commentary," *Proceedings of the IEEE,* **60:** 10 (Oct. 1972) pp. 1200–15.

8. Nils J. Nilsson, *Problem-solving Methods In Artificial Intelligence* (New York: McGraw-Hill Book Company, 1971).

9. Bernard Meltzer and Donald Michie, *Machine Intelligence* (New York: John Wiley & Sons) (annual).

10. Feigenbaum et al., "On Generality and Problem Solving: A Case Study Using the DENDRAL Program," *Machine Intelligence,* Vol. 6 (1971), pp. 165–80.

11. Lederberg and Feigenbaum, "Mechanization of Inductive Inference. . .," chapter seven in Kleinmuntz, *Formal Representations for Human Judgment* (New York: John Wiley & Sons, 1968).

People and Problems

8

The final component we need to add to all of the hardware and software in order to make a real working system is *people*.

Hardware and software do not, after all, do anything unless people read in data and programs and push the buttons that set them going. Thus in order to have a complete general understanding of computer-based systems, it is important to consider the roles, responsibilities, and limitations of the people involved with them.

Since large projects must be divided and computer personnel usually perform specialized tasks, there are many opportunities for misunderstandings, errors, and irresponsibility, which can turn a well-conceived and socially appropriate system into anything from a minor annoyance to a menace. We will first describe the division of labor and the

way work around computers is usually done to provide a context for a discussion of the ways errors arise.

Personnel

As one might expect in any field, there is a division of responsibility among specialists in computer work and also between highly skilled and less skilled personnel. First of all, we must make a basic distinction among three separate groups:

☐ People who create the systems
☐ People who operate the systems
☐ People who use the systems

Those who design the systems, write the programs, and test and install them are most likely to be specialists. Normally, they will have no more to do with the system once it is operational. Then a new set of people becomes involved: those who fill in the forms, punch the cards, update the data base, ask for reports, change magnetic tapes, and operate the computer. The users of the system are the executives, scientists, policemen, administrators, or military officers who use the information the system produces.

A large organization—a corporation or a government agency, or even a hospital or large school district—is likely to have all or most of its computer-related affairs centralized in a data-processing department. On an organization chart this department might look like figure 8-1.

Of course, there are as many different kinds of organizations as there are uses for computers, and there are also as many ways of breaking down their functions and grouping their personnel. However, we can regard this organization chart as typical so that we can go on to examine the functions of the various people involved in computer use.

Figure 8-1 is the chart of a relatively large department. (Smaller organizations with smaller computers and more limited budgets will have simpler data-processing departments, of course. But the same functions must still be performed, even if a single person has to occupy several positions.)

The Manager. The data-processing department manager has the usual administrative responsibilities of supervising the department's personnel, making up and checking budgets, planning for future needs, and so forth. But the manager's most important function is to keep the department serving the needs of the organization as a whole.

The data-processing department is a service department; that is, it performs functions at the request of and for the assistance of other parts of the organization. The manager serves as the principal link to these other parts, which may be viewed as customers of the data-processing department. On the basis of a general knowledge of the corporation's affairs, the manager will suggest possible applications for computers to them. When the head of the accounting department, for example, feels that some computer assistance might lighten the load on the accounting staff, he or she will mention this idea to the data-processing manager. The manager will say whether the idea is feasible or not, how soon work might begin on such a system, about how much it will cost, and so forth. When they decide to look into the question more carefully, they will assign the task to technical personnel on both their staffs. But the responsibility to see that data processing serves the goals and interests of the total organization basically rests with the data-processing department manager.

Because the manager's responsibility is to the goals of the organization, he or she will be trusted to make wise decisions and not to recommend automating functions and introducing computer use solely for the sake of keeping the staff busy or making the DP department larger.

Systems Development Staff. The left half of the organization chart in figure 8-1 is devoted to the systems development staff. This group could be organized in many different ways; in actuality, it probably has no very permanent structure. There are staffs of analysts, programmers, and coders, who are organized into projects as the need for them arises. As a job of creating a system is completed, the project team responsible for it dissolves

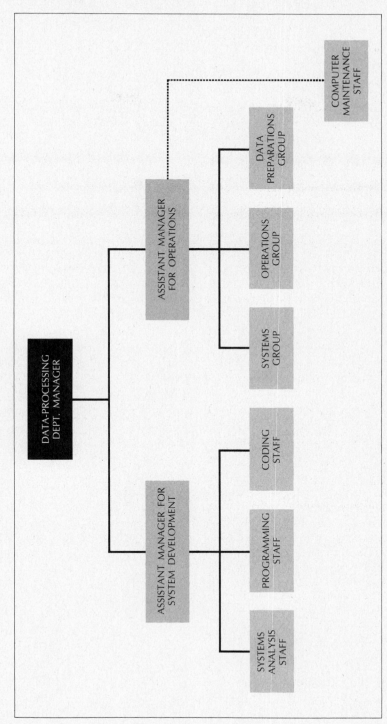

Figure 8-1 A typical data-processing department

and the personnel are assigned to new projects to create other systems. The project will go through many phases, not unlike the processes of engineering design and construction.

Requirements Analysis.   How does such a project work? Let us consider a typical case. It has been decided to investigate the feasibility of a new cost-accounting system. Analysts will begin by discussing how the system will affect the staff of the accounting department. The analysts will point out areas where new techniques might be used and warn of areas where large expenses may be incurred in computer processing. The results of their analysis will be a document called the *requirements analysis,* which will state explicitly what the needs for the system are: what data will be maintained in the data base and for what purpose; what reports will be printed and on what schedule; what information will be input to modify and update the data base and with what frequency. Usually, the analysts will also be re-

quired to make a first estimate of the costs of creating and running the system. This may be difficult, particularly for those systems that have not existed before. Still, the estimate must be made so that the responsible managers can decide whether it is "worth it." The systems analysts can estimate costs, but estimates of benefits will have to involve the staff and management of the department that will use the system.

System Specifications. Once a requirement analysis has been approved by all concerned as a complete and true statement of the user's needs, programmers will be asked to take the next step. On the basis of the analysis, they will design a system to satisfy the requirements stated. They will specify the format in which data is to be entered (Last name first? What about incomplete addresses? What abbreviations can be used?); the format in which the information will be maintained in the actual data base (Will birthdate be month-day or days since January 1? Will year of birth be

in decimal or binary?); and the structure of the data base (Will personnel records be sorted alphabetically by last name? Or by social security number? Or by zipcode?). They will make these decisions on the basis of how the information is going to be used and what is most convenient and economical for machine processing. For example, if there is some chance of name duplication or misspelling, social security number is probably a better clue to identity than name. If the file is going to be used to prepare mailings to people over a wide area, it will be convenient to store them in zipcode order. Considerations of security must be made: How will unauthorized access to the files be prevented? How can company information be kept secret?

The programmers will also design the main structure of the program, breaking it down into segments or modules. They will specify which program language is to be used and document their decisions in a document called the *system specifications.*

The system specifications can then be given to less-experienced programmers, sometimes called *coders,* who will describe in detail how the modules will work (in terms of flowcharts or some other form of coding specifications). Based on this, they will then write the programs in the language specified by the system specifications—perhaps FORTRAN or COBOL.

Testing. The system definition has now proceeded from a general statement of need gradually to more specific statements of what the system will do, how it will do it, and the actual coded programs. It is now necessary to test the programs to see whether they actually perform the functions they were designed for, and thus to test the total system. This is done by a series of steps similar to the steps used to create the system, but in the opposite order. At each step of the way, conformity to documentation at the appropriate level is tested. Figure 8-2 is a representation of this process.

The first step after the program has been written is compilation. As we pointed out in chapter five, the compiler itself makes some tests for errors in syntax and logic. This is the first test of the program. Errors the compiler detects are corrected, the compiler accepts the program, and a binary form of the program that can be run then exists.

The second test is made by the coder against the flowchart or coding specifications. In order to do this, he or she makes up a series of test cases to conduct his code check or *debug* the program.

For example, suppose the module being tested is to compute the age of any specified individual in the file. It will locate the individual's record in the file, extract the date of birth, locate today's date (which the operating system maintains), and compute age in years, months, and days. The coder will supply the module with a few cases that may be expected to exercise its capabilities: first, a few dates will be chosen almost at random. The coder will compute age from these by hand to see whether his module does it correctly. If so, he or she will consider more difficult cases to be sure that nothing unexpected will happen even in unusual circumstances. For example, what happens if there is no record of the person's birthdate—will the program say he or she is nearly two thousand years old? What happens if a person is born on February 29? Will the program work if the person was born today (that is, if he is 0 years, 0 months, and 0 days old)? What happens if, by some accident in data input, such as typing the year of birth as 7950 instead of 1950, the person's age is computed to be negative? When the coder is confident that the module works, the code check is complete.

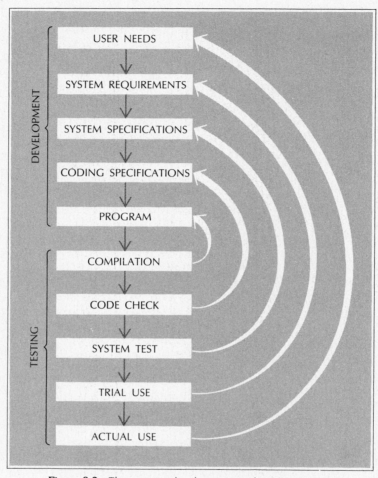

Figure 8-2 The systems development and testing process

The tested modules can now be assembled into the complete system to see whether they will work together. Perhaps the author of the age-computation module expected to be given the name of an individual, but the author of the module he communicates with expects to give the social security number. These communication errors between people must be located and corrected in the systems test. At the conclusion of this stage, the programmers and coders should be quite confident that the assembled program matches exactly what they said it would do in the system specifications.

Up to this point, the system has only been tested with very small data samples and simple problems. When it is time for a more realistic test, actual data is put through the system, which is then required to produce the reports and answer the questions stated in the requirements analysis.

Now the system faces the final test: Does it actually help the user perform a job? Does it supply the needed information on time and at a cost the organization can afford? If not, the analysts have erred in interpreting the user's needs and writing the requirements analysis.

Figure 8-3   A typical computer operator at work

Thus the analysts, programmers, and coders bring the system from the abstract down to the most concrete in a series of stages. They then test it back up to the very abstract and general level in order to be assured that it will work under all foreseeable conditions and is, in fact, the useful tool the users had anticipated.

Operations.   The assistant manager for operations has a different view of the system. He or she views all computer users as customers who are to be supplied with access to the computer when they require it. But real access to the computer—a key to the computer room door, for instance—is not what such customers really want; they want mediated service. For example, the head accountant does not want to go to the computer personally, type problems out, wait for an answer, and go away. Therefore the operations staff includes data-preparation personnel such as keypunch operators and typists who will convert information such as the head accountant's query into machine-readable form.

In addition, the computer, like any other machine, needs operators. Computer operators perform a number of functions. Some of them are simple, such as making sure the printer has an adequate supply of paper, checking to see when the ribbon needs to be changed, getting tapes and disk packs from the library and putting them on the machine as they are required, putting input cards into the hopper, and taking completed work (cards, tapes, printout) from the machine and delivering it. The computer operator may do some accounting, such as keeping a log of how many minutes each job takes, but the computer's operating systems will do most accounting functions automatically. The operator does have more critical functions to perform, however. When machine malfunctions occur, he or she is expected to notice the situation at once and call a maintenance engineer to fix it. Under conditions of high load—

when there is more work to do than there is machine time—the operator will have to make decisions about what work to do and what to leave undone. (In a large organization, this decision will be made by the operations manager, or at an even higher level.)

In large installations, there may be three or four computer operations personnel present at the machine at all times. One or more of them will be responsible for loading and unloading tapes and disks. One person may have responsibility for getting tapes out and putting them away; he or she will be the tape librarian. The chief operator or console operator will be responsible for monitoring the operation of the computer itself and seeing that work flows smoothly from the pile of input jobs waiting to be done to the pile of output waiting to be returned to the users.

Notice that none of these operations people are concerned with the nature, accuracy, or effect of the programs that are run on their machines. They run a computing factory.

The operations staff may also include a systems group composed of experienced programmers with a detailed knowledge of the system software. These people are available if there are any problems with systems programs or if modifications are required. Since the operating system keeps the computer going from job to job, its functioning is understandably critical. However, most computer centers use system software that was produced elsewhere, and therefore systems programming is often not performed in the user organization at all. Instead, problems are usually referred to the organization that provided the programs. Similarly, applications programs are usually also maintained by the people who wrote them.

Systems programming (the task of writing compilers, operating, and time-sharing systems) is an extremely technical specialty. Such programmers must be very knowledgeable about the detailed design of the hardware so that they can produce the best and most economical programs for the purposes specified. In designing the *interface* (the means of communication) between object programs and the operating system, a systems programmer affects the design of each individual program. Often, the privacy protection for a computer-based system is left to the operating system, which is one of the systems programmer's responsibilities. Thus, although the job is highly technical and all but incomprehensible to the layman, it is critical to all who use the machine and depend on these protections.

Error

The computer hardware, the software that supports it, and the personnel needed to adapt it to specific problems and to run it, taken together, constitute an impressive system. It may be viewed as a large and complex tool that an administrator in government, industry, or research can apply to his or her objectives. Whether the use of the tool is beneficial to society or harmful is, as we have argued before, primarily a question of the user's intent—not of the tool itself.

Although this statement is essentially correct, it does oversimplify the situation somewhat. A system composed of computers and communication networks, software systems, programmers, and other personnel is a more complex tool than a hammer or an automobile or even a factory. Because such a system is so complex and because the user may not understand it sufficiently, it may not always be completely under control and totally at the service of his or her objectives. Furthermore, since the process of bringing such a system into operation requires many different specialists and stages of documentation, the final system may not be exactly what was desired. Errors may occur that change the system from what the user intended. In systems that affect people, these errors may have social consequences.

In a system as complex as the hardware-software-personnel system described here, a number of errors may occur. Several classes of error should be distinguished:

☐ Errors in design
☐ Errors in programming
☐ Errors in data
☐ Errors in procedure
☐ Errors in hardware operation

These types of errors illustrate the way a system can malfunction despite the intention of the administrator or executive who is responsible for it.

Errors in Design. As we have seen, the system development process starts when the systems analyst begins asking the user what his or her requirements are. The analyst must produce a detailed and clear description of what the system will do. The process of systems analysis is difficult and presents a number of dangers. The first problem is this: the user may not really know what is needed—at least not in detail. The user may know what should be accomplished but cannot say precisely what information is needed or what kinds of uses the system will be put to two years from now, when it is in operation. The analyst and the user must try to work out such questions as what kinds of information will be needed and what will not, what data will be presented in detail and what will be summarized, and what informa-

tion would be useful but is not really necessary.

As we will see in later chapters, this process of forcing explicit answers to questions like "Who is going to get what information and what are they going to do with it?" can ultimately raise larger and more important questions—like "Who is in charge of what?" This can be both disruptive and instructive to the user organization.

A second problem is this: the user may know very little about computer systems and how they work. Talking about numbers of bits, sorting keys, or disk versus tape storage may be bewildering and confusing, yet the system must be designed within certain limitations, such as those of time and cost. The analyst understands these things and must attempt to explain them and convince the user they are important. Sooner or later, responsibility for the system will pass from the analysts and programmers to the users. The transition may be difficult and subject to many problems if the user has not been involved in the development process.

Third, the user probably has a full-time job and can probably devote only a small amount of time to helping the analyst and participating in the analysis. This, coupled with a lack of understanding of the technical aspects, may result in the user's leaving the analysis for the analyst to do alone.

Fourth, the analyst may have only a shallow understanding of the actual use to which the system will be put. After all, his or her profession is analysis not the user's field. In a year or two, the analyst will be involved in something altogether different. Analysts usually have neither the time nor the inclination to learn in depth about cost accounting in the shoe business or personnel records in welfare or banking. They try to grasp the essentials as quickly as possible and to formalize them in the analysis. They have to depend on others to guide them in areas where the analysis must reflect subtle interpretations of the needs and goals of the user's organization.

This gap between the user and the analyst may cause errors in design. When, months or years later, the system is produced, the user may discover that it is not in fact the best means of accomplishing the goals it was intended for. But what can be done? The time and the money have been spent; it is not possible to start over. The user will probably try to make do with what has been produced, possibly with minor changes. An error that occurs at the design level usually makes the tool imperfect for its purposes. In some cases, it may even be unusable. Most likely, the system will be considered "good enough"—because who wants to admit to having designed the wrong system? It probably will be used despite its failings and inadequacies.

Errors in Programming. Each of the stages of programming and coding involves testing to see if the program does what it is supposed to. But how much testing is enough? No matter how exhaustive the tests, cases may arise years later that were not considered and that will bring hidden flaws to light.

Consider this hypothetical case. In a system to maintain confidential credit references on individuals, the programmer assumes that the initial value of all the items in the file—before any data have been input—is zero. When a new name is put in the file, it has no record other than the name itself. The system works well until, as time passes, some names are deleted and the slots they occupied are reassigned to new names. Because of the way the program was written, the new names assume the credit records of the names that preceded them. Mr. X (a new name) finds his

applications of credit rejected; he may never learn why.

A not unusual area of difficulty has to do with the bill-paying habits of some customers. A programmer may assume that people either pay their bills or they do not. Although this is true of the overwhelming majority of customers, it is by no means true of all. Some customers will round off their bill to the nearest dollar, paying a few cents more or less than required. Clearly the machine has to have instructions on what to do about payments that are in error.

Errors in mathematics may be small enough to slip past even fairly close checking. Vast studies have been made of the problem of maintaining accuracy in computer calculations. A simple case will do as an example. When computing bills to be submitted or payments to be made, it is normal to round the result to the nearest cent. The alternative is called *truncation,* where all digits beyond the cent are ignored. For example:

	ACTUAL	ROUNDED	TRUNCATED
	$5.71324	$5.71	$5.71
	7.84501	7.85	7.84
	1.59999	1.60	1.59
Sum:	15.15824	15.16	15.14

While in this example the sum of the truncated numbers is only two cents lower than the sum of the rounded numbers, it can become a larger error when there are more numbers to be added. On the average, almost a half cent is lost in every truncation. The difference between the code for rounding and truncation in most programming languages is a matter of only one or two letters; it is an easy matter for the programmer to truncate when he or she should round.

Does this matter? Perhaps not to the individual who receives the bill or the check. But the system may send out millions of bills each month (public utilities do), half of which are in error by one cent, thus depriving the organization of thousands of dollars. The error may also work the other way, of course, depriving millions of people of pennies that accrue to the organization. There is one recorded case of embezzlement by a programmer who credited an accumulated truncation error for thousands of dollars to his own account, much to the surprise of the bank.

When systems are put into actual use, they are observed closely to see whether errors will crop up. But in the case of some systems, such checking is impossible. Consider military or space systems, for example. Although there may be much testing in simulated operational conditions, programs to guide a flight to the moon or a ground-to-air missile will never encounter real use until it is necessary for the users to place complete faith in them. When they are used, it will be too late to correct errors that affect their performance. Personnel involved in programming for systems like this are acutely aware of the problem, for they understand better than any of us the things that might go wrong and the potential cost of such errors. For example, during the manned space-flight of Apollo 13, the on-board computer erroneously reported an overload condition although none existed. Luckily, the astronauts recognized it as an error and overrode the alarm.

When a software company produces a program for a user, it is understood that it will be reasonably free of errors. A number of software companies have recently been sued by their customers because of errors and inconsistencies in programs they have delivered.

Errors in Data. People who prepare data for input to computers make mistakes, too. And, despite every precaution, some of these mistakes remain undetected and become part of the data base. Clerks who type or keypunch data make the kinds of errors that all typists do: they transpose characters, they omit one character or one word or one line, they mistake look-alike characters (G and 6, 1 and I, and so forth), or they hit the wrong key. Proofreading detects many of these errors. Retyping by another person and machine comparison detect others. Still, a few errors remain. It is easy to miss an error in proofreading, especially when proofreading something you have typed. Unaccountably, two typists may make the identical error when typing the same material.

A well-considered system will always examine its input for credibility before the data is used. If part of the input, for instance, is date of birth, the program should check that the month is a number no greater than 12 and that the date is less than 32. It may also check the year against some reasonable limits—today and one hundred years ago today, perhaps. Social security numbers will be checked to be sure that they consist of nine digits with no blanks and no letters. This kind of checking does not, of course, guarantee that the data is correct, but only that it is credible and within the bounds of reason.

If an error is made by a typist, missed by a proofreader, made again by a second typist, and passes the credibility check, it is in the system. Such an error is unlikely and is bound to be rare; it is not impossible, however, and its frequency can be computed on the basis of tables of probability.

Commercial agencies that punch cards normally guarantee only that there will be fewer than five percent errors in unverified cards and fewer than

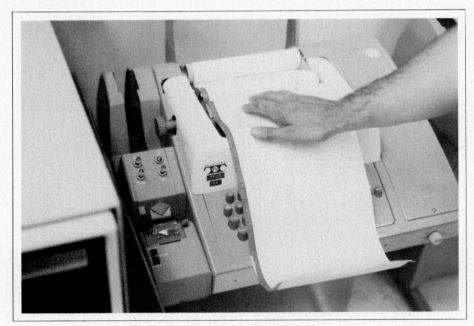

Figure 8-4 A Braille terminal

one percent in verified (double-checked) cards. Thus even with two separate keypunch operators typing identical material, we must assume that one card in every one hundred is in error.

Any large data base has such errors among its data. In a credit-checking system, for example, which may have some twenty million records, there is simply no way to remove such errors economically or even to hunt for them manually. If there are 1000 characters per record, this could mean 2,500,000 errors in the file. However, one can do more than merely hope that these errors are not too important. Double verification before input can reduce this error percentage by a factor of at least five.

Errors in Procedure. Procedures set up for system operation are designed to insure that errors cannot be introduced by the personnel who operate the system. But like every other step of the way, these too are seldom foolproof.

In some cases in which input is in the form of cards, the order in which the cards appear is highly significant. If they are accidentally shuffled or if one drops out and is replaced in a different position, its meaning may be changed. For example, suppose a deck of cards consists of personnel records. The first card of each group is the name/address card and the following cards represent facts about that individual. One of the fact cards accidentally placed behind the wrong name would change the computer's records of two individuals.

Tape is the ultimate storage medium of most large systems. Although frequently needed information will usually be stored on random-access files, a backup file will be maintained on tape. When the machine is being repaired or is undergoing periodic maintenance checking, the content of random-access files may be destroyed and may have to be refreshed from tape.

Thus the tape library is the backbone of the information collection. Because tapes all look

Figure 8-5 A fire-damaged tape library

alike, they are also subject to being misfiled, interchanged, and so forth. If all the tapes are kept in one place, the library is of course very vulnerable to such catastrophes as fire. For this reason, many installations keep copies of their most important tapes at locations far from the computer center itself.

Errors in Hardware Operation. All the potential errors cited so far are errors made by people. But don't machines ever make mistakes and introduce errors? Surprisingly seldom. Although electronic components are indeed subject to transient (occasional) and catastrophic (final) failure, computers and related equipment are designed with these characteristics in mind and every effort is made to detect errors immediately when they occur and, if possible, to correct them. We are concerned here not with catastrophic errors, like power failures that disable the hardware altogether, but with such errors as the transient failure of a single transistor that might be expected to introduce an error into the data.

Errors may occur in the transfer of information from one part of the computer to another: from the memory to the central processing unit or back, from an input device to the memory, or from the memory to an output device. The simplest and most economical method of detecting such errors is by the use of *parity checking,* which is now almost universally used for internal checking. In this method, an extra bit is added to every word (or even every byte, in some cases). If, for example, a computer has sixteen bits per word available for storage of information, the word in the memory will actually consist of seventeen bits. This extra bit is used to maintain an odd parity in the word— that is, if the number of ones in the sixteen-bit word is odd, the extra bit is set to zero; if the number of ones in the word is even, the extra bit will be a one. Thus, as shown in figure 8-6, the total number of ones in the seventeen-bit word is always odd. After every transfer of a word, its parity is checked. If the parity is even, an error has occurred: either a one has turned into a zero or a zero has turned into a one. The transfer is attempted again, and if after several tries, the error remains, it is called a *solid error* and the operation must be halted for repairs to the computer.

If two errors occur in the same word, of course, the parity will be correct and the error will go undetected. This is not a serious possibility in modern computers. Suppose that the chance of a single error is one in 1,000,000,000 (a reasonable figure for internal transfers). The chance of two simultaneous errors is one in 1,000,000,000,000,000,000. In a machine with one microsecond memory access, the expected time between single errors is 1000 seconds or about fifteen minutes; the probable frequency of double errors is one per thirty thousand years.*

The concept of parity can be used as a check on the correctness of most operations that take place in the CPU, the memory, and in storage units (such as tapes and disks) where information is maintained in binary form. However, parity cannot extend to input/output devices that do not allow for extra bits. For instance, when information is to be printed, the parity bit must be discarded at some point. What if an error occurs after this point? Usually a method called *echo checking* is

---

*William Gear, *Computer Organization and Planning* (New York: McGraw-Hill Book Company, 1969), p. 64.

WORD	PARITY BIT
1 0 0 1 1 1 0 1 0 0 0 1 1 1 0 0	(1)
0 1 0 1 0 1 0 0 0 1 1 1 1 0 0 0	(0)
1 0 0 0 0 1 1 1 1 0 1 0 0 1 0 0	(0)
1 0 0 0 0 0 1 1 1 0 0 1 0 0 1 0	(1)

Figure 8-6   Parity

employed. After a character has been printed, the printer sends information about what it was back to the computer. The computer's error-checking circuitry compares this with the character that should have been printed. If they are not the same, an error has probably occurred. (The error-checking circuitry could also have made an error.) Since the error (if there was one) is now printed on paper, it is no longer under control of the computer. Depending on the design of the system, it will either print the same line over again, hopefully error-free this time, or stop and signal the operator that something has gone wrong.

In the case of input devices the method is much the same. Each card is read twice and the information received by the computer must be identical. If not, an error has occurred.

The techniques of error detection in communications are much the same as those described for internal operations within the computer itself. If the transmission is critical and redundancy is low, parity and echo checking may be used. In some cases, where the line is very noisy and multiple errors are possible, more elaborate codes, such as a two-out-of-five code, are employed to introduce redundancy. In this code two bits of every five must be ones, and the other three are zeros. This detects a high proportion of errors transmitted. Figure 8-7 gives an example of a two-out-of-five code.

	0 1 2 4 7
1=	1 1 0 0 0
2=	1 0 1 0 0
3=	0 1 1 0 0
4=	1 0 0 1 0
5=	0 1 0 1 0
6=	0 0 1 1 0
7=	1 0 0 0 1
8=	0 1 0 0 1
9=	0 0 1 0 1
0=	0 0 0 1 1

Figure 8-7 A two-out-of five code

Table 8.1 Communications Error Rates

CHANNEL TYPE	RATE (bits/sec)	BIT ERROR RATE
50-band Telex	50	1 in 50,000
100- or 200-band subvoice grade lines	150-200	1 in 100,000
Public voice lines	2400	1 in 100,000
Public voice lines	1200	1 in 200,000
Public voice lines	600	1 in 500,000

Thus if 11000 were transmitted as 11110, a two-out-of-five check would detect it while a parity check would not.

Some types of communication may be very noisy and therefore seldom used for computer work. Radio, for instance, may have a bit error rate of 1 in 1000 or worse. For media more typical of computer networks, Table 8.1 gives expected error rates.*

Summary

In this section we have considered ways in which errors can inadvertently enter a computer system and result in it doing something other than what it was intended to do. We saw that error detection and correction circuitry, which is ten to fifteen percent of a computer's circuitry, makes it extremely unlikely that the hardware will produce

undetected errors. And, in fact, as the importance of error detection goes up, more hardware can be introduced in order to reduce the probability of undetected errors still further.

We have not discussed the question of sabotage or the deliberate introduction of error. Nor has the question of failure been discussed. In some systems, errors are less important than failure; they would better be operated with some incorrect data than not operated at all. Consider the case of an air traffic control system. If errors occur, there may be some inaccuracy in the information the system has about the location of aircraft and consequently in the instructions that are given for aircraft maneuvers. However, if the system fails altogether, the air traffic controllers may (depending on the system's design) know nothing about aircraft location and would not be able to offer guidance to any of the pilots. In such a case, failure for more than a few seconds simply cannot be tolerated.

In systems like this, further circuitry—even the complete duplication of all the hardware—will be necessary to insure that the system will not

*See James Martin, *Teleprocessing Network Organization* (Englewood Cliffs, N.J.: Prentice-Hall, Inc., 1970).

suddenly stop. If errors begin to occur and it appears that the system is malfunctioning badly, procedures may be instituted to close it down. In the air traffic control system, for instance, all aircraft that cannot be landed immediately can be sent to other airports.

By and large, however, such problems apply only to control systems. Most information systems can be allowed to fail when hardware, software, or procedural errors occur. This will cause inconvenience and annoyance but not catastrophe. Of considerably more importance and interest are the kinds of errors we discussed earlier in the chapter, which introduce false or misleading information that passes for truth.

Exercises

1. Does your school have a data-processing department? How is it organized? What are the functions of its personnel? Do they correspond to those in the text? What accounts for the differences?

2. Many cooperative organizations in the computer field (in particular, the Data Processing Management Association and the Business Equipment Manufacturers Association) have published material on what computer personnel do, what backgrounds they should have, and how much they earn. Locate some of this material and fill in some detail about the hypothetical data-processing department in the text.

3. As an example of specifying a process in complete detail, consider the problem of telling a person who has never used a pay telephone how to do it. You must "program" the person's actions so that the call can be completed no matter what the response is (such as busy signal, recorded announcement, losing his coin, and so forth). Write the specifications for this process.

4. Test this program by having someone else try to follow your instructions.

5. Murphy's Law states that anything that can go wrong will. You have now had an introduction to what can go wrong. Find an example of a system that went wrong and see if you can find the reason. What could have been done to prevent it?

6. Schemes like parity and two-out-of-five coding are called *error detecting*. What can you find out in the library about error-*correcting* codes?

7. Relate the job of the computer operator as described in this chapter to the work performed by the operating system, as described in chapter five.

8. Suppose you were a criminal who wanted to penetrate a very valuable time-sharing system. Whom would you bribe?

For Further Information

The Psychology of Computer Programming (1) is the first book to make a serious effort to look into the question of what programming is really like, how people do it, and why. People who have read it—whether they are programmers or not—have responded very enthusiastically and the book is highly recommended. A few other books take a more technical look at the process by which systems come into being; three are included in the list below (2–4). The paper by Christopher Strachey (5) shows how a person might go about solving a programming problem; although difficult to follow in places, it is worth the effort.

Two books are included (6 and 7) that deal with the matter of organizing and managing the personnel involved in a complex computer-based system.

Error detection among human beings seems to be a subject learned by experience, not from books. Although the subject is given brief mention in many programming texts (see the references in chapter two), there is little that is worth considering. For information about machine errors, we have drawn on two books (8 and 9) in this chapter. You may want to look at them, too.

References

1. Gerald M. Weinberg, *The Psychology of Computer Programming* (New York: D. Van Nostrand Company, 1971).

2. M. J. Alexander, *Information Systems Analysis* (Chicago: Science Research Associates, Inc., 1974).

3. Perry E. Rosove, *Developing Computer-Based Information Systems* (New York: John Wiley & Sons, 1967).

4. Van Court Hare, Jr., *Systems Analysis* (New York: Harcourt Brace Jovanovich, 1968).

5. Christopher Strachey, "Systems Analysis and Programming," *Computers & Computation* (San Francisco: W. H. Freeman, 1971).

6. Frederic G. Withington, *The Organization of the Data Processing Function* (New York: John Wiley & Sons, 1972).

7. R. Yearsley and R. Graham, eds., *Handbook of Computer Management* (New York: Halstead Press, 1973).

8. William Gear, *Computer Organization and Programming* (New York: McGraw-Hill Book Company, 1974).

9. James Martin, *Teleprocessing Network Organization* (Englewood Cliffs, N.J.: Prentice-Hall, Inc., 1970).

If every instrument could do its own
work, if the shuttle should weave
of itself and the plectrum play the
harp unaided, then managers would
not need workers and masters
would not need slaves.

ARISTOTLE
The Politics, 350 B.C.

PART THREE

What Is Their Influence on Society?

Computers in Use

9

In Part Two we presented the outline of a technology. We covered the computers themselves, the programs and systems and people around them. We treated the technology more or less as a world of its own, without considering its relations with other activities of men and women. In Part Three, the focus of our attention will shift and we will concentrate on what this technology is used for, how it is applied to useful work, and its moral and legal implications on some critical issues. This book obviously cannot include a complete survey of computer applications. We will have to omit many of the most important and most striking uses. For example, we will not cover the way in which scientific research has been revolutionized by computer techniques, nor the modern techniques of engineering in which buildings and bridges and roads (and computers) are designed

in detail by computer programs. The use of computers in libraries is another important topic we cannot touch on here. And the computer in printing and publishing is another important and growing application area we have no time to discuss. Yet the *New York Times* has transferred its complete index to a computer-based file, linked that file to an information management system, and offered access to this system on a subscription basis: a total automated newspaper "morgue."

In this chapter we will discuss the effects of computers on people and organizations. In succeeding chapters we will cover, in some detail, computer applications in business, health care, education, public administration, and the administration of justice.

Computer technology does not in fact exist in a world of its own. It survives and grows and engages

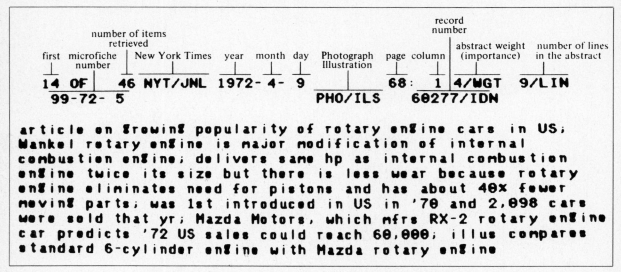

Figure 9-1 Output from the *New York Times* computerized index

our interests because it can be used to help us achieve our objectives. It has made activities that were once expensive more economical. It has allowed some things to be done that had previously been impossible. Along with other modern technologies, it has permitted people to seek objectives that had been only dreamed of—like going to the moon. It has made our lives different, sometimes in striking ways. Like all the gifts of the gods, it has two faces, improving some aspects of living and degrading others.

Before going on to consider the social implications of computing in broad philosophical and legal terms, it will be helpful to take another look at computers themselves, but this time in the environments in which they work. We will examine what computers are in fact used for. In presenting a survey of computer applications, many of the concepts presented in earlier chapters will reappear: simulations and models, control systems, information management, time sharing, minicomputers, programming and analysis, terminals and communications. You will be able to recognize similar features in many application areas.

The computer, once invented, did not simply appear in the offices and factories of America. Its introduction was a long and difficult process. We will be focusing on how the computer is used today, but some of the lessons learned in getting to this point will help you understand why and how it is used.

First, the invention of the computer produced a fiercely competitive industry. This competition has led to much improvement in the hardware techniques, software aids, and cost reductions. But it has also led to many problems. Since the industry grew rapidly and the technology continually changed, there were barely enough competent trained professionals to go around. Today, in contrast, there are specialists in one programming language, one operating system, or one application area.

However, before our current abundance of computer professionals and experience in applications developed, there were many (and there still are some) disappointed users whose budgets and schedules were badly disrupted by premature and overambitious projects. In part, these situations occurred because of exaggerated claims made by salesmen, but many were caused by some of the things we discussed earlier. The computer and its use are a complex matter. The division of labor required to create a functioning system often leads to misunderstandings about what is needed. There are many opportunities for mechanical mistakes also. It was very difficult to rapidly analyze and design data-processing systems to replace processes that had evolved over twenty years. They obviously didn't always work. The net effect of this was that users learned to be cautious.

However, there were some subtle things that had to be learned about the organizations that used computers. It was discovered that all parts of an organization are related, knit together by the information the organization uses. If one part of the information handling system is automated, it soon affects other areas, some of which turn out to be more important than the original area. Thus analysts learned early that they had to consider the whole organization at once. But it took many years before users were prepared to let systems analysts study their organizations as a whole. In any organization there is a natural progression and refinement of raw data into finished information from the bottom of the organization to the top. Any organization that is so big that it must manage by reports rather than observation must use the natural data flow. Organizational planning and research must be based on this flow, not on some artificial source. Thus this flow from raw data to finished information that serves operations, planning, and management becomes an integrating principle in an organization's use of computers.

You will see here and in other accounts of computer applications a historical sequence of events: routine clerical operations are automated and huge standard reports are produced; more uses

for the system are discovered; ultimately the organization's total information requirements are analyzed and an online system using management by exception rather than standard reporting is created. (*Management by exception* refers to the practice of using the data-processing system to signal abnormal events that need attention rather than standard reports.) This progression can take five or even ten years as trained personnel, management experience, and confidence in the system accumulate.

So the computer didn't go easily from the drawing board into actual use. Its users went from early naïve optimism and excessive expectations to disappointment, skepticism, and cynicism—and finally cautious practicality. The sophisticated user of computers now lays out a schedule of very detailed project goals and carefully evaluates these as accomplished. (You, the student, should ask of every advertised computer application "Is it real? How long has it been in use? Or is it research that may some day succeed?")

It is important to make what may be an obvious point here. By and large, the use of computers has proven to be profitable. If it had not, computers would have been abandoned. Complaints about the costs and problems in using them sometimes hide this fact.

So far, the computer hasn't really revolutionized the world. As you read the rest of this chapter and the accounts of applications that follow, you will find, for example, that the computer hasn't changed the functions that organizations perform as much as they have changed *how* they perform these functions. This isn't to say they won't. It is only to caution you, the reader, that there is a big jump, say, from computer assisted typesetting to replacing all publishing functions by home TV "newspapers." Similarly, there is a big step from banks and credit companies using computers to a "cashless society." These kinds of revolutionary changes may come, but they haven't yet. The revolution that has taken place is far more subtle.

We will start our discussion of computer impact at the personal level.

A Day in the Life

How do computers affect our lives? Computers are, as we have seen, very expensive. They are complex. Though there are many of them, they are usually kept in windowless, air-conditioned laboratories; most people have never even looked at one. We thus might be tempted to assume that such an exotic machine could not affect the lives of any but a few specialists.

But if we take a look at the facts, we will see that the computer intrudes on our lives to a surprising degree. Consider today's mail. It is delivered by a very human postal worker, after having been sorted and handled by any number of other real people. (The U.S. postal system has not made remarkable advances based on information technology.) But look at the material in the mailbox more closely: What is it? Where does it come from? First, we may find a magazine or two. The address label was prepared by a computer from a data base that contains information about the subscriber and the subscription. The magazine may have been edited for people in this region specifically: "demographic editing" uses computer analyses of local characteristics to determine which articles and which advertisements the people in Florida should see that will be of no interest to those in Oregon. The several pieces of junk mail that are surely in the mailbox are also addressed by computer. Even junk mail is expensive, and

companies do not mail out their literature at random; they select people on the basis of what can be learned about them from computer-based information systems.

But in the first-class mail, most of the envelopes are also addressed by a computer. There will be some bills, a solicitation for a donation (although the letter begins Dear Mr. Smith, few people are fooled—it was not typed by a human secretary), and perhaps a bank statement. In all of these cases, the material was printed out by a computer and the pages were separated and folded by another machine, stuffed into a envelope, stamped, and mailed, without any involvement of a human being. A postal clerk is probably the first person to touch the individual piece of mail.

At least your replies to these letters, you may think, will be human and personal. But your checks, inquiries, change-of-address notices, and replies to ads, will all ultimately be translated into machine-readable form. One or more computer-based systems will be a buffer between you and any large organization with which you are likely to deal.

This situation is not restricted to your mail, of course. Computers affect your relationships with organizations even when you deal with them in person, and computers' involvement is invisible. For example, if you go to the bank to cash a check, the teller will ask a computer about the balance in your account. When you register to take a class, a computer is usually involved in making sure that there is an opening, that you have the prerequisites for the course, and that the teacher is promptly informed who you are. When you apply for (or use) a credit card, register to vote, are stopped by the police, go to the hospital, or apply for a job, it is almost certain that computers will be asked for information about you and will be informed of any action taken that may be of interest in the future.

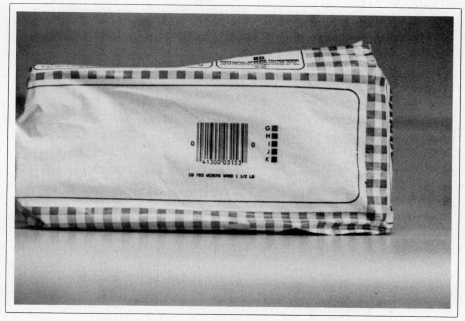

Figure 9-2 A computer-recognizable price code

We have come, as a society, to depend so much on computers that it is hard to imagine how our lives could continue at their current level of complexity without them. However, there is a negative side to be considered here. The total effect of a new system on people is difficult to predict. It can save them time, money, and inconvenience, or it can produce delay, frustration, fatalism, and damage to health, reputation, and finances. We will consider all of these, but immediately there are two kinds of situations that concern us: those that present us with no choice and those that can be changed only by a major change in the data-processing industry itself.

No-Choice Areas. People have a choice when there are alternative organizations providing comparable services. If, say, the Diner's Club's data-processing system makes an error and alienates a customer, there is always Carte Blanche

or American Express. However, if a private citizen has an argument with the local telephone or electric company, he or she does not have the same choice. A public utilities commission is not much help; regulatory agencies do not protect the private individual from abuses by public utility monopolies. Similarly, banks, although not monopolies, have quite an edge in their arguments with the public: they hold the money, they have the computer to process the records, and they referee the argument.

Potentially, the most threatening computer-based industry is the credit- and check-verification business. They are as necessary to the economic health of our country as credit itself, but they also encourage undisclosed and uncontrolled sharing of information among banks, department stores, and many other organizations. The credit companies are not responsible for the accuracy of their information: they hold their sources of credit

Figure 9-3 A computer-produced library catalog

information (those same banks or department stores) responsible for the accuracy of the data. If, for example, after a dispute between a department store and an individual over a bill or the quality of some merchandise, the department store fails to acknowledge to the credit company that the dispute has been settled, a person's credit can be ruined, damaged by default, or simply remain in doubt. The person has no choice. He or she may find out about it by having credit denied, and then must trace down the source of the problem and try to get the department store to acknowl-edge the settlement to the credit company. The burden of proof is on the person, not on the credit-checking company. He or she may not have the resources to reverse the situation and thus the person's credit is ruined.

Changes in the Computer Industry. The second class of problems is those whose correction would require economically important changes in the computer industry itself. Suppose that the com-puterized credit-checking industry became monopolistic and its security practices became

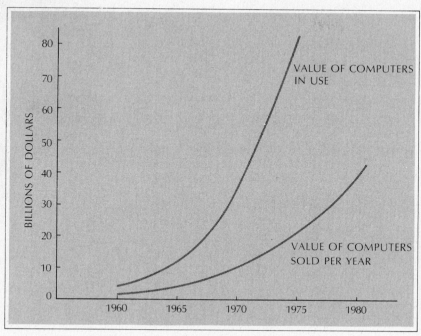

BILLIONS OF DOLLARS

VALUE OF COMPUTERS
IN USE

VALUE OF COMPUTERS
SOLD PER YEAR

Figure 9-4 Growth of value of computers

totally inadequate to deal with computerized wiretapping. Suppose a public furor over the misuse of the stolen information grew to such heights that it was decided to use super-secure communications equipment at all computer terminals that had access to the credit data base. This change could increase the cost of credit in the same way (if not to the same extent) that changing the smog-producing characteristics of the internal combustion engine has increased the cost of operating a car.

Although the computer industry and, say, the credit industry are not as large as the automobile industry, they are very big. No issue of social significance has threatened the hardware and software industries at this writing to the point that they have combined to fight together. If they do, they will be formidable. An indication of *how* formidable is given in figure 9-4.

In 1970, computer sales exceeded $10 billion; in 1980, the total will be approximately double that, and the value of all the computers in operation in the United States will be about $80 billion. The size of the industry argues for effective self-protection if not self-policing. The intense competition in the industry provides some controls. In 1973, several companies sued IBM, the largest computer manufacturer, for engaging in unfair pricing and leasing practices and for withholding technical information. One of these companies, Telex, was awarded $259.5 million in damages by the U.S. District Court. (This decision was later reversed.) Another suit, by Control Data Corporation against IBM, was settled out of court for $60 million. As one condition of this settlement, Control Data agreed to destroy a computerized index to a massive file of IBM documents it had produced in preparing its case. Because this index might have been of great importance in a number of cases pending (including a government antitrust suit against IBM), the action was criticized and condemned by representatives of the Department of Justice and the computer industry. By then, however, the information had already been destroyed.

In actions like this, the computer industry looks like a battleground of warring giants. While industry representatives have cooperated fully in such matters as congressional debates on the right of privacy, you should be aware that the social impact of computers may not be the major concern of an industry almost as monopolistic and big as the telephone company.

The Impact on Organizations

Installing a computer in an organization for the first time is in a way similar to the ancient ritual of proving innocence by passing one's hand through fire. The arrival of the computer has a way of causing problems in an organization to rise to the surface. This happens because the design of the computer system forces the company to state exactly the purposes for which information is collected and used. This in turn requires that the responsibilities and authorities of personnel also be defined in detail.

It also makes different kinds of organization possible, since a little bit of everyone's function disappears into the computer and whole new functions become possible. Further, high-speed digital communications between parts of the organization allows for physical growth, geographical dispersion, personnel mobility, and internal complexity. Let us examine these changes briefly.

Growth. Before the arrival of computers, an organization with more than a few thousand employees was large, cumbersome, and likely to be inefficient. Modern management methods involving the computer have changed this situation; now, large organizations are often more efficient than smaller ones. As a result, organizations have grown and combined with one another to create the large corporations, businesses, and government enterprises we find today.

Growth in size, geography, mobility, and complexity is the natural course of an organization's life. It is certainly more difficult to maintain quality, dedication, and clarity of purpose as an organization grows. The loss of such characteristics ultimately stops growth. In communications and transportation the increased availability of facilities has led to greater use and demand for more facilities. The same has happened with computers. In part, the natural tendency for growth has led to an increased use of computers, and in part the increased use of computers has led to growth.

Distribution. As an organization grows, it establishes branch offices; digital communications between central and remote processors allows both decentralized control and centralized management. This is possible because remote locations can supply a central operating data base for top management to review. In the transportation and entertainment business, reservation status can be maintained centrally and accessed accurately from many parts of the world. This has resulted in fewer vacancies and more efficient operations.

Mobility. Because of cars and jet aircraft, people are more mobile. Computers allow them some of this freedom to move about and carry data with them, such as credit cards, social security numbers

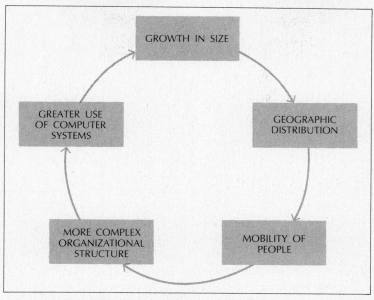

Figure 9-5 The growth pattern of organizations

and unemployment file numbers. Similarly, criminals are much more mobile, but computers are being used to limit their freedom. Thus computers allow some organizations (like the Social Security Administration) to cope with mobility, and mobility plus computers have created a market for other organizations, such as credit card companies.

Complexity. Everything is more complex now than in the past. We have many more choices about many more things. Payrolls have far more deductions for taxes and social services, techniques of organization management are more complex, and relationships among people, government, and industry are more complicated. Computers help cope with all of this complexity.

Other Effects. When the computer becomes a basic part of an organization, other possible side effects occur that are not necessarily the consequences of automation—such as depersonalization,

rigidity, errors, and misuse. We will discuss each of these in turn.

Depersonalization. By *depersonalization* we mean that coldness which convinces a person that the organization he or she is dealing with doesn't care. It can come about in a variety of ways. The organization's employees may be busy or disgruntled. The bigness that computers encourage can also make personal treatment more difficult. Depersonalization often occurs in any organization that tries to make communications between its computers and its customers more efficient. The convenience of the computer is often given more consideration than that of the customer. However, the computer need not contribute to the depersonalization of the relation between the individual and the organization. A computer can save employees time for more personal treatment of the customer and can even handle more exceptional cases than a manual clerical operation can. You will see this when we examine the area of health care. Nurses now have more time for patients since they don't have as many forms to fill out.

Rigidity. Organizations tend to get rigid as they age. A computer can contribute to this rigidity when an organization has a great deal invested in files and software. Change is expensive. If the conditions required for computer use reduce the opportunities for human judgment, the system will indeed be rigid. However, a well-designed system will allow for growth in volume and change in structure. Whether it will make an organization rigid is a matter of how well it is used rather than any basic property of information systems.

Errors and Misuse. There are many errors and abuses that can occur in the use of data-processing systems. Their interaction with the public can be confusing, forbidding, error-ridden, or fraudulent. Control over file contents can be loose or non-existent, permitting anyone to destroy or modify anything maliciously or inadvertently. Controlling the computer programs and auditing them to be sure they are working properly may also be lax. When a computer-based system is at the heart of a company's financial processes and only a few specialists know the details of that system, the company is ripe for fraud and embezzlement. Computer systems can be used to print reports that look impressive but are too detailed or too complex to be examined closely. For example, many people feel that, because their bills and bank statements are produced by a computer, they must be right.

Most companies are well aware of the problems of protection, security, and error. However, in many cases the price of solving these problems may just be too high. Remodeling a data-base system to limit access to the information and to make

periodic checks of which records have been modified may increase the costs of operation to the point where it is no longer economical to operate it at all. Thus management must choose between a poor system and no system at all. A careful audit of financial programs to be sure the employees are not stealing from the company or its clients may not appear to be worth the cost. If errors exist, their seriousness and the organization's purpose must be considered together. In fact, some errors may be allowed to persist because they are so infrequent or small that they are not worth correcting.

The design flaws in systems that make them inconvenient, unpleasant, and awkward are also based primarily on economics. More thought, more careful system design, and a more expensive product would probably have taken care of these flaws. But in order to produce a cheap system, some corners have to be cut. Interaction with the public is often considered such a corner.

The penalty for errors that annoy, harrass, or punish people should be established at a high enough level to force computer users to spend the money to correct them. Controls to guard against the use of computer-based systems for spying, sabotage, and embezzlement are also coming into being and will be discussed at greater length in later chapters.

Maintaining Distinctions in Society

Some writers believe that the strength of such distinctions as between labor and management, government and private industry, public welfare and private philanthropy, and public law enforcement and private protection systems is vanishing and that the United States is becoming one giant interlocked and self-perpetuating bureaucracy. If this bureaucracy—whether for convenience or efficiency or whatever—chooses to share information gathered about people, then the threat of the *universal dossier* becomes real.

Some information sharing is legitimate. For example, state taxing agencies share information with the Internal Revenue Service. However, many educational, health, criminal, marital, financial, and recreational records develop around one person from birth to death. In the hands of the greedy, the paternal, or the authoritarian, they could be dangerous. These records could be economically integrated: if not now, almost certainly by the year 2000.

The single most powerful protection we have is the insistence that the information that organizations keep about people be strictly relevant to their purpose—and that in order to decide what is *relevant,* we must reinforce the distinctions among the institutions in our society. For example, juvenile authorities should be maintained independently from adult authorities. The safety of Social Security, Internal Revenue, and Census Bureau information could in one way be strengthened by long-term appointment of the heads of these organizations. The credit-checking industry should be kept at arm's length from the banking industry. Law enforcement officers should need a court order before delving into a private computer file.

Impact on Government. As you will see in the chapters on the administration of justice and public administration, the computer affects government both directly and indirectly. Directly, it tends to make government operations larger and information gathering more dispersed and more complex just as it does in business operations. Indirectly, its added effects on business and on individuals ultimately wind up at the government level, since government must react to changes in society.

There are inherent dangers in law enforcement systems. For example, juvenile records may become mixed with adult criminal records. However, juvenile authorities are well aware of the files being developed about their juveniles, and protection is being given so that records will not get into the hands of adult authorities. Another common concern related to police files is the problem of mistaken identification. Regardless of how much information there is in a computer about a person, the only proof of identity accepted as certain is the fingerprint.

Still, one may ask, is it good that these files exist and are accessible to law enforcement officers of all kinds? From the point of view of law enforcement, yes. Thus the question is really "Is improved law enforcement worth the risks?"

The risks, first of all, are mostly conjectural. There have been few recorded misuses of such systems yet. The conjectured abuses fall into such categories as unauthorized access, intimidation, difficulty in erasing trivial mistakes of the past, and violation of individual privacy. You will read more of these matters in the chapter on the administration of justice, and later we will discuss the various protections available and in use.

Dependence on Computers. A less dramatic but perhaps more serious consideration is the extent to which government will become dependent on computers. There is a tendency to use automated systems in government, with the consequent growth in areas such systems encourage: bigness, dispersion, and complexity. In fact, the very attempt to improve the government operation may, some conjecture, cause a change in the function and meaning of government.

The use of modern management methods in government has proven to be extremely valuable. It has weeded out many inefficient and unnecessary operations and made more important and useful projects possible. However, a blind drive to make government more efficient may not be consistent with its objectives. Our government's operation is not intended to be a well-run business. The intent in the Constitution was to create a system in which various forces could act on one another and serve to control and balance one another. There is a limit to the amount of streamlining of the vehicles of government that can be performed without changing this balance and compromising the basic goals. As you read the section on public administration you will find areas in which computers are widely used, but few developments that indicate basic changes.

Summary

The effects of computers are as diverse as their applications. The closer a particular application comes to dealing with people and questions of values, policies, and national priorities, the more possibilities it has for both great good and great evil.

Accounting for and managing resources holds little such potential. Well done, it is efficient; badly done, it is wasteful. Rigidity, depersonalization, and misuses in business—at least in a free-enterprise economy—mean, at worst, individual business failures. Other businesses will arise. The same symptoms in government are far more serious because government failure takes far longer to weed out and reorganize.

What we have attempted to do in this short chapter is to expose you in a general way to the array of social concerns that arise from computer applications. We invite you to read the next five applications chapters with these in mind. After those chapters, we will return to a discussion of the concerns for privacy, unemployment, loss of individuality, and the effect on power.

Exercises

1. Our protection from politicians comes from such things as our secret ballot, two-party system, free press, and balance of powers within government. Can you think of a way that a computer could be used to keep a corrupt politician in office?

2. As the computer contributes to growth it forces us to test our values. Growth brings both vitality and disruption. Stability brings stagnation and relief from the pressures of change. Decline in size can be seen either as decay or as preparation for an advance in a new direc-

tion. These generalities can have different meanings depending on whether you are considering the growth of nations, governments, businesses, or individuals. Pick any one of these four and offer your value judgments about growth and the computer.

3. Select a half-dozen people you know and ask them about their experiences with computers and their attitudes about the effects of computers. On the average, do they think computers are a help or a hindrance? Do their attitudes seem to go along with your knowl-

edge of computer-related affairs? Do they correlate with some other aspects of their experience?

4. Do you agree with our statement that "the single most powerful protection is the insistence that the information organizations keep about people be strictly relevant to their purpose—and that in order to decide what is *relevant,* we must reinforce the distinctions among the institutions in our society"? What better methods of protection against the universal dossier can you think of? What *other* consequences of reinforcing the distinctions among our social institutions can you think of?

5. You are now the president of a large corporation that sells books by mail order to the public. Your public relations department tells you that there have been a number of lawsuits against similar corporations for unfair computer billing practices, and you would like to head off such a catastrophe for your own company. How would you go about finding out about what is going on in your own company? What do you expect each of the concerned department heads to tell you, and how do you expect to get at the truth?

For Further Information

This chapter will serve as a good point to introduce you to some more general bibliographic references. A very valuable periodical in the computer literature is *Computing Reviews* (1). It is a monthly publication of the Association for Computing Machinery and contains reviews of a large part of the literature of computing. This is a good place to look for information about a particular subject of interest. The reviews are arranged by subject. You may find it interesting to look through a few issues, learning how the subject matter is arranged and how to make use of the publication.

Applications of computers—a subject introduced in this chapter and one that will be expanded upon in the next few chapters—are treated in Part Three of each issue of *Computing Reviews*. There is an extensive literature of how computers are actually used in various fields. Some of the periodicals mentioned earlier are good sources

of such information as well. Two books, *Applications of Digital Computers* (2) and *Computer Usage Fundamentals* (3) present a range of applications and how they work, generally in more detail than the cases we have presented in this book.

A small but growing number of books has attempted to deal seriously with the general subject of the implications of computer technology for social institutions. Edmund Berkeley's text (4), is now somewhat out of date, but it stands as the first serious attempt to state the computer professional's responsibility for taking an interest in the effect of technology on people and society. An article in the *Communications of the ACM* (5) is a very provocative checklist of problem areas, with a list of questions that need to be addressed. Weizenbaum's paper (6) is a briefer and more personal look at the computer's impact.

The Information Utility and Social Choice (7)

contains a series of papers about the implications of the concept of a computer utility, in which information services are readily available to everyone. *Computers, Communications, and the Public Interest* (8) also is a collection of papers on a similar topic, so that a number of points of view are represented. *Computers and the Problems of Society* (9) presents a somewhat different perspective: how computer-based techniques can be applied to pressing social problems. The report by Roy Amara (10) is a thorough review of the issues, although your library may not have a copy of this one. *The Digital Villain* (11), finally, is a very personal statement on the ethics of person/machine relationships with a number of interesting and unusual insights.

Most of the interesting and valuable studies of the impact of computers and technology on society have been shorter pieces; the anthologies listed below contain a wealth of material, especially some of the older works that are worth preserving. *Automation* (12) is available in paperback, and you may want to have a copy for your personal library. The next two books (13 and 14) are more recent collections and contain a good cross-section of the materials that are available. The Teich book (15) also has some important pieces and is worth studying.

References

1. *Computing Reviews*, monthly.

2. W. F. Freiberger and W. Prager, eds., *Application of Digital Computers* (Boston: Ginn and Company, 1963).

3. Eric A. Weiss, *Computer Usage Applications* (New York: McGraw-Hill Book Company, 1970).

4. Edmund C. Berkeley, *The Computer Revolution* (Toronto: Doubleday & Company, Inc., 1962).

5. ACM Committee on Computers and Public Policy, "A Problem-List of Issues Concerning Computers and Public Policy," *Communications of the ACM* (September 1974) **17:**9, pp. 495–503.

6. Joseph Weizenbaum, "The Impact of the Computer on Society—Some Comments," *Science* (May 1972) **176:**4035, pp. 609–14.

7. Harold Sackman and Norman Nie, eds., *The Information Utility and Social Choice* (Montvale, N.J.: AFIPS Press, 1970).

8. Martin Greenberger, *Computers, Communications, and the Public Interest* (Baltimore: The Johns Hopkins Press, 1971).

9. H. Sackman and H. Borko, eds., *Computers and the Problems of Society* (Montvale, N.J.: AFIPS Press, 1972).

10. Roy Amara, *Toward Understanding the Social Impact of Computers* (Menlo Park, Calif.: Institute for the Future, 1974).

11. Robert M. Baer, *The Digital Villain* (Reading, Mass.: Addison-Wesley Publishing Co., Inc., 1972).

12. Morris Philipson, ed., *Automation, Implications for the Future* (New York: Random House, 1962).

13. Zenon W. Pylyshun, ed., *Perspectives on the Computer Revolution* (Englewood Cliffs, N.J.: Prentice-Hall, Inc., 1970).

14. Irene Tavis, ed., *The Computer Impact* (Englewood Cliffs, N.J.: Prentice-Hall, Inc., 1970).

15. Albert H. Teich, *Technology and Man's Future* (New York: St. Martin's Press, 1972).

Business Applications

10

The first computers were applied to scientific and engineering tasks. However, it was not long before it occurred to some people that these machines could also be applied to the repetitive clerical operations that occupied so much time and effort in large business organizations—the transactional systems to which punched-card accounting machines had already been applied. These machines began to be replaced by digital computers almost as soon as they became commercially available. The Remington UNIVAC computer was the first machine to be programmed for a business application when General Electric applied one to computing a payroll in 1954. Other machines quickly followed. Within a few years most large businesses were using computers for their routine clerical and accounting operations. It also became evident that this was the largest potential market for computers. Most of the computers now in existence are used primarily for business data processing.

All large corporations today depend upon computer processing in their clerical operations. Most medium-sized companies (100 to 1000 employees) are also using computers. Many smaller companies (less than 100 employees) are finding it profitable to use a computer for some of their operations, too. They frequently use the hardware and software made available by a bank or service bureau. They do not need to have the computer in their offices and they do not need to have programmers and other computer support personnel on their payrolls. They prepare the data for their computer runs in a prescribed format, deliver these sheets of paper to the service center, and their reports are returned to them the following morning.

But what do computers do in business offices? The most obvious applications are those that demand only simple logic and arithmetic but require that the same operations be performed many, many times on similar individual transactions. Because these were the easiest to imagine being performed by machines, they were also the first to be programmed. Such operations include issuing utility bills on the basis of meter readings, preparing dividend checks for stockholders, maintaining inventory records, and calculating and writing payroll checks. These operations had already been defined and procedures had been established for clerks to follow, so the simplest way to design the computer-based system was to follow the manual procedures as closely as possible. Such an approach produces a usable system but rarely takes full advantage of the computer's capabilities.

Effective Business Systems Analysis. A more sophisticated analysis considers the real current needs for the system and designs programs to meet them. However, this requires a fairly detailed analysis of the company's operations and perhaps a total redesign of procedures. A survey performed by McKinsey and Company of the profitability of industrial computer use found that those companies that merely automated existing clerical operations had gained far less from their computers than those that had analyzed their total information needs and designed a completely new system to suit them.*

*The survey findings were published by McKinsey & Co. in a report titled *Getting the Most out of your Computer* (1963). A later study titled *Unlocking the Computer Profit Potential* (1968) describes the bad effects on profits of managers' abdicating control of their computers to staff specialists.

Some information systems just grow. Like building a house one room at a time, bits and pieces are added as they are needed. Dissatisfied with this approach, many companies have now made a careful study of the information needs of their entire business before implementing any system. Such businesses are likely to find that their managers acquire, in the course of this analysis, a much clearer understanding of the firm as a whole and the way it functions. This understanding and the revised policies and procedures that it leads to may be more valuable than the computer application itself. As a case in point, a story is told about a consulting firm advising the government of India about the possible uses of computers in the federal offices of that country. After studying the problem, the consultants concluded that India could get a large share of the benefits of a computer by doing the planning required to use a computer—and then *not* getting one.

This phenomenon is neither mysticism nor is it a case of systems analysts exaggerating their own importance. The manual information-handling system that evolves over a number of years is shaped largely by what data can be collected easily, what tasks people can perform consistently, and what collections of people can be organized into departments. When a thorough analysis of information needs is done, most often it is found that many departments collect somewhat the same data and that no one is completely happy with the reports that are produced. Reports are too detailed or not detailed enough and are rarely on time. When the opportunity arises to redefine the information needs of a business organization, the analyst thinks about the problem primarily in terms of functions like data collection, processing, and reporting rather than in terms of the existing organization. Thus he or she thinks about the problem differently than anyone in the organization ever has before. This is why the development of an automatic data-processing system produces a fundamental understanding of an organization's information needs and in turn leads to a fuller utilization of data processing.

A Typical Application. It will help to clarify business applications if we examine a few of them in a little detail. A good one to start with is the payroll—because every business has one, because its basic function is easy to understand, because it is a function so widely performed by computers, and because it is more complicated than it looks.

In many businesses, the payroll is in fact the first clerical task to be assigned to the computer. We have already mentioned that this was the case with General Electric, the first company to employ a computer in its business operations. Several reasons can be given for the primacy of the payroll among computer applications. First, it is a repetitive task that must be done for each employee and for every pay period: in the course of a year, a large corporation issues a very large number of paychecks. Second, there is the obvious requirement for accuracy and also a need for speed: the complete information about the payroll is not available until the last day of the month (in the case of a monthly payroll) and the employees expect to be paid on the first of the month or very soon thereafter. Finally, there are many records and reports that must be prepared in addition to writing the paychecks themselves. The payroll program (or the series of programs that ends in the preparation of the checks) will include most of the following functions:

☐ Update the employee file by making additions of new employees, deletions due to termina-

tions, and changes in the records of ongoing employees (new address, name change, amount of deductions, number of dependents, and so forth);

☐ Keep track of sick leave and vacation;

☐ Compute wages for each employee on the basis of regular and overtime hours worked;

☐ Make deductions for each employee: federal withholding tax, state and local taxes (different for each state and city the company operates in), annuity or retirement funds, union dues, health and life insurance, social security, savings, charity, credit union debts, government bonds;

☐ Keep an up-to-date record of the amount of wages paid and the amount of each deduction for each employee so far this year;

☐ Allocate labor costs to various departments, projects, or fund accounts;

☐ Print employee W-2 forms for tax purposes at the end of the year;

☐ Produce reports of various kinds for management use and auditing purpose;

☐ Print the checks.

It would be misleading, of course, to assume that the computer actually performs the entire payroll function. It plays a key role, and does much of the repetitive processing, but a great many people are involved, too. The personnel office prepares forms on new employees and employees leaving the company. The clerks in that office copy information about those employees onto special forms, for use in the payroll process. In addition, this office is also responsible for forms indicating changes in employees' salaries when it receives notification of such changes from the various departments. In addition, it will receive each month notifications from employees about other changes to their files: new addresses, changes in amounts of deductions, and so on. At the close of the month, all of these changes will have been prepared on special forms, keypunched, and verified. They are now ready to be used in the payroll process. At the same time, each department is responsible to see that a timecard is prepared for each employee. At the end of the month (or other pay period), the time cards are checked for accuracy and are signed by some responsible administrator in the department. These, too, are then forwarded to the personnel department and are keypunched and verified. These forms include the employee's name and personnel number, the hours worked under various conditions (at regular time, time-and-a-half, and double time), and the projects or departments that are to be charged for all or parts of the employee's time. In the tape library of the company's computer center is a tape which is one of the products of last month's payroll run. It contains the master payroll file—a record for each employee, with as many as fifty to a hundred items of information about each: personal information (name, address, marital status, and so forth), pay rates, taxes and deductions, year-to-date totals, quarter-to-date totals, and other information. Not all of the data is, strictly speaking, relevant to the payroll itself. However, since this is the major file maintained by the personnel department on the computer, it is easier to add the few additional items of information than to create a whole additional file just for things like telephone number or spouse's first name.

Once the data is ready, the first activity is to update the master file. The change cards the personnel department has prepared are read by the computer. However, these are usually in the order in which the personnel office received the information, not necessarily the order in which the master file is maintained. Because it will be easier to make the changes if the two files are in the same order, the change cards are now sorted. Once that is done, the master file is read, the changes are made in the appropriate records, and a new file is prepared. A report is also printed, indicating which records were changed and how. This report is returned to the personnel office for checking, to be sure no error has been introduced on the way.

The payroll program itself may now begin. The cards containing the time and department information for each employee are now read. They too must be machine sorted. Then, one by one, the records are processed. Gross wage is computed on the basis of the hours worked (from the input card) and the rate to be paid (from the master file). Deductions are calculated on the basis of information in the master file and the gross wage. Year-to-date totals are updated and the employee's complete new record is written on the new master file. Information about current wages is put in a temporary file, so that the payroll register, the journal, and the paycheck can later be printed.

If this document appears satisfactory, the checks can be printed. They are not printed on ordinary paper, of course, but on paper preprinted as checks, with the bank and company name on each. Each of the checks will have a unique number as well, so that no blank ones can disappear without the loss being apparent. The paper must be aligned so that the information the computer will print will go in the right places on the checks. At the end of the check printing run, totals are printed out again. These should, of course, be the same as the totals on the payroll register.

Now it only remains for a few additional machines to finish the job. One machine will supply simulated signatures to each of the checks. The checks, which are still in a continuous sheet as they come from the computer, must be torn apart and then finally stuffed into envelopes by another machine. The checks will have been printed in an order to speed their delivery by whatever means are used. Those that are to be mailed will be in zipcode order, those that are to be delivered to offices will be arranged in batches for the various offices, and so on.

Summary reports may now be printed for the maintenance of manual files, and further summaries will be left on tape or disk for further processing. For example, taxes withheld must be reported (and paid) periodically to appropriate government agencies. Other programs will perform these functions. The new master file is sent to the tape library to be saved until the next pay period. The old master file and all of the input files are also saved for security purposes—in case the new master file is accidentally destroyed, for instance. These tapes may even be sent to a different physical location to protect the company from losing all the copies of its records during a fire or other disaster.

These few paragraphs about payroll processing have necessarily glossed over many of the details, particularly error detection and correction and the ways the individual wages and deductions are computed. Still, this example may give you an idea of the complexity involved in the entire process of preparing the payroll. Attempts to produce general-purpose payroll programs—to suit the needs of many different companies—have been difficult because so many details of the process depend on the needs and policies of the individual companies and the peculiarities of individual state laws.

A comment should be made, too, about the number of places people can check the computer output. One might think it is unnecessary to check whether the computer has done the job right. This task is necessary because of people, not because of the machines. In most companies the payroll is the largest single financial obligation. It varies from month to month, and thus it offers an excellent opportunity for embezzlement. If there were not checks and balances, a dishonest employee could slip in the name of a nonexistent employee, or dummy overtime cards, or (say) modify the program to add the fractions of cents lost in rounding on to his or her own check. Manual reviews of the computer output are necessary to be sure that this does not happen.

The Development of Business Systems.   A business data-processing operation consists of many such applications. And these are not separate and distinct but usually are closely interrelated. In order to consider how such systems develop, let us consider the case of a company that maintains an inventory of electrical appliances such as toasters, frypans, fans, irons, and so on. The company, let us suppose, has already been using a computer for the payroll and some other financial processes. Now it is experiencing some difficulty in managing the warehouse: it always seems to run out of some items while others are overstocked. Despite the large amount of money invested in inventory, it does not seem able to keep up with demand and is losing sales because of this. The management of the company is considering whether the use of its computer could help in this process. What will be involved in this decision? A systems analyst, or a team of analysts, will be asked to look into the question. They will talk to people involved in inventory control, so they can gain an understanding of how the process is conducted currently and what seems to be wrong with the system. After they have spent some time on this investigation, they will report back to management their estimates on such topics as these:

☐ What will the functions of the new computer-based system be?
☐ What will it cost to produce this new system?
☐ How long will it take to develop and install?
☐ What will it cost to run, relative to the manual system it is replacing?

If the analysts are totally frank, they will be forced to admit that the last question is difficult to answer. An experienced analyst will be able to estimate with some accuracy the cost, in dollars and months, of producing the system. But estimating its effect on the company's operation will be difficult.

Inventory Control. The inventory control procedure that is being considered by our appliance company is somewhat more complex than the payroll system we examined earlier. It is not so easy to say what the computer-based system will and will not do. Still, the systems analyst will have to prepare a specific set of functions for management to consider.

What, first of all, is the function of inventory management or control? It is, in simplest terms, to find the most economical compromise between two conflicting goals: maintaining a large stock so that the warehouse is never out of an item when it is needed, and maintaining a very small stock, minimizing storage costs and capital tied up in inventory. In order to perform this function, good managers use information they have about present stocks and the behavior of their suppliers; they use their experience about seasonal and other variations in customer demand; and they use their knowledge about things external to the business as well—their expectations of general business conditions, for instance.

A computer program for performing the functions of inventory control is going to have to use much of the same information and make similar kinds of decisions. The system to be automated has three major components: inventory file maintenance, demand prediction, and order analysis.

Inventory file maintenance is the first component, the basic program in the system, and the easiest to describe. It maintains an up-to-date list of what is really in the warehouse. For every item that is stocked, a record is kept: its name and number, how many are in stock now, how many are on order, when those on order are due to arrive, and other facts needed for the demand prediction and order analysis programs. In order to keep this list up to date, entries must be made every time stock is ordered, received, or shipped. Other data and changes must also be entered periodically. Basically, it is not unlike the first part of the payroll system: keeping the basic file that will be used by other programs.

Besides maintaining the files, this program will produce periodic reports. It will print out, every few months, a complete stock list. This will be used to take a physical inventory of the warehouse, to discover if all of the items believed to be in stock are actually there. Summary reports will be produced more often: the stock of various types, the value of the inventory, and so on. This will be used by management to evaluate whether the inventory control process is proceeding smoothly or whether some changes to the system are needed. It will also produce some "exception reports"—notifications of unusual activities. If, for example, far more stock of a certain kind is being shipped than was predicted (or far less), then management should be informed so that they can investigate and take appropriate action. Similarly, breakage and pilfering can be detected at this point.

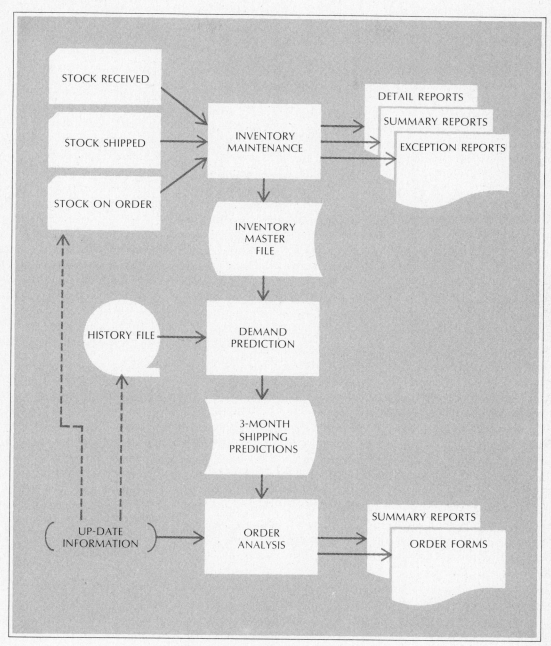

Figure 10-1 An inventory control system

The procedure to perform demand prediction logically follows. The basic question to be answered is this: On the basis of factors known, how many of each item will be ordered over the next three months? The data in the file for each item will include these:

☐ Seasonal variation code
☐ Quantity shipped, per month, for the past twelve months

The analysis program will take a weighted average of demand over the past year, giving more weight to the more recent data. It will then multiply this average by a suitable factor for the period in question; this is the seasonal variation code. Just because air conditioners are popular items in the summer, we must not let the procedure assume that they will sell as well at Christmas. Thus the predicted demand for the next month will be made. The procedure will make predictions for each item for three months into the future.

Predictions, however, are not decisions. The third component of our system—order analysis—must perform further work before decisions can be made as to what additional stock to order. For each item of inventory, this program must analyze current status. If the inventory is sufficient for the next three months (the prediction period of our example), nothing needs to be done. If not, further examination of the question is called for. How long does it take to get an item, once is is ordered? If it only takes one month to get an order and if we will not run short for two months, then it is too early to order; this item can be left until next month.

But in the case of some items, we will run out unless we order now. Therefore, orders must be generated for these items. But how much should we order? A crucial analysis must now take place, called Economic Order Quantity (EOQ) analysis. In the case of most items, the cost is less if we order in large volume, so it saves money to buy large lots. However, it costs money (in space, insurance, and use of capital) to have items in the warehouse. What is the proper number to order? If the price break is at, say, 100 items, then we will consider ordering 100. We will compute the money saved in ordering 100 of this item. Call this quantity, the money saved, N. What will it cost to keep the 100 items until they are used up? This will depend on how long they will last (back to our prediction model), what they cost, and how large they are. Call this quantity M. If M is less than N, then we should order the item in lots of 100; otherwise, we should order a smaller number.

The output of the order analysis will be the orders themselves, on preprinted forms, ready to be sent to suppliers. There will also be summary reports, of course, indicating how much money will be spent, when it will have to be paid, and so forth. Other data are provided that will be used to update the inventory file (so that we do not reorder the item again next month) and the history file, used in the demand prediction phase.

This description has focussed on the computer's role in the process. We should not ignore some important human inputs, however. People must specify the "seasonal variation codes" and the rules by which the program will predict demand. The computer program can be no more accurate in its predictions than these critical factors permit. The program, as we have outlined here in very general terms, makes no allowance for some aspects of prediction that may be critical, such as general economic conditions (in a depression, people buy fewer luxuries), fashion (the older models are not the latest style), and competition (another company has just introduced a comparable item at half the cost). Unless human judgment involves these considerations in the decision, the computer program can do no more than assume that every year will be just like the one before it.

But if programs like this are used judiciously and are not assumed to be wiser than the people who created them, they can be very effective and economical tools of business. Because it is possible to make more detailed and frequent analyses, many companies have found it possible to reduce warehouse space requirements by fifty percent or more with computer-based inventory control. Perhaps more significant, they have fifty percent less capital invested in their inventories. This is more than enough to compensate for the costs of system development and computer use.

Further Applications. In discussing the payroll program and the inventory management system, we have spoken as though each such program or group of programs were independent and could be designed, evaluated, and implemented on its own. It is worth noting, however, that this is not altogether true. Each such development interacts with other actual and potential computer operations. For example, in order to maintain the inventory file, an invoice must be prepared and keypunched whenever something is shipped from the warehouse. The billing system, therefore, should prepare its output in a form in which the inventory system can use it. Both the payroll and the inventory system are involved with financial matters, so their output files must be in a form in which they can be used by other programs. Thus all the financial functions of the company are involved: accounts payable, accounts receivable, ledger and journal, invoicing, sales, ordering, purchasing, receiving, and inventory.

Related areas are shipping and transportation

(closely allied with warehouse operations and thus with the inventory control programs), planning and scheduling of factory operations, credit control, market analysis. . . . The list appears unending. In fact, the applications of computers to this or any business are not a series of isolated areas but a closely integrated web, as demonstrated in figure 10-2. This fact has several implications. First, the design problem is difficult because each application and each file must take into consideration implications throughout the system. Changes or hasty decisions in one area can create problems all over. Second, computerization of one part naturally encourages computerization of others. If the computer is used in inventory, there will be compelling arguments to apply computers in ordering, billing, and shipping procedures as well. Third, the entire system becomes so complex that its advantages and disadvantages are almost impossible to measure. If a company begins using the computer, where will the process end? If it is leading to large-scale automation of office procedures, what does this mean for the operation of the business as a whole? Will it save money? Will it improve operations, staff satisfaction, customer approval? Those responsible for the decision can usually only guess. Once the computer is in the door, new plans for its use spring up almost immediately. When a significant part of the data about the company and its operations is on the computer, various methods can be applied to supply more information to management and, hopefully, permit the company to run more smoothly, more economically, and more efficiently.

Control and Planning. The applications mentioned so far have been at a level sometimes called *transactional* or *operational*. Further refinements and more elaborate systems support the functions

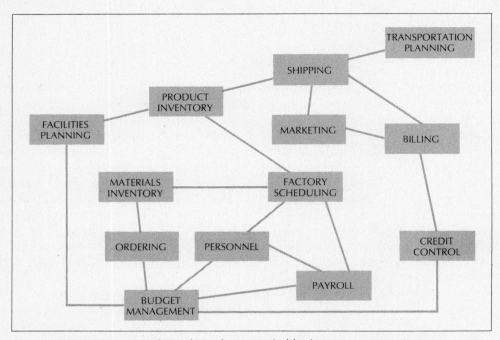

Figure 10-2 Interrelationships of some typical business computer systems

of management: the *control* of the organization's operations and the important function of *planning* future activities.

Specifically, information management systems and simulations can be used for management support. The massive amount of information about what the company is doing constitutes a data base that can be used as an information system to determine the effects of past decisions and current trends. This information can, in turn, be used as a basis for decisions about the future. It may be desirable to construct a model of the company's operation and its relationship to its customers and competition. This can be used to estimate the effects of alternative policies: new products, modifications to the advertising budget, raising or lowering prices, and so forth.

Thus the computer, once it enters a business,

is soon found to be doing something never done before because there was no way to do it. The computer makes new things *possible,* in the business office as elsewhere. Does it save the company money? If we look at the amounts being spent on computers and their supporting machines, systems, and personnel, the answer must surely be no. On the other hand, computers allow companies to become bigger and more complex, to make wiser and faster decisions, and to become responsive to their consumers' desires. In the light of these facts, the answer must be yes. The company is simply a different enterprise than it was or would be without it.

Effects on People. Another way of estimating the effect of computers in business is to look at the situation in more personal terms. Rather than looking at the computer's operational and economic impact on an organization as a whole, we might ask these questions:

☐ How does the computer affect the company's managers?
☐ How does it affect the employees?
☐ How does it affect the customers?

The answers to these questions are complex, too. The managers are given more information about the affairs they are managing; they can thereby exert more control. One prediction for the long-range effect of computers in business is that top management will be able to control the organization in more detail and that middle management will thereby become less important. But this need not happen. The additional information and ability to control can be used to make better plans for the future and to provide better considered and more controlled long-range planning.

By and large, the effect of introducing computers on the workers will be that the company will employ more technicians and fewer clerks, more highly skilled and fewer unskilled employees. Generally, more skills (and thus more and better education) will be required. This will be discussed in more detail in chapter eighteen.

The effects on customers will vary. A better-run business, based on accurate information about what customers want, can be more responsive, producing better products at lower prices. On the other hand, computers often seem to intrude themselves between the customers and the people who run the system. Customers whose accounts are maintained in a computer may find it very difficult to get information when they think they have been cheated or when they simply have a

question. They may find that they cannot contact a single human being who has any authority or real knowledge about their problems. It is small wonder that they come to believe a mechanical brain has taken over their bank, their department store, or even their supermarket. While this unfortunate way of using computers is neither necessary nor inevitable, it does happen often enough to be mentioned.

Information-oriented Businesses

The example of the appliance manufacturer was presented as a typical case of an organization that uses information to perform its primary function—the manufacture, sale, and distribution of something else. There are other organizations whose primary function is information, and here the computerization of information handling has had a profound influence.

A primary example of such an industry is banking. Its very large clerical function is to adjust symbolic records of accounts and to use its files to make decisions in the course of day-to-day operations. It has been estimated that eighty to ninety percent of the clerical operations involved in banking are now automated. Checks with magnetic ink characters are sorted by machine. Deposits and withdrawals are entered and new balances are determined by computer. Online systems permit a teller to learn the balance in an account simply by keying in the account number at a terminal.

Besides such clerical operations, a bank may have a range of more sophisticated programs performing such functions as:

□ Cost accounting
□ Budget management
□ Credit scoring
□ Loan analysis
□ Investment analysis
□ Portfolio selections
□ Market research

Many banks have also developed general-purpose programs to perform routine accounting and clerical tasks that they offer as an added service to customers. Thus small businesses that cannot support a computer or staff of their own may contract with their banks to keep their accounts, send their bills, and write their payrolls.

A Bank's Information System

The Northern Trust Company of Chicago, Illinois, provides a good example of modern banking automation. Northern Trust was established in 1889 and now ranks as one of the forty largest banks in America, with a full range of banking and trust operations and services. Its computer operations are based on a moderately large IBM/360 system, with many online applications utilizing more than 100 terminals throughout the bank's offices. Nearly 100 employees are involved in the design, development, and operation of information systems at the bank. They are a very important part of the bank's operation.

The current system, which began to be installed in 1970, replaces a series of earlier computer applications that were oriented primarily to batch processing and clerical automation. The present system design emphasizes a series of interrelated data bases, a sophisticated range of management information applications, and the ability to perform the bank's clerical operations online from the many conveniently located terminals.

In chapter six (Applications Software), we indicated that Information Management Systems are large, complex, and expensive to produce, and that many users will choose to adopt an available general-purpose system rather than to create one of their own. The Northern Trust uses such a system as the backbone of its computer operations: IBM's IMS/360. Data bases implemented on this system include full files of information on most of the bank's major operations: commercial loans, savings accounts, demand deposits, and trusts. Customer information files and personal loan data files are in the planning stage.

In each of the application areas, the basic pattern is as follows. As activities take place, those responsible (tellers and loan officers, for instance) enter the information by means of their terminals. They indicate the kind of transaction they wish to perform; the system tells the person at the terminal the information that must be entered by a "fill-in-the-blanks" format on the display. As soon as the information is entered, it is inserted in the data base and is available to be used by anyone in the bank. Thus the data base always has current information.

Inquiries about current status can also be made from these same terminals: a teller can inquire about current balance of an account, for example, or a loan officer can ask for detailed information about all of the loans and accounts that concern a particular individual or company. In addition, the management of the bank can request reports, either detailed or summary, on any of the affairs reported in these data bases.

The various parts of the bank's overall system were developed in phases. The system started with an online data base for response to inquiries. Once

Figure 10-3   A banking application

this was operating successfully, file maintenance and data entry procedures were added, until the application was fully developed. This series of steps has taken place in one application area after another. The advantage of such an approach is that parts of the system can be used almost immediately, without waiting for the total system to become operational. This may take many years.

A major component of this system is the commercial loan operation. Commercial loans at the Northern Trust are valued in excess of $1 billion, with 3000 customers and literally millions of separate pieces of information. The employees of the bank update the file immediately each time the status of an account changes. They also are able to get up-to-the-minute information on any phase of

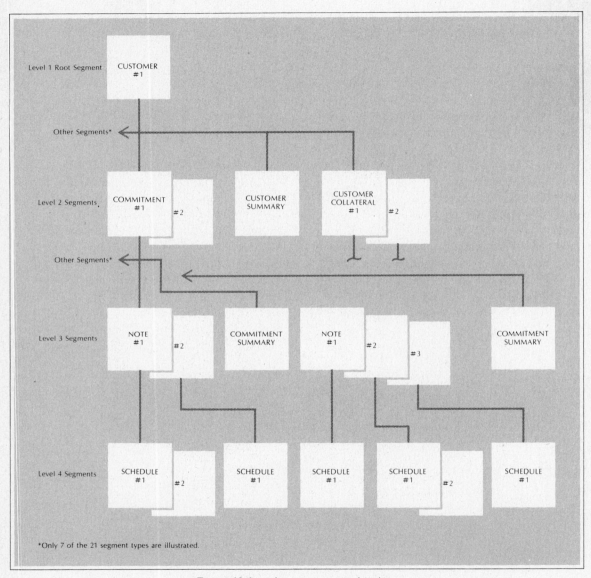

Level 1 Root Segment — CUSTOMER #1

Other Segments*

Level 2 Segments — COMMITMENT #1 #2 — CUSTOMER SUMMARY — CUSTOMER COLLATERAL #1 #2

Other Segments*

Level 3 Segments — NOTE #1 #2 — COMMITMENT SUMMARY — NOTE #1 #2 #3 — COMMITMENT SUMMARY

Level 4 Segments — SCHEDULE #1 #2 — SCHEDULE #1 — SCHEDULE #1 — SCHEDULE #1 #2 — SCHEDULE #1

*Only 7 of the 21 segment types are illustrated.

Figure 10-4 A loan company's data base

the operation. About 1700 transactions and inquiries are processed every day.

The data base itself is very highly structured, with data on customer information, loan descriptions, plans for payment, collateral, and relationships among loans and customers all carefully detailed. Maintaining this highly structured file is the work of the general-purpose management system. Figure 10-4 shows a small portion of this file, indicating how each customer (at level 1) can

would do as well. When the customer locates a flight he or she wants, with available space, the ticket is sold and the inventory for that flight is appropriately reduced. Customers can thus get immediate response to their inquiries without having to wait hours or days. The airline can sell exactly the number of available seats, without either overbooking or turning customers away unnecessarily.

Currently, airlines have a total of more than $250 million invested in these reservation systems. They are primarily concerned with making reservations and providing the documents and records related to the passenger lists.

American Airlines' SABRE is the best known of these systems. It maintains an online file of information relating to flights for the next 320 days. Each day represents approximately 5000 flights for this airline. For each flight in this period, records are maintained for each scheduled passenger: name, address, telephone, special requirements (children, special diet, wheelchairs, and so forth), connecting flights, car and hotel reservations, and ticketing and payment information. At any of the airline's offices, an inquiry can be made about a particular reservation, and it can be modified or a new reservation can be entered. Records of past flights are retained on tape for sixty days and are then destroyed.

In 1968, a magazine article* claimed that the SABRE system could be (and frequently was) used by law-enforcement agencies to check up on the movements of travelers. A query could be made about a specific person, according to this article, and the computer would produce a complete list of his or her trips, including the person's traveling

companion. The story was widely and threateningly quoted before a more careful investigation discovered it was totally false. The system is designed to satisfy the requirements of an operating airline and is not a surveillance system: queries must cite a specific date and flight number. There is no provision for answering more sweeping questions, nor could there be without total reprogramming, which would probably, among other things, make the system more inefficient in performing the job for which it was created. Further, the cost of searching a file of this size (nearly two million flights) would be considerable—and it would only provide information on a single airline and only for a few months.

Other examples of online systems can be cited. One that should be mentioned is in retail sales. A point-of-sale (POS) terminal that also performs the functions of a cash register can immediately transmit information about a transaction to the central computer for processing. Charge accounts can be checked and debited automatically. Sales slips are printed at the time of the sale and the information is recorded for later processing. You may have seen such terminals. Similar procedures are now followed in many libraries when patrons check out books.

Industrial Applications

We have discussed the use of the computer both within the business office and by clerks and agents who deal directly with customers. A few paragraphs must be added about the use of the computer in the shop, the laboratory, and the factory.

In a number of industries, a product is manufactured by a continuous process: raw materials are fed in, modified by machines of various kinds, transformed into a final product. Chemical

---

*"The Computer Data Bank: Will it Kill your Freedom?" *Look,* June 1968.

Figure 10-6 A process control system

plants, oil refineries, electrical power plants, paper mills, and steel mills are industries that use this kind of process. The actual transformation from raw material to finished product is made by machines that require constant monitoring and control. The use of computers in this area is called *process control*. In a chemical plant, for instance, it is necessary to monitor the state of many kinds of meters such as thermometers, flow meters, and pressure gauges. When certain conditions are reached, the system's behavior must be modified.

For example, when the temperature in a certain vat reaches 87°, a heater must be turned off; or if the flow of one material into a vat is greater than another, the valve must be closed until the flows are equal. The computer can be directly connected to the meters, heaters, and valves, and make such changes rapidly. (These applications are also discussed in chapter six under "Control Systems.")

A final example of computer use in industry is in the field known as *numerical control.* Many machine parts, tools, and dies are produced by machines that cut complex shapes from blocks or sheets of metal or some other material. The machine operator guides the machine to produce the desired shape.

We now frequently see such machines controlled by a computer-produced magnetic tape rather than by a human operator. Special computer languages have been developed for these applications. (APT is one of the best known of these; it allows a programmer to describe the shape that is to be produced relatively easily.) The computer program translates this description into sequential commands the machine tool must follow. Such numerically controlled machines are more accurate

For Further Information

The use of computers in business organizations has been dealt with from all points of view in a great many books, articles, and reports. The references below contain only a few that we think will be of particular value. *The New Science of Management Decision* (1) is a thoughtful book and scholarly study of the effects that computers are having (and will have) on the management of business organizations. *The Computer Age* (2) is a review of the state of the art intended for an audience of managers. The books by Withington (3) and Sanders (4) are also excellent surveys of the field. Boutell's more recent book (5) is also recommended.

Information Systems in Management (6) is an introduction to management information systems that is clear and understandable even to a layman. *Business Computer Systems and Applications* (7) is particularly noteworthy for its detailed and informative presentations of some actual application systems.

References

1. Herbert Simon, *The New Science of Management Decision* (New York: Harper & Row, 1960).

2. Gilbert Burck and the editors of *Fortune, The Computer Age and its Potential for Management* (New York: Harper & Row, 1965).

3. Frederic G. Withington, *The Use of Computers in Business Organizations* (Reading, Mass.: Addison-Wesley Publishing Co., Inc., 1966).

4. Donald Sanders, *Computers and Management* (New York: McGraw-Hill Book Company, 1970).

5. Wayne S. Boutell, *Computer-Oriented Business Systems* (Englewood Cliffs, N.J.: Prentice-Hall, Inc., 1973).

6. K. J. Redford, *Information Systems in Management* (Reston, Calif.: Reston Publishing Co., 1973).

7. Alan Eliason and Kent D. Kitts, *Business Computer Systems and Applications* (Chicago: Science Research Associates, Inc., 1974).

Health Care

11

The economic nature of medicine is for the most part, entrepreneurial. Most doctors are self-employed businessmen; most hospitals are profit-making organizations; druggists are usually small store owners. This is not to deny the humanitarian nature of their work, but to emphasize one basic restriction on their activities—economics. Thus the computer has had to gain its admittance to the area of health care against strict standards of economy. For this reason the principal use of computers in this field has been in large hospitals, where computers do the same things that have been found cost-effective elsewhere: inventory control, billing, personnel files, and general management. In addition to these recurring applications, we find imaginative innovations: the monitoring of life symptoms in intensive care units, the automatic processing of electrocardiograms (which holds the promise of life-saving warnings of a heart attack), the automation (with its promise of fewer errors) of blood and urine tests. The applications that come closest to our personal welfare both attract our attention and raise our fear of the computer taking over.

Since we started with cost improvement as an important reason for the use of computers in medicine, let's look at the costs of medicine today. In total, medical care in the United States costs roughly $90 billion a year. This is nine percent of our trillion dollar gross national product. To put this in the context of growth, while our population was doubling from 100 million in 1933 to 200 million in 1973, the total cost of public and private medical care went up by a factor of twenty. On a per capita basis, per year, the average person's yearly expenditure for medical care went from $79 in 1949 to over $400 in 1973.

We have over 300,000 doctors and twice as many nurses. Contrary to our national expectation of being best at everything, worldwide we are tenth in doctor-patient ratio. We have one doctor for every 700 patients, and, as with all averages, in some areas the ratio is very much worse. It has been estimated that fifty percent of our population finds it difficult or impossible to get (or pay for) adequate medical care. Of course, it must be recognized that our high general state of health has increased our expectation for good medical services. There are over 8000 hospitals in the United States, with something in excess of two million beds. They admit about 32 million patients per year at a cost of nearly $32 billion. They are big businesses and big generators of paperwork.

The high cost of medical care in the United States forces health care professionals to accept changes that can reduce expenses. There are also other computer innovations in medical care that were motivated by the discovery or cure of serious illness. Many of these are still experimental and have more the flavor of the ethical and humanitarian mission of medicine.

Although it has been traditional to view medicine as one of the sciences, in general the medical researcher deserves the title of scientist more than the practitioner. Medical practitioners get their educations in a very concentrated way while they are relatively young, and from then on their practices are intuitive and descriptive rather than precise and analytical. Their aim is to cure patients, not to create a body of new knowledge. One of the direct benefits of accumulating medical records in computers is to widen a doctor's basis for intuitive diagnosis through access to a broader range of records than an individual practice allows.

We will first discuss those applications that are basically intended to improve economy: hospital automation, multi-phasic screening, automation of clinical laboratories, and psychiatric record processing. We will then cover new forms of individual treatment that would not be possible without computers. Last, we will look into the medical world of the future.

There can be no pretense of completeness here. The large number of uses for computers in medical care forces us to omit many useful applications, such as training, information storage and retrieval, and medicare administration, that are not substantially different from those we have discussed in other fields.

Cost-effective Applications

Hospital Automation. In the following paragraphs we will discuss four specific successful hospital automation projects. All of them divide their data-processing resources between administrative and patient record processing. Administrative functions include accounting, billing, and inventory control. Drugs are controlled to prevent theft and misdosage. Most hospitals also automate employee payroll, bed allocation, x-ray, surgery, and other facility scheduling.

The patient data handling system extends from admissions to discharge. As in so many other systems that you have seen and will see in the remainder of the applications chapters, it is this operational data—the patient's medical dosages, their diets, room, surgery, and x-ray records—that generate the administrative control data that

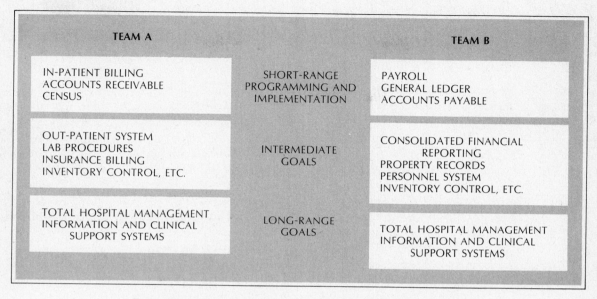

Figure 11-1 Data-processing staff at Daughters of Charity Hospital

hospital administrators use. (In the area of law enforcement, in contrast, arrest and investigation records generate the administrative data that police management uses to run the police department.)

Daughters of Charity Hospitals. The Daughters of Charity of St. Vincent de Paul is an order that staffs fourteen hospitals in the eastern part of the United States. These hospitals are linked into a computer communications network with the IBM 360/20. To develop this network a problem had to be solved that also bothered law-enforcement management in the early development of their systems: the scarcity of systems analysts who really understood the area. Care was taken to educate medical personnel in data processing and include them in the development process. Because they were pioneering, no one knew how much of the system to build at first. For this reason, it was built with what is known as a modular approach. Individual applications were divided between two teams and then were divided into short-range,

intermediate-range, and long-range goals as shown in figure 11-1. In this way, the hospital could get early results to prove the system's usefulness to a management anxious about such a new and expensive venture. The system has many components (modules): financial control, billing, accounts payable, payroll, and so forth. We will give you an overview of just one of those subsystems: financial control.

When a patient enters one of the Daughters of Charity Hospitals, a computer record is opened and continuously maintained until his or her account is closed by final payment. The record contains the patient's identification number, room number, birth date, doctor, guarantor's name and address for billing purposes, and financial class. All charges, like daily charges, receipts, and adjustments are made to this record. This information is then used to produce reports on the patient's status, treatment, and financial obligation to the hospital. The daily census report is used by the dietary department and the clergy. The same basic information is used to produce admissions and discharge listings, in-patient billing status, and an accounts receivable record. From this you can infer the obvious. Large hospitals have trouble losing patients in the system (like the jails and the Army and any large people-processing institution), and they also have a problem that jails don't have: the inmates sometimes don't pay their bills.

Rockland State Hospital.   Rockland State Hospital in New York is a mental institution with a 6500-bed capacity and a staff of about 2000 employees. As a mental hospital, much of its treatment is drug therapy. Thus keeping track of the use of drugs is important to the hospital both to analyze the effects of its treatments and as a matter of operational control. Rockland State started using computers in 1963, and in 1968 its drug-monitoring program went into effect. Like the Daughters of Charity Hospitals, it is part of a multi-state, multi-facility network of mental hospitals and community health centers that uses a computer communications network to share data and data processing facilities.

The Rockland State drug-monitoring system provides a complete record of the patient's pharmacological treatment. Record is kept of the ward location, treating physician, legal status, diagnosis, and drug therapy. The basic input documents are patient status and location change forms and the drug order form.

Let us follow a typical patient into the system. When he arrives at the reception center, the evaluation of his illness and therapy begins. He may stay at the reception center anywhere from a week to several months, and that is where the record begins. That patient's history and results of the mental exam are recorded. His need for medication is determined by a doctor and recorded

by the computer, and the computer also completes a number of legally required forms. When the patient's stay at the reception center ends, he may be transferred to one of the treatment centers, discharged from the hospital, or moved to another dormitory. All of these changes are recorded in the computer, which fills out the appropriate forms. When a patient is transferred from one building to another, his drug orders are cancelled and new ones must be created by a doctor, thus preventing inappropriate treatment. Any change in the patient's drug regime is instituted by a doctor giving an order to the computer. If the patient is given leave to visit home, the number of days of absence granted is noted in the computer. If he doesn't return on the scheduled date, his drug orders are cancelled.

In many people-processing systems the basic transaction involves a legal document. The drug order form is a legal document that must be part of the patient's medication orders. The administration of the hospital takes great care to check these orders by hand and uses many administrative review steps to be certain that errors of type and dosage are not made. For example, each week, lists of every patient's drug regime are produced for each physician and supervisor, by building and ward. The nursery staff also uses this same list for individual patient treatment.

Again, the operational data provides the administrative data. An inventory of drugs is kept at the pharmacy and in each building. Each patient's drug dosage is subtracted from this record. Monthly physical inventory and records of drug use are checked to determine reorder levels and budgets required to buy drugs. This kind of tight control also helps prevent theft. Figure 11-3 shows how drug inventory control works.

After many years of use, the hospital has estab-

NAN GOLUB

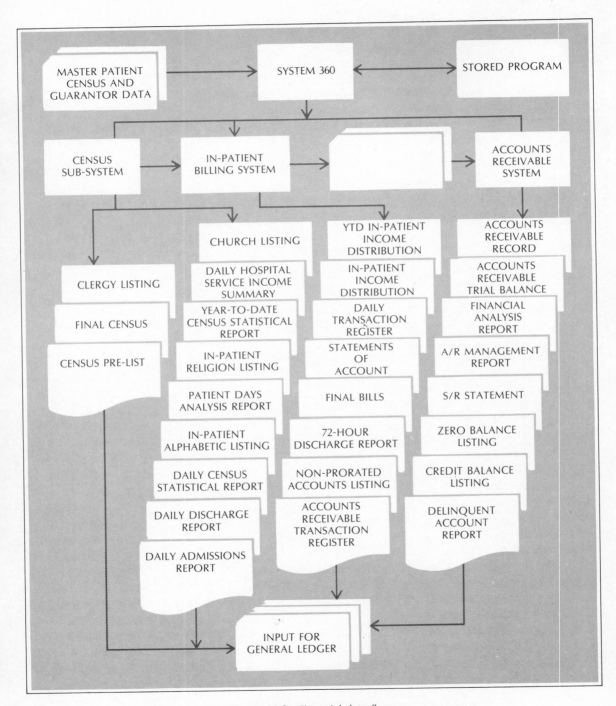

Figure 11-2 Financial data flow

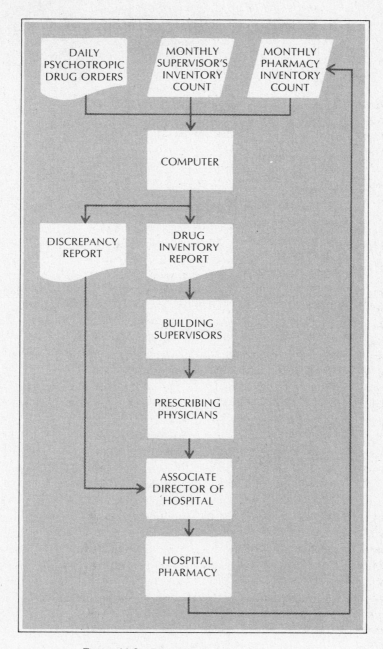

Figure 11-3 Drug inventory control system

lished the advantages of their drug control system: relief from routine, time-consuming paperwork, accurate reports on the drug regime and history of each patient, close administrative control of the stocking and use of drugs, and statistical analysis of the results of treatment.

Loyola University Hospital.   The Loyola University Hospital in Maywood, Illinois, had the opportunity to design its data-processing support as an integral part of its new building, recognizing that the quality of patient care depends heavily on the speed and accuracy of patient information. The hospital did a systematic study of its information requirements before developing the system. Thus it is able to state concrete statistics: an average of twenty documents are initiated for each patient admission and at least thirty more documents are created during each patient's stay. This is for just a 450-bed hospital. But even such a small hospital treats 50,000 outpatients a year and provides service for about 20,000 patients a year. Therefore over a million medical records a year are developed at this hospital, and this is fairly typical.

Loyola University Hospital uses an IBM 360/40 and telecommunications links to twenty-two remote terminals. The system performs all the standard functions of a hospital automation system. One of its unique features is that every transaction that is entered at the terminals is monitored and compared against a standard set of comprehensive orders. Any order that isn't consistent with the standards is rejected as a potential error. It is estimated that as much as fifty percent of the nurses' time had been taken up in preparing reports and filling out forms; much of that time is now available for patients.

Another hospital, Monmouth Medical Center in Long Branch, N.J., using essentially the same system, estimates that seventy-seven percent of all patient-related paperwork is handled by their computer more accurately and fifty percent is handled faster than by their manual system. Formerly, a nurse had to fill out five or six slips of paper for each medication order. To get a lab test done he or she had to select one of twenty-four forms to fill out. Now, the computer handles ninety-seven percent of the hospital's paperwork. Monmouth estimated that the installation of their computer increased the daily cost of patient care by three to four percent in the first year of operation. But it expects to see the computer help level off the total cost of hospital operation in about three years after it was installed. That expectation is reasonable, but it will be difficult to confirm because other increasing costs for manpower and supplies could well mask the computer savings.

Multiphasic Screening.   A large percentage of a doctor's time is spent with well people or with people whose illnesses have stabilized to the point that the doctor need only be concerned with testing for changes. Much of this testing can be done automatically. The general movement to mass testing began with mobile tuberculosis units, and then testing for diabetes became widespread. Now there are a number of places in the country—like the University of Florida, the Good Samaritan Hospital in Cincinnati and the Kaiser-Permanente Hospital in Oakland, California—with large multiphasic screening installations that use computers to process the data from mass testing. In addition, private industry is installing these systems for the use of their own employees. The advantages of using a computer to process the data are more rapid reporting, quick decisions about further tests to be made on the patient, improved accuracy in data recording, and, of course, saving nurses' and doctors' time. The computer can also give immediate notification of measuring instrument failure, calibrate the instruments, and convert the measurements into meaningful terms for the doctor. Last, by retaining the records of patients from previous visits, it can do studies of the individual patient's medical history.

To go a little further into detail, we will describe the Kaiser-Permanente Automated Multiphasic Screening Program in Oakland, California. This system registers patients at the rate of two every five minutes, and the examination takes two to two and a half hours. It is accompanied by an internist's investigation, and a group of specialists is available for other exams, such as gynecological cancer detection. The automatic test includes:

☐ Electrocardiogram
☐ Phonogram
☐ Cardiovascular test
☐ Height, weight and other body measurements
☐ Chest X-ray
☐ Breast X-ray
☐ Visual acuity
☐ Ocular tension (for glaucoma)
☐ Retinal photograph
☐ Lung measurements
☐ Pain reaction
☐ Hearing test
☐ Health questionnaire
☐ Blood chemistry
☐ Personality questionnaire
☐ Blood hemoglobin
☐ White cell count
☐ Blood group
☐ Test for syphilis
☐ Latex test
☐ Urine test

Of course, the physician in attendance is responsible for any diagnosis. In fact, the system is aimed at screening specific diseases, not for general-purpose diagnosis.

Clinical Laboratory Automation. Seventy-five percent of all chemical and fifty percent of all blood test data in the typical modern clinical laboratory is generated by automated instruments. There is a shortage of trained laboratory technicians who can organize the workload for these instruments, watch them for malfunctions, and translate the raw data into final test results—so this is a natural area where computers can be used. The results of this application are increased productivity, higher quality control standards, and quicker response to the physician's request for test data on each patient. As in the case of other hospital information systems, such systems relieve the laboratory technician of much paperwork.

Multi-state Information Systems for Psychiatric Patients. It has been estimated that one out of ten people in the United States will spend some time in a mental hospital. That surprising and stark figure is an enormous commentary on both the state of our civilization and the facilities that our society offers its mentally ill. Psychiatry is at best an approximate science. The evaluation of individual patients is subject to error, and these mistakes affect both the patient and society in general. However, if a wider data base of psychiatric data can be accumulated, both the patient and our society will benefit. Individual treatment will be improved and society will be spared exposure to those who still need hospitalization.

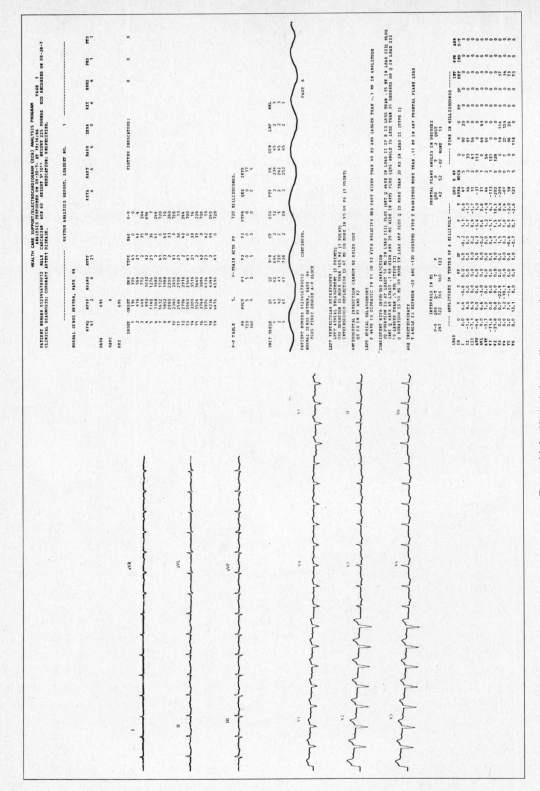

Figure 11-4 Clinical data collection–admissions form

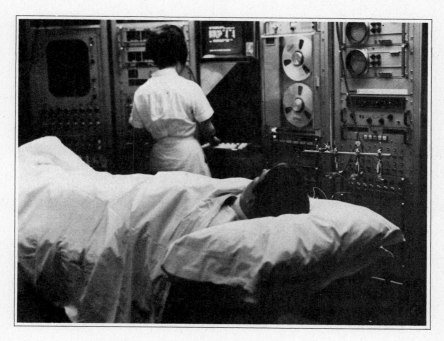

Figure 11-5 A patient-monitoring system

The newspaper attests daily to crimes and suicides by mental patients who have been prematurely released.

A special computer-based system that has been developed, called the Multi-state Information System for Psychiatric Patients, can eventually provide the data base that will improve the basis on which institutional psychiatry is practiced. At the same time, it poses the same kind of social problems with privacy and personal control that you will see in police information systems. Let us first examine the system itself and then discuss its social aspects. It is installed at the same Rockland State Hospital we discussed above. The hospital has an IBM 360/50 that directly and indirectly serves 850 state and local psychiatric hospitals, mental health centers, and halfway houses. The system handles records for about 300,000 patients a year—roughly twenty percent of the number of patients in the state-operated mental hospitals in the United States. Again, the system collects detailed information about each patient and his or her treatment, and this mass of data in turn serves hospital administrators in planning facilities, managing them, and evaluating their effectiveness. To give some examples of the system's use, an administrator can ask for the number of in-patient days to claim for reimbursement from Medicare and Medicaid. A researcher can obtain an alphabetic listing by age and sex and diagnosis of patients on a given treatment program. (Those persons responsible for choosing where to build new mental hospitals require such records to assure that mental health facilities are equally available in different regions of the country.) Another example of the diverse ways that such records can be used is an actual case history in which a patient in a particular hospital was discovered to have amoebic dysentery, a serious and sometimes fatal disease. In order to avoid an epidemic, it was necessary to use the system to track down every other patient that had been in

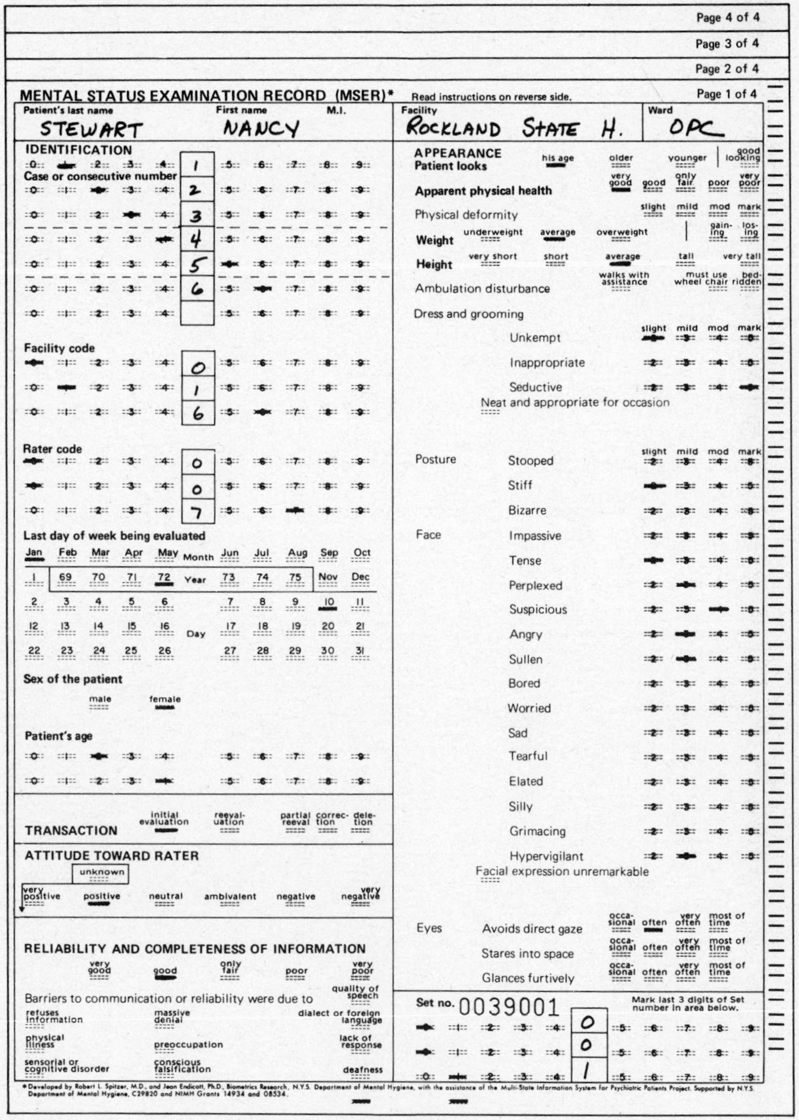

MENTAL STATUS EXAMINATION REPORT

PATIENT: STEWART, NANCY
CASE NUMBER: 123456

DATE OF EXAM: JANUARY 10, 197—
FACILITY NO.: 16
RATER NO.: 7

INTRODUCTION

THIS IS A REPORT OF AN INITIAL EVALUATION FOR THIS ADMISSION OF A 24 YEAR OLD FEMALE PATIENT BASED ON INFORMATION COLLECTED USING THE MENTAL STATUS EXAMINATION RECORD. HER ATTITUDE TOWARD THE EXAMINER WAS POSITIVE. THE RELIABILITY AND COMPLETENESS OF THE MATERIAL IN THIS REPORT ARE CONSIDERED GOOD.

APPEARANCE

THE PATIENT LOOKS HER AGE. SHE APPEARS TO BE IN VERY GOOD PHYSICAL HEALTH. SHE IS OF AVERAGE HEIGHT AND WEIGHT. IN HER DRESS AND GROOMING SHE IS SLIGHTLY UNKEMPT AND MARKEDLY SEDUCTIVE. HER POSTURE IS SLIGHTLY STIFF. HER FACIAL EXPRESSION IS MODERATELY SUSPICIOUS, MILDLY PERPLEXED, ANGRY, SULLEN, AND HYPERVIGILANT, AND SLIGHTLY TENSE. OFTEN SHE AVOIDS DIRECT GAZE.

GENERAL ATTITUDE AND BEHAVIOR

HER BEHAVIOR IS MODERATELY WITHDRAWN, AND SLIGHTLY UNCOOPERATIVE. SHE SHOWS MODERATE IMPAIRMENT IN FUNCTIONING IN GOAL DIRECTED ACTIVITIES. SHE SEEMS SLIGHTLY SUSPICIOUS. SHE SHOWS MILD OVERT ANGER. SHE HAS BEEN CRITICAL OF OTHERS AND SULLEN. SHE HAS MADE AT LEAST ONE SUICIDAL THREAT. SHE IS MILDLY GUARDED AND COMPLAINING. THE PATIENT HAS A HISTORY OF MILD DRUG ABUSE INVOLVING HALLUCINOGENS. SHE IS SEXUALLY SEDUCTIVE.

PATIENT: STEWART, NANCY
CASE NUMBER: 123456
RATER: NUMBER 7

POTENTIAL FOR SUICIDE OR VIOLENCE

IN THE EXAMINER'S JUDGMENT, THIS PATIENT'S POTENTIAL FOR SUICIDE IS MODERATE, AND POTENTIAL FOR PHYSICAL VIOLENCE IS LOW.

INSIGHT AND ATTITUDE TOWARD ILLNESS

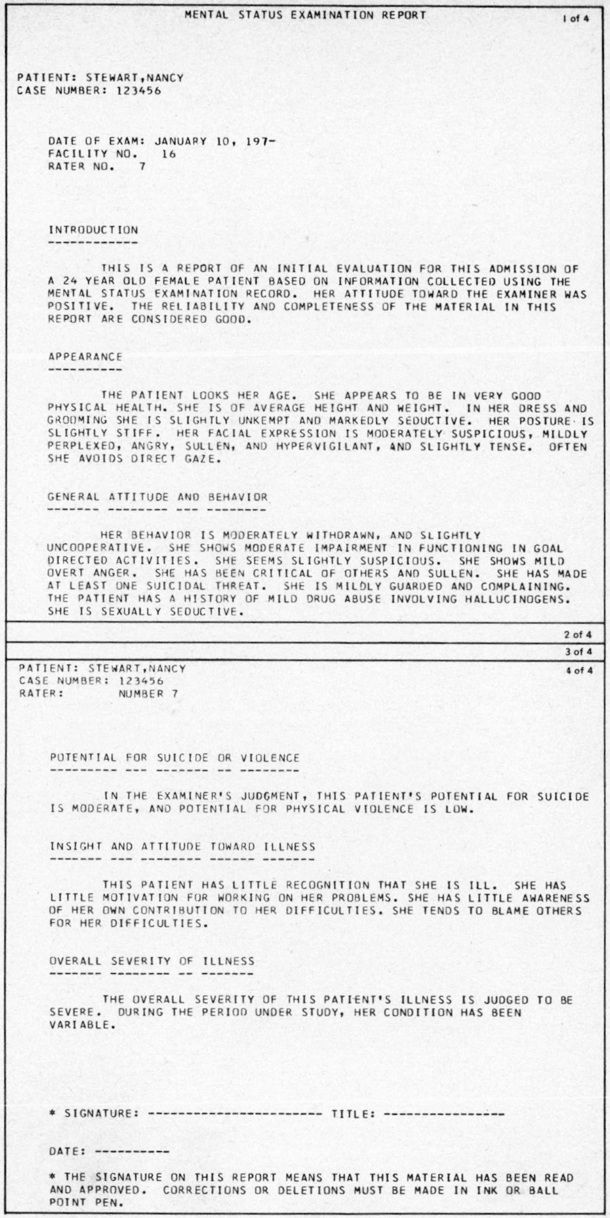

THIS PATIENT HAS LITTLE RECOGNITION THAT SHE IS ILL. SHE HAS LITTLE MOTIVATION FOR WORKING ON HER PROBLEMS. SHE HAS LITTLE AWARENESS OF HER OWN CONTRIBUTION TO HER DIFFICULTIES. SHE TENDS TO BLAME OTHERS FOR HER DIFFICULTIES.

OVERALL SEVERITY OF ILLNESS

THE OVERALL SEVERITY OF THIS PATIENT'S ILLNESS IS JUDGED TO BE SEVERE. DURING THE PERIOD UNDER STUDY, HER CONDITION HAS BEEN VARIABLE.

* SIGNATURE: ------------------ TITLE: ------------------

DATE: ------------------

* THE SIGNATURE ON THIS REPORT MEANS THAT THIS MATERIAL HAS BEEN READ AND APPROVED. CORRECTIONS OR DELETIONS MUST BE MADE IN INK OR BALL POINT PEN.

MENTAL STATUS EXAMINATION RECORD (MSER)*

Patient's last name: STEWART First name: NANCY M.I.

Facility: ROCKLAND STATE H. Ward: OPC

Read instructions on reverse side.

Page 4 of 4
Page 3 of 4
Page 2 of 4
Page 1 of 4

IDENTIFICATION

Case or consecutive number

Facility code

Rater code

Last day of week being evaluated

Sex of the patient

Patient's age

TRANSACTION

ATTITUDE TOWARD RATER

RELIABILITY AND COMPLETENESS OF INFORMATION

Barriers to communication or reliability were due to

Set no. 0039001

* Developed by Robert L. Spitzer, M.D., and Jean Endicott Ph.D. Biometrics Research, N.Y.S. Department of Mental Hygiene, with the assistance of the Multi-State Information System for Psychiatric Records Project. Supported by N.Y.S. Department of Mental Hygiene.

APPEARANCE
Patient looks

Apparent physical health

Physical deformity

Weight

Height

Ambulation disturbance

Dress and grooming

Posture

Face

Eyes

Figure 11-6 Clinical data collection—mental exam

that particular ward during the disease's incubation period. This was done successfully.

Almost all of the information in the system has been collected by the use of simple multiple-choice questions. This means that the answers can be put in machine-readable form by mark-sensing equipment. However, the system makes its information available to its users in text form. Figure 11-6 shows a sequence of examples from the history of a fictitious "Nancy Stewart." At each stage from admission to discharge, the doctors' observations on Nancy are entered into the system. Figure 11-6 shows the forms and the computer translation of these forms.

Psychiatric records, like medical records in general, benefit from the doctor-patient confidentiality privilege. However, these records can be subpoenaed in legal cases like disability suits, and are relevant for determining medical benefits from the government, private insurance companies, and welfare support. It is for this reason that the state of New York had to pass an amendment to their Civil Rights Law in 1972 providing that the out-of-state patient records that resided in the Rockland State Hospital computer would not be treated as public records and would be confidential and not subject to subpoena. Otherwise hospitals in other states would not have permitted their records to reside in a computer in New York. The history of protection of medical and psychiatric records has been generally good. The place where patients' civil rights might be infringed would be if such rights conflicted with the state that possessed their psychiatric records.

Treatment

Outside of hospitals, a patient receives treatment from specialists, general practitioners and paramedics. We will discuss these in that order.

Specialties. Radiology is the study of the human body, using the x-ray machine. The x-ray photograph is a difficult and subtle record to interpret. The same techniques that are used to improve aerial reconnaissance and space photographs are being used to get the most out of an x-ray photograph. This isn't to say that computers can do a better interpretation, but rather that they can help get more data out of a photo. The radiologist still makes the interpretation. Surgery, always the most dramatic of the specialties, has the promise of computer-directed laser surgery. Another application is the use of equipment and techniques to monitor life signs during surgery. The computer integrates the information for the purposes of both the surgeon and the anesthesiologist. Thus the strategy taken in any surgical procedure can be changed during the operation. Also, anesthesiologists can better control the depth of anesthesia by monitoring the arterial and venous blood pressure, blood oxygen saturation, body temperature, pulse and respiration rates, and brain, heart, and muscle electric potentials. The heart specialists, of course, want to be able to process electrocardiograms with increasing sophistication and can do this easily using computers. Therefore someday we may be able to institute mass dataprocessing that will provide norms for treatment and diagnosis of heart illness. The benefits are consistency of interpretation, cost savings, and speed (two to five times faster).

General Practice. As of this writing, the use of computers by individual doctors is still a matter of conjecture. The prospect of universally organized, standardized patient medical records that accumulate with the aging of the person seems distant. These would permit study of one person's health over a long period of time and ultimately would constitute the precise medical history of a population. However, this possibility is likely to remain remote for some time because of excessive costs and the habits of data gathering (highly individualized, confidential, and incomplete) in this profession. Similarly, the use of time-shared medical instructional materials for on-the-job-training and consulting by physicians is still in the future. Sadly enough, for lack of an imaginative approach to financing, this opulent group of professionals is denied certain benefits. To date, the most obvious application is the one used—billing.

Paramedics.   The use of computers in paramedical areas spans a range of application programs—from straight scientific computation of dosage limits for x-ray technicians, to storage and retrieval of dosage requirements for prescription drugs for pharmacists, to file management systems with donor files for blood banks. One of the more unusual applications is being used by paramedical first-aid groups. There is now a technique for attaching ECG sensors to a heart-attack victim and telemetering the ECG by radio or telephone to a computer that is monitored by a doctor at all times. He or she can then prescribe immediate treatment for the paramedic to apply.

The Future

In the future, computers in medicine will be applied both in the same areas we discussed above and in new ones as well. Present technology is already being adapted to life-saving use. These applications include such developments as computer-controlled automatic respirators for premature babies. The principal results of the use of computers in medical research remain to be seen in the future. We will know more about the molecular structure of amino acids (and thus protein) through the use of computer studies. Automated processing of chromosome photographs will tell us more about genetics. The simulation of neutral networks will tell us more about our nervous systems, and the simulation of the heart will tell us more about heart failure. If this research is successful, our future is bound to be healthier. There is no other field of science, with the possible exception of chemistry and physics, in which the computer is being used so extensively as a research tool as medicine.

Exercises

1. Research and describe computer applications in medical training.

2. Research and describe the impact of computers on the profession of nursing.

3. We have briefly alluded to the potential conflict of a patient in a state mental hospital with the state over medical records. Suppose a mental patient in your state was committed involuntarily and sought release. Would he or she have access to hospital records the way a criminal or a credit petitioner would? Each state's laws and practices are different. Research this question.

4. If you were a hospital administrator considering the use of computers, what would your first half-dozen questions be?

5. The field of medicine is one of the least controversial areas of computer application. Although scientific applications have often been criticized, rarely has medical practice been condemned for its use of computers. However, many doctors have been sued for malpractice. The consequences of this have been so great that insurance companies have raised their premium rates for malpractice insurance to the point that some doctors have been forced to retire. Some insurance companies have ceased to sell malpractice insurance because these suits have cost them a great deal of money. How do you think a computer could be used to help this situation? As a hint, think about it from the point of view of three people—an insurance actuary trying to find a fair way to charge doctors premiums based on their actual experience, a legislator trying to pass a law creating no-fault medical malpractice insurance, and an attorney trying to get the most for his or her client in a malpractice suit.

For Further Information

To research the literature of medical applications, you find yourself in a different part of the card catalog and thus in a different part of the library. While your library will catalog some of this literature under Data Processing or Computers, most of it will be under Medicine. In general, this happens when an application area is well developed. This body of literature isn't too complex in terms of computer technology, but be prepared for a shock when it comes to medical terms. For a general introduction, (1), (2), and (3) are good places to start. (4) has some interesting work on the simulation of neural networks that was too detailed for this book, but you may be interested in pursuing it. If you would like to find out more about the use of computers in teaching medicine, (5) is a good place to start. (6) is a collection of papers, all of which are interesting, but Victor Fuchs' article starting on page 95 is the best. (7) and (8) are rather specialized, but if your library has them you might scan them for interest.

References

1. E. E. Mason and W. G. Bulgren, *Computer Applications in Medicine* (Springfield, Ill.: Charles Thomas, Publisher, 1964).

2. Enoch Haga, ed., *Computer Techniques in Biomedicine and Medicine* (Philadelphia: Auerbach Publishers, Inc., 1973).

3. R. S. Ledley, *Use of Computers in Biology and Medicine* (New York: McGraw-Hill Book Company, 1965).

4. R. W. Stacy and B. D. Waxman, *Computers in Biochemical Research,* vol. I (New York: Academic Press, 1965).

5. Donald A. B. Lindberg, *The Computer and Medical Care* (Springfield, Ill.: Charles Thomas, Publisher, 1968).

6. John B. McKinsey, *Economic Aspects of Health Care* (New York: PRODIST, 1973).

7. "A Complete Interview for Emergency Room Patients," *Computers and Biomedical Research* **6:** 3 (June 1973) pp. 257–65.

8. *Automation in Medicine: Selected Papers from a Seminar on Automation in Medicine,* (Mt. Kisco, N.Y.: Futura Publishing Co., 1973).

Applications in Education

12

Of all areas of computer application, none is more fascinating or of greater potential significance than education. Part of the reason for this is that education is so important in our society. Other reasons will become apparent as you read this chapter. Since you are probably going to school while you are reading this book, you have a very fine opportunity to make your own observations on the extent of computer use and the ways it affects both students and teachers. In reading the following pages, you may want to make some investigations and draw some comparisons with your own institution.

The methodology of education is at a critical point in its development. In general, modern technology has had little effect on it. Although television, and films have been used somewhat, the primary medium of education today is, as it has been for hundreds of years, the lecture and the quiz. The teacher explains the material to a group of students, asks questions to assess their grasp of it, and either goes over it again or moves on to something new. Students do some independent work, reading books and writing papers, but most of their instruction takes place in a class. They are in lock-step with their classmates; no one can move ahead faster than the rest of the group and no one can fall very far behind. If a student has trouble keeping up, he or she receives a poor grade; those who keep ahead of the class get an A. If a student is interested in pursuing a different aspect of the subject or investigating it in greater depth, he or she usually is allowed to do so only if it will not interfere with classmates' activities.

Another problem in the methods of education has to do with teacher effectiveness. In most fields of work today, a person can perform much more work than in the past, thanks to machines. But because technology has not been applied in the same way to education as it has to production, the cost of education (relative to other human activities) continues to rise. At the same time, the scope of human knowledge has been extended dramatically, so that there is more to teach.

A third problem area concerns students. Many of them find the slow pace of the traditional classroom dull—sometimes too dull to bear. These students leave school before their training is complete. Today, students are accustomed, outside the classroom, to having large amounts of information thrust at them very quickly. Students often engage simultaneously in several activities that have high information content: reading and listening to music, for instance. They accept and make frequent use of such technologies as automobiles, telephones, records, television, radio, and movies. An hour in class seems to move at an impossibly slow pace. Accustomed to considerable freedom in so many activities, the modern student is likely to be further annoyed or even totally alienated by traditional lock-step instruction.

The computer has by no means supplied a solution to all these problems, but it does give us some tantalizing possibilities. Many of these possibilities, it must be stressed, have not yet been realized. Perhaps they never will be. Yet the promises of the application of computers to education have attracted the attention of some of the finest minds both in computer technology and in education over the past twenty years.

Let us look at some of these possibilities. If the computer is programmed to act as a tutor, the lock-step can be broken: each student, sitting at a terminal, can proceed at his or her own pace. Unlike a book, a computer program can be flexible, adapting itself to a student's need. It can provide more detailed information when the student seems to want it, or go over the material more quickly if the student already appears familiar with the subject. The impersonality of computer-based systems has been found, in some cases, to be a boon rather than a hindrance: students feel they are being treated equally. Also, no one need fear the teacher's scorn at a stupid answer or impatience when the same fact has to be repeated over and over again before the student masters it.

Applications in education cover a considerable range. In most schools, computers first enter through the back door, as workaday machines that assist in the considerable data-processing activities of the school as a business. Many of the functions discussed in the chapter on business applications pertain to schools and colleges as well: keeping track of financial records, planning, inventory control, and maintaining records. A second broad area of application is to be found in some of the administrative tasks that have no parallel in other industries: student admissions, registration and academic record processing, grading examinations, and keeping track of library books. Third, the computer has been used in the instructional process itself. Students at many schools, at all levels, use the computer as they would a tape recorder or an adding machine or a television set. This chapter will present an overview of these three areas: instructional applications, business applications, and educational management.

Instructional Applications

How can the computer aid in the instructional process itself, substituting for the teacher or helping students when they are studying on their own?

Figure 12-1   Students interacting with a computer

There are several different answers to this question. A computer, as well as a teacher, can provide much of the help a student needs. A teacher is available to the student only at scheduled times and must be shared by many. A computer terminal can give individual instruction to the student on a schedule that is most convenient to him or her.

There are numerous examples that demonstrate the use of computers in instruction. It is significant, however, that only in very few cases has an effort been made to automate a course completely: some parts of instruction are almost always felt to be more appropriate to a human teacher than to a machine.

Computer training.   Four classes of instructional applications of computers deserve to be mentioned. The first is the most obvious: teaching students to use computers in various ways. Many students will, when they graduate, take jobs that require them to use computers, and they must be trained for this. Some will become involved with computers directly as systems analysts, programmers, computer salesmen, or machine operators. Others will become users of computers who will need to know something of programming and computer operations: accountants, chemists, engineers, bankers, statisticians, and business people. Since this is a fairly obvious application of computers in education, we will say no more about it.

Drill and Practice. A second class of application uses a computer to automate a fairly simple level of instruction, commonly called drill and practice. You have engaged in it yourself when you and a fellow student have quizzed one another on a set of facts that had to be memorized, such as the multiplication table, definitions of new words, or historical dates. The process is simple. The tutor (or the computer) has a list of questions and answers. Questions are asked in random order and, if they are answered correctly, are not asked again. If the pupil fails to give the correct answer, he or she is told what the answer should have been and then, later in the learning session, is asked the same question again. This technique has been computerized in many areas with considerable success. Since it is a relatively simple process, a very large or expensive computer is not required. A grade-school student can be drilled in arithmetic for less than fifty cents per fifteen-minute session.

Tutorial. The third application is called *tutorial,* and is somewhat more complex. Rather than just drilling the student, the computer actually teaches something. The student sits at a terminal to learn about a new subject—perhaps Newton's third law

of physics, for example. The computer begins by asking a few questions to determine the level of the student's understanding, much as a human tutor might. If the student cannot answer them, perhaps he or she will be advised to take a different lesson first. But if the student appears to have the prerequisite skills, the lesson will begin. Some facts are presented to the student, either at the terminal itself or by means of a slide projector. After the student has read them, he or she answers a question asked by the computer. If done correctly, the lesson proceeds; if not, a more extensive presentation is made, spelling the facts out in greater detail or in a different way.

The student who moves ahead quickly and seems to get all the answers right may be assumed to be somewhat familiar with the material; the system may give him or her shorter explanations or skip some of the intermediate steps. Thus the fast student is taken through the material as quickly as possible, the average student proceeds at the best pace for him or her, and the slow student is provided with extra tutorial material to help in understanding the concepts. Since each student works independently with a separate terminal, there is no need to keep all the students together, all doing the same thing. Such techniques provide individualized instruction beyond the capability of any classroom teacher, since the teacher can devote only a fraction of his or her time to each student as an individual. The teacher in such a computerized system is free to counsel the students individually, to provide special help for the student who is having difficulty, and to suggest additional lessons or tasks for the fast-learning student who is getting ahead.

At its best, computer-aided instruction of this kind may be equivalent to having a master of the subject as a tutor. The student learns quickly, and

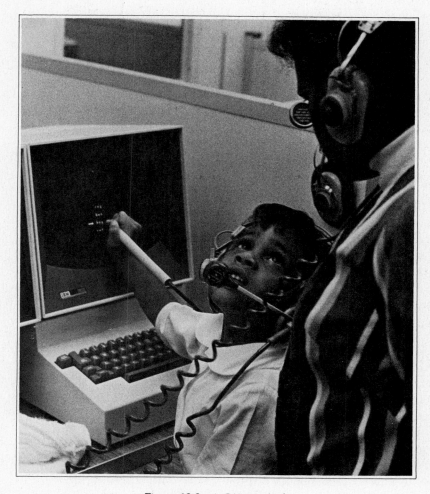

Figure 12-2 A CAI terminal

the human teacher is presented with detailed analyses of how his or her students are progressing. Even at its best, however, no one can claim this system is the equivalent of a good human teacher. And at its worst, it may be unacceptable to the whole range of students who are exposed to it. The bright student may feel that the exposition is dull and the questions are stupid. Finding the whole instructional process mechanical and insensitive, he or she may decide the subject itself is uninteresting and not worth the bother. Slower students are in a worse predicament. They find themselves subjected to a maze of meaningless presentations: they don't understand the information being given and they cannot answer the questions. But they are caught in a mechanical and apparently never-ending circle. The only escape is to give up, leave the terminal, and probably drop the course. How can a student explain to the teacher that he or she was defeated by a machine? Most computer-based instruction, of course, is at neither of these extremes.

Advanced Instructional Applications

Although computers are not as good in some senses as human teachers in tutorial applications, there are some applications where they are better. Our fourth category of computers in instruction includes those cases where the computer is used to do things that human teachers cannot do. As in many other areas of application, in education computers are first used to perform functions that parallel very closely those of humans; but as the people who are using the computers come to understand them better, imaginative and sometimes totally novel applications emerge.

In many fields, instruction consists very largely of telling students how to do something and only in a small degree in letting them practice and learn by their own mistakes. The reasons for this are obvious in many cases. Students of business administration cannot be presented with their own company to practice on; medical students cannot be supplied with human beings so that they can learn by their own mistakes. Some scientific experiments are too dangerous (nuclear chemistry) or too time-consuming (genetics) or too expensive (space travel) to allow students to perform them. A computer-based technique already discussed—simulation—seems ideally suited for use in such situations. Instead of lecturing students on how something is done, they can be allowed to practice and improve their skills in simulated environments. A few examples will help illustrate this point.

A management game. A well-known instructional program in this category is the Harvard Business School Management Simulation Game. This game is widely used in business schools, and others have been developed that follow the same general format. The game is played by a group of twenty or more students. The goal is to have them exercise skills in marketing, finance, and production management as individuals and also to learn to work together with their teammates to solve problems too complex for one person to deal with in the time allowed.

The class is divided into groups of four or five students when the game is played. Each of these groups manages a complete business. The four or more businesses made up by the class compete for the available market for their products. The actual nature of the business is not important; it is usually assumed to be a variety of consumer products (such as small electrical appliances) in the $5 to $50 price range.

Each group is presented, when the game starts, with a financial statement, a market survey, and some historical data for their company. They review this information together and make decisions on budgets (how much to produce, prices, advertising and research, and so on). These decisions are input to the computer; the output of the computer program is a new set of accounting statements, three months later. The students then review these, make new decisions, and submit their budgets once again. Each of these periods takes about three or four hours, and a complete game may take twelve or more such periods.

The students behave much as they would if they were actually operating businesses, although of course on a much shorter time scale. The computer simulates everything outside the executive conference room: the factory, the personnel, the market, and the world at large. Most students find such games to be interesting and valuable parts of their education.

Laboratory simulation. A rather different kind of simulation is represented by laboratory models.

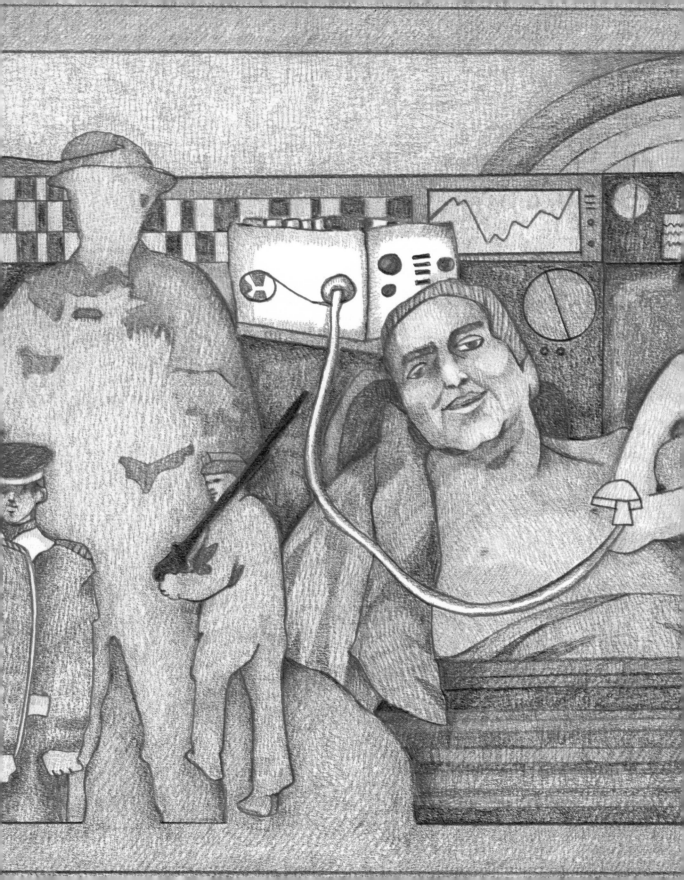

NAN GOLUB

Figure 12-3 Teaching with a computer

The purpose of a laboratory for student use in the sciences is to allow the students to practice the skills that are being described to them in their lectures and textbooks and to pursue scientific investigations on their own. Those students who will actually pursue a career in science must learn the skills of manipulating the laboratory equipment and materials and to master the actual procedures. But for most students, the experience is intended primarily to exercise their abilities to think logically, to acquire information experimentally, and to make decisions rationally and scientifically. For these students, a simulation of the laboratory is quite satisfactory, and in some cases cheaper and easier to arrange. Figure 12-4 illustrates a portion of a dialog between a student and a computer during a laboratory lesson in quantitative analysis. You will see that the process of reason required of the student is very similar to that of a student standing at a laboratory bench. Other programs are sometimes used in teaching medical students the very similar process of physical examination and diagnosis, as well as for experiments that require more time than is available in a typical laboratory session or school term.

Social science applications. This kind of laboratory experience is not limited to the physical sciences. A set of programs and data bases developed at Dartmouth College, called IMPRESS, provides a similar kind of experience for students in the social sciences. These programs are not in fact simulations but are more closely related to what we have called here information management systems.

An important technique in the social sciences is the analysis of large masses of data in the form of surveys, census reports, election returns, economic indicators, and so on. Project IMPRESS gives the student an opportunity to learn these techniques. Students are given a range of data bases to work with, a convenient language for describing the information they want, and interactive access by means of a computer. They can deal with a large set of data, such as the returns of a major election, or even several independent collections of data—perhaps surveys on the same question over a period of time. Access to such information allows them to analyze and investigate relationships. For example, one might ask for the distribution of political party preference in a given survey by race or age. The teacher can suggest questions that the student may then attempt to answer by conducting research on the available data. How much the students learn in this environment depends on the ingenuity of the instructor's questions and on the students' ability to find ways to make the computer work for them.

An important consideration in learning techniques such as this is that the process of instruction is basically and radically altered: rather than being told how scientists do research and find answers to questions, the students are presented with an opportunity for doing it themselves. This seems, to many experts, to have great advantages for the student.

Limitations. There are factors limiting these interesting and imaginative applications in education, however. One is the high cost. Computing continues to grow less expensive, but at many colleges, a student may easily use $50 or more in computer time in a single course. This is more than many schools can afford. Another is the fact that new methods of instruction require teachers trained in new technologies, teachers with a fairly sophisticated knowledge of computers and their application to education. This resource may even be in scarcer supply, in some cases, than money.

Business Applications

The people who manage a school have budgets to keep, bills to pay, raw materials to order and stock, and payrolls to maintain. They are concerned about the quality of their product and the economy of their operation; they prepare documents and tables of figures that summarize such facts. When students pay fees, the school must have an accounting function that sends bills and keeps track of who has paid them and who has not. Schools at all levels are required to prepare reports to government agencies responsible for monitoring educational performance.

In doing these things, the academic administrator acts as any responsible executive does, and most of the techniques he or she uses will be

```
COMPUTER:   Observation. A yellow precipitate forms. Specify an analysis
            action.
STUDENT:    Conclude.
COMPUTER:   You do not have sufficient information at this point to make a
            conclusion. Answer again. Specify an analysis action.
STUDENT:    Add.
COMPUTER:   Reagent?
STUDENT:    NaOh.
COMPUTER:   O.K. Concentration?
STUDENT:    6M.
COMPUTER:   Good. How much?
STUDENT:    8 drops.
COMPUTER:   The precipitate dissolves. Specify an analysis action.
STUDENT:    Conclude.
COMPUTER:   You still shouldn't make any conclusions. Specify an analysis
            action.
STUDENT:    Add.
COMPUTER:   Good. Reagent?
STUDENT:    HAc.
COMPUTER:   O.K. Concentration?
STUDENT:    6M.
COMPUTER:   Good. How much?
STUDENT:    Until acidic.
COMPUTER:   Good. A yellow precipitate forms again. Specify an analysis
            action.
STUDENT:    Conclude.
COMPUTER:   O.K. What is your conclusion?
STUDENT:    Lead is present.
```

Figure 12-4   Dialog between a student and a computer in a chemistry problem

drawn from those of business administration. These applications therefore do not differ much from those described in the chapter on business applications. The purposes of a computer are those it serves elsewhere in business data processing: getting the necessary work out with the least expense (in terms of both time and money) while at the same time assuring high accuracy and prompt action. The trend to more computer use in academic administration has been accompanied by a fairly recent demand that schools be run in a more businesslike way. For many decades, it was fashionable for schools (particularly private colleges) to be run very casually. The feeling was that education was everyone's primary concern, and efficiency of operation was a very secondary matter. However, most institutions today feel that an institution's educational goals can best be achieved when the business aspects that accompany them are managed frugally and not left to fend for themselves. This trend has encouraged the use of computers and, correspondingly, their availability has made more businesslike operations easier to achieve.

Another important development in education—particularly in higher education—that has supported the extensive administrative application of computers is the growth in the size of these institutions during the past few decades. At the same time that computers were becoming available, many institutions found themselves with rapidly expanding enrollments that made computers necessary for repetitive operations and file management. They had more students and

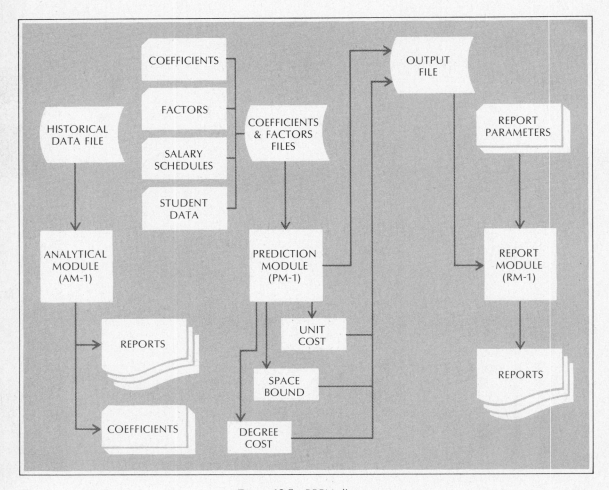

Figure 12-5 RRPM diagram

courses and classrooms to keep track of, more staff to pay, more books to buy and bills to collect. These things meant either an army of clerks or some automation of these processes.

More sophisticated management techniques, including management information systems and prediction models, have not been overlooked in education, either. The National Center for Higher Education Management Systems (NCHEMS) has developed, for example, a computer-based simulation model called the Resource Requirements Prediction Model (RRPM). This model is used by many colleges and universities to help those responsible for the resources (classrooms, money, personnel) to understand the implications of decisions made in the planning of these institutions. Another well-known and widely used model, called CAMPUS, was developed by a Canadian company. It functions in a basically similar way.

The input to the RRPM or CAMPUS model takes the form of estimates of the numbers of students who will be enrolled in the institution's various programs. The model estimates (on the basis of data that must also be supplied) the resources required to support these students: faculty, class-room space, materials, laboratory supplies, athletic equipment, and so on—and then evaluates the cost. Using this model, administrators can find tentative answers to such questions as the cost of adding a school of nursing over the first five years, or the money that would be saved by reducing the foreign languages program, or the implications of a drop in applications for admission to the school of social sciences. Those schools that have seriously attempted to use these models have found them to have a powerful effect on the school's ability to make realistic plans. Such models are not, however, easy to use. The information they require as input may be difficult to find in many institutions, since records are usually not kept with the accuracy required.

Here pause and recall a general statement we made in chapter ten. There is a natural flow of data from the bottom of the organization to the top. Management and planning must be based on this natural flow. Attempts to initiate a single isolated management or planning tool such as the modeling done in RRPM or CAMPUS will necessarily fail or be at best awkward if they are not part of a total system based on this natural flow of organizational data.

Educational Management

Some of the data-processing problems of a school are different from those of other kinds of enter-prises and present unique problems. A few of these will be mentioned here as examples. You may be able to find others on your own campus.

Using computers to score tests and examina-tions is now a fairly routine application, particularly at institutions with large classes. If students are given multiple-choice questions and put their answers on mark-sense cards or sheets, the com-puter can grade them quickly and accurately. Besides the savings in time, the teacher gets a few additional benefits. Most such scoring pro-grams provide statistical information on the performance of the students. Some items in the test may turn out to have been misinterpreted by the students or to be ambiguous. If, for instance, all those students who had the highest *average* score for the quiz got item #17 wrong, perhaps there is something wrong with that item. The teacher can change the way he or she wants this question graded and run the entire stack of answer sheets through the computer again. The advantages to the student are faster results and (because of the information the teacher gets on how good the questions are) fairer tests. The disadvantage, of course, is that it encourages teachers to use multiple-choice questions in preference to essay-type tests, because they are the only kind that can be graded in this way.

One of the most important computer applica-tions at most medium to large colleges and univer-sities is in the registration process. The assignment of students to the classes they wish to attend, and in which there is room for them, is a con-siderable problem in data management. It is also one in which the computer has been applied (at least in many cases) to everyone's benefit.

The un-computerized registration process usually works something like this. The student examines the catalog of courses to be offered, decides the ones he or she would like to take, making sure there are no conflicts in scheduled meeting times. On the appropriate day, he or she visits the departments offering the courses. If there

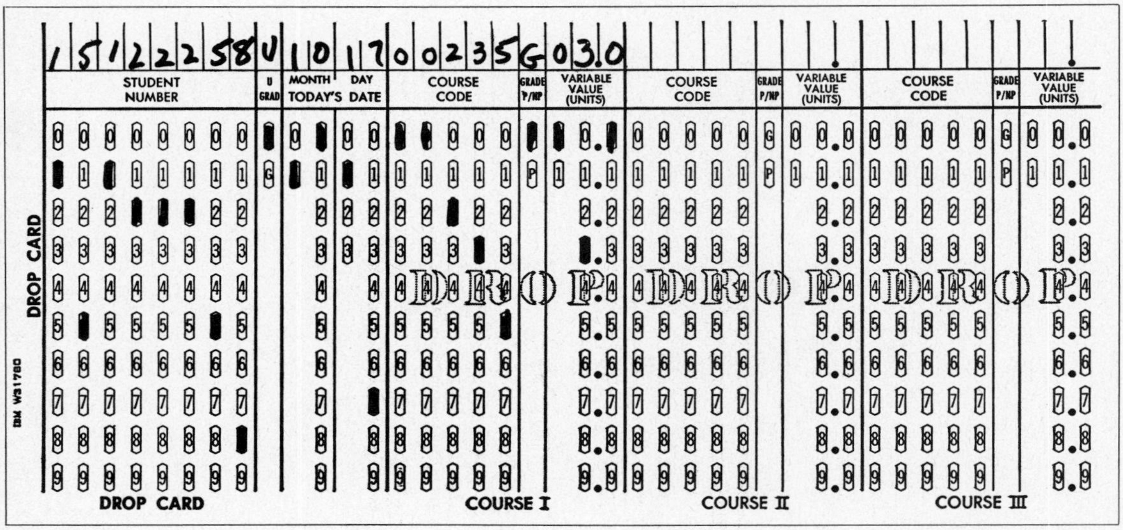

Figure 12-6 A mark-sense card filled out by a student wishing to drop a class

is an opening, the student's name is put down by a departmental secretary for that course. If that course (or that section of the course) is filled, the student may have to reconsider his or her entire schedule, possibly going back to offices that have already been visited in order to make changes. It is a long and frustrating experience for the student. The departments have only manuscript (and probably inaccurate) lists of the students who plan to take their courses. It may be days or weeks before the registrar has complete and accurate lists of all courses. If an error is made when the secretary writes down the student's course selection, the semester will be well advanced before the student, the teacher, and the appropriate administrative offices know what class the student is really in. This system is obviously inconvenient from the student's point of view. But it also means a great deal of work for the teachers and administrators involved as well. Efforts to make systems like this more flexible for the students have usually failed because of the excessive workload (and long delays) that would be involved.

At many institutions, a straightforward automation of this process has taken place, with considerable advantage. The student sits at a terminal or talks to a clerk who actually types in the data. The student first supplies his or her name and student ID number. The computer checks to make sure that person is in fact a student and has no pending problems such as overdue library books or unpaid bills. It may ask whether the address and telephone number are still correct. Once these preliminaries are over, the student types in the courses wanted.

The computer checks to make sure the student has not requested classes that conflict, and that he or she has the necessary prerequisites for those classes that require them. Then it will add the student's name to the class lists and complete the registration. But suppose that the student asks to enroll in section 3 of History 102 and that this section is full. The computer will tell the student that sections 1, 2, 5, and 7 are still open and that, of these, only section 2 will fit his or her schedule. The student can either select that or modify the schedule in some other way to get the best program. When the student is satisfied that the program is satisfactory, he or she so indicates to the computer and is enrolled in the specified classes. At the end of the registration period, class lists are prepared for the teachers and the registrar, and the summary information is immediately available to various offices.

This program follows closely the procedures of manual registration: the student makes the same kinds of decisions but quicker and more conveniently. Like the manual system, this places a great premium on early registration. When students have registered and left, they cannot be asked to make small changes to accommodate students who will arrive to register later.

Some schools have attempted to go farther, and remove from the student the necessity (and the freedom) to juggle courses around in order to see whether they can fit them in. The student specifies only the courses he or she wants to take; the computer tries all possible alternative combinations of sections to see whether they can be fitted in. If they cannot, it may go back to try to reschedule some other students in order to maximize the number of students who get what they ask for. This kind of registration system, of course, means all the students must be scheduled at once: the students must submit their lists of courses and then, a day or so later, pick up their schedules.

In one such system, which may be taken as typical, students fill out cards indicating the courses (and the sections) they wish to take. These are then keypunched and the complete set of information for all the students makes up one of the three files necessary for the processing. A second file contains the names and student numbers of all the students entitled to register for courses, along with such personal information as address, telephone, and so on. In addition, the file contains the student's major department and level (freshman, sophomore, junior, senior). A third file contains information about the courses: name and number, day and time of each meeting, and the maximum allowable size.

Student requests are processed one at a time (starting with the seniors and working back to the freshmen). A student is enrolled in his classes and his name is added to the class rolls. Eventually, however, a student wants to enroll in a class that is already full. A rather complex set of decisions ensues.

First, all the student's other classes are scheduled, if this is possible. Then the unavailable class is examined again. Is there another section? If so, all the sections are checked to see if there is an opening and if one of them will fit into the hours the student still has free. If the schedule will not allow him or her to be enrolled in one of these sections, the program reexamines other classes the student has been scheduled for. Can he or she get all the classes they want by rescheduling some of these? This may involve a fairly complex effort, particularly since the largest classes are generally the freshman classes and are the last to be treated.

Eventually, if even this effort fails, a note is added to the student's schedule, indicating that he or she will not be able to take the course in question.

The decision-making process attempts to perform in a general way what most students would attempt in a manual system: to work out a schedule allowing them to take the courses they want, by trying different ways of fitting them all in. The development of this system (from requirement analysis to programming and testing) took about two working years: the equivalent of two people working full-time for a year.

The program, as it has been described here,

Figure 12-7 Students working with a computer project

makes some assumptions about the student's desires. If the assumptions are correct, then the decisions made for the student are probably appropriate. But if they are not, some of the student's freedom is taken away. It assumes, for instance, that if a student wants to take History 102, he or she would prefer to take any section of it than none at all. But some people may want to take it only if they can have Professor Jones or only if they can take it after 10 o'clock in the morning, and this program does not allow them to specify these criteria.

The intent of all such registration programs is to simplify and expedite the very complex and confusing registration process—for the students, for the teachers, and for the administration. In doing so, it takes from the students some elements of freedom. For very large colleges, it is hard to imagine registration without computers. In most cases, and for most students, the automation of registration must be regarded as a success. But for those few who want to do things the system does not allow, it must appear a mechanical and dehumanizing procedure.

Summary

The computer has moved naturally and quickly into use as an aid in clerical and business applications in schools. It has also been applied to educational management in such areas as registration. The consequence of these applications is similar to that of applications in business: they have made schools more efficient in operation and they have allowed administrative processes to deal successfully with much larger numbers of students than before. As a consequence, schools (particularly colleges and universities) have been able to grow much larger, and they have sometimes become more impersonal and mechanical in the ways they deal with their students.

The computer in the classroom is something different, however. It presents a totally new set of tools that can be applied to education. The challenge to educators is to find ways of using these tools to make instruction better for the students: richer, more meaningful experiences in learning, more individualized instruction and less rote learning; more learning by practice and less by example; more effective utilization of human resources. Progress in finding the way to make this all come about has been slow, however. Computers in instruction are expensive; they require new skills on the part of teachers and administrators. The actuality, in all but a handful of schools, is well below the potential and the opportunity.

Exercises

1. It has been suggested that using a computer, like using a library, is a basic skill that all students should learn. Suggest some arguments for and against this position.

2. Visit administrative offices in your own school or college and compile a list of computer applications in administration and educational management.

3. Select one administrative application of computers. Find out how it is performed on your campus. If computers are not used, try to find out why.

4. Are computers used for instruction on your campus? Find out what these applications are, why they were implemented, and how successful they have been. Try to talk to both students and teachers about their evaluations.

5. Talk to some computer people about what they think are the potentials of the computer in education. Also talk to some educators at the primary and secondary level as well as in college. Try to analyze and explain the differences of opinion you find.

6. On the basis of what you now know, what do *you* think would be the advantages of computer-based instruction?

7. Select some portion of this course and describe how it might be effectively taught by a computer.

For Further Information

A thorough introduction to the real and potential role of the computer in education, particularly higher education, will be found in *The Emerging Technology* (1). The Gerard and Holtzman books (2 and 3) are useful additional references, since many of the papers in them present more detailed examinations of specific types of applications. Two books have dealt with the problems facing those who attempt to apply computers in the classroom: *Run, Computer, Run* (4) is a brief, readable, common-sense approach to the limitations of technology; *Factors Inhibiting the Use of Computers in Instruction* (5) is a careful analysis of what has slowed down the expected development of this application area. Both have a lot to say.

The book by Hussain (6) is designed for the administrator and explains how information systems are developed in the context of education. *The Management Game* (7) describes at length the business game that was used as an example in the text of this chapter.

There are several periodicals in this area that your library or some member of the faculty may subscribe to; three are listed among the references (8–10).

References

1. Roger Levien, *The Emerging Technology* (New York: McGraw-Hill Book Company, 1972).

2. Ralph Gerard, ed., *Computers and Education* (New York: McGraw-Hill Book Company, 1967).

3. Wayne H. Holtzman, ed., *Computer-Assisted Instruction, Testing, and Guidance* (New York: Harper & Row, 1970).

4. Anthony G. Oettinger and Selma Marks, *Run, Computer, Run* (Cambridge, Mass.: Harvard University Press, 1969).

5. Ernest J. Anastasio and Judith S. Morgan, *Factors Inhibiting the Use of Computers in Instruction* (Princeton, N.J.: EDUCOM, 1972).

6. Khateeb M. Hussain, *Development of Information Systems for Education* (Englewood Cliffs, N.J.: Prentice-Hall, Inc., 1973).

7. F. Warren McFarlan, James McKenney, and John A. Seiler, *The Management Game: Simulated Decision Making* (New York: Macmillan, 1970).

8. *Data Processing for Education* (monthly)

9. *Journal of Educational Data Processing* (bimonthly)

10. *THE Journal: Technological Horizons in Education* (monthly)

Computers in Public Administration

13

The United States is a federated system of government. This means that most of its citizens live under at least five levels of government, each with its own elected officials, taxes, and bureaucracy. These are, typically, city, school district, county, state, and the federal government, and there may be more. Over the country as a whole, there are 80,000 units of government, although this figure may have declined through consolidations and incorporations. They all compete for power and yet with the possible exception of the national government, none of them are big enough to solve our problems. This is because these problems—urban decay, air and water pollution, health care, civil rights, transportation planning, housing, crime, poverty, and energy shortages—are interdependent and respect no arbitrary physical boundaries like state borders, congressional districts or county lines. Thus their solution demands a quality of cooperation and a common set of values that is difficult to achieve.

In 1964, in the Godkin Lectures at Harvard University, Nelson A. Rockefeller presented an idealistic statement of what might best be called the goals of our many-centered form of government. He described it as ". . .a concept of government by which a sovereign people, for their greater progress and protection, yield a portion of their sovereignty to a political system that has more than one center of sovereign power, energy, and creativity. No one of these centers or levels has the power to destroy another. Under the Constitution, for example, there are two principal centers of government power—state and federal. As a practical matter, local government, by delegation of state authority under the principle of 'home rule,' is a

> The skill in structuring problems,
> the ability to communicate with the machine,
> and the speed of calculation, now impose
> demanding responsibilities in the design of
> techniques for ordering information. In...

DATA PROCESSING

Organizing basic information
to be handled by routine procedures.

 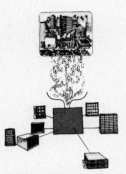

the computer helps bring order to the flood of information our society is producing.

As this mass of collected data grows, so does the task of locating needed information...

third such key center of power. . . . It puts into play a sharing of powers not only among different levels of government, but—on each level—a separation of powers between the legislative, executive, and judicial branches of government. . . . It demands faith in—and an environment for—the free play of individual initiative, private enterprise, social institutions, political organizations, and voluntary associations. . . ." Rockefeller asserted— from the vantage point of the governorship of one of our largest states—that the federal idea fosters the diversity of the states' individual differences within a concept of national unity; permits and encourages creativity in satisfying the needs of the people; gives scope to many energies, beliefs, initiatives, and cultures; prevents excesses of

Figure 13-1 The United States capitol

power and encourages home rule and free enterprise. The extent to which these goals are achieved varies, of course, with the times and to the extent that the leaders we choose believe in them.

Typically, our national approach to solving problems has been to design specific "programs." For example, in recent years we have had Project Headstart and the Poverty Program. The successful programs become major bureaucracies. The role of the computer in this area hopefully is to provide the mechanism that can cross political boundaries, assist the analysis of population needs, and evaluate the effectiveness of new programs and projects. Last, as the bureaucracy grows in size, the computer is used for operational needs in much the same way as in other large organizations.

This use of computers is extensive. If we could count all of the computers in these nearly 80,000 units of government, we would find thousands. We will discuss this usage in terms of national,

state, and local governments; then we will discuss its effects. Justice systems, uses in education, and to some extent uses in health systems, are also governmental uses of computers, but we will not discuss them here, as they are covered elsewhere.

The National Government

The function of the executive branch of the national government is to administer laws passed by Congress. Effective administration of laws, such as those concerned with education, labor, poverty, and welfare, requires data collection. Fund transfers between various levels of government require matching funds, and these in turn require accounting. This all implies data processing. There are now over 6000 computers in use for the national government.

Almost any department of the federal government has vast data-processing problems: the Labor

Department is responsible for up-to-date employment statistics; the Treasury disburses thousands of checks daily; the Veterans Administration runs, among other things, a very large insurance business; Social Security maintains records on virtually all Americans who are working or have ever worked. In these areas, office automation—such as was discussed in the context of business and industry—has found a natural home. Payroll calculations, accounting, and inventory control are as important, as expensive, and as time-consuming in a government agency as they are in a bank, a factory, a school, or an office. The business of some agencies, however, involves so great an amount of data handling that the computer becomes more closely integrated into the work. The most obvious example is that of the Census Bureau.

The Census Bureau.   The Census Bureau conducts a wide range of surveys and produces a large number of statistical analyses. Some of these are conducted more frequently than the ten-year census of population. Data about trade, employment, business, and agriculture is produced periodically. However, the mammoth job of counting the United States population, which occurs every ten years, is the largest processing problem the Bureau faces.

It was previously mentioned that Hollerith's punched cards were first used in the 1890 census. As the census problem grew larger, newer machines and ideas had to be employed. The first commercially produced computer, a Univac, was installed in the Census Bureau in 1951, in time to be used in processing the data collected in the 1950 census.

The use of the computer to tabulate the data once it is collected is understandable; you can well imagine what such an information system must be like. The problem of collecting the many millions of individual reports (one for each household) and converting them into machine-readable form is still a considerable manual task, however. Gradually, more and more of this job has been automated.

In 1960, an optical sensing device known as Fosdic was installed. It allowed the forms that had been coded by hand to be processed directly. Because of this capability, the number of full-time Bureau employees was reduced from 9500 to 4000. In the 1970 census, most households were given a form they could fill in and mail, further eliminating the need for manual processing.

The Census Bureau has become the focus of public attention for two reasons. First, can the information it collects be construed as a threat to the privacy of the citizen? Actually, the Bureau has very elaborate procedures to control the release of information. There are large numbers of requests from researchers in government and industry for special processing of census data. Before any such data is released, the Bureau makes certain that the numbers of people involved in the sample are so large that no inferences can be drawn about any particular person or company.

Second, why are such personal questions asked? Government and private industry are exerting pressures to learn more about people. The statistical information is of considerable social value, although it is sometimes difficult for individual citizens to appreciate the social value that can be gained from a loss of individual privacy.

Internal Revenue Service.   Another major federal computer user is the Internal Revenue Service (IRS), which collects taxes from individuals and businesses. Every individual or married couple

Form 1040

US Department of the Treasury—Internal Revenue Service
Individual Income Tax Return **1974**

For the year January 1–December 31, 1974, or other taxable year beginning _____, 1974, ending _____ 19___

Name (If joint return, give first names and initials of both)	Last name	COUNTY OF RESIDENCE	Your social security number

Present home address (Number and street, including apartment number, or rural route)		Spouse's social security no.

City, town or post office, State and ZIP code	Place label within block	Occu-pation Yours ▶ Spouse's ▶

Filing Status (check only one)

1 ☐ Single
2 ☐ Married filing joint return (even if only one had income)
3 ☐ Married filing separately. If spouse is also filing give spouse's social security number in designated space above and enter full name here ▶
4 ☐ Unmarried Head of Household (See instructions on page 5)
   ▶
5 ☐ Widow(er) with dependent child (Year spouse died ▶19 __)

Exemptions

Regular / 65 or over / Blind
6a Yourself . . . . . . ☐   ☐   ☐   Enter number of boxes checked ▶
 b Spouse . . . . . . ☐   ☐   ☐
 c First names of your dependent children who lived with you _____
   Enter number ▶
 d Number of other dependents (from line 27) . . . . ▶
7 Total exemptions claimed . . . . ▶

8 **Presidential Election Campaign Fund** . . . ▶ Do you wish to designate $1 of your taxes for this fund? . . . ☐ Yes ☐ No
If joint return, does your spouse wish to designate $1? . . . ☐ Yes ☐ No
Note: If you check the "Yes" box(es) it will not increase your tax or reduce your refund.

Please attach Copy B of Forms W-2 here

Income

9	Wages, salaries, tips, and other employee compensation (Attach Forms W-2. If unavailable, see instructions on page 3.)	9
10a	Dividends (See instructions on pages 6 and 13)$ _____, 10b Less exclusion $ ____, Balance ▶ (If gross dividends and other distributions are over $400, list in Part I of Schedule B.)	10c
11	Interest income. [If $400 or less, enter total without listing in Schedule B] [If over $400, enter total and list in Part II of Schedule B].	11
12	Income other than wages, dividends, and interest (from line 38)	12
13	Total (add lines 9, 10c, 11, and 12)	13
14	Adjustments to income (such as "sick pay," moving expenses, etc. from line 43) .	14
15	Subtract line 14 from line 13 (adjusted gross income)	15

● If you do not itemize deductions and line 15 is under $10,000, find tax in Tables and enter on line 16.
● If you itemize deductions or line 15 is $10,000 or more, go to line 44 to figure tax.
● CAUTION. If you have unearned income and can be claimed as a dependent on your parent's return, check here ▶ ☐ and see instructions on page 7.

Tax, Payments and Credits

16	Tax, check if from: ☐ Tax Tables 1–12 ☐ Tax Rate Schedule X, Y, or Z ☐ Schedule D ☐ Schedule G OR ☐ Form 4726	16
17	Total credits (from line 54)	17
18	Income tax (subtract line 17 from line 16)	18
19	Other taxes (from line 61)	19
20	Total (add lines 18 and 19)	20
21a	Total Federal income tax withheld (attach Forms W-2 or W-2P to front) 21a	
b	1974 estimated tax payments (include amount allowed as credit from 1973 return) . . . . b	
c	Amount paid with Form 4868, Application for Automatic Extension of Time to File U.S. Individual Income Tax Return c	
d	Other payments (from line 65) . . . . d	
22	Total (add lines 21a, b, c, and d)	22

Pay amount on line 23 in full with this return. Write social security number on check or money order and make payable to Internal Revenue Service.

Balance Due or Refund

23	If line 20 is larger than line 22, enter **BALANCE DUE IRS** . . . . ▶ (Check here ▶ ☐ , if Form 2210, Form 2210F, or statement is attached. See instructions on page 7.)	23
24	If line 22 is larger than line 20, enter amount **OVERPAID** . . . . ▶	24
25	Amount of line 24 to be **REFUNDED TO YOU** . . . . ▶	25
26	Amount of line 24 to be credited on 1975 estimated tax. ▶ 26	If all of overpayment (line 24) is to be refunded (line 25), make no entry on line 26.

Sign here

Under penalties of perjury, I declare that I have examined this return, including accompanying schedules and statements, and to the best of my knowledge and belief it is true, correct, and complete. Declaration of preparer (other than taxpayer) is based on all information of which he has any knowledge.

Your signature _____ Date _____

Preparer's signature (other than taxpayer) _____ Date _____

Spouse's signature (if filing jointly, BOTH must sign even if only one had income) _____

Address (and ZIP Code) _____ Preparer's Emp. Ident. or Soc. Sec. No. _____

Please attach Check or Money Order here

Figure 13-2 A familiar form: 1040

with a substantial income must file an annual income tax return. In addition, estimates and quarterly installment payments may be filed. Further, employers must report on taxes withheld and income paid to individuals, banks and corporations must submit reports on interest and dividends paid and received, and so on. People move from one city to another during the year, change jobs, marry, divorce, and change names. The task of pulling together all the documents corresponding to a particular individual or family is a difficult job—so difficult that, until recently, it could not be attempted for large numbers of taxpayers.

Within the past few years the IRS has totally revised its system. Several changes were necessary. First, all records had to be gathered at a single centralized location where they could be sorted appropriately. Second, so many millions of documents were involved that the information had to be totally converted to machine-readable form and the work done by computer. Only in this way could a tax return from a man in California be associated with the estimate he made when he lived in Chicago, the withholding tax paid by his employer in New York, and the dividends paid to him by a company in Utah.

The IRS system has three levels: the district office, the regional center, and the national center. The district office deals directly with the taxpayer, answering questions, making inquiries and investigations, and so on. Tax returns and other IRS documents are sent to the regional centers. There are ten of these, each of which has several hundred terminals for direct data entry. Under peak load, each center is capable of handling from 120,000 to 180,000 documents per day. The information it receives is keyed into the computer, validated and verified, and written on magnetic tape. These tapes are then sent to the national center without further

processing. The computers at the regional centers are small and unsophisticated. Although time-shared among many terminals, the amount of data processing they do is very small. There are plans to convert these to more sophisticated systems.

At the national center, an eighty-million record file (one for each taxpayer or taxpaying entity) is maintained. The computer there updates the file on the basis of the input tapes received from the regional centers and produces several outputs: a refund tape (which is sent directly to the Treasury Department, where another computer reads the tape and produces the checks), bills and delinquency notices (which are printed by the computer and then mailed directly to the taxpayers), and indexes and lists of accounts to be audited (which are sent to the district offices). The national center employs less than 200 people to maintain all of the tax records in the United States.

One noticeable effect of this automation is less tax cheating. A very positive aspect from the point of view of tax policy is that the IRS can now begin to assess the effect of tax legislation in advance and can indicate to Congress how hard various classes of people and businesses will be hit by new tax proposals. This, to some extent, has taken the guesswork out of the tax debates in Congress. Whether it has resulted in fairer taxes or less taxes is still a matter for which congressmen and senators must take the credit or blame as the case may be.

Bureau of the Budget. The Bureau of the Budget has another important use for computers. The federal budget is a very complex affair, amounting to hundreds of summary tables and thousands of pages of text. It is prepared every year in a period of about three months. The inputs from various agencies and departments about their projected activities are tabulated and summarized; project funds that cut across departments are cross-checked for accuracy and consistency. Once the budget is completed, changes may have to be made. The president's office may want to know what would happen if one item is increased or another is eliminated. This may have effects on numerous other departments and agencies, so many of the calculations have to be made again.

The Budget Bureau uses an information management system for all these purposes, maintaining a master budget file of approximately three million characters. Within this system, the budget can obviously be computed and cross-checked more easily than by hand. More important, perhaps, alternative forms of the budget can be created and questions of the "what if" variety can be answered easily and cheaply. An unmanageably complex set of information can be manipulated and studied before it is approved and published. The significance of this use of computers is that the federal budget is the single strongest statement of national policy in the United States.

Military Applications

If the federal government is the largest user of computers in the world, the largest user within government is the Department of Defense. When it is considered that this department includes the Army, Navy, and Air Force, this fact is hardly surprising. The data processing required to maintain so large a collection of personnel, machines, and material, scattered around the globe, is considerable. The bulk of the computing power in the Department of Defense is used, not for exotic tactical and strategic systems, but for the same payroll, accounting, and inventory problems faced in other government departments and in business and industry. However, some of the problems faced by the military establishment are unique and are worth reviewing.

The Defense Supply Agency. The Defense Supply Agency maintains a computer-based inventory system on a grand scale, involving a centralized supply control system with decentralized distribution. Records are maintained on 1.5 million different items. The central system handles the stock records (how many and where?), requisitions (do we have one? where is the closest one to the user?), material levels, reorder status, and so forth. The distribution centers handle the problems of receiving, storing, and shipping materials as directed by the central control system.

The Air Force SPADATS. The Air Force also has a unique use for computers. When the U.S.S.R. and the United States first began launching artificial satellites, it appeared that some American agency should keep a catalog of what was up there and where it was likely to be at any given time. The Air Force was given the responsibility of creating a satellite detection system that would keep track of all artificial objects in space, note when new ones appeared, and predict the paths of old ones. This activity was called Project Space Track, and the system created is known as SPADATS, for Space Detection and Tracking System.

SPADATS involves a worldwide network of observation stations that check to see whether the old objects are still where they are expected to be, when they will re-enter the atmosphere, and whether any new objects appear. This system has some characteristics in common with more elaborate command and control systems, but its objective is purely informational: to detect, track, identify, and catalog all artificial space objects. It

Figure 13-3   A command and control center

is designed to prevent the more sensitive attack warning systems from putting the country accidentally on alert because of a harmless spacecraft.

Weapons Applications.   Also, computers are basic to many weapon systems. Ballistic missiles use them for guidance computations, anti-ballistic missiles use them for intercept calculations, and computers on board surface ships and submarines use them to keep track of where they are. High-performance aircraft also use computers as an intermediary between their supersonic speed and the inadequately slow reaction time of the pilot.

Command and Control Systems.   Finally, some mention must be made of computer-based systems that are more exclusively military in conception and intent. An earlier chapter mentioned the SAGE air defense system as a prototype of a command and control system. Several such systems exist at different levels of command.

Military operations are a complex subject. The responsible military agencies are unable to publish detailed information about the capabilities of their systems because of the help this might be to potential enemies. It is hardly surprising, then, that people have imagined such systems to be more powerful and more dangerous than they really are. These systems are, in large part, information management systems, for a military commander is a manager, too. He or she faces an information handling problem, like the manager in many of our previous examples. Information comes from many sources, much of it, like radar, electronic in origin, so that it must be interpreted. Fact analysis must sometimes be made in great haste so that a decision on how to proceed can be made in a matter of seconds or minutes.

Military data-processing systems are in part process-control systems also, for much of the military commander's power and force is in the form of machines, which can be controlled more conveniently by computers in the hands of personnel rather than by people alone. With faster, more complex, and more sophisticated weapons systems, the military commander needs faster, more complex, and more certain means of controlling them.

Implications of Military Applications. Although such systems are not without attendant dangers, the threat of push-button warfare has sometimes been overdramatized. In fact, in military operations as elsewhere, greater volume and speed of information flow places greater control rather than less over the subordinate decision maker. Important decisions do not have to be made on the spot by the person in charge of local operations; they can be made at the highest military level or even at the super-military, or political, level. The consequences of overt military action are so great today that civilian control of the military has become complex. The president must be continuously informed about any action that United States forces are in or near, whether it be the Sixth Fleet in the Mediterranean, the Strategic Air Command, the Air Defense Command, or our forces in the Pacific. This requirement has probably more than any other escalated the military use of computers. Thus if one were to choose a principle that computers have contributed to, it is the civilian control of the military.

Computers and Congress

At present, Congress does not use computers in a major way, although many bills have been introduced to facilitate computer use. A number of questions are asked whenever the issue is raised: Would computers in Congress change the structure of the institution? Would they increase the bickering and change the balance of power among the branches of government? Would they make Congress more efficient? Threaten the committee system? Decrease the importance of seniority? Or would the old traditions and familiar procedures continue to prevail? Before any serious effort to use computers in Congress can be started, these questions must be faced.

Let us look at some possible, though hypothetical, effects of employing computers in the legislative branch of government. First, by making more relevant information available, computers could facilitate the creation of more informal ad hoc study groups, such as the one that formed around the 1970 antiballistic missile debate. Such committees would compete with existing congressional committees and subcommittees and perhaps would strengthen the entire committee system through vigorous competition. Young, talented, and aggressive congressmen would become familiar with computers and the congressional data base and might be advanced in committee assignments over more senior congressmen. Furthermore, broad information access might further democratize Congress by offering equal information to all members, not just to those on particular committees or with great personal wealth.

Congressmen or senators have to spend a great deal of time responding to constituent requests, attending endless meetings, and informing themselves on substantive matters. They must remain aware of the current needs and desires of their constituencies. By using information systems they can receive more relevant data rather than just more data. However, the central theme of politics concerns values, not mere information. The problem is not essentially one of mechanical and physical assists to Congress; it is more one of establishing priorities and program effectiveness. While computer assistance will not influence Congress' value system, it can provide congressmen with better information on which to base these important judgments.

Computers and the Budget. One might expect that executive branch concern over congressional harassment through questions raised by computer-supplied data would cause that arm of government to attempt to block these kinds of developments. However, the situation is quite the contrary. For example, the Bureau of the Budget is now preparing a budgetary and appropriations data base for use by Congress. Making such extensive data available to congressmen can only serve to broaden their viewpoint. Such awareness could not help but strengthen the congressional case in dealing with the executive branch.

Further, to the extent that modern information systems can make the budgetary process more explicit, they will expose conflicts and disagreements that have never been adequately debated because of obscurity. Since budget processing is easily within the state of the art, it can easily be used to help Congress. As it now stands, except for new programs and a few special analyses, Congress can only compare this year's expenditures with past expenditures. In fact, there are probably fewer than a half-dozen people in Congress today who can develop a comprehensive view of the total budget.

Congress usually has only six months in which to evaluate the president's proposed budget. A computer assist in this area would make its evaluation more meaningful and perhaps even force the executive branch to counter-evaluate the budget and discuss it with Congress.

Implementing a Congressional DP System. The legislative reference service of the Library of Congress started to explore computer possibilities for Congress in the 1950s. Progress has been slow and tentative. The large-scale introduction of computers into Congress can be done in a number of ways. Preferably, a requirements analysis should be performed, and then a preliminary system designed. However, unless the analysis is done properly, the values and priorities that are Congress' real concern will not be revealed and illuminated by the data-processing system, and any system thus created will simply become another source of semi-relevant facts.

The more diverse purposes a computer must serve, the more difficult is the task of developing the system to serve them. Without exaggeration, assessing the information requirements of Congress is the most complex task of this type yet faced because these requirements encompass most of the major goals and objectives of the United States. It will be difficult to select error-free, mechanically compatible, relevant, current information from among the available data bases. Further, a Congress that is dependent on a presidentially designed or program-oriented data base must worry about bias. The net effect of these difficulties has been to slow the process.

Other Benefits. Payoffs have already begun to appear. Increased quality of information is now available to Congress for tax consideration. The ability to manipulate social science data through a

National Data Bank has already been offered to Congress, but progress has been blocked by questions of privacy. The Library of Congress now receives and publishes the status of bills biweekly, and the system has a text editing capability that saves typing time. Eventually this text system will feed directly into an electronic photocomposing system for printing bills.

Figure 13-4 is an accumulation of the lists of proposed applications. A number of these applications have already been tried in state legislatures, and none are so revolutionary that they threaten the power structure in Congress.

Will Change Take Place in Congress?

Motivation for reform and improvement is strong. Time is being wasted, congressmen and their staffs are overworked, the need to be well-informed is becoming more urgent, and, last, the imbalance of power between the legislative and executive branches has been steadily increasing for many years. Congress has been losing the initiative in legislation, in public policy formation, and in the detailed inquiries into the facts of the executive management. Although it can call experts from every walk of life and summon testimony from all executive branches, the executive can outstaff Congress on any given issue. This disadvantage leads to a very real problem of trust and control between the two branches of government. Also, strict constitutional theorists fear for the traditional balance of powers; use of the computer represents one of the few opportunities for Congress to change that balance.

While it is clear that the potential benefits are great, information systems may have more to offer than Congress can accept immediately. At the basic level, the mechanical assists (scheduling meetings, storing and retrieving bills, and so forth) can be easily recognized and implemented with clear payoff and little political conflict. However, as we have seen, such areas as budgetary processing have real political significance for Congress and the executive branches and as such will be more difficult to achieve. Assessing Congress' real information needs for committee and subcommittee action will be the hardest technical and political task. However, it should have the greatest payoff, for it can have a real effect on the totality and range of congressional understanding of the needs and functioning of the nation.

An Overview. There are three basic ways in which information technology can aid Congress: as feedback, for predictions, and as a way of better understanding the enormous complexity of our country.

To learn how to solve the massive problems the United States faces we must be able to assess the results of the solutions we try. Information systems can feed back results of new programs in such a way that both success and failure can be more easily understood.

But, more important, we must learn about problems while they are still manageable. There is an old adage that government cannot plan but can only react to crisis. Crises indeed influence elections and re-elections, but to focus on crisis implies that noncritical matters get less attention. Furthermore, the nature of some of these problems (smog, for instance) is such that by the time they are obvious enough to affect the political fortunes of a congressman or senator they are so locked into our socioeconomic fabric (mobility, automobile design, gasoline production) that they are nearly impossible to solve or have acquired such momentum that they are too expensive to stop. It is possible to decrease crisis-type legislation by

LEGISLATIVE FUNCTIONING

- Authorization, appropriations, and expenditures data
- Committee-oriented substantive data bases; topical research information, survey, and statistical data available on demand.
- Status of pending legislation, including:
  Indexes to congressional documents and the *Congressional Record*
  Calendars
  Witness lists
- The content and statistics of pending legislation
- Pre-vote information on major issues
- Post-vote analytical information
- Information on fiscal managements, including federal contract awards.

ADMINISTRATIVE FUNCTIONING

- Lobbyist activity information
- Mailing lists, including:
  Constituent interest file
  Constituent correspondence file
- Current congressional telephone book

Figure 13-4 Congressional applications

developing better socioeconomic warning indicators and monitoring systems.

The problems of a modern country obey no arbitrary boundaries. Crime, smog, pollution, inequality, education, welfare—these concerns overlap district, regional, and state lines as well as the bureaucratic boundaries of government. The solutions to many of our problems are dependent on understanding the interrelatedness of our society. Education must be improved while we are also working on our crime and health problems. The reduction of smog must be carried out while we are devising better means of transportation. How do proposed budgets or laws relate simultaneously to the negative indicators and the quality of life and economic health of the country? In our opinion, the computer can assist Congress in understanding such questions. Planning solutions requires a wise view of the future. Well used, computers can make a contribution to this interrelated and long-range perspective.

State Government

To most people, state government is remote. With the exception of the highway patrol, state government usually isn't obvious. However if you are a barber, a doctor, a lawyer, a CPA, a schoolteacher, a liquor distributor, a beautician, a nurse, a hunter, a fisherman, a boat owner, a driver or owner of an automobile, it is to the state that you have to go for a license. In most states, this licensing is done by computer. Less obvious are the finances of state government. Most states collect money that they don't spend and spend money that they don't collect. That is to say that states serve as a switching center for the disbursement of federal funds to local government. In addition, states disburse money for workmen's compensation, dependent children, Medicare, the aged, aid to education and school lunch programs. These collections and disbursements of money are done with the help of computers.

Although state governments were slower to get started using computers, as you can see, they are now very involved with them. In general, state governments started out with many small computers. Any department that needed one and could afford it, bought it. In the large states this grew so unwieldy that master plans for data processing were developed, consultants hired, and state data-processing resources centralized. Some of this planning has produced ways of linking units of state government through data sharing and computer sharing. The most outstanding example is in the areas of the highway patrol and drivers' license applications. This linking is done mostly for reasons of efficiency and economy, but it also is recognition of the interrelatedness of the social problems faced by state government. It is truly difficult to deal with our social dislocations through the separated functions of government. Unfortunately, integrating departments of state government through data sharing is difficult (for reasons that follow), and most state data processing is done within the well-prescribed jurisdiction of established departments.

The use of computers often reflects the nature of the environment they are used in. State government is a highly "political" environment. The governor, unlike the president of a large corporation, does not simply issue orders that force the executive departments to fall right in line. There are cases in which some executive departments are independent of the governor because they have sources of tax revenue that the governor can't control. The most common case is highway departments that operate on gas taxes. In other cases, executive departments develop their own relationships with the legislature to protect their own budgets. It is for these reasons that in this environment, statewide plans for integrating data bases or sharing computer resources are often only partial successes. Data and computers are viewed as a source of departmental power, and they are. To illustrate this point further, most states keep statistics on a long list of items. The following short list is typical.

☐ Insurance claims
☐ Land use
☐ Fish and wildlife
☐ Highway accidents
☐ Tourism
☐ Crime
☐ Students
☐ Revenue
☐ Employment
☐ Health
☐ Pollution
☐ Commodity and industrial production
☐ Traffic violations

Most often these are kept in independent departments. It is this data base, if integrated, that could provide a total view of the state's problems and opportunities. This is one of the possibilities that tempt statewide planners to try to integrate the data if not the data processing in state government. Although most of what states do with computers is what any large organization does, (research, personnel records, budgeting, facility management, billing, reporting, scheduling, engineering, forecasting, accounting, inventory control, and test scoring), there are some unique opportunities in state government for uses of simulation.

Simulation. The use of simulation for various purposes at the state level is, if not common, at least not unusual in the larger and wealthier states. Models are used to examine in detail the social and economic impact of highways, water, or land use plans. They are used to evaluate the relations between materials and products entering and leaving the state's economy and can also be used to evaluate potential changes in the mix of industries in the state. Traffic flow models are used for street and highway planning, and models of industry and residential movement help in estimating power requirements.

State Legislatures. Although legislatures are slower than businesses in adopting computers, as of this writing over forty of the fifty states are using them. There are statute retrievel systems, bill drafting systems (editing, typesetting), reapportionment calculations, and budget processing. Arizona, for example, has developed a model of the effects of a school finance law on local school districts.

County Government. Intermediate between state and city government, there is county government. For example, in California, Alameda County has established what they call their People Information System, which is a computer service bureau for all of the county governmental agencies. The list of available services and programs runs to more than

sixty pages; their center is always open. Their customers are the various county departments that use computation: tax collectors, engineers, hospitals, law-enforcement agencies, and auditors. One of their major files is a central index of 200,000 people served by welfare, hospitals, health, and probation agencies.

Municipal Data Systems. Ever since the early 1960s municipalities have been experimenting with the use of computers. As of this writing, over 300 cities are spending more than $40,000,000 per year on computers. This experimentation was forced by their growth, their increasing difficulty in delivering services to the public, and their belief that computers would provide an easy tool for the improvement of management. They saw their problem as too much responsibility (and thus saw the need to narrow the individual bureau chief's span of control) and an inability to control their budgets (and thus saw the need to be able to relate their expenditures directly to public services). Unfortunately, the early application of computers did nothing to help these problems. Their focus was on reducing clerical staffs in payroll, bookkeeping, utility billing, check preparation, and budget status reporting. As such, costly efforts fell short of expectations. Even those attempts at providing a centralized data bank that cut across all city departments' needs for (say) real property data proved to be expensive and rarely relevant to operating and management needs. Early simulation and modeling were similarly narrow in scope and scarcely used in decision making.

These early failures were not due to an inadequate effort or a primitive use of technology; they were caused by the genuine difficulty of municipal government's problems.

Consider the problem of highway routing. It is quite possible for a team of mathematicians and computer programmers to model the effects of a highway passing through a city on a given route. Costs of property acquisition and construction can be estimated for a variety of routes. It is also possible to calculate the effect on traffic on other surface streets. However, the problem of the decision maker is not that simple. He or she must propose a route, say, to a city council, which must in turn open the decision to public debate. Each alternate route affects the value of homes and business prospects along that route differently. Neighborhoods are destroyed and new ones are created. Human values are involved. These are far more difficult decisions than those involved in running a business or the design of equipment. The intellectual cliché that a nation that could go to the moon could surely solve the problems of the cities was misleading. The problem was not simply to technically improve the standard way of doing business. The cities had to undergo a conceptual revolution.

This took place over the last half of the 1960s and resulted in 1969 in a program sponsored by the Housing and Urban Development Department. They issued grants to six* cities between 50,000 and 500,000 to develop information systems.

There are four basic concepts (and this is the conceptual revolution) in these new systems:

☐ The information technology must be integrated with both routine and high-level decision processes.
☐ There must be departmental reorganization to take advantage of the new technology.

☐ There must be improved understanding of the role of officials.
☐ There must be the development of new skills and, in particular, an understanding of information technology.

In part, the scope of a city's responsibilities and this new integrated view of data processing can be seen in figure 13-5. It groups functions, in the outer circle, by major agency. The next inner circle reports through an inner circle of techniques to the decision-making functions of operating, planning, and managing. The techniques circle has a few blocks that are not self-explanatory: PERT/CPM, PPBS and Geo-Coding. We will explain briefly.

Geo-Coding refers to a unique problem in city management. Any house in any city in the country is likely to be in a half-dozen different "districts." It's in a city, a county, a fire district, a school district, a police precinct, a tax region, a zipcode area and so on. And the house next door may be in one or more different districts. City records are kept by different departments in different districts. The Geo-Coding technique, aided by a computer, allows street addresses, for example, to be translated from district to district, and thus allows for communication between the files.

PERT/CPM (Program Evaluation and Review Technique/Critical Path Method) is a technique for scheduling complex projects by representing each project as a network of interrelated events. The periodic event reporting is then related to the network that represents the total project, and a new schedule is produced. For complex projects a computer is required.

PPBS (Program Planning and Budgeting System) is a system of accounting for costs of operation in such a way that the total costs of government

*Charlotte, N.C.; Wichita Falls, Tex.; St. Paul, Minn.; Long Beach, Ca.; Reading, Pa.; Dayton, O.

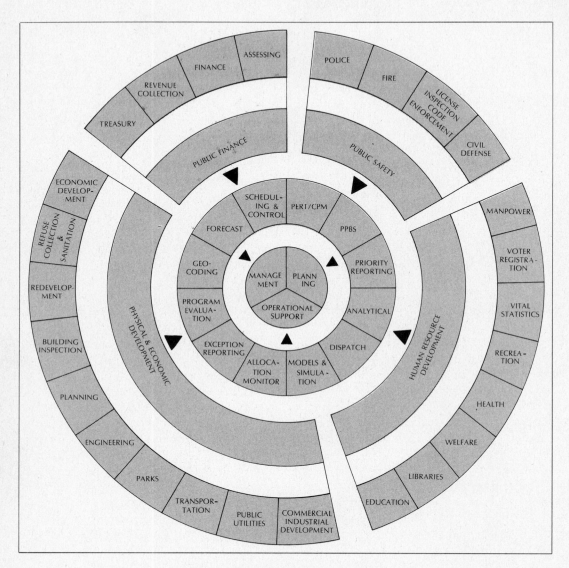

Figure 13-5 Municipal data processing

are allocated to the specific services that are delivered to the public. As budgets are refined, it takes a computer to calculate the effect of planned changes in services on the many departments involved in producing a given service. For example, if juvenile delinquency is viewed broadly, then in addition to the police budget, added efforts to reduce the problem would involve the areas of education, health, welfare, recreation, and parks.

Thus it must be possible to process all department budgets according to the common purposes of their service.

The types of planning that advanced cities have primarily been involved in are for transportation, sewage, school attendance, and air pollution purposes.

The benefits to date have been both specific and general:

□ Cost reduction and avoidance of future costs
□ Improved administration
□ Improved public service

Today, the cost of personnel is sixty to eighty percent of the cost of city government. Without automation, city personnel costs tend to rise as fast as the city population grows. If, for example, a city has an assessment and tax system that is capable of automatically processing 20,000 parcels of property, the cost of handling 40,000 parcels of property is only slightly greater. Some of the improved services reported are: faster response to calls for help from the police, less paperwork required to deal with city agencies, and fairer property taxes.

Impact on Government

The computer affects government both directly and indirectly. Directly, the computer tends to make it possible for government operations to get larger without great expense. A serious consideration is the extent to which government will become dependent on computers. There is a tendency to use automated systems in government, with the consequent growth in areas such systems encourage: bigness, dispersion, and complexity.

There is a reasonable doubt as to whether all of this has made government more effective. It is certainly more efficient at what it does already, but it can't be claimed to be more responsive to the needs of the people except in a mechanical sense. This can be seen even more dramatically in the social welfare programs that came out of the turmoil of the 1960s. By now the judgment on most of them has been negative. Thus it can't be expected that introducing a new tool would revolutionize public service. However, the computer has certainly helped.

Exercises

1. Pick any area not discussed in this chapter in which government uses computers, such as in county welfare data processing. Find out what they do with it and what information they store. What social issues does this system pose? How does it affect people?

2. Assume that you are the head of a local poverty agency that is running a job training program. You have limited funds, so you cannot accept every applicant. What information would you want to have about the trainees and what limits would you place on releasing this information to your trainees' prospective employers?

3. One of the problems in keeping the cities habitable is maintaining open space for parks. A city's zoning affects its ability to attract new industry and thus tax revenue to run the city. Neighboring cities compete for new industry. What information would you need, as planning commissioner, to select a new area for a park? What departments of the city would you go to for this information? What problems would you expect to find in getting this data? (If you want to research this question, look in the literature of "land-use" studies.)

4. Information from the 1970 census is available in the form of computer tape as well as in printed

documents. Who uses this kind of information? In what way is it more convenient than books?

5. If you were a citizen of Alameda County, what would you say were the arguments for and against a "People Information System" such as the one described? Would you be for it or against it? How do you think your own position (wealth, age, job, social station) would affect your decision?

6. Recall the chance remark by the aide to the mayor of a large city we quoted anonymously in the first chapter who expected that if he had access to all the data kept in the city's data bank, he could keep his boss in office forever. What do you think of that possibility now?

7. Do you see any relationship between our "federated" form of government and the threat of computers?

For Further Information

In general, the best place to find out about government in the library is in the government publications room. There you will find magazines like (1), the Public Administration Services issues, (2), and (3) and special studies like (4). The work that we quoted Nelson Rockefeller from (5) is also likely to be found there too. It is short and well written. The first comprehensive work in this field was the Hearle and Mason book, (6). It is still worth reading and, sad to say, some of the fine goals they foresaw have still not been realized. A more recent publication by Hearle (7) gives an extensive introduction to the literature of the field as well as a view of this lack of progress. (8) is a rather protracted study of bureaucratic processes and it is generally easy to read, if dour. By way of contrast and realistic hope there is (9). (10) gives an insight into the use of computer simulation in social decision making with some case studies in which large-scale simulation models were used to aid planning and development in San Francisco and Pittsburgh. (11) gives a description of some thirty-five federal information systems. (12) isn't much as bedtime reading, but browse through it just to see how extensive the use of computers in government is. (13) and (14) give some concrete details of the question of computers in Congress, which we have had too little space for. If you want to go farther in a more complex book on computers in public administration, try (15). Similarly, if you want to know more about command and control systems, start with (16), but don't expect to find Dr. Strangelove there.

References

1. J. E. Dever, "A Comprehensive Municipal Management Information System," *Public Management* (May 1973).

2. *Public Administration Review* (monthly)

3. Kenneth L. Kraemer, "The Evolution of Information Systems for Urban Administration," *Public Administration Review* (July–Aug. 1969).

4. *Automated Data Processing in State Government, Status, Problems, and Prospects,* a Study by the Council of State Governments and Public Administration Service (Chicago, Ill.)

5. N. A. Rockefeller, *The Future of Federalism* (Cambridge, Mass.: Harvard University Press, 1964).

6. Edward F. R. Hearle and R. Mason, *A Data-Processing System for State and Local Governments* (Englewood Cliffs, N.J.: Prentice-Hall, Inc., 1963).

7. E. F. R. Hearle "Information Systems in State and Local Governments," in C. A. Cuadra, ed., *Annual Review of Information Science and Technology,* vol. 5.

8. K. C. Laudon, *Computers and Bureaucratic Reform* (New York: John Wiley & Sons, 1974).

9. "Information Systems: The Search for a New Approach," *Nation's Cities* (January 1972).

10. Garry D. Brewer, *Politicians, Bureaucrats, and the Consultant; a Critique of Urban Problem Solving* (New York: Basic Books, 1973).

11. Saul Herner and Mathew J. Vellucci, eds., *Selected Federal Computer-Based Information Systems* (Washington, D.C.: Information Resources Press, 1972).

12. *Inventory of Automatic Data Processing Equipment in the United States* (Washington, D.C.: U.S. Government Printing Office, 1971).

13. Kenneth Janda, "Features of an Information System for Congress," *Proceedings of the ACM Conference* **21:**361–72.

14. Ernest C. Baynard, "Computers In the Congress," *The Honeywell Computer Journal,* **6:**4 (1972).

15. B. G. Schumacher, *Computer Dynamics in Public Administration* (Washington, D.C.: Spartan, 1967).

16. "Command and Control," *Science and Technology* (October 1948).

The Administration of Justice

14

In this chapter, we will look into the area of justice in the United States and its administration by law enforcement, the courts, and corrections. All of these areas have been involved with computers, but the field of law enforcement has shown far more interest and has obtained far more benefit from their use. Therefore most of our discussion will focus on the ways the police use computers. In order to understand how computers have affected law, order, and justice in our society, we must first look at the size of the crime problem and the practical difficulties faced by the police. Then we will review a capsule history of law-enforcement use of computers before we discuss specific applications. Last, we will consider the social impact of this use of computers.

Crime costs the United States an estimated fifty billion dollars a year. Property damage due to crime is estimated to be one hundred million dollars a year. At the present time there are about two million people in jails and prisons, and this represents two kinds of losses: We lose the productivity of two million people and we have to support them while they are in jail. Inestimable in numbers is the loss to people who are afraid to take a walk at night, shun strangers, and fear the streets.

Arrayed against this problem are some forty thousand law enforcement agencies, with over two hundred thousand sworn officers, nearly twenty thousand judges, and four thousand detention centers that cost the public approximately one billion dollars in taxes a year.

The Practical Difficulties

Applying the computer to law enforcement shows what a problem this area is. Law enforcement is largely a local function. Cities, counties, and states elect or appoint their own officials and pass their own laws for them to enforce. These laws vary considerably; what is a felony in one district may be only a misdemeanor in another. Each agency has a high degree of independence. Yet on many matters, like narcotics enforcement, more than one agency may become involved in the same investigation. This involvement may or may not be cooperative, and on occasion a lack of cooperation has even resulted in officers from different organizations shooting at each other. The limits on cooperation may be caused by pride in their own organizations, a desire for individual recognition, or distrust of each other's honesty.

The criminal in this century is highly mobile. Forgers, burglars and murderers cross state lines in stolen cars, change identities and launder money with great ease; thirty percent of the criminal records show offenses in more than one state. It is for these reasons that the police have looked to computer-communications networks to combat the mobile criminal. The independence of law-enforcement agencies and the institutional difficulties they have in cooperating is what puts the computer-communications network at the center of so many public controversies.

Just on the basis of what has been said so far, it is not hard to understand why police protection is imperfect, incomplete, difficult, and laden with errors and injustices. However, this becomes even more evident when we consider the sociology of the police.

Police departments, as we know them, are relatively recent. It wasn't long ago that protection was a matter of private force or hired thugs. Historically, police departments have been the haven of spoilsmen, and some are still corrupt. The police present an interesting dilemma. Most police officers work alone or in pairs. Thus police departments need highly trained individuals who can react intelligently and independently to a variety of situations; yet they are essentially military organizations depending very much on rank, rule, and discipline to function well. In many cases, police departments are isolated from the community they serve by a misunderstanding public and by their own belief that no one but the police can understand their problems. They are under intense public scrutiny, and often it is hostile.

Individual police officers must risk their lives for very little pay, and surviving spouses collect little. In many cases the police officer contacts criminals with a great deal of money. These circumstances hold the potential for graft and corruption. The police are subject to both the standards and expectations of the community they serve. Thus they are sometimes in the position of having to overlook illegal activities like gambling and prostitution if that is what their community wants. They are expected to be brave, forgiving, and psychologically sensitive—all for perhaps $10,000 a year. In almost every other field of services, the public is able to accept the maxim "you get what you pay for"—except this one.

Many times in the history of our country, the suggestion of a national police force has arisen. A national police force, with uniformity of standards, enforced cooperation, and less cost through duplication would, it is suggested, better solve our crime problem. However, our country deliberately accepts an imperfect system of law enforcement rather than take the risk of tyranny that a national police force brings with it. In fact, it is a deliberate recognition of the imperfections of our system of justice that biases the processes toward the release of the guilty rather than risk the imprisonment of the innocent.

The Role of Technology

In the last decade, the police have looked to new technology to make them more efficient, less subject to error, and faster to respond to calls for help from the community. The courts and correction authorities also are using information technology to be better informed about the people that they process. In addition to computers, many new techniques have been considered. Non-lethal weapons and voice printing are two. In the future, automatic classification and searching of fingerprints may be used also, but this expectation is at least as remote as the automatic recognition of handwritten script discussed in chapter seven on artificial intelligence. Communications technology has contributed almost as much as computers. Improved communications from the central station to the cars in the field, from the cars to patrol officers, and between states and nations, have all improved the chances that criminals will be captured and have contributed to the safety of officers in the field.

Nationwide, the use of computers varies, depending on the availability of money, the degree of local interest, crime rates and patterns, and the sophistication of the local police department. Most departments are low on money and are relatively unsophisticated, but some, like Chicago, even have officers who are competent programmers and analysts. In this regard, the FBI is a good model.

Until the early 1960s the use of computers by the police was mostly limited to punched-card processing of individual files, and even that was rare. The first event of real significance, oddly enough, was not generated by the police but by an Eastern branch of organized crime. In 1957, in a small town in upstate New York called Appalachin, a meeting of organized crime figures was discov-

ered. The investigation and prosecution of that conspiracy stretched out over a number of years and drew the principal prosecutor into the files of over two hundred police departments. That man, Eliot H. Lumbard, conceived the idea of connecting the nearly 4000 independent police agencies of the state of New York in one integrated network for sharing and improving information for investigative purposes. In 1963, the System Development Corporation undertook an initial assessment of the problem, and by the late sixties the system was operational under Dr. Robert Gallati. It is called the New York State Identification and Intelligence System (NYSIIS).

The development of the FBI's National Crime and Information Center was conceived in 1966. It started with fifteen control terminals and one field office. In 1967 the first computer-to-computer link was established with the California Highway Patrol, and the tie to St. Louis, Missouri, followed soon after. The FBI's system started with five basic files: wanted persons, stolen vehicles, license plates, guns, and property, and grew in 1968 to stolen securities and aircraft. In 1969, a stolen boat file was added, and in 1971 the work on criminal histories of convicted offenders began. There are now NCIC terminals in each state. The NCIC will be covered in more detail below.

Along with these systems developments, a key event took place in 1965. The then governor of California, Edmund G. Brown, let a number of contracts to aerospace corporations in California to study, among others, the problems of crime and delinquency. Space General, a California aerospace corporation, did a groundbreaking analysis of the problems of justice. It was the first time that a technical study had looked at all the institutions of justice and tried to assess the costs and benefits to society if our arrangements for law, order, and justice were changed. The study was criticized as naïve, and in some ways it was, but its contribution was its idea—the process of justice had to be looked at as a whole rather than in conventional parts.

This was followed by a 1967 study by President Johnson's Crime Commission of, among other subjects, the contributions that technology in general could make. This led to the establishment in 1968 of the Law Enforcement Assistance Administration under the Safe Streets Act of 1968. This branch of the U.S. Department of Justice was given funds to help provide new technology to local law-enforcement agencies. This single act has done more to promote the upgrading of law enforcement's use of computers than any other development.

Thus with this necessarily brief survey, we will examine some details of the use of computers in law enforcement. We will describe the NCIC today; the Santa Clara County (California) Information Control System; the Kansas City, Missouri, ALERT I-II Enforcement Response System; the data processing done in the courts in Philadelphia, Pennsylvania; and the Connecticut Department of Corrections' data processing. Last, since so much of the police's time is taken up with matters having to do with automobiles, we will describe the Vehicular Traffic Control System of Wichita Falls, Texas.

Applications

NCIC. Since 1908 it has been the FBI's responsibility to investigate violations of federal criminal statutes. It has investigative responsibility for some 185 matters that include bank robbery, kidnapping, interstate auto theft, internal security, organized crime, and airplane hijacking. With a budget of about $300 million, the FBI employs 19,500 people who conduct roughly 1,000,000 investigations per year. It has been possible, in the past, for the FBI to justify this budget solely by the value of the property it has recovered.

For about fifty years the FBI has exchanged information with local law enforcement. The FBI's National Crime and Information Center, which is the modernization of this exchange, has, as we said, been in existence for some time. Before we go into detail, consider these case histories of the system in action:

The Arlington, Texas, police department arrested a man on a local "suspicious persons" charge stemming from a citizen's complaint. Because of lack of background information on the man's status, the police asked for an NCIC check with the available identifying data they had. They were informed that the man in their custody was a fugitive from Alabama.

An example of the advantage of having stolen property placed in the NCIC files involved a burglary in a small Midwestern town that resulted in the loss of four expensive hunting guns. The descriptions of these guns were entered in the NCIC. Four months later, an officer of the Missouri highway patrol investigated an automobile accident and found two hunting guns in the wrecked car. This officer made an inquiry of the NCIC on the serial numbers of the guns and immediately learned they were loot from the previous burglary. Further investigation solved the burglary and revealed that two of the guns had been subsequently sold to an innocent purchaser.

Another example of the NCIC's valuable contribution to the recovery of stolen property occurred in Arizona. The Tucson police department makes NCIC inquiries on all major items pawned in local pawnshops. During one month, they recovered a

Figure 14-1 NCIC

radio stolen in Vermont, a television set stolen in New York, a rifle stolen in Pennsylvania, a tape recorder stolen in Illinois, two rifles and a pistol stolen in different cities in California, and two guns stolen in a local theft.

A New York state police officer stopped a vehicle with an out-of-state license plate, and, while talking to the driver, discovered ammunition in the glove compartment. A search uncovered three pistols and a sawed-off shotgun. An NCIC check through the New York State Police Information Network disclosed that two of the pistols had been stolen in North Carolina and one in Florida. The five occupants of the car were arrested, and a further search of the car revealed thirty-eight payroll checks stolen in an Indiana burglary and seventy-five checks taken in a Florida burglary. The five occupants, it was determined, were wanted in Indiana on felony larceny charges. One of them was on parole from both Indiana and California—the California charge being homicide. This one

vehicle stop and NCIC check by the New York state police officer resulted in thirty-three felony and ten misdemeanor charges.

The system also serves to protect law-enforcement officers by warning them when they are dealing with dangerous felons. Those who doubt the necessity of this need only consider that every year hundreds of officers are killed in the line of duty.

In the following paragraphs, we will discuss the NCIC itself, its protections, and the social questions its existence raises.

System Description. As of this writing, the computer installation at FBI headquarters in Washington consists of an IBM 360 Model 65 with a two-million byte memory; IBM, Telex, and Calcomp disks; and IBM communications transmission control units. This equipment communicates with forty-eight computers and manual terminal devices. These serve thirty-one state agencies and

Table 14.1 National Crime Information Center Annual Transactions, 1968–74

	ENTRIES	INQUIRIES	CLEARS	OTHER	YEARLY TOTAL	DAILY AVERAGE
1968	923,000	3,274,688	400,036	2,427,373	7,025,097	19,194
1969	1,351,095	7,844,670	541,348	3,849,267	13,586,380	37,223
Percent increase over 1968	46.4	139.6	35.3	58.6	93.4	93.9
1970	1,632,749	11,515,851	580,416	5,901,217	19,630,233	53,781
Percent increase over 1969	20.8	46.8	7.2	53.3	44.5	44.5
1971	1,887,564	14,364,308	664,148	8,187,063	25,103,083	68,776
Percent increase over 1970	15.6	24.7	14.4	38.7	27.9	27.9
1972	1,936,435	20,008,408	715,510	10,491,519	33,049,644	90,547
Percent increase over 1971	2.60	39.3	7.73	28.1	31.7	31.7
1973	2,082,230	22,690,866	766,054	14,995,311	40,529,174	111,039
Percent increase over 1972	7.52	13.4	7.10	42.9	22.6	22.6
1974	2,298,152	28,272,976	761,679	21,938,498	53,271,305	145,949
Percent increase over 1973	10.4	24.6	.057 −	46.3	31.4	31.4

SOURCE: *FBI Law Enforcement Bulletin,* February 1972 (revised March 1975)

seventeen metropolitan area systems providing online access to six thousand law-enforcement agencies in the United States and Canada. The communications lines are fully dedicated (non-dial-up) and there is no dial-up service allowed.

The growth of this system can be seen in table 14.1, which gives the last published history of transaction rates from 1908 to 1971. By the time you read this, the daily transaction rate will be close to 100,000.

The size of the system's files is shown in table 14.2. This growth was accomplished mostly by online entry by state and local agencies. The tremendous growth rate both in transactions and file size is caused by the system coming into use, not by increases in the crime rate.

One measure of success of the system is the number of times that inquiries result in the identification of a wanted fugitive or an item of stolen property—a "hit." As of this writing, the number of hits exceeds 700 per day. Other benefits are the decreases in the necessities for communicating through a nationwide law-enforcement teletype system, posting of wanted notices manually, and maintaining files manually.

Independent of the previously mentioned files, in 1968 the FBI began to consider a criminal history file (distinct from the wanted persons file). It took three years to work out the answers to some very hard questions like degree of centralization, record content, standard classification of crimes, and security and confidentiality protections. The final NCIC criminal history record that evolved is a brief index to state records, not a centralization of all criminal records in the country. This is possible because seventy percent of all criminals confine their efforts to one state. The entry of records to the NCIC can be made only by a responsible law-enforcement agency authorized to make entry into the system. Such computer entry must be supported by a criminal fingerprint card. Only convictions of serious crimes are recorded in the criminal history file. Thus excluded are: juvenile offenders, drunks, vagrants, traffic offenders, gamblers, loiterers, and those who disturb the peace and break curfew. There are exceptions, of course. For example, traffic violations involving arrests or manslaughter, driving under the influence of drugs or liquor, and "hit and run" are included. Social history data (narcotics, civil commitment, or mental

Table 14.2 National Crime Information Center, File Growth, 1967–74*

	TOTAL RECORDS	WANTED PERSONS	STOLEN VEHICLES	STOLEN LICENSE PLATES	STOLEN FIREARMS	STOLEN ARTICLES	STOLEN SECURITIES	STOLEN BOATS	CCH**
December, 1967	346,124	18,676	130,304	31,118	121,245	44,781			
December, 1968	743,950	30,082	246,640	81,800	191,371	141,107	52,950		
Percent increase over 1967	114.9	61.1	89.3	162.9	57.8	215.1			
December, 1969	1,447,148	50,913	393,156	146,819	254,085	319,763	281,554	858	
Percent increase over 1968	94.5	69.2	59.4	79.5	32.8	126.6	431.7		
December, 1970	2,453,662	77,118	584,894	208,352	343,220	513,373	724,326	2,379	
Percent increase over 1969	69.6	51.5	48.8	41.9	35.1	60.5	157.3	177.3	
December, 1971	3,330,220	114,497	755,879	252,735	441,591	715,444	1,045,629	4,445	
Percent increase over 1970	35.7	48.5	29.2	21.3	28.7	39.4	44.4	86.8	
December, 1972	4,252,129	117,481	837,523	288,235	549,858	865,502	1,344,504	6,809	242,217
Percent increase over 1971	27.7	2.60	10.8	14.0	24.5	21.0	28.6	53.2	
December, 1973	5,014,385	138,955	898,515	344,397	669,549	990,274	1,526,728	8,842	437,125
Percent increase over 1972	17.9	18.3	7.30	19.5	21.7	14.4	13.6	29.9	80.5
December, 1974	5,556,382	154,954	958,495	342,276	799,388	1,176,886	1,607,088	11,325	505,970
Percent increase over 1973	10.8	11.5	6.67	0.61–	19.4	18.8	5.26	28.1	15.7

* 12/1/67 through 12/1/74

**The Computerized Criminal History File (CCH) became operational November, 1971.

SOURCE: *FBI Law Enforcement Bulletin,* February 1972 (revised March 1975)

hygiene commitment) is not included unless it is part of the criminal justice process. The record contains personal identification, descriptive data, number of times arrested, charges, corrections, last arrest, and court and custody status.

System Protection. The system is protected to the maximum extent possible against error, subversion, and misuse. The protections against error include elaborate procedures for doublechecking and periodically reviewing records submitted by the control terminal agencies. This is done both at the FBI and the control terminal agency, both manually and automatically. The NCIC is physically protected and its personnel are screened. The use of dedicated communications lines restricts penetration through the use of the telephone. Use logs are maintained to identify users. The FBI insists that all computers that communicate directly with the NCIC be under the management control of a responsible criminal justice agency. This causes a difficulty in those states that are too small to justify a computer dedicated solely to law enforcement. Only criminal justice agencies are permitted to use these records. Finally, the subject of these records can challenge their contents. It is a matter of stated policy that the FBI will not knowingly act in any manner to infringe upon an individual's right to privacy.

Social Questions: What Are They? One indication of the degree of concern for the effect of this system and the criminal history file in particular is the number of official bodies investigating it. The vice president of the United States heads a domestic council committee on the right of privacy. The Senate committee on the judiciary has a subcommittee on constitutional rights concerned with it. The House of Representatives has a similar com-

mittee. These are all considering legislation dealing with various aspects of the problem—rights to challenge, sealing of records, the accompaniment of arrest by court disposition data, expunging records, and the use of criminal records by licensing agencies. These issues have been influenced by court decisions as well. For example, in 1971, the federal district court in Washington, D.C., in the Menard case, ordered the FBI to cease distributing criminal history information for licensing and employment purposes. Congress reversed this order in 1972.

At present, the administration of the system is essentially in the hands of the FBI with relatively little clear guidance from Congress. This is more of a tribute to the complexity of the matter than negligence. Each issue at hand involves fifty sets of state laws and the basic question of civil rights versus efficiency of law enforcement. In chapter eighteen, we will go further into detail on the efforts of Project Search and the NCIC advisory board to resolve some of these questions.

Santa Clara County, California

Santa Clara County has in recent years evolved from an agricultural region to a giant urban complex. This growth has brought with it problems of drug abuse, congestion, and alcoholism, as well as urgent needs for public assistance, mass transit, and improved law enforcement. In response, the county government and the sixteen city governments have joined in an effort to develop a Criminal Justice Information Control System. In order to take advantage of this new tool, these seventeen independent political bodies had to learn how to cooperate. They did, and today in Santa Clara County it is possible to monitor the progress of a defendant through the entire criminal justice process. A network of eighty online terminals processes thousands of bookings and complaints a day. This system has two objectives: improved criminal justice operations and support of comprehensive justice planning.

The person-case information includes booking; charges; future court appearances; jail release dates; notices to the probation department of arrested probationers; and custody, complaint, calendaring, probation, and disposition information. These are the records created as the person passes through the justice system. This data base, in turn, supports institutional planning and staffing; law enforcement deployment; budgeting for courts, corrections, and the police; and eventually an evaluation of the effectiveness of these decisions. The statistics compiled are used for probation recommendations and crime prevention models. The Law Enforcement Assistance Administration provided the funds for this development. The work began in 1970 and evolved through the following stages. The first part of the system to be developed was the criminal justice operation concerned with the individual progress from booking through final disposition. The next phase brought in adult probation, the district attorney, courts and other police departments. Then the system progressed to direct connection with AMIS (the California State Department of Motor Vehicles System), AUTO STATIS (California's system for keeping track of stolen, wanted, and recovered cars and license plates) and the NCIC. The next stage provided bail-setting information for judges, witness and attorney scheduling information, and full court recording. The last part of the system to be developed was the juvenile component.

Let's follow a suspect a little way into the system to see how it works. When an arresting officer

stops a suspect, he or she radios a dispatcher requesting identification of the suspect. A computer terminal operator uses whatever information the officer provides: driver's license number, social security number, name, date of birth, height, weight, place of birth, race, and sex to check against 120,000 of the county's own records. An NCIC check can also be run. Let us assume that the computer finds that the suspect is currently on probation. The system's response must guide the officer's choice of action and consequent risk. If the suspect is identified as a felon, the type of felony record must be given to the officer in the field. If the suspect is indicated as dangerous, he or she must be treated as such. Many an officer has been killed in the field for lack of this information. If the circumstances warrant, the officer transports the suspect to jail where he or she is booked. The booking officer institutes another search of the files for this suspect, and more than one probable identity may be found. To obtain all possible identities, the system uses a name-processing system that comes up with all possible names that sound the same as that given by the suspect. The 120,000 records represent 285,000 possible names, aliases, nicknames, and alternate spellings. The booking officer must use other information to narrow the choice of identities until fingerprint identification makes final identification possible. If no previous arrest record is found, the terminal operator must start a new one. If there is a previous booking record, the operator updates such statistics as last known address, weight, and marital status. The booking time, date, agency, arresting officer, and charge are recorded; vehicular specifics are entered, and the suspect is formally booked.

The information provided so far now may be used to notify Probation of the involvement of one of their probationers, the public defender may be notified of a need for his or her services, and the police department now has a record of the officer's activity. A record is kept of the facility where the suspect is housed, special hospital data, status information (such as misdemeanor, juvenile, drug, sex offender, etc.), and release date. Thus the public defender's office can use the system to locate its clients, and the prosecution can locate persons in custody for questioning.

The significance of the Santa Clara County system is that it links cities, counties, and state in a sharing of information that does not threaten the independence of any of these agencies. Secondly, the opportunities for nightmarish errors such as prosecuting a person for the wrong offense or losing someone in the system are reduced. Last, it is most difficult to analyze the improvement in order and justice. It is much easier to document disorder and injustice.

Kansas City, Missouri

The police department of Kansas City is the twenty-fifth largest in the nation. It serves a population of 500,000 people spread over 316 square miles. Kansas City is ranked eighteenth in crime rate in the United States. Its law-enforcement system has many of the same goals and problems as Santa Clara County's. The first difference can be seen on the map (figure 14-2) showing Kansas City's communications system. It has an interstate communications link with the nearby state of Kansas. Secondly, its workload is higher than Santa Clara County's. On a monthly basis, it handles 650,000 transactions for its region and 141,000 to the FBI system in Washington, D.C. It, like Santa Clara County, communicates with its statewide system and the highway patrol.

The history of this system began in 1965 when Chief of Police Clarence Kelley (now director of the FBI) saw the need for a real-time computer system to support the police officers in the street; this orientation has remained throughout development. By 1968 the system had gone operational with an IBM 360/40 and by 1971 it had grown to a larger computer with the smaller one becoming a back-up computer. Since police computers are on duty twenty-four hours a day, seven days a week, this "back-up" role of a second computer becomes very important.

Kansas City has successfully tested mobile computer terminals in squad cars that can communicate directly with the central computer. Thus officers in a squad car do not have to go through a terminal operator to get information from the computer. Figure 14-3 shows such an installation.

The Kansas City system has been developed in two phases. The first, called ALERT I, is designed primarily to serve the officers in the field and secondarily to provide management reports on offense, arrest, and traffic statistics and daily intelligence summaries, pick-up reports, case clearances, and stolen auto data.

The second part of the system is called ALERT II. It serves the prosecutor and the courts. Since the aspirations of ALERT I are very similar to those described in Santa Clara, we will describe their support to the municipal court under ALERT II.

This court tries 9000 traffic cases and 2500 general ordinance cases each month. To help it do this, the system promptly and accurately determines the nature of the defendant's prior criminal involvement for the court, the city prosecutor, prosecuting attorneys, probation department, and the Alcohol Safety Action Program. It provides this information online to all these agencies. Further use of the system can be seen in figure 14-4.

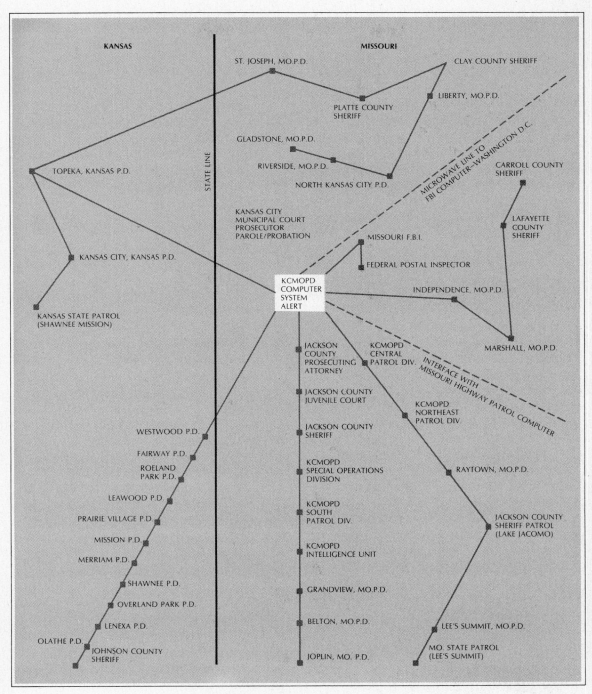

Figure 14-2 The Kansas City system

Figure 14-3 A terminal in a squad car

Long before the public became alarmed by the police's use of computers, Kansas City instituted a system to protect the security and privacy of its records that is outstanding in the United States. It has done this by a combination of policy, procedure, and disciplinary actions for the infringement of civil rights.

In summary, this system serves forty agencies within its area, two states, and the FBI. Kansas City credits, at least in part, its ability to operate with only four police officers per square mile (as compared to a national average of 7.3 for cities of its size), to the existence of this system.

Philadelphia, Pennsylvania

The staggering workload and case backlog of the courts today acutely hinder a defendant's right to "speedy" justice. In many parts of the country, it takes months to bring a criminal case to trial, and civil cases can wait six years and more. This delay contributes to the crime rate, because some defendants out on bail are free to commit more crimes. This can happen when the court doesn't have the resources to check a defendant's record before granting bail. The unfairness of this delay can be seen in the cases of people who are too poor to make bail and must serve time before being acquitted or, say, those injured people who have to wait for many years for a court to force an insurance company to pay their medical bills.

The Common Pleas Court of Philadelphia has installed an IBM 360/40 principally to schedule and operate the court. It has significantly reduced the court's backlog. Criminal cases are now on a two to four-week cycle, and the civil case backlog has been shortened by as much as two years. The computer schedules judges, courtrooms, and attorneys. It prints lists for prison deliveries, indictment list-

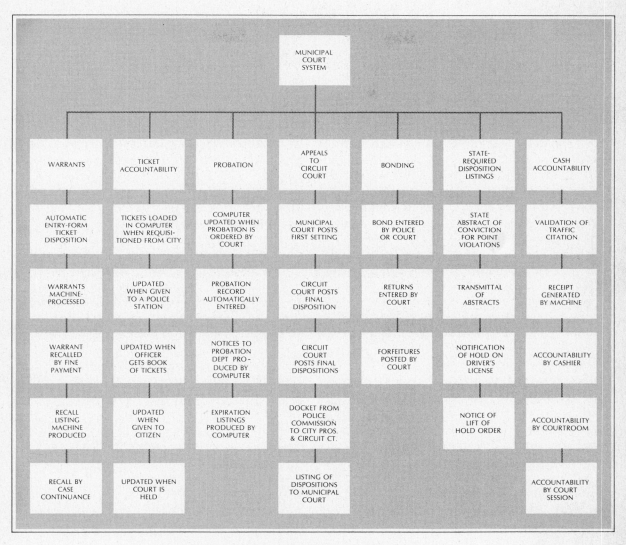

Figure 14-4 Data-processing support to the courts

ings, subpoenas, and trial calendars—thus reducing the clerical workload. It supplies the police department with case disposition records and notices of when officers are to appear at trials.

As in the case of police information systems, the main operational data of the court system can be used for other management purposes. In this case, for example, investigations disclosed that only a very few of Philadelphia's 6000 attorneys did most of the work with the courts and thus were a major source of the delay since they carried such a large workload.

The heart of the system is an IBM 2314 disk storage device with 200 million characters of memory. A video retrieval system with terminals located at the Criminal Clerk's Office and the Civil and Criminal Listings Offices provides access to the status of civil or criminal cases, who the attorney is, cases pending for a given attorney, the charges against any defendant, the judgments outstanding in a civil case, and arbitration cases outstanding.

To use this system, the attorney for a case files a Certificate of Readiness, which is keypunched and read into the computer. From these records, the computer produces a daily conflict-free trial listing of the top 250 cases in the order of their priority. This list is delivered to the Philadelphia legal newspaper, which publishes it. Attorneys for the top twenty cases notify the court of their readiness or ask for a postponement. Of the top twenty cases, usually fifteen or so are found to be ready for trial and twelve are assigned to courtrooms. The computer also produces a worksheet of the pertinent data for each trial, which the judge uses to record the disposition of the case. Cases held over continue to appear on the trial list until settled. Settlement notices and trial results are entered into the computer, which produces the daily summary case reports. The computer also produces daily conflict-free conference schedules for up to five judges, involving as many as fifty meetings. Thus only trials that are truly ready to appear take up the court's time. Figures 14-5 and 14-6 show the civil and criminal data flow.

Further computer applications are being planned now that this operational data base has been accumulated. For example, simulation of the court system in operation should provide a useful management tool.

As of this writing, the Philadelphia court system is the most advanced in the country. There is nothing technically innovative about the system at all. What was required for this advance was that the court abandon its traditional way of doing things.

The State of Connecticut

The State of Connecticut operates six correction centers (jails) housing 1400 persons, five prisons with another 1900 inmates, and has jurisdiction over some 1000 people out on parole. In addition, there are some twenty to twenty-five thousand admissions to these correction centers each year. These short-term sentences are served by inmates waiting arraignment, indictment, or bail determination. Then there are those who are unable to make bail, who are in various stages of trial, or have been convicted and not yet sentenced. Thus while Connecticut is a small state with a small prison population, it has a high rate of turnover. Until it installed a computer and standardized its record-keeping practices, it had no way to measure the effectiveness of its treatment programs and no indication of how long inmates were being held pending trial, sentencing, or bail. For most of you, the penalty of prison can only be imagined, and it may add little to your imaginings to describe it as a total lack of freedom and self-determination, and constant monitoring, drabness, and boredom. But the outrage of having to spend more time in prison than you deserve should be obvious to all.

The CORRECT system (Connecticut Online Records and Research for Effective Criminal Treatment) has now established a common and extensive data base for all inmates at all facilities, reduced bookkeeping by the custodial staff, and

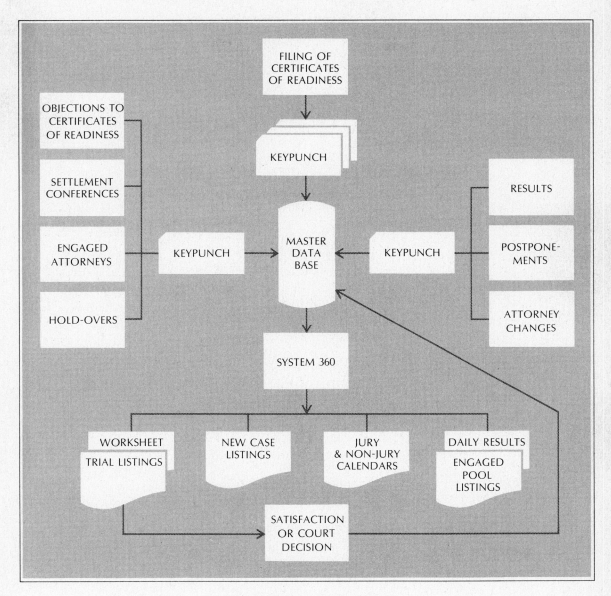

Figure 14-5 Civil data flow

provided quick access to the basic prison records. It now has a communications terminal at each corrections center connected via telephone lines to the central computer at the State Data Center in Hartford.

The system allows searches by prisoner name; outputs court appearance listings; prepares the paperwork for release, transfer, and court appearances; and produces a variety of management reports. It began in 1970 and as of this writing had

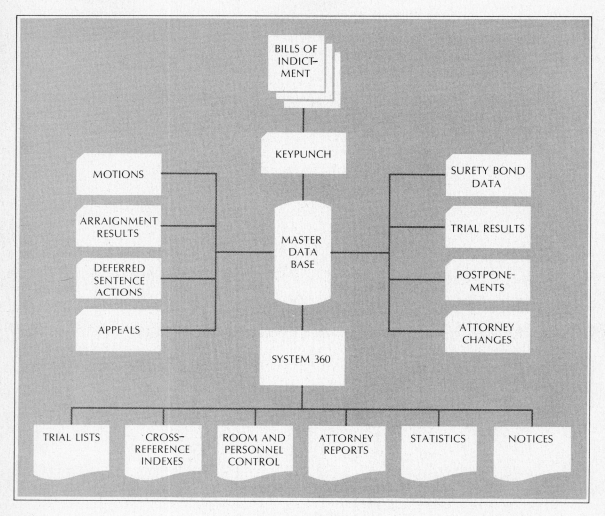

Figure 14-6 Criminal data flow

eleven terminals connected with the state welfare, motor vehicles, police, and judicial processing systems. CORRECT is believed to have contributed to fairer treatment of prisoners as well as greater institutional efficiency. A hopeful bit of irony: part of the software was produced by six or seven inmates with only a two-day programming course in the prison training program.

Wichita Falls, Texas

Much of the police's time is taken up directing traffic, and, similarly, a fair amount of the court's time is taken up with automobile accidents. As such, anything that can be done to improve traffic control and reduce automobile accidents frees time for other matters. Wichita Falls, Texas, is one of the growing number of cities that is using computers for traffic control. We selected it to show that automatic traffic control is feasible and profitable even in cities as small as 115,000 people.

The problem of traffic control gets worse and worse because roughly eight million new cars are added to the streets each year. Wichita Falls installed loop and pressure detectors at seventy-seven intersections, using existing traffic signals and intersection controllers. A cable system connects this equipment to an IBM 1800 computer and display system. The total cost was $250,000. The system checks the status of the traffic at these intersections sixty times a second and automatically selects the most suitable overall signal pattern. It can be expanded to cover 500 intersections. It monitors itself and gives immediate notification of failure. The patterns that it responds with can be changed if the city grows or the flow of traffic changes in major ways. Most significant, it considers the traffic flow in the city as a whole rather than one corner at a time.

Specifically, the vehicle stops have been reduced by sixteen percent and average delay by eighteen percent. It has been estimated that this saves the citizens of Wichita Falls $50,000 a year in automobile operating costs and 19,500 hours of travel.

Social Impact

You have now seen a range of examples of how our system of justice uses computers. Of these cases, it seems to be only the police systems that arouse public fears of invasion of privacy and injustices caused by errors in the system. The police are also concerned about these same problems and others as well. We will first discuss our concerns for privacy.

The basic problem is that data in police information systems are useful for other purposes, such as credit checking, pre-employment inquiries, licensing investigations, crime reporting, and Department of Defense security investigations. Each local law-enforcement agency collects its own information and is subject only to local laws, so it can do anything it pleases with its data. The problem is complicated when networks of computers exchange information with no ability to correct the information once it is out of the local hands. Responsible law-enforcement officials see the need to protect this information, and in later sections we will discuss the measures Congress and the FBI are taking to safeguard the exchange of such information. However, at this point we can say that it will be some time before these concerns are totally satisfied, because there are so many politically independent agencies involved. It must be said that the police have considerable experience in protecting sensitive juvenile records (because of laws protecting children) and vice and organized crime information (because disclosure would disrupt investigations). Thus even if there were more restrictive laws concerning the distribution of information, the police could still act effectively. On the other hand, if the police are to be held responsible under the law to protect private information, then the civil service regulations that they administer personnel under must change. For example, consider the case of the sheriff of a large county who discovered the wife of a narcotics peddler working in his records section. The woman was using police records to assure her husband that he was not dealing with undercover narcs. However, under civil service regulations, the sheriff was unable to fire the woman.

Responsible police officials have all these concerns for their computer systems and then some. They also see them subject to destruction and sabotage by anarchists, criminals, and civil disorders. They worry about the corrupting influence of private detectives, crime reporters, and respectable businessmen who would like to use their files for their own purposes. The progress that enforcement has made in solving these problems will be described when we discuss Project Search.

A broader and less specific set of public concerns adds up to the fear of doing anything that makes the police more powerful. To this kind of fear we can give only the most general of answers. The police have very stringent rules that must be followed to justify detaining or searching people, searching premises, and admitting evidence. The computer simply helps them get complete information in a hurry. The conviction of innocent people is what our court system is designed to prevent. The extent to which the court system and law enforcement are separate and opposed can be seen in the whole history of recent Supreme Court decisions that restrict law enforcement. In our view, the use of the computer has done nothing to change the balance of power between the courts and the police.

On the positive side of the ledger, you have seen how computers have helped make law enforcement safer for the police, reduce the possibility of mis-identification, prevent the release from custody of criminals wanted in other districts, improve the probability of apprehension, reduce court delays, make sentencing fairer, and reduce foul-ups in prison.

In some people's opinion, the question of social impact should be viewed as a balance between the very high cost of crime (roughly fifty billion dollars a year in the United States) and the human misery that crime costs its victims—and the personal lives of a relatively small number of criminals. One might argue that the task of justice is to punish the guilty at the least cost to the innocent. Of course, the ultimate answer to our problem is to administer justice to both the innocent and the guilty. This is not a problem for computers. Guilt or innocence is an absolute matter. If a court convicts a person, he is guilty; if not, he is innocent. However, the grey area in between is where the police must operate. Often there will be enough information about a person to convince a police officer of his or her guilt but not to obtain a conviction in court. Should we prohibit the retention of information that is not evidence and just keep histories of criminal arrests that are matched by convictions? The police argue that such information is useful for later investigations. Civil libertarians argue that it is prejudicial.

In the case of police intelligence squads that focus on organized crime, the question gets even harder. One of the most insidious things that organized crime does is corrupt public officials. Thus elected officials must be assured that the people they appoint to public office are not in the pay of organized crime. For that matter, the political parties that nominate persons to run for public office need the same assurance. To obtain such assurance requires that police check on the associations of those who may be appointed to public office. This obviously puts the police in a politically powerful position, since they could discredit an innocent person. The police must be able to distinguish between political nonconformists and the criminally dangerous, such as hijackers, bombers, and assassins. Thus police investigations into radical groups requires subtlety and wisdom. Similarly, the records of these investigations must be handled carefully.

Now we have the question down to a contest between values of the same type. We are no longer comparing a small number of criminals with 200,000,000 innocent people, but the need for security at the risk of political surveillance. In the latter case, the surveillance does not necessarily involve collecting more information, just using it. Deciding between these alternatives is a job that you must do for yourself. Chapter fifteen will elaborate the privacy aspect of the problem.

Will the advent of computers do anything to remedy police abuses of power? Probably very little in the short run, but over the long run, by recording more of what happens as a suspect goes through the system, it will be harder to hide the false arrests, the beatings, and the illegal entries that so outrage the public and police administration. In the same sense, the rulings of dishonest judges and the deals of corrupt prosecutors will become more public and thus will be restricted. We detail these flaws in our system of justice not as an indictment of it but to show just how intimately information (and thus computers) becomes involved in the institutional problems of those who use it.

Exercises

1. In this chapter we have discussed an example of the concern for efficiency in government at the possible expense of human values. In the case of the court's use of computers, the right to a speedy trial is denied by the delays of overcrowded courts. The solution, in part, is to waste less of the court's time with cases that aren't ready—that is, to make its scheduling more efficient. This is cheaper than building courthouses and paying more judges. However, this is done at the possible expense of justice. Speed may replace wisdom. A computerized summary sheet on the relevant facts in a case or a person's record may so oversimplify the human events that justice becomes impossible. To research this question properly you will need materials that your school library probably won't have. However, how would you go about assessing the social impact of this computer system if you could visit the court and talk to everyone concerned?

2. This question is similar to the first one. We are going to ask you to think about *how* you would answer a question rather than answer it. Again the question is concerned with human values. Does making the police more efficient make law enforcement more just? How would you go about finding out whether the Kansas City system contributes to the protection of the innocent as much as the apprehension of the guilty? Think of yourself as an investigative reporter.

3. You are a bright and rising young attorney in the district attorney's office. The city police, quite by accident, discovered a meeting of organized crime figures in a motel in your city. They raided the motel and arrested those present on charges of conspiracy. Your job is to research the background of all the suspects. You must find out what they have in common to bring them together to a meeting. What

sources would you go to? Do any of those sources use computers?

4. One of the sensitive questions concerned with the use of police information for non-enforcement purposes has to do with identifying potential young offenders before they commit serious crimes. If you had access to police, school, health, welfare, and psychiatric records, how would you do this? What do you think of the idea?

5. You are a detective faced with a series of brutal killings in the skid row section of Kansas City. You have no description of the suspect. The killings have narcotics overtones. The victims are all males in their twenties. Up until ten days ago, there has been one murder a night. Then they ceased. How would you use the information system to find possible suspects?

6. Suppose that you are a member of organized crime, who is concerned with penetration of your syndicate by undercover police. How would you try to use a police information system to your own advantage? How would the police, in turn, protect against this?

7. Suppose that you are a revolutionary activist violently opposed to the police. How would you go about trying to destroy a police information system? How would the police protect against this?

For Further Information

The best place to start to gain an appreciation of the overall impact of crime on our society is still the report of the president's Crime Commission (1) and its task force report on science and technology (2). For more detail on the use of computers in law enforcement we suggest first (3) and then Whisenand and Tamaru (4), which is used extensively in Police Science departments around the country. The FBI regularly issues reports like (5) and (6), and they are obtainable directly from the FBI or can be found in the government publications room of your library. (7) and (8) are a little obscure and not likely to be found in your library, but (7), the Space General Report, can be obtained by writing the state of California Library in Sacramento, California. Alan Westin did a detailed study of the NCIC in (9), and you may be interested in pursuing that. (10) is a study of the improvements possible in courts through the use of computers and its author is a genuine expert in the field. Adams has been working in court automation for over ten years.

References

1. President's Commission on Law Enforcement and the Administration of Justice, *The Challenge of Crime in a Free Society* (Washington, D.C.: U.S. Government Printing Office, 1967).

2. Institute for Defense Analysis, Task Force Report on Science and Technology, *A Report to the President's Commission on Law Enforcement and the Administration of Justice* (1967).

3. "Criminal Justice Information Systems," *Datamation* (June 15, 1971).

4. Paul Whisenand and Tug Tamaru, *Automated Police Information Systems* (New York: John Wiley & Sons, 1970).

5. "National Crime Information Center," *FBI Law Enforcement Bulletin* (January 1974).

6. Clarence M. Kelley, Director of the Federal Bureau of Investigation, "A National Need: The Security and Privacy of Criminal History Information," an address before the National Association of Attorneys General (1974).

7. *Final Report: Prevention and Control of Crime and Delinquency,* prepared for the Youth and Adult Corrections Agency, State of California, by Space General Corporation (1965).

8. *SDC Magazine* (October 1965).

9. Alan F. Westin and Michael Baker, *Databanks in a Free Society* (New York: Quadrangle Books, 1972).

10. Eldridge Adams, *Courts and Computers* (American Judicature Society, 1972).

Privacy and Individuality

15

You have now seen an array of computer applications, each created in the belief that it would improve an organization's operation, make people more effective in their jobs, or improve the level of service the organization is able to provide. No one deliberately designs computer-based systems with the intention of creating inefficiency, hurting people, or damaging the organizational and social structures within which the system operates. The disadvantages, the dangers, and the damages that accompany computerization are all by-products: on the way to reaping some benefit, other unforeseen and undesirable consequences also appear.

Many of these problems and concerns have been mentioned in passing in earlier chapters. In this chapter and the one that follows, we will examine a few major social issues with greater scrutiny.

Two issues that have received considerable attention are *privacy* and *individuality*. They are separate questions and are usually treated independently. However, placed side by side, they appear to have much in common. The privacy question has to do with our right to keep part of our lives to ourselves; the individuality issue has to do with the conditions under which we spend much of our lives in communion with other human beings. We will treat the issues separately, beginning with privacy; then we will consider the two together.

Privacy

The need for privacy is no longer the special urge of the artist or the eccentric. In the context of our modern society and its use of computers, privacy

has become the name of many problems: criminal records unfairly causing more punishment than the law provides; welfare recipients being exposed to degrading inquiries; and insurance, loans, and credit being denied because of errors in semi-relevant data gathered for other purposes. It is a problem of all people—the rich and the poor, the majority and the many minorities.

What is Privacy? Privacy is a voluntary withholding of information that is reinforced by a willing indifference to others. This indifference can be a lack of caring about the other person, but more often it is a conscious recognition of the right of others to be let alone. Secrecy, by contrast, is the compulsory withholding of information, reinforced by punishment for disclosure.

Privacy cannot be considered independently of two other forces in our society: secrecy and publicity. All three interact with each other. In his book *The Torment of Secrecy,* Edward A. Shils puts it this way: "If America is to find a balance between publicity, privacy, and secrecy which maintains liberties, it must avoid the temptation to honor those who stand at the poles of enthusiasm for the sacred or hatred of the diabolical." This balance shifts from time to time and is viewed with different values in other countries. Alan Westin draws an interesting comparison between the totalitarian state—where the state has all the privacy (actually secrecy) and the citizen has none—and the liberal democracy where the opposite is (or should be) true.

Privacy involves a number of concepts. The first

is the freedom to keep the past from interfering with the future. This is, in a sense, the ability to pick one's self up and start over again. The only anonymity that we can obtain today comes in part from the urbanization and mobility of our society and in part from the separations between our present information systems. However, it would seem more appropriate for freedoms to derive from wisdom rather than confusion.

The ability to control the degree to which our history and activities are known influences the extent to which we can make a measured investment of ourselves in an ideal, in another person, or in an organization. It is too commonly thought that anything less than complete commitment is equivalent to disaffection, and this tends to make the protection of privacy even more important.

Similarly, a person needs the ability to control his or her confidential communications. The intimacy of our relationship with our loved ones or the intimacy of the relations among a small group of people depends on the ability of all concerned to be assured that confidences are limited to those they are intended for. The denial of the rewards of intimacy is the best control over the privacy of personal communications. But this control is not possible when the individual deals with the massive institutions of government and industry.

Why is Privacy Necessary?

All of us occasionally feel very strongly the need to be left alone to enjoy solitude, self-contemplation, and freedom from stimuli and inquiry from the outside. This is how we develop and maintain a personal sense of autonomy, the freedom of emotional release, and the process of self-evaluation and self-improvement.

Very few people can live in absolute devotion to an ideal; most must change sometime, to some degree. But, people being the way they are, we resent our deviations being monitored and recorded. Ultimately we become so hostile that we revolt against both our watchers and the rules themselves. Furthermore, not only deviations from the rules warrant privacy. Acts of delicacy, consideration for the feelings of others, and legitimate plans can be ruined by lack of privacy. What is true of the needs of individuals is also true in large part about groups of people and businesses.

How Does Privacy Stand in Our Society?

As our country grew, the process of decision making changed. Industry developed, and a small number of industrialists influenced how people lived by deciding where to build a railroad, which product to sell, or which resource to exploit. Today, the single most important decision maker is government. This shift in power has been accompanied by a change in the way decisions are made. The basis is no longer individual self-interest—it is collective self-interest (the greatest good for the greatest number), as understood by government. There is vast disagreement about this statement. There are segments of our population that argue that this change is desirable. Others see it as the only salvation in a complex world; some feel that it is necessary but poorly done. Still others would argue that there is no single large government that is dominating our lives, but a diversity of governments, each sensitive to local needs. Our only point is that this change accounts for the government's concern for predicting the behavior of, exercising control over, and providing for the welfare of people. This rationale and its well-

established institutions—such as the census, the income tax system, and the social security system, lead to the gathering of tremendous amounts of information about people.

All of these government functions involve the collection of and distribution of highly personal information—which ultimately brings up the question of the potential invasion of privacy and the control of human beings. However, there is nothing new about these practices. Such information is of considerable social value, although it is sometimes difficult for individual citizens to appreciate the social value that occurs from a loss of individual privacy. Although computers may be used to assist government in these functions, it is the functions of government that intrude on people's lives, not the computers. However, such extensive and efficient intrusion would be impossible without the computer. Increasingly, federal agencies are turning to computers to make available, at the

touch of a button, information on millions of Americans. Some major examples:

Social Security Administration.   In these files are earnings records on nine out of ten jobholders in the United States. They also contain information about all those receiving Social Security and Medicare benefits.

Internal Revenue Service.   Tapes store details from all taxpayers' tax returns, which are available at cost to all states and the District of Columbia.

Secret Service.   Its computer tapes hold names of persons who might attempt to harm or embarrass the president or other high government officials.

Federal Bureau of Investigation.   Chapter fourteen (The Administration of Justice) described the NCIC files. In addition, the FBI has extensive fingerprint files gathered from both criminal and non-criminal proceedings.

Department of Agriculture.   Keeps data on all borrowers and investors in programs of Farmers Home Administration, as well as records of all farmers buying federal crop insurance.

Department of Transportation. Keeps on file names of all citizens who have been denied driver's licenses or whose permits have been suspended or revoked.

Pentagon.   Has files on all present and past military and civilian personnel who have been subjected to security, loyalty, criminal, and other types of investigations.

Veterans Administration.   Preserves files on all veterans and dependents who are now receiving benefits or have received them.

Department of Labor.   Has files on all persons in federally financed work and training programs, coded by Social Security numbers.

Department of Justice.   "Databank" has names of key individuals who have been involved in riots and civil disorders since mid-1968.

Department of Housing and Urban Development. Maintains records on all Americans who bought homes with loans guaranteed by the Federal Housing Administration. There is also an "adverse information" file on builders and other businessmen.

Thus information on just about every American is stored away in one agency or other. And with the federal computer network spreading, there is virtually no limit to the volume of information that can be filed for quick retrieval.

Computer technology and practice have created a situation in which government organizations, such as tax agencies, find it cheaper to share some information rather than collect it independently. It is usually cheaper to maintain an integrated file on a person rather than regather much of that information every time the person has any contact with the government. There are many good reasons for collecting personal information, and good reasons to combine these collections. These aggregations of information may or may not have names attached to them. For some purposes, like research, names are not necessary. In the political debates that have swirled around these files, they are labeled "dossiers," and that is an emotionally loaded word that brings to mind totalitarian images like the Gestapo, the NKVD, and *1984*. We will now trace the history of this debate up to the Federal Privacy Act of 1974.

The Recent History of the Right to Privacy.   First, to summarize what we have said so far, privacy seems to be a collection of vague concepts, but they are no less vital to our society for their vagueness. Like the freedom of the press, privacy has certain practical limitations. Our government in numerous ways affects people's privacy for many individually justifiable reasons. The increasing availability of the computer has forced us to examine carefully the purposes for which information is collected and how it will be used.

In the late 1960s and early 1970s, privacy became the focus of a good deal of attention. Popular writers like Vance Packard (*The Naked Society,* 1964) and Arthur Miller (*Assault on Privacy,* 1971) wrote about the subject, and congressmen and senators like Gallagher and Ervin held extensive hearings. These investigations tended to have a common pattern. They were based partly on fact. Their assertions of the numbers of files in the hands of government agencies were correct. Their statements of the fallibilities of the law and current protections were right. Their alleged intentions were to create a "climate of concern." But, in our opinion, they went too far in their inferences about the evil intent of computer application. During the same period, there was a proposal for a National Data Bank. Its purpose was to integrate economic information from a number of federal agencies to facilitate economic research. The proposal was attacked as a "dossier" file and destroyed because of its lack of attention to the privacy problem.

Out of the sensationalism that surrounded the public debate on the National Data Bank, there arose several serious students of the problem of privacy, and a number of key laws that we will describe later were developed. In his book *Privacy and Freedom,* published in 1967 and begun before the congressional hearings, Alan F. Westin gave some clarity to the problem. He defined privacy as the claim to determine communications about yourself to others—where "you" may be a person, a small group of people, or a large organization. He discussed privacy as if it were a need like the needs for social stimulation, curiosity, surveillance, and self-disclosure.

Westin detailed the danger that a citizen's absolute right to privacy poses to a democracy in terms of anonymous influence on public life such as campaign contributions, criminal conspiracies, and threats to national security. His thesis was that privacy is not an absolute right but rather a balance that must be struck between the needs of people and the needs of government. Integrate too many files, merge too many functions, and you can create a dossier monster with such potential for surveillance and control that people may be oppressed. Cripple the files with excessive costs for protections, severely delimit access individually and interdepartmentally, and you hamper government's ability to plan, research, and operate.

In the nongovernmental field, credit versus privacy was an easier issue to resolve. In 1971, the Fair Credit Reporting Act was passed after far less sensational hearings. It restricted credit agencies' data gathering, made them responsible for the dissemination of their information, and granted people access to their own credit files.

Databanks in a Free Society. In 1972, the National Academy of Science published the results of a study aimed at evaluating the impact of computerized record-keeping on the right to privacy. The study was directed by Alan Westin, whose earlier book on this subject has already been mentioned. In the study, Westin and his associates visited fifty-five organizations—government agencies, commercial enterprises, and nonprofit organizations. In addition, they surveyed many other organizations and individuals. The conclusions of this extensive study are striking: basically, it was

Figure 15-1 The TRW credit bank

found that the computer has had little effect on the way information is used or the way organizations function. The dire predictions made by many (including Westin himself) who surveyed the *potential* of the use of computers and information systems had just not come to pass—yet.

Managers of organizations surveyed had developed a more realistic approach to computer technology than they had in the past. They no longer were willing to accept all of the claims made by computer enthusiasts. And there was a growing awareness and concern among them over the heavy financial costs of computer-based systems.

All fifty-five of the organizations studied closely had computer-based files of people-related information. Most, however, were not involved or interested in the creation of centralized, shared databanks. Their files were very restricted in scope and purpose. In the case of many organizations, plans for centralizing and creating unified systems had been abandoned, modified, or at least delayed: the difficulty and expense of merging separate functions into one huge system turned out to be greater than anticipated. Although central data banks had been much discussed a few years earlier, none of the organizations studied had brought theirs into existence. Quoting the report:

> These organizations indeed had automated files in operation, but their central databank projects had either been discarded or had been converted into what was usually called "subsystem development leading to the prospect of a unified data bank in the future," an embarrassed way of saying that things were going to take a lot longer than they had expected and there was no central databanking yet. (p. 236)

Just as the actuality of databanks was less than had been anticipated, the investigators found no justification for many popularly held beliefs about the invasion of privacy. In a majority of the organizations studied, a large increase in the amount of information being collected had not followed computerization. The organizations had no need for additional information; the intent of their systems was primarily to make the information already being collected more quickly accessible in more usable form.

Even in those cases where more information was desired, it was not collected for the sake of having more detailed information about individuals. Rather, it was to serve as a basis for statistical analysis for general evaluation and planning. However, the confidentiality of the individual reports was found to be largely a matter of faith in the system.

But how confidential is information, once it is in a computerized system? Who has access to it? Is more data shared more widely? To put these questions in perspective, it is important to note that in the pre-computer era much data was shared and many people had access to files. Much of the same kinds of sharing still go on: ". . . we found that nothing in computerization itself has produced a sharing of identified information to a broader class of users within multi-bureau organization or among organizations than before computers." (p. 255) Informal exchanges, evident in manual systems, still go on, and may have increased with computerization in some cases.

In fact, the dangers that people see in computerized personal information systems are present in all information systems. They are implicit in the notion of systematic record-keeping itself. Computers have not made such systems more prevalent, more prone to error, more detailed and complete, or more likely to be misused. Computerization has created no revolutionary new powers of surveillance—as yet.

Records, Computers, and the Rights of Citizens. The fact that abuses are possible in manual systems does not, of course, lessen the significance of the abuses of computerized systems. The fact that dangerous computerized systems have not yet been developed does not mean that it is too early to express concern about their ultimate development. As a matter of fact, at the same time that Westin was conducting his study, the Department of Health, Education, and Welfare convened a committee to consider the privacy issue. In 1973, its report, called *Records, Computers, and the Rights of Citizens,* was issued. This report viewed the potential of computerized systems as a real danger to personal liberty and proposed some concrete and specific acts the government should take in order to protect citizens' rights.

Under current law, the report concluded, a person's privacy is poorly protected against arbitrary or abusive record-keeping practices. It recommended the need for a federal "Code of Fair Information Practice" for all automated personal data systems. Such a code should rest on five basic principles:

☐ There must be no personal data record-keeping systems whose very existence is secret.
☐ There must be a way for an individual to find out what information about him or her is in a record and how it is used.
☐ There must be a way for an individual to prevent personal information that was obtained for one purpose from being used or made available for other purposes without his or her consent.
☐ There must be a way for an individual to correct

or amend a record of identifiable information about him or her.

☐ Any organization creating, maintaining, using, or disseminating records of identifiable personal data must make sure that data is reliable and must take precautions to prevent its misuse.

The report also considered the growing tendency to use the Social Security Number (SSN) as a standard universal identifier—a means of identifying a particular individual uniquely, for ease in associating a person with a file or one file with another. It recommended that the use of the SSN for this purpose be restricted: "We recommend against the adoption of any nationwide, standard personal identification format, with or without the SSN, that would enhance the likelihood of arbitrary or uncontrolled linkage of records about people, particularly between government and government-supported automated personal data systems."

Differing in their outlook from that of the Westin study group, the HEW committee concluded that computerization does encourage organizations to increase their data-collection activities and make record-keeping a more important function of the organization. A second effect, according to the committee, is that it makes access to information easier and therefore more frequent. It further grants access and control of this information to a new group in the organization: the computer technicians. As a result, the ability of people to control the way information is used is gradually lessened.

> Record-keeping organizations must guard against insensitivity to the privacy needs and desires of individuals, preoccupied with their own convenience or efficiency, or their relationships with other organizations. They must not overlook the

effects on people of their record-keeping and record-sharing practices. They have the power to eliminate misunderstanding, mistrust, frustration, and seeming unfairness; they must learn to exercise it. (p. 46)

The Federal Privacy Act of 1974. While there has been a great deal of legislative activity at the state level, the biggest single legislative event in the history of privacy is Public Law 93-579, enacted December 31, 1974. It reflects the point of view of the HEW committee that produced *Records, Computers and the Rights of Citizens,* if not all its recommendations. Section 2 (b) asserts the intended purposes as:

. . . requiring Federal agencies, except as otherwise provided by law, to—

(1) permit an individual to determine what records pertaining to him are collected, maintained, used, or disseminated by such agencies;

(2) permit an individual to prevent records pertaining to him obtained by such agencies for a particular purpose from being used or made available for another purpose without his consent;

(3) permit an individual to gain access to information pertaining to him in Federal agency records, to have a copy made of all or any portion thereof, and to correct or amend such records;

(4) collect, maintain, use, or disseminate any record of identifiable personal information in a manner that assures that such action is for a necessary and lawful purpose, that the information is current and accurate for its intended use, and that adequate safeguards are provided to prevent misuse of such information;

(5) permit exemptions from the requirements with respect to records provided in this Act only in those cases where there is an important public policy need for such exemption as has been determined by specific statuory authority; and

(6) be subject to civil suit for any damages which occur as a result of willful or intentional action which violates any individual's rights under this Act.

Among the exemptions from the law are the law-enforcement and intelligence agencies. In addition to spelling out how these purposes are to be accomplished the law also creates a commission empowered to study those problems that are not covered by it. These are such thorny problems as state and commercial systems, interstate transfer of information, and the use of Social Security numbers.

Summary. Those men and women whose initial intent was to create a climate of concern suc-

ceeded. The issue of privacy has struck a chord that reverberates deeply in the American character, and predictably, these laws that we have described briefly will evolve and improve with time.

Individuality

There is a justifiable concern on the part of many that our rights to privacy are being abraded by computerized record-keeping. But at the same time, some of us feel that we are becoming too private, that we are being isolated from other human beings in a world of machines. Another quotation from the same HEW report, *Records, Computers, and the Rights of Citizens,* will serve as an introduction to the second major social issue we will consider: individuality.

> It is no wonder that people have come to distrust computer-based record-keeping operations. Even in non-government settings, an individual's control over the personal information that he gives to an organization, or than an organization obtains about him, is lessening as the relationship between the giver and receiver of personal data grows more attenuated, impersonal, and diffused. There was a time when information about an individual tended to be elicited in face-to-face contacts involving personal trust and a certain symmetry, or balance, between giver and receiver. Nowadays an individual must increasingly give information about himself to large and relatively faceless institutions. . . . (pp. 28–29)

Men and women have a right to be treated as strangers on some occasions. Yet they also need to be treated as neighbors on others. Such essential human contact is missing from many of our affairs. The impersonality of computer-based systems has generated some of the most violent reaction and opposition to computers. One of the most eloquent statements of this position was a placard carried by a student during the riots at the University of California at Berkeley in 1965. It said, "I am a human being. Do not fold, staple, or mutilate." The implication is that large organizations are often more concerned about the damage to punched cards than about the damage to human lives.

Maintaining Individuality Against the System. Few adults in our society have not had at least one duel with a computer system. People tend to emerge from such conflicts feeling hostile both to the specific system and to the computer in general.

In one case known to the authors, a well-known mathematician and computer specialist persisted for six months in his effort to have a $27 erroneous charge removed from his bill. He wrote countless letters and included photostatic copies of documents proving the error. Not one of his communications was answered. He received only the series of bills, statements, threatening letters, and finally a cancellation of his account and a demand that he return his credit card.

The case is not unusual, but the analysis made by the victim is. He argued as follows: a large international credit card agency, such as the one with which he had had his dispute, does not create errors deliberately; nevertheless, when an error does occur, the most cost-effective course of action is to ignore it.

If a company ignores a letter complaining of an error in a bill, what is likely to happen? Perhaps the customer will eventually pay the bill anyhow. In that case, reading the letter and replying to it would have been a waste of money. Perhaps the customer will sue the company, but this possibility is so unlikely that it can be ignored. Such a suit

would cost the customer thousands of dollars and he or she would probably lose the case anyhow. Finally, the customer may refuse to pay and cancel the account.

Thus the company may lose a customer. Is this bad? That depends on several things, principally this: does it cost more to save the customer or replace him or her? Carrying on an extended correspondence, correcting the computer-based records, and so on can cost as much as $100. But for $50 invested in advertising, the company can get a new customer. Thus the most reasonable and cost-effective means of dealing with letters from customers is to throw them away unread. The argument appears somewhat fanciful, yet the hypothetical attitude of the corporation is far from impossible or unusual.* Many companies present at least the appearance of total indifference to human values and to the dignity of their customers.

Many people are first exposed to large computer-based systems in school. For example, a

---

*After October of 1975, the victim in such stories will no longer be totally at the mercy of the creditor. The Fair Credit Billing Act stipulates that if the individual writes the creditor within sixty days giving his or her name and account number, and explaining what he or she thinks is incorrect, the creditor must reply within thirty days and resolve the complaint with supporting evidence within ninety days. Until the complaint is resolved, the debtor cannot be reported as delinquent to a credit-reporting firm. If the creditor tells the credit-reporting firm that the amount is in dispute, the debtor must be notified that the information has been passed along. Furthermore, until the inquiry is resolved, the creditor may not send letters demanding payment, threaten adverse credit reports, or charge interest on the uncollected amount. Failure to comply forfeits the right to collect the disputed amount and is subject to a fine of at most $50.

graduate of a small high school may go to a larger college where he or she knows no one. The student will be handed forms to fill out for the computer to process and will receive in return dormitory assignments, class schedules, and bills—even (at the end of the term) grades in the form of computer printouts. No one in either the administration or the faculty seems to care about the student as an individual. To them, he or she is no more than a statistic; the only individual attention comes from the computer.

Patients in modern hospitals complain of the same isolation. They are alone and worried and cannot find a human being to reassure them. No one has the time, the responsibility, or the interest to see them as anything but a statistic. Doctors and nurses visit hurriedly to take their temperatures or deliver medication. If their condition is serious enough to require constant attention, they may be linked online to a computer that will monitor their heartbeat and respiration.

Experiences like these, repeated again and again, have convinced some people that human beings have lost control, that no one cares any longer for contact among human beings, and that individuality and personal freedom have been lost. A number of writers have presented this point of view with some eloquence. Among the most important and intellectually substantial spokesmen for the view that technology is robbing us of our identities are Jacques Ellul and Lewis Mumford.

The Technological Society.   Ellul's book *The Technological Society* is a long and detailed analysis of the effects of technology on society. It deals with technology in very broad and general terms and the computer, as such, is hardly mentioned. Yet Ellul's concepts are particularly applicable to the issues we have been discussing.

The central concept in Ellul's argument is that of technique. Technique, according to him, is a concept much broader than that of technology or automation. It is the process by which technology and machines come into being, the process by which new and more efficient methods are invented and come into use. It is the standardized way of achieving a given goal by the most expeditious method; it is "know-how." In some of his discussions, one is tempted to suggest that his notion of technique is not unlike that of programming: the process of dissecting problems and stating a clear, unique, and logical solution.

Technique, Ellul argues, has gradually been applied to more and more of our activities; agriculture, science, and manufacturing have all been routinized and standardized. As technique takes over, it creates an inhuman and mechanical atmosphere. Depersonalized factories, banks, offices, schools, and hospitals are a consequence of the relentless application of technique: everything human and spontaneous and imaginative must be brought under control so that it can be mechanized. What cannot fit into the mechanical, technological picture must be destroyed.

Thus we are gradually becoming adapted to a world of machines rather than nature, since the natural is too spontaneous and unreliable to fit into the technological world. In fact, we ourselves are being changed as we, too, are "programmed" to think in terms of technique, in terms of know-how and improved methods, rather than in historic, humanistic terms.

This application of technique has expanded not only into the fields we normally think of as technological, but into social fields as well. Social, economic, and political affairs are subjected to the same brutalizing analysis and redesign that has revolutionized the factory and the business office.

Thus, having transformed the world and made us and our institutions over in its image, technique becomes a power in itself. Society becomes dominated by rationality, logic, and the drive to find the one best method of doing everything. Spontaneity, creativity, and nature are excluded from this artificial world. The process, once begun, is no longer under our control: it is self-perpetuating, all-embracing, and irreversible. The result is a world of efficiency and order, with no exceptions and no irrelevancy. Civilization becomes a closed system in which we, since we are a source of error and unpredictability, can have little responsibility.

Lewis Mumford's concern is, like Ellul's, the dehumanizing potential of technology. He too deals with the broad subject of technology as a whole, but he also devotes some of his attention to automation and the computer in particular.

The most dangerous effect of automation, Mumford argues in *The Myth of the Machine,* is that the individual will become subordinate to the system. Personal confidence in making independent judgments or resisting the system is undermined; rather, the behavior that is reinforced and encouraged is that of the organization person who takes orders from the system and does not deviate from the program. Thus we become victims of the relentless advance of automation toward control of the world.

Unlike Ellul, however, Mumford sees some indications that this process can be changed. In fact, he says, as human nature is pressed into the mold of automation, it threatens to spring back with a vengeance and assert our primal, irrational energies. The violent reaction against the establishment may be viewed as just such an affirmation of basic humanity—"I am a human being; do not fold, staple, or mutilate."

A Spokesman for the Counter-Culture. The reaction that emerged in the 1960s when young people began to express their rejection of much of the established and generally accepted ideals of our society found a spokesman in Theodore Roszak. He has combined the anti-technological stand of Ellul with a critical analysis of contemporary American culture and an interpretation of the disaffection of youth. His best-known and most influential work is called *The Making of a Counter-Culture.* It presents two major concepts: first, that science and technology are responsible for the trend in our society away from human values to those of sterile mechanization; and second, that the alienation of many young people from the society and politics of their elders is in fact a revolt against the domination of science and scientific values. It is the first of these concepts that will concern us here. The second is equally important to Roszak's argument, and, if you are interested, we urge you to look into this fascinating book yourself.

Books like those of Roszak and Ellul that speak eloquently on behalf of the emotions and the irrational element in human psychology are difficult to summarize or reduce to a few paragraphs of argument. Their appeal is largely to the emotions; their thesis is that the use of only rational argument, instead of other elements of reality and human thought, is a basic failing of our culture. The following summary will therefore rely heavily on quotations to give you a feeling of Roszak's argument.

"By the technocracy," he writes,

I mean that social form in which an industrial society reaches the peak of its organizational integration. It is the ideal men usually have in mind when they speak of modernizing, up-dating, rationalizing, planning. Drawing upon such unquestionable imperatives as the demand for efficiency, for social security, for large-scale co-ordination of men and resources, for ever higher levels of affluence and ever more impressive manifestations of collective human power, the technocracy works to knit together the anachronistic gaps and fissures of the industrial society. . . . So we arrive at the era of social engineering in which entrepreneurial talent broadens its province to orchestrate the total human context which surrounds the industrial complex. Politics, education, leisure, entertainment, culture as a whole, the unconscious drives, and even, as we shall see, protest against the technocracy itself: all these become the subjects of purely technical scrutiny and of purely technical manipulation. . . .

In the technocracy, nothing is any longer small or simple or readily apparent to the non-technical man. Instead, the scale and intricacy of all human activities—political, economic, cultural—transcends the competence of the amateurish citizen and inexorably demands the attention of specially trained experts. . . . For our purposes here it will be enough to define the technocracy as that society in which those who govern justify themselves by appeal to technical experts who, in turn, justify themselves by appeal to scientific forms of knowledge. And beyond the authority of science, there is no appeal. (pp. 5–8)

Technology grows to include more and more of human affairs and is embraced by the leaders of every faction: liberals as well as conservatives, communists as well as capitalists, artists and religious leaders as well as teachers and politicians. It is based on the appealing assumptions that the basic human problems are technical, that the techniques exist (or will soon exist) to solve these problems, and that those in control of our social institutions are those who understand how to apply these techniques to the solution of our

problems. However, Roszak argues that the really important problems are the ones that technology cannot treat: but they are replaced by artificial problems that can be solved technically.

Whole areas of human life are degraded in this process of absorption and change. Education is changed from the life of the mind to brainwashing; free enterprise becomes market manipulation; democracy turns into a matter of choosing between equally noncommittal candidates whose appeal is basically the same.

Computers and information science are in a very real sense, a culmination of this technocracy. Roszak describes his understanding of the place of the computer in our technology-dominated culture:

So then: if muscle power can be replaced by a mechanism, how much more desirable still to replace the mind behind the muscle with a mechanism! . . . "Artificial intelligence" is the logical goal toward which objective consciousness moves. . . .

Why should we not invent machines that objectify thought, creativity, decision making, moral judgment . . . ? Let us have machines that play games, make poems, compose music, teach philosophy. To be sure, it was once thought that such things were to be done for the joy of the playing, the making, the composing, the teaching. But scientific culture makes no allowance for "joy," since it is an experience of intensive personal involvement. Joy is something that is known only to the person: it does not submit to objectification.

So we come to the ultimate irony: the machine which is a creature of the human being becomes—most fully in the form of the computerized process—its maker's ideal. The machine achieves the perfect state of objective consciousness as Jesus incarnated the Christian conception of divinity. Under its spell, a grand reductive process begins in which culture is redesigned to meet the needs of mechanization. If we discover that a computer cannot compose emotionally absorbing music, we insist that music *does* have an "objective" side, and we turn that into our definition of music. If we discover that computers cannot translate normal language, then we invent a special, more rudimentary language which they can translate. If we discover that computers cannot teach as teaching at its most ideal is done, then we redesign education so that the machine can qualify as a teacher. If we discover that computers cannot solve the basic problems of city planning—all of which are questions of social philosophy and aesthetics—then we redefine the meaning of "city," call it an "urban area," and assume that all the problems of this entity are quantitative. In this way man is replaced in all areas by the machine, not because the machine can do things "better" but rather because all things have been reduced to what the machine is capable of doing (pp. 228-31)

The charge is a sweeping one, against all of science as well as technology.

Mitigating Factors. In opposition to Ellul, Roszak, and Mumford, one can argue that computers individualize us. For every example they cite, one may cite a contrary example. For example, Ellul refers to the cold and impersonal efficiency of the modern hospital but he does not bother to remind his readers that fewer people die in this cold efficiency than in the more sympathetic but less technical hospital of the nineteenth century.

Computers make bigness possible, and bigness means impersonal relations between organizations and individuals. But it also means that these organizations' services and products can be made available to many more people than would have been conceivable a few decades ago. Banks are much larger and more impersonal because of computers, but an equally important cause of their size is that there are more people with enough money and credit to use the services they provide. Since the computer makes larger organizations possible, it to some extent encourages them. But other forces in society have made them necessary also. Larger schools and hospitals and increased production of food, machinery, and luxuries are not desired simply because the computer makes them possible but because our society desires equality and a universally high standard of living.

It is indeed deplorable that a young person entering college feels that the college is like a machine and that he or she is being processed like a punched card. But what is the alternative? Higher education in the nineteenth century was much more personal and more enjoyable, but it was available only to a small aristocratic minority. The choice has been between this kind of restricted educational opportunity and expansion at the risk of degrading some of the more pleasant but perhaps less essential characteristics. The latter choice has been made. The job we now face is to improve the quality of education.

Technology in general (and computer technology in particular) has achieved a momentum that seems frightening at times. Changes come so fast that people have trouble adjusting to them and thus may condemn them immediately. Some problems are inevitable when change is so much a part of our lives; however, we can avoid some of them, change others, and find a solution to most. In fact, careful analysis and study will probably indicate a way out of our current problem. If we want a solution seriously enough to work for it, we can direct technology towards the goals we think are important.

Individuality and Technology

Before going further, let us review what we mean by individuality. Individuality, we might say, is the recognition that each of us is different from every other person, that each person is totally unique. An individual is an entity that is more complex and more real than the information in the files of corporations and government agencies. One cannot define a human being completely by describing his or her history, family relationships, and job.

The Right to Individuality. The ideal of individuality is that all people should believe this both of themselves and of every other person. An individualist believes that everyone has the freedom to make decisions and is responsible for his or her own choices. The individualist respects this right in others and expects it to be respected in return. To many people in the world today, this seems a natural right and any threat to it must be an absolute evil. However, this right has, in fact, a fairly brief history. The freedom to behave as an individual has belonged to only a very small minority of the human race throughout most of history. Individuality is very expensive. It requires education, information, and the freedom to move about and to meet other people as one chooses. In the highly individualistic society of the ancient Greeks, it was granted to "all citizens"—but not to women or to slaves (who far outnumbered their masters). In all societies, it has historically been a right of the aristocracy and some other small minorities, but it has been a right purchased with the labor and bondage of the majority. The effort to create an environment in which individuality is possible for all seems feasible only in a world improved by technology. The freedom and the resources (education and information) that individuality requires can be bought only with the work of others or with automation and technology.

Thus one can argue that individuality for large classes is a technologically induced phenomenon. We have used technology to move from an elitist society toward a democratic one. If the move is not complete and not without attendant problems, what seems to be needed is more ingenuity and more and better technology applied to the goals that we consider important.

At a more detailed level, having now seen what is involved in analyzing and programming a problem for a computer, you are in a position to appreciate both sides of this issue. The whole method of analysis—flowcharting, defining your data base, finding the best solution—is an example of what Ellul called technique. It is easy to see how it could be used shallowly to bring about oversimplified and offensive ways of dealing with people. However, you have also seen that there is nothing inherent in the computer that means it has to be used badly.

It is possible to strike a balance between such negativism as Ellul's and the naïve notion that any thing new must be better. Technology and computers have introduced changes in our society, some of them with consequences not totally desirable. The depersonalization of human relationships is one of these. Technology, as the expression of human ingenuity, can be used to solve these problems, but only if it is guided by informed concern.

Privacy and Individuality: A Summary

Privacy is a real human need, and in our society we have the right to restrict parts of our lives to a limited audience. Individuality, if not a legal right, is a long-cherished American value. Threats to our individuality and privacy limit our public and private behavior—our total behavior. Despite this strong emotional appeal, both issues are a matter of balance rather than absolutes. Total privacy and individuality for all would result in anarchy and chaos. Complete exposure and uniformity would guarantee the slavery and psychosis of *1984*. Thus we sacrifice some of each for the benefits of living in an organized society, and we watch carefully to see that the balance between sacrifice and benefit is fair, just, and in our interests. Each of us sees this balance according to his or her own values.

Exercises

1. If you were a personnel manager hiring a computer systems analyst to do a requirements analysis for an application that requires sensitive interaction with the public, what characteristics would you look for in the applicants that you interview?

2. The concepts of this chapter are of necessity very general. Do you have any feelings or personal experiences that would tend to confirm or deny these concepts for you as an individual? Describe them.

3. A strong sense of privacy, individuality, and the hatred of authoritarian power are characteristics of the American character. Pick a person from the current American scene whose life represents an effort to maintain one or more of those characteristics. Write a short essay on his or her efforts.

4. How did the concepts of privacy, publicity, and secrecy trade off with each other in the context of the war in Vietnam or Watergate?

5. Privacy is not an absolute right. Consider the following borderline cases:
   a. Disclosure of personal campaign contributions made by a candidate
   b. A reporter's ability to protect his or her source when revealing a crooked judge
   c. A priest's obligation to respect the privacy of confession of a murderer
   d. A mental patient's right to read his or her psychiatric file
   Where would you stand on each? Why?

6. Does your school require you to state your Social Security number? What happens if you refuse?

For Further Information

The discussion of privacy in this chapter has relied on two first-rank recent publications: *Databanks in a Free Society* (1) and *Records, Computers, and the Rights of Citizens* (2). They are clearly the first books you should read if you are interested in pursuing the question at all. After that, you may be interested in pursuing some further references. Westin's earlier book (3) is an important one. (4)

is written by Carl Kaysen, one of the participants in the National Data Bank debate and is interesting history. Some of the shorter papers in the reference list (5) and (6) also provide useful insights into the question. The literature in this area is growing rapidly, and it will repay you to check for publications more recent than those included in this list. There is, for example, a monthly newsletter (7).

Much of the presentation on individuality was based on the work of Mumford (8,9), Ellul (10), and Roszak (11,12). Two papers critical of Roszak's

analysis are also included in the bibliography (13 and 14). These writers are major spokesmen, but many other references can be cited to writers who have questioned the value of technology to our society. *The Children of Frankenstein* (15) is a well-written survey of the history and present role of computers in our society and is decidedly pessimistic. The other references (16–19) present a range of views and express the current concern with individuality in our society.

References

1. Alan F. Westin and Michael A. Baker, *Databanks in a Free Society* (New York: Quadrangle Books, 1972).

2. *Records, Computers, and the Rights of Citizens.* Report of the Secretary's Advisory Committee on Automated Personal Data Systems (Washington, D.C.: U.S. Department of Health, Education and Welfare, 1973).

3. Alan Westin, *Privacy and Freedom* (New York: Atheneum Publishers, 1967).

4. Carl Kaysen, "Data Banks and Dossiers," in *The Public Interest* (Spring 1967).

5. Donald Michael, "Speculations on the Relation of the Computer to Individual Freedom and the Right to Privacy," in *George Washington Law Review* (October 1964).

6. "Privacy and Efficient Government," *Harvard Law Review* (1968), p. 399ff.

7. *Privacy Journal* (monthly)

8. Lewis Mumford, *The Myth and the Machine: Technics and Human Development* (New York: Harcourt Brace Jovanovich, Inc., 1967).

9. Lewis Mumford, *The Myth and the Machine: the Pentagon of Power* (New York: Harcourt Brace Jovanovich, Inc., 1970).

10. Jacques Ellul, *The Technological Society* (New York: Alfred A. Knopf, Inc., 1964).

11. Theodore Roszak, *The Making of a Counter-Culture* (New York: Doubleday and Company, Inc., 1969).

12. Theodore Roszak, *Where the Wasteland Ends* (New York: Doubleday and Company, Inc., 1972).

13. J. A. Passmore, "Anti-Science: A Misunderstanding," *Science* (July 27, 1973) p. 327.

14. Charles Frankel, "The Nature and Sources of Irrationalism," *Science* (June 1, 1973), pp. 927–31.

15. Herbert J. Muller, *The Children of Frankenstein* (Bloomington: Indiana University Press, 1971).

16. Donald Michael, "The Individual: Enriched or Impoverished?" in *Information Technology: Some Cultural Implications for Decision*

Makers (New York: The Conference Board, 1972).

17. Charles Frankel, *The Love of Anxiety* (New York: Harper & Row, 1961).

18. David Riesman, *Individualism Reconsidered* (New York: The Free Press, 1954).

19. Erich Fromm, *The Sane Society* (New York: Holt, Rinehart & Winston, Inc., 1955).

Leisure and Power

16

The issues of privacy and individuality are concerns that affect all of us and our relations with one another. Two more issues that have attracted attention will be discussed in this chapter. The first has to do with the balance of work and play in our lives: If computers do more of our work, what should we do with the hours when we are released from labor? The second concerns power and influence in our society: By making information and sophisticated processing more available, do computers alter the balance of political and financial power? As with the issues discussed in the last chapter, there are no pat answers. We will try to make the questions clearer; the answers will have to be worked out over a period of years and even decades.

Work and Leisure in an Automated World

The introduction of steam engines and power machinery in eighteenth-century England led to a dramatic shift in the social and economic structure. The promise (or threat) of a similar upheaval has led some writers to refer to the present era as a second industrial revolution.

The Industrial Revolution represented a process of mechanization: machines replaced human (and animal) muscle power. The use of general-purpose computers and other self-regulating devices is more than an extension of mechanization. It replaces human control of processes and machines; it augments a person's mind. This new phenomenon is called *automation*.

Machines alter or replace labor. Control machinery replaces people in the operation or control of mechanical power. We may reasonably expect the general introduction of automatic machinery in many industries and trades to lead to some changes in employment patterns. In many industries work conditions, salaries, and the levels of required skills have begun to change. It is also reasonable to conclude that if a machine is doing the work a person formerly did, the person must be doing something else.

What are these workers doing? Some are unemployed; some have found new jobs. All (or almost all) spend less time at their work than their parents did: the increased capacity of machines has bought them leisure with which they can improve their knowledge and abilities, amuse themselves, help others, or kill time.

Actually, the impact of automation is quite complex and has been widely studied and analyzed. Of all the issues associated with computers, it has received the most attention. However, it has been surprisingly difficult to estimate the overall effect of automation on employment. Investigators seem to disagree about these most important questions:

1. *Does automation provide more or fewer job opportunities?* On the one hand, automatic machinery and computers do work formerly done by people, thus limiting the jobs available. On the other hand, vast new industries and new job opportunities have been created for the manufacture, sale, use, and maintenance of these machines.

2. *When a machine takes over a job performed by people, it is ultimately to be viewed as the removal of a burden or the imposition of a curse?* People have had to work for a living in one way or another since the beginning of time; idleness and unemployment are a threat that we are not used to dealing with. On the other hand, much of the work that machines now do was formerly drudgery for humans to perform. Since machines can now do it, we are free to engage in more noble pursuits.

3. *Does the use of machines raise or lower the level of skills people need?* The tasks of designing and building computers are elaborate and highly technical; they demand highly developed skills. However, many skilled persons, such as keypunch operators, are often involved in dull repetitive work, doing little more than assisting the machines.

4. *Over the past twenty years, what has been the effect of computers on employment?* Here, too, opinions differ. One expert claims that computers create one new job for every five they destroy. Another study estimates that computers displace 40,000 people per week. A more detailed study by the U.S. Labor Department reviewed twenty companies that had introduced computers and directly affected a total of 2800 employees. After one year, one-third of the employees had been reassigned to new positions in the companies, one-sixth had retired or quit, and the majority remained at their old jobs. Nine people were laid off after a year of automation.

Analyses of productivity increases indicate alternatively that two percent of the population will be able to produce more goods and services than ninety-eight percent can consume, and that we will need the labor of all. The petroleum industry is noted for the extent to which automation has been adopted. Large-scale process-control systems have been installed in most major refineries. In the decade from 1950 to 1960, employ-

"Good morning, everybody!"

ment in this industry dropped from 257,000 to 252,700—less than two percent—while production increased fifteen percent. In the same decade, which saw the great expansion of the use of automatic machinery in the telephone industry, employment there rose from 594,800 to 696,500.

A major problem is being able to define what we want to measure. In the face of the very great changes that can affect a company or an entire industry over a few years, it is difficult if not impossible to isolate those changes for which automation alone is responsible.

Factors That Affect Employment

A number of factors can be considered to affect automation and employment. We will describe eight significant ones.

1. *Computers and related machines displace some workers from their jobs.* A computer in an office does work formerly performed by clerks. A numerically-controlled machine tool replaces the work of machinists. Numerical control would not be economical if this were not true.

2. *Computers and related machines increase the productivity of some workers.* Where workers have not been displaced, their productivity has been extended; one person can do the work that would otherwise have taken several. An accountant with a computer can do more work in a week than he or she could have done in a month without it.

3. *Much of what computers do is novel; it is work never done before.* Complex business reports and industrial and scientific simulations would have formerly been too costly and too time-consuming to do by hand; before computers were available, such reports could not even be considered. Thus the computer's availability, speed, and low cost create work for it to do. Factories that use numerically-controlled milling machines can now make a profit doing work that was too intricate for production facilities in the past.

4. *The computer industry employs many people in new jobs.* The demand for computer engineers, systems analysts, programmers, operators, and maintenance personnel is a consequence of the use of computers. The buildings, air conditioning, electricity, cards, paper, and magnetic tapes computers need are also the products of industries that have prospered with the advent of computers and automation. In 1970, this was an 11.6 billion-dollar industry; it did not exist in 1948.

5. *The demand for goods and therefore the need for production continue to rise.* At least part of the increased production potential for which automation has been responsible is absorbed by increased demands. As we become a wealthier nation, individuals demand more goods of more and different kinds. In addition, the increasing population requires increased production. Thus in many industries, employment has not fallen even though productivity per employee has risen.

6. *People work shorter hours and retire sooner than they formerly did.* In many trades, a person can do much more work in an hour than he or she did in the same length of time fifty or even ten years ago. But the six-day week has been reduced to a five-day week. In some industries, it has been reduced to four. The ten- or twelve-hour day has been reduced to one of seven or eight. As of 1970, the average work week was thirty-seven hours. Vacations are longer. In 1972, eighty-seven percent of American workers received more than four weeks vacation. People stay in school longer and retire at an earlier age. Increased production capacity is thus converted (at least in part) to leisure rather than increased production.

7. *A shift to service industries and away from production industries has occurred.* In the past half-century, the percentage of the work force active in certain industries (in particular, agriculture, mining, and transportation) has gone down. In wholesale and retail trade and those

activities known as service industries (such as repairs, hotels, restaurants, medicine, education, entertainment, and so forth) the percentage has risen. More people are needed in these trades where customers require the individual attention of a human agent and where automation has had little effect on employment.

8. *Society has found new activities to absorb productivity.* Space exploration, scientific research, and many government activities have possible social value, create new jobs, and absorb people. Such activities use the efforts of many individuals who are no longer required to produce the necessities of life.

The Overall Effect

In the face of these complex shifts in the employment pattern, we can see why the extent of only one of them—job displacement—should be hard to isolate and measure. In fact, it now appears that the original question, "To what extent does automation displace the worker?" is unanswerable. But there is still the broader and more basic question "Is the effect of automation, on the whole, to the advantage or the detriment of the people concerned?" Things are changing in a complex way. Can we at least say whether they are getting better or getting worse?

Some answers to this question are possible. They are, however, incomplete, tentative, and not without some internal contradictions. Once again, a difference of attitude and perspective affects the way people look at facts and the conclusions they reach. If we look from the point of view of the clerk whose job is in jeopardy, the answer is likely to be negative. However, the computer programmer or the manager who uses computer data may see things in a different and more positive light. Finally, the sociologist or historian viewing the situation in terms of large processes and time spans will see automation another way altogether. Let us start by considering the problem of the person whose job can now be done by a machine.

The Displaced Individual

No matter how socially beneficial a change may be, if you are personally threatened you are liable to be less than enthusiastic. Consider Miss A who is a file clerk at an insurance company, or Mr. B who works in the accounting department of a large manufacturer, or Mrs. C who maintains a factory's inventory records. They have learned to do their jobs well. Nevertheless, the functions they have performed are now to be taken over by the computer and they will have to do something else.

From the simultaneous factors listed above, one can conclude that Miss A, Mr. B, or Mrs. C could get jobs in the computer industry (if their abilities and education are adequate), they could retire early (if they are old enough), or they could learn a new trade (if they are young enough). Unfortunately, for many people, none of these options is open. Such people bear the brunt of automation. For them, being replaced by a computer is not a liberation; it is a loss of both income and pride or self-respect.

Fear of automation, of being replaced by a machine, is probably a factor in many people's lives: how many, no one can say. This fear has been more or less directly responsible for the careful studies made of its effect and the large share of publicity the problem has received.

Further, the study and the publicity themselves have affected the situation, softening many of the hardships that might be expected. Concern for Miss A, Mr. B, and Mrs. C has influenced both organized labor and management. In many cases when computers are introduced, special efforts are made to locate new jobs for displaced individuals. The development of an information system can take years; thus there is time for a careful and gradual shift of personnel. Many industries and government agencies insist on personnel plans as well as plans for system development.

If a drop in the staff is necessary, natural attrition often solves the problem. Some people quit to care for young children, ambitious people leave to take jobs elsewhere, or older ones retire. Because they are not fired, they are not counted among those whose jobs are lost because of automation. However, when such employees leave, new people are not hired to replace them, and their positions disappear. Because the overall effect on the job market is the same as if they had been laid off, this practice of not hiring has sometimes been referred to as silent firing.

Changes In The Job Mix

Besides being concerned for the security of individual employees, government agencies have been interested in whether and how automation changes the job mix—the ratios of people with different levels of training required to operate the nation's industries and trades. For example, when office employees are replaced by computers, there will be work for engineers and programmers, probably at a higher education level, and for computer and keypunch operators, possibly at a lower level. What is the sum total of this effect? Statistics seem to indicate that there is a real change although it, too, is not so great as one might expect.

A major government study in 1966 concluded that the "overall demand for less-skilled workers will not decrease over this eleven-year period (1964–75), although it will decline somewhat as a percentage of the total."* Some observers have suggested that jobs in the middle are disappearing. The need for low-level workers to fulfill routine tasks persists: there may be fewer file clerks but there is a greater demand for computer operators and tape librarians. The need for highly-trained personnel increases. Thus although the average may be the same, skills may be distributed in a new way, both top- and bottom-heavy.

The Growth of Leisure

About one fact there can be no dispute. A clear and evident consequence of automation and the mechanization that preceded it has been the decrease in the amount of work required of individuals. People on the whole have more free time. In the two decades from 1940 to 1960, the average

*National Commission on Technology, Automation, and Economic Progress, *The Outlook for Technological Change and Employment,* vol. 1 (Washington, D.C.: U.S. Government Printing Office, 1966) Appendix.

worker acquired 155 hours more of leisure per year. Steelworkers have suggested the possibility of thirteen-week vacations. Some estimates suggest that by the year 2000 the normal work week may be as low as fifteen hours, which implies an unlikely increase of 260 percent in productivity.

Although the trend is indisputable, there is some difference of view about its meaning in terms of human values. Leisure can mean idleness, with no activities of interest and value. It can also mean freedom from the necessity for meaningless labor, with expanded opportunities to pursue meaningful and valuable interests. Let us look at both sides of the case.

The Curse of Work. Throughout history, the concept of Utopia has been associated with freedom from labor. Work has been seen as an unavoidable curse. The upper classes, the wealthy, and the powerful—those who were able to avoid work—avoided it whenever possible. Automation provides the first glimmer of hope that all people can one day be released from this bondage and become free to pursue the tasks that interest them. What is done out of joy, interest, and love is not work but pleasure. The tasks of making clothes, working in a garden, or carving wood are work when they are done out of economic necessity, but they are creative acts when done in freedom. The appreciation of great art and the study of history and science will be open to all when machines take over the burden of work.

The Challenge of Leisure. All this is true, but it is only half the picture. When Aristotle suggested that all people would be free when a loom could weave by itself, he could not have imagined that in two thousand years looms would do just that.

Freedom from the obligation to engage in a regimented pattern of tasks is sometimes better to imagine than to experience. The sad fact is that few of us are prepared to find an alternative to work that is meaningful, rewarding, and satisfying. Leisure has already increased to a point where we can see how some people have reacted to this freedom. Some have found leisure pleasurable and satisfying; others have not. Symptoms of the inability to cope with free time are easy to find. Workers who retire while they are still robust and healthy enough to lead an active life soon find time hangs heavy on their hands. After a few months of freedom, many look back with longing at the routine that previously regulated their lives. Although many take second jobs or moonlight because they need the extra income, others simply feel the need to be occupied and are unable to find rewarding leisure activities.

And some take their leisure as seriously as they take their labor, and work just as hard at it. They get up before dawn and play golf and drive hundreds of miles over crowded highways on a tight schedule to accomplish the maximum number of activities possible in a three-or four-day weekend. With more leisure, they will be forced to even more energetic feats to fill their hours with compressed experiences. They seem to labor under a belief that free time must be used in some constructive way, and that they must have accomplished something to justify the existence of the free time. Their leisure is built on the model of their work.

Effects of Leisure. It has been argued that the compulsion to work or at least to engage in work-like activities is part of the Puritan tradition in American history. According to this theory, all our early training has schooled us to believe that work is good and idleness is bad, that what we do not earn by our labors we do not deserve, that "the devil finds work for idle hands." America was built on this tradition and it is hard to break: people feel guilty if they are not working hard.

Proponents of this theory point out that some primitive societies where leisure is possible do not react as we do. Members of Pacific island cultures are content to be idle, to have the freedom to do nothing at all. They are not bored by the absence of work or of the kind of games we invent to compensate for its absence. Perhaps the inability to cope with leisure is only a passing phenomenon of our highly-industrialized society; perhaps these attitudes can change.

This theory contains some truth and some oversimplification. In discussions like this, one must beware of the trap of the *fallacy of homogeneous man*. Almost nothing we can say about the needs, attitudes, and desires of people is true for all of us. In any society, ours among them, there are people content to do no work and others who must be totally occupied all of the time. Most of us are in between and can adjust a certain amount in either direction. It is also an oversimplification to infer that the workload is being reduced equally for all members of society. The reductions in work that account for the statistics apply mostly to hourly and salaried employees whose responsibilities can be measured in terms of the number of hours they spend on the job. Others who measure their output in other terms may work many more hours—such as the salespersons who estimate their accomplishments by the number of sales they make, doctors who serve all who come to their offices, artists, scientists, or scholars who make their own goals, or executives whose responsibilities are to manage and control the affairs of their companies. The work of these people is certainly not going to be reduced to fifteen hours per week. People will work as hard and as long as they need to, to support their goals.

Education for Change. Many people are not ready to handle the rapid and far-reaching changes that we now know we must expect. As technology advances and new products and processes replace old ones, former crafts and skills disappear. A worker who sets out on his or her first job at the age of twenty or so must realize the job may disappear before retirement forty years later. He or she must also expect to spend less time at his job than his parents; there will be many hours, days, and weeks of free time. Filling them will be the worker's responsibility, not the employer's.

These facts point at the educational institutions in our society. If young men and women are to be prepared for the world of the future, education must prepare them. Educators have been considering this problem carefully, and some efforts are being made to modify the educational process to reflect the needs of late twentieth-century automated America. Three specific goals have been identified.

First, it is no longer adequate to train workers-to-be in a single specific trade. They must be prepared for the fact that the jobs they will hold ten years out of school do not even exist at the time they are in school. What they must learn, then, is *how to learn* so as the world they live in changes they can pick up the ideas and skills they need to live in it.

Second, it is no longer sufficient to consider a school as a place for young people only. People must become prepared to continue their educations all of their lives. The amount of information in the world, it has been estimated, doubles in ten years. Engineers who have been out of college for a decade know only half (if that much) of their trade unless they have periodically renewed their education by learning on their own or by going back to school. Thus the opportunities for adult education, or continuing education as it is more properly called, must be expanded.

Finally, students must have an opportunity, while they are in school, to find areas in which they can spend their leisure time constructively and happily. Leisure activities adequate for a few hours of relaxation after a day of hard work are not sufficient for the needs of people with more free time. The practice and appreciation of the arts, politics, and science must be presented to students not as courses to be taken once and forgotten, but as introductions in the true sense—the beginnings of acquaintanceships that can be expanded and explored in years to come.

The problem of creating an educational system to satisfy these needs is, of course, great. Here we have had the space to describe only what needs to be done. But perhaps it will serve as an introduction.

The Abuse of Power

Another aspect of the computer's impact on social institutions is its effect on the organization and distribution of power. First, computer-based systems may give some individuals power and influence over others that they could otherwise not attain. Second, the computer may become a power in its own right and we may all be under the threat of falling into its dominion—or, as it is sometimes put, computers may be taking over. In this section, we shall discuss these two aspects of the issue of computers and the power structure.

Centralization and Organization. As we have seen, computers allow greater centralization and control of information. In previous chapters, we noted that using a single large file of information is more valuable than using a number of smaller ones: there is less redundancy, the file is easier to update, and it allows information from a wide geographic or subject area to be combined and compared.

In an organization, top management has more control if all of the information about its affairs is centralized. Thus enterprises that use computers are likely to become more tightly organized. By and large, this situation is extremely useful to management, of course. A manager who is responsible for the conduct of a government agency or a corporation wants to use all the information and the power and control he or she can to exercise his or her responsibilities and do the job. If a clear view of the future, more information, and more centralized control mean better service to the customer, more economy of operation, and more accurate and thorough work, then it is to the advantage of any organization to create situations where this is possible. As long as this power is directed toward socially useful goals, the situation is desirable. However, excessive power in the hands of a few individuals also creates dangers of accidents and deliberate abuses.

Government and Public Systems. Government information systems provide centralized and easily accessible information on a wide range of topics such as personnel, organizations, plans for the future, policies, and strategies. Those with access to these files face occasional temptations to misuse them to their personal advantage.

There are two ways in which the kind of information contained in government files can be misused. First, information about individuals can be used to blackmail, or at least to intimidate them. Second, information about groups of people can be used to manipulate them. The use of information about individuals overlaps the question of rights of privacy that has already been discussed. Therefore we shall only touch on the issue briefly with a few hypothetical examples.

Mayor A is running for re-election and needs the support of prominent citizens, like Mr. B. Mr. B and his wife were not legally married at the time their first child was born. If this information were published, it could embarrass the Bs' and damage Mr. B's business. If B does what the mayor wants, the information will remain confidential.

A civil servant discovers in a tax file that Mr. C, a member of a commission deciding the location for the new civic center, has a financial interest in some of the property concerned. She urges Mr. C to resign from the commission and points out that if the decision is made to C's financial advantage, she will reveal the information she has.

In both of these cases, information in files maintained for one reason is put to use for another purpose—to make individuals change their behavior. Those in possession of the information, the mayor and the civil servant, had information that gave them power over others. In the first case, we would say that the mayor acted badly. We would probably decide that the civil servant in the second example acted in the public interest. But she too used information for a purpose for which it was not intended.

In the investigation of campaign tactics that followed Watergate, the very real question of the use of tax-return information by the party in power arose. It is possible (although not ethical) for politicians to use the information available to them to keep them in their position. The question of what constitutes legitimate use of public and confidential government data is difficult and complex. Few legal precedents can guide us. It is of small comfort that those whose misuse of power is represented by the word *Watergate* didn't require a computer for their abuses.

Political Campaigning

An extremely important use of computers and information technology is in political campaigning. Politicians who run for office present themselves and their ideas to the electorate, which then compares each with his or her opponents and decides who it wants to represent it. The politician's problem can be viewed as one of presenting a personal image attractively. Thus information about the electorate is of enormous value to politicians. Computer techniques may be used in a number of ways to deal with the numerous problems faced in a political campaign. It is a very common practice, even in small local elections, for candidates to use mailing labels prepared by a computer from lists of registered voters. In such a case, the computer not only sorts the addresses by zipcode and address, but will only prepare one label when there are several voters with the same last name in the same household. Commercial firms prepare such lists for candidates at a surprisingly low cost. They also produce "walking lists," an important tool in local elections: voters are listed by street address (odd separated from even), so they are in the right order for a campaign worker who is walking along the street, visiting each voter.

Candidates for more important offices, with larger budgets, can do more. They can use computers to analyze questionnaires and survey results, simulate voter responses to different positions and strategies, manage large files of information about issues and personalities, and prepare individualized letters. Some actual cases will make these techniques clearer.

Rockefeller's Campaign. Winthrop Rockefeller was one of the first politicians to use a computer in his campaign for governor of Arkansas in 1966. He faced formidable problems as a candidate: he was new to politics, never having held office. He was a Republican in a Democratic state. There was very little information about the voters. Before that year voters were not required to register, so there was not even a voter list.

It was decided to find out who the voters were and to concentrate the effort on personal contacts to key groups. First, the voters had to be found. Lists of names and addresses, such as telephone records, were used to start with. By phone and by door-to-door contact, information about these people was acquired—who they were, how they voted, what their interests were. For the 1966 campaign, these detailed records were assembled for approximately ninety percent of the adult population in the most important counties.

Next, a computer analysis was performed to identify voters important to the candidate. First, those who were pro-Rockefeller but who were not registered were contacted and urged to register to vote. Individual contact as opposed to advertising in newspapers or television appearances was used wherever possible. Special-appearance letters were prepared for various groups of voters. For each name in the file, a letter was typed, literature selected, and a mailing label prepared—all by computer. Thus an individualized appeal was sent from Mr. Rockefeller to each voter (or, at least to each voter who appeared, by computer analysis, to be worth the effort).

Griffin's Campaign. Other campaigns that used both similar and different techniques can be cited. The campaign of Robert Griffin for senator in Michigan in 1966 used a somewhat different technique based on polls of voter interest and opinions rather than on individualized data files. Like Rockefeller in Arkansas, Griffin entered the race a virtual unknown. Only a small percentage of the voters had even heard his name. Intensive polling was conducted to answer three questions:

1. What are the geographic areas where voters are undecided and therefore are worth working on?
2. In each of these areas, what are the issues that seem most important to the voters?
3. In each of these areas, who are the Republicans most admired and respected?

Once answers were obtained to these three questions, the strategy was simple and straight-forward: in each of the key areas (question 1), make sure that the voters hear from people they admire (question 3), who speak to them about the issues of concern to them (question 2), on behalf of the candidate, Griffin.

In 1973, Kevin White ran for re-election as mayor of Boston using a campaign based almost totally on computer-generated personalized letters. Well before the election, campaign workers collected information about a large number of voter households by means of a door-to-door canvass. The information covered the issues of importance to each voter. Once this data base was in the computer, machines turned out personalized letters directed to just those issues. The mayor reported directly to the individual voters on the issues they cared about.

The campaign included almost no public advertising, no mass rallies, no radio or television broadcasts. Thus there was almost nothing the mayor's opponent could respond to; White was essentially invisible to his opponent and to the press. How was the opposition to fight such a campaign? "That," said one of the workers for the mayor, "is our opponent's problem."

Computer Concepts in Campaigning. In each of these cases, the computer played an important role, processing masses of data totally unmanageable for humans, and doing it quickly and economically. It is perhaps equally important to note that even if computers had not been used at all, computer concepts certainly were: all the strategies were based on the idea of the programmed manipulation of information.

In each of these campaigns, the strategy was to concentrate on contacting individual voters or small groups and not to make massive public appeals. This technique took the opposition (and the press) by surprise. In more conventional campaigns the press follows and reports on the candidates' public appearances. An individual reporter (or voter) can then assemble a reasonably complete picture of what the candidate has said and where he or she stands on issues. If, however, the candidate does not speak on television or in large public meetings, but concentrates on "personal" letters and phone calls, no agency or individual really knows what he or she is saying. Does the candidate say the same thing to all the voters? Or does he or she change position depending on what the voter wants to hear? The campaign becomes a personal one, between the candidate and the individual voter; the traditional role of the public press is weakened, if not destroyed.

In the cases described, a computer performed relatively simple tasks such as sorting large bodies of information, typing letters, and addressing envelopes. The use of simulation is a more sophisticated technique. Simulation techniques permit a candidate and his or her staff to consider alternative policies and strategies to see which would be the most effective. During John F. Kennedy's campaign for the presidency, a group of scientists built a model of the electorate using the historical records of a major public opinion sampling firm. This model was used to analyze the effect of different campaign strategies. Their most important effort was the analysis of the religious issue. Kennedy was a Catholic, and many feared that this issue, if handled badly, might cost him the race. The simulation team's analysis, which they presented to the Kennedy staff, was that the candidate should treat the matter openly rather than try to ignore it.

There is no published information as to the extent to which this information influenced the campaign strategy. However, the decision, for whatever reason, made by Kennedy's staff was to do precisely what the simulation team recommended. Post-election analyses indicated that this was the proper strategy; Kennedy's forthright approach to the issue probably won him more votes than he lost due to religious prejudice.

The net effect of this brand of politics is to enable young inexperienced politicians to compete with old experienced pros. However, in the same sense that television campaigns require huge sums of money, these newcomers will require similar sums for computers. This then leads to another kind of centralization of power: it reinforces the role of money in elections.

Politics and Marketing

The techniques described above remind us of the techniques used by manufacturers and their advertising representatives to market products to the public. The effort to contact large numbers of people, the use of media, and the studies to locate the proper market and the proper approach are strikingly similar. Richard Nixon's 1968 presidential campaign has been analyzed in just these terms. The concept of selling political candidates as though they were deodorants or laundry soap is unpleasant and shocking to most people. We conceive of commercial marketing at its worst as being an effort to sell people what they want (or think they want), whether it is good for them or not. Cigarettes are a prime example.

To pursue the analogy, in politics or in commercial marketing, information can be used in two ways. A company interested in marketing a detergent can begin by asking what people want to buy and concentrating its efforts on creating such a product. By and large, this technique works to everyone's advantage. Some of the qualities buyers look for may not in fact be important but, over time, the buying public and the manufacturers together can create a good and successful product.

Another sales approach is to find out what subtle psychological measures can be used to convince a buyer to select a given product. An advertiser may learn, for instance, that the middle-aged women who constitute a major market for laundry products yearn to look young and slender and have beautiful hair. Then the problem is simply one of finding some means (short of straightforward lies) to suggest to the purchaser that people who use this detergent are young, slender women with beautiful hair; if she uses this product, she too will look young, slender, and so forth.

What implications for politics can be drawn from these examples? All market research cannot be considered immoral. It is both desirable and important for politicians to know what the electorate is interested in and what its views are on issues of concern. They can use this information to be sure they are addressing the electorate's opinions on these issues. In this way, information can be used to make the politician more aware of the community and the community more aware of the politician and his or her ideas.

However, when politicians use the information simply to make themselves attractive to the electorate by promising to repair the roads and bring in more federal jobs, or by claiming to agree with group A when they speak in Ayesville and with group B when they are in Beesville, the community is not becoming more aware of the politicians. It is becoming more aware of a deliberately false image the candidates are projecting. Knowing what people want to hear can be used by politicians to create lies and distortions of fact that will keep them in office—to serve their goals rather than those of their constituents.

The computer is not the only thing that makes this kind of manipulation possible; however, it does make it easier and more effective. Ultimately, the computer allows candidates to make the best use of their resources. Used wisely, the computer and the resources of information management and simulation will tell candidates how best to use their time, money, and people. It is reasonable that they would attempt to find the people who have open minds and address their attention primarily to them rather than to people who have already made up their minds. It is also reasonable that candidates should address their electorates on the issues the electorates feel are important.

Norbert Wiener was one of the first people to see the social impact that the computer might some day have. He recognized it would bring a hope for the betterment of people and society, but he was also deeply aware that it meant a contribution to the concentration of power. And, he adds, "power . . . is always concentrated, by its very conditions of existence, in the hands of the most unscrupulous."* This view, it seems to us, is unnecessarily pessimistic about the rational use of power in a democracy. While powerful people are not always morally upright and do not think endlessly of the general good, neither can they all be tarred with the same brush. The success of our form of government depends on a complex series of controls to prevent the accumulation of excessive power of the sort that Wiener imagines. In fact, our whole form of government is based on the idea that we are imperfect. We are well prepared for the election of an occasional crook or self-styled dictator. Furthermore, despite all the cynical efforts of market researchers or computer specialists, the practical results of a politician's term of office cannot be disguised from the public.

New technology, new ideas, and new methods mean only that new thought must be given to existing controls. Our protection must be continuous awareness of possible misuses of power and perpetual readiness to thwart them.

The Power of Computers

Let us look at another aspect of the question of power. Computers mean increases in power; but, as some have argued, increased power does not mean increased control of that power. The entire structure of our complex society today depends on computers to run it. They are our slaves, it is true; but, as with any society that uses slaves, we are totally dependent on their slavery to survive. We can no longer live without them. Without computers, our factories would not run, our banks would not open, checks would not be written and

*Norbert Wiener, *Cybernetics: or Control and Communication in the Animal and the Machine* (Cambridge, Mass.: The M.I.T. Press, 1961) p. 39.

mailed, food would not be processed, and electricity would cease being manufactured. In our large and crowded cities, disaster would soon strike in the form of cold, hunger, sickness, and death.

Systems Failures. Is such dependence a bad situation and should we try to do something about it? We think such dependence is not, in itself, a bad thing. However, computers are subject to malfunction and deliberate sabotage. In an earlier chapter we discussed small errors that could creep into a system and not be detected. Cases are known in which disgruntled employees, before leaving their jobs, have deliberately destroyed information in their employers' files. Another danger is colossal failure, which is easy to detect but difficult (if not impossible) to correct. For example, a fire in the tape library, whether caused by accident or deliberate action, can destroy the funds of information an agency has built up. Cases can also be cited in which three copies of the same tape have been destroyed within a matter of minutes by a combination of accident and carelessness. However, the other side of the dependence issue is that computers don't cause city-paralyzing strikes or require inflationary cost-of-living increases.

Military systems offer the greatest—or at least the most dangerous—threats of this kind of error. It is for this reason that they are so elaborately protected. For example, in 1971 during a routine test of the air defense warning system, the wrong communications tape was put into a teletype machine and a warning of an attack was sent out. The machine operator detected the error immediately and the order was cancelled before any military counteraction was started, but not before large numbers of people were needlessly frightened. Other systems may not be monitored as well.

A classic example of a failure occurred in the Ballistic Missile Early Warning System (BMEWS) in October 1960. Radar returns were interpreted by a computer-based system to be a flight of missiles approaching North America over the North Pole. When the headquarters of the Strategic Air Command called the radar site for confirmation, there was no answer to the call. (A submarine cable had accidentally broken just after the first message). The North American Air Defense commander, however, considered the attack so unlikely that he insisted on contacting the radar site before he took action. What had happened? BMEWS had not been programmed to distinguish between the moon and a flight of missiles.

The chance of a serious error occurring in a military system and of irreversible action being taken is extremely small, but it can never be claimed to be nonexistent. Combinations of errors—a programming error, a broken cable, a human misjudgment—may cause such a system to misfire. The chance is small but the consequence would be disastrous.

Considering the Consequences. Once again, we must turn to Norbert Wiener for a well-written statement of the pessimistic case. He points out the flaw in the argument that "computers do only what they are told to do." Wiener cites several examples in literature to illustrate the point that "doing what we tell them" is not equivalent to "doing what we want." The famous story by W. W. Jacobs, "The Monkey's Paw,"* tells of a family granted three wishes. They wished first for $200 and then received a message that their son had been killed and that there would be an insurance pay-

_____
*W. W. Jacobs, *Lady of the Barge* (New York: Dodd, 1902).

ment of $200. They wished for their son's return and were visited by his ghost; their third wish could only be that he go away.

Such disasters, Wiener points out, are not to be found only in fairy tales. When we tell computers to achieve given goals without sufficiently considering the consequences, we will see similar disasters on a much larger scale. "Any machine," he writes,

> constructed for the purpose of making decisions, if it does not possess the power of learning, will be completely literal-minded. Woe to us if we let it decide our conduct, unless we have previously examined the laws of its action, and know fully that its conduct will be carried out on principles acceptable to us. For the man who is not aware of this to throw the problem of his responsibility on the machine, whether it can learn or not, is to cast his responsibility to the winds, and to find it coming back seated on a whirlwind.*

No one could argue that the dangers Wiener envisions do not exist. The debatable question, of course, is how great they are and to what extent the controls and safeguards that are possible to us will protect us from reaping the whirlwind. The passage quoted above was written in 1948; it is a small but real consolation to know that the danger does not appear significantly greater now than it did then, or the disaster more imminent. When Wiener wrote, he conceived that the greatest role that would be assigned to computers would be in control systems. In fact, however, their role in this area has been small in relation to their use in information management. If the growth of control systems had been as great as that of information systems, and if they had been allowed to grow with as little care for the direction and nature of their growth

as information systems have, it is quite possible that Wiener's words might have been no exaggeration.

An Overview. Part IV of this book will comment in detail on ways in which technology can be controlled for the public good. It seems important here, however, to point out some facts to counteract the rather ominous tone of many of the examples and statements in this section.

The basic fact that must be remembered is that technology itself provides the tools to protect us from its own misuse. Computers do give people power to misuse information, but they also provide a means of monitoring who is examining which files. For example, they provide new opportunities for embezzling funds, but they also provide the ability to audit accounts accurately and frequently.

Computers, polls, and television give the candidate for office greater opportunity to lie and achieve votes by manipulating information. But the same technologies give the public at large the ability to follow candidates, discover their lies, and publish their deceptions.

Summary

Computers are our slaves and we depend on them. They do our work, monitor our machines, and help us control the progress of our society. Increasing population, urbanization, and all forms of technology make our lives more complex, but computers are the tools best suited to help us manage complexity.

Each of the four major issues raised in chapters fifteen and sixteen is closely related to the impact of computers on American society. Evaluating these areas is a rather subjective process, however. Social

---

*Wiener, *Cybernetics,* p. 253.

issues are not generally subject to controlled experiments and quantitative results. But it would be unfair not to note that the same issues are also being raised in the context of other technologies: employment is endangered by all labor-saving machinery; privacy is endangered by wiretapping and lie detectors; individuality is threatened by mass transportation and mass production; the control and use of television affects political power far more profoundly than the computer does.

Each of these issues is a major problem of our society, and the computer is part of the problem. The problems are a function of the growth and development of our society; technology—computer technology—is an important key to solving them.

Exercises

1. Describe an industry that did not exist ten years ago. What gave birth to this industry? How many people are employed in it? How does this compare to the total U.S. work force?

2. Compare the numbers of people involved in the manufacture of computers (about 200,000), the use of computers (about 400,000), and the numbers of computers (about 60,000) with the total work force of the United States. Are these in any sense a significant fraction of the work force?

3. The discussion of automation suggested reasons why the computer put people out of work and why it created new jobs. On the basis of your experience and your reading, do you think it is more of a danger or a help to people?

4. How do you feel about the relative importance of work and leisure in your future life? Do you think your attitude is different from your parents'? Your grandparents'?

5. The concepts of chapters fifteen and sixteen are necessarily very general. Do you have any feelings or personal experiences that would tend to confirm or deny these concepts for you as an individual? Describe them.

6. Do some library research and write a report on computer use in a political campaign other than those mentioned in the text, such as the presidential campaigns of 1972 or 1976.

For Further Information

Perhaps the best introduction to the subject of leisure, work, and automation is a factual government report (1); it contains a wealth of useful material. In particular, it has a paper by Paul Armer, "Computer Aspects of Technological Change, Automation, and Economic Progress," which is particularly valuable. A more emotional statement and one that presents a good case for the dangers of automation is *Cybernation: the Silent Conquest* (2). This important and influential essay has been reprinted in a number of anthologies, including the ones by Pylyshyn and Philipson cited in the bibliography of chapter nine. *Automation and Technological Change* (3) contains a number of thoughtful papers on the impact of automation in different areas of society. *The Shape of Automation* (4) has three excellent essays, the first of which, "The Long-range Economic Effects of Automation," is particularly recommended in the context of this chapter. Two further books, by Silberman (5) and Seligman (6), present rather different philosophical outlooks on the problems and potentials of automation and round out the list. As indicated in the text, the most authoritative author on the power of computers has been Norbert Wiener. *Cybernetics* (7) is his most important book; it deals with scientific as well as social aspects of the subject. *The Human Use of Human Beings* (8) is a more popular treatment of the subject and most readers will find it considerably easier to master. In addition, there is a brief article (9) that is extremely interesting. You may be interested in following it up and reading a rebuttal published in the same journal a few months later (10).

The Social Impact of Cybernetics (11) contains several papers on different aspects of the subject. In the context of this chapter, those by Neisser and Rickover are recommended in particular.

The use of computers in politics has had considerable documentation. *The New Politics* (12) describes several different campaign techniques, some of which use computers. The book by Ithiel de Sola Pool and his associates (13) describes the technique they employed in assisting John F. Kennedy in 1964. *The 480* (14) is a fictional account of a campaign using these strategies. Finally, *The Selling of the President* (15) is a report on the techniques of Richard Nixon's campaign in 1968. Chartrand's book (16) is intended as a handbook for politicians and political managers on how to make good use of this new tool: it discusses what information should be included in your data base, how much you will have to pay for different kinds of service, and so on.

References

1. "The Outlook for Technological Change and Employment," *Technology and the American Economy, The Report of the National Commission on Technology, Automation, and Economic Progress* (Washington, D.C.: U.S. Government Printing Office, 1966) vol. 1, Appendix.

2. D. N. Michael, *Cybernation: The Silent Conquest* (Santa Barbara: The Center for the Study of Democratic Institutions, 1962).

3. John T. Dunlop, ed., *Automation and Technological Change* (Englewood Cliffs, N.J.: Prentice-Hall, Inc., 1962).

4. Herbert Simon, *The Shape of Automation for Men and Management* (New York: Harper & Row, 1965.)

5. Charles E. Silberman, *The Myths of Automation* (New York: Harper & Row, 1966).

6. B. B. Seligman, *Most Notorious Victory, Man in an Age of Automation* (New York: The Free Press, 1966).

7. Norbert Wiener, *Cybernetics: or Control and Communication in the Animal and the Machine* (Cambridge, Mass.: The M.I.T. Press, 1961).

8. Norbert Wiener, *The Human Use of Human Beings* (Boston: Houghton Mifflin Company, 1950).

9. Norbert Wiener, "Moral and Technical Consequences of Automation," *Science* (May 6, 1960).

10. Arthur L. Samuel, "Some Moral and Technical Consequences of Automation—A Refutation," *Science* (September 16, 1960).

11. Charles R. Dechert, ed., *The Social Impact of Cybernetics* (New York: Simon & Schuster, Inc., 1967).

12. James M. Perry, *The New Politics: The Expanding Technology of Political Manipulation* (New York: Clarkson N. Potter, Inc., 1968).

13. Ithiel de Sola Pool, Robert P. Abelson, and Samuel L. Popkins, *Candidates, Issues, and Strategies: a Computer Simulation of the 1960 Presidential Election* (Cambridge, Mass.: The M.I.T. Press, 1964).

14. Eugene Burdick, *The 480* (New York: McGraw-Hill Book Company, 1964).

15. Joe McGinnis, *The Selling of the President* (New York: Trident Press, 1969).

16. Robert L. Chartrand, *Computers and Political Campaigning* (New York: Spartan Books, 1972).

True, from a low materialistic point of view, it would seem that those thrive best who use machinery wherever its use is possible with profit; but this is the art of the machines — they serve that they may rule. . . . How many men at this hour are living in a state of bondage to the machines? How many spend their whole lives, from the cradle to the grave, in tending them by night and day? Is it not plain that the machines are gaining ground upon us . . . ?

SAMUEL BUTLER
Erewhon (1872)

PART FOUR

How Can We Control Them?

The Control of Business and Government

17

An important theme of this book has been the great potential of the computer for both improving the human condition and damaging it. An overriding consideration must therefore be how we, as a society, can control this technology: how we can reap the benefits without falling prey to the dangers. In this chapter and the one that follows we will discuss this consideration. The control of computer technology is in part a technological problem—that of designing and building the mechanisms to protect, monitor, and control computer systems. This is the subject of chapter eighteen. The control of the users of large-scale information systems—business and government—is the subject of this chapter. Since this is a very new problem, and one with little precedent, the analysis that we will offer seeks a footing in a wide range of legal and political controls. Because we will range widely, it seems appropriate to give you our plan of attack.

We will first look at the general subject of control: government commissions, the ombudsman, the media, the class action suit, and legislation that already exists to control computer users. Considering the computer professionals as professionals, we will look at their efforts to regulate themselves, and the subject of licensing. The experience that has been gained in controlling other technologies is relevant and we will explore it also. We will then discuss individual responsibility as a control. Last, we will examine some actual cases of computer abuse.

The Context of Control

A new technology demands new kinds of laws and controls to restrict abuses. The creation of new laws and regulations for the control of a highly specialized technical field in the face of powerful interests is not easy and is not accomplished quickly. A natural place to begin our discussion of controls is by considering the parallel controls that exist in other fields. Let us examine some of these.

Government in the United States is controlled by the press, the balance of powers within government, the competition of the political parties for power, public opinion, and pressure groups. Federal, state, and local governments compete for power and thus provide checks on each other as well.

The processes of our form of government have three characteristics that have been granted the status of virtues. The first is slowness or (alternatively) deliberateness of government action. In making important decisions, in the courts as well as in legislation, to be right is more important than to be fast; in other words, no action is better than rash action. Speed is not considered important in righting social wrongs if there is a danger of creating a second wrong while righting the first.

A second virtue is that we have many social or economic forces that compete openly. In such competition, we are presented with all sides of the issues and can therefore make theoretically better decisions.

Third, judicial fairness (in the long run) is expected from the hierarchy of courts that review lower court decisions.

This slowness, pluralism, and apparent indecisiveness make the establishment a ripe target for critics who claim that no action is being taken on critical issues and that people in power are deliberately delaying needed actions. However, one alternative is speedy, unilateral, and final decisions that have no allowance for error. Governments with highly centralized seats of power are capable of very rapid action, but sometimes with disastrous results. Consider, for example, the early Soviet experimentation with collective farms that cost the lives of millions of Russians.

The Regulatory Commissions. Within the government, there are seven prominent federal regulatory agencies:

☐ The Interstate Commerce Commission (ICC)
☐ The Civil Aeronautics Board (CAB)
☐ The Federal Maritime Commission (FMT)
☐ The Securities and Exchange Commission (SEC)
☐ The Federal Power Commission (FPC)
☐ The Federal Trade Commission (FTC)
☐ The Federal Communications Commission (FCC)

In general, they are set up separately from the executive branch in order to provide a form of political independence. The commissioners are appointed, but long terms of office (five to seven years) give them political independence also. Because commission considerations involve matters that require more technical expertise than can be expected of most judges and courts, commissions are set up independently of courts but are subject to court review. The pattern of their proceedings is very judicial in nature: they hear disputes and make decisions based on a pattern of rules and regulations, on a case-by-case basis.

Commissions are usually created out of debate between public and private interests. The regulatory statutes that these debates produce are usually as vague (or as concrete) as the national economic policy at the time, since these commissions are usually involved in economic affairs. Typically, a long time is required before sufficient concern is accumulated in any given area to produce regulatory statutes. For example, before the Securities and Exchange Commission was established the stock market crash of 1929 and the subsequent Senate investigations into fraud and dishonesty in the securities market had to occur. The creation of the Interstate Commerce Commission took twenty years, during which a coalition was gradually built among farmers, small shippers, and merchants to oppose the railroad interests. Finally, the ICC was created to control railroad rates and discriminatory practices.

The Federal Communications Commission was established in 1934 to regulate commercial communications by radio and wire. Commercial television became a reality in the early 1940s and the FCC assumed regulatory control, putting a freeze on new station franchises so that an orderly growth could be planned. This plan took four years to write, which is relatively fast action for a new industry. However, the plan's weakness became clear later when it failed to promote educational uses of television or to provide for such potentially valuable alternatives as community antenna television (CATV).

In general, the experience with regulation by commission has shown that the commissions are:

☐ Excessively influenced by the groups subject to regulation
☐ Too easily used to protect private versus public interest
☐ Seriously hampered by the political competition between the president and Congress

Any regulation of the computer industry is going to be a technically complex matter and thus will be beyond what can reasonably be expected from many judges and courts. However, there is as yet insufficient cause to force the creation of a regulatory commission for the computer industry. It further seems unlikely that a case-by-case, judicial-style approach to remedying computer offenses

will work because, by their very nature, such offenses will affect very large numbers of people.

Computer Regulation and the Commissions. The computer industry has encountered regulatory control so far only through its association with communications and the antitrust actions taken by the Department of Justice against IBM, the largest company in the industry. A 1969 FCC inquiry concluded that there was no need or demand for the regulation of the data-processing industry.

Those computer applications most likely to be subject to FCC regulation in the near future will be those services that involve message switching (distributing messages through a central computer to many terminals) or data communications networks in which the central computer receives a message, modifies it slightly, and relays it. This regulation will probably occur because such services will compete with common carriers; it will not apply to the substance of the messages or the nature of the modifications.

In another vein, if large data banks, such as credit-checking ones, that represent considerable economic power begin to constitute monopolies, they will become subject to antitrust regulation. The practices of concern would be those that act in restraint of trade; for example, selling credit service to only one department store in a region, thus limiting the other department stores from a credit class of trade. Racial discrimination would be prevented by another set of legislation.

A Suggestion for Control: The Ombudsman

The responsibility of the executive branch of government in a democracy is to administer the laws passed by the legislature. However, the legislature cannot review administration in complete detail.

The courts, while very capable watchers, can act only on individual cases. They are dependent on the desire and the financial ability of people to begin lawsuits. Thus they are essentially passive.

Early in the nineteenth century, Sweden established the concept of the *ombudsman*, an arbitrator in disputes between an individual and the government. Although the ombudsman is appointed, not elected, he or she is independent and free from government control. The ombudsman's decisions are usually only recommendations, but they carry considerable weight.

In a broad series of published lectures delivered at Harvard and expanded for publication under the title *When Americans Complain*, Walter Gellhorn has described and analyzed the office and practice of ombudsmanship. According to him, the ombudsman is basically an instrument of the legislature with no connection to the executive branch. Since ombudsmen have complete and unlimited access to administrative papers, they are free to express an ex-officio expert opinion about the actions of government and the reaction of the public.

The ombudsman can gain public acceptance of his critical views only if they reflect accepted social norms. He must explain his views carefully in terms of those norms. He cannot redesign public policy and reshape public administration to his own concepts; he can only try to match society's expectations. Thus the ombudsman inherently has trouble coping with subtle problems involving broad changes in public opinion.

Historically, such critics have strengthened rather than weakened public administration. In practice, they have been more successful when dealing with the omission of specific services of the state than when attempting to design new government policies or to correct generalized failures in the administration of law. Issues that concern the public at large are apparently better left to political controls than to ombudsmen.

Ombudsman Functions in the Federal Government. Congressmen are ombudsmen of a sort. Constituent casework is a heavy part of the representative's duty. However, this casework tends to produce short-term solutions to individual problems rather than long-term solutions to general problems. Response to constituent complaints has become such an important aspect of elected representatives' workloads that the Office of Coordinator of Information has been created to provide information for House members, telling them to which agency they should go to obtain expert help.

Representative Henry S. Reuss of Wisconsin has proposed an americanization of the ombudsman system in the form of the Administrative Council of Congress to "review the case of any person who alleges that . . . he has been subjected to any improper penalty or that he has been denied any right or benefit to which he is entitled . . . or that the determination or award of any such right or benefit has been . . . unreasonably delayed as a result of any action or failure to act on the part of any officer or employee of the United States."[*] This has been proposed in such a way that it would not come between a congressman and his or her constituents. Such an administrative council would have only slight powers. It would initiate no inquiries on its own and would not be capable of anticipating problems. However, despite the modest aspiration for such a council, this proposal has made very little progress in Congress.

_____

[*]Walter Gellhorn, *When Americans Complain* (Cambridge, Mass.: Harvard University Press, 1966), p. 87.

Ombudsmen at the Local Level. It has been argued that the ombudsman idea works well only in small countries; perhaps a smaller community is needed for the ombudsman's recommendations to be heard and heeded. Perhaps the function of ombudsmen at a local level would be more feasible. The ombudsman concept in state government is only as good as the state government itself, and this is a highly variable matter. An ombudsman cannot renovate a decayed structure; he or she can only tidy up a well-built house. The real problem in correcting an administrative wrong at the state or local level is the matter of public confidence. Too many people feel it is impossible for individual citizens to exert influence; consequently, they do not try.

The problem of knowing where one can go for help, given the multiplicity of helpers available, is a further difficulty. Most people do not know how government functions. In recognition of this, in 1965 Governor Rockefeller of New York set up a Citizens Information Service in major cities just to put citizens in touch with the right officials or agencies of their government. Many cities have established central offices in which complaints can be lodged, and some enlightened public officials set aside a fixed amount of time to "sit in the marketplace and talk with the people."

One of the most controversial questions in the field of public control of the government is the police review board. It has been characterized as anywhere from the ultimate in hope to the ultimate in hoax. Gellhorn concludes that: "The police can control the police. The police should control the police. If the responsibility is not well borne by those who have it, the appointing power must find others to replace the failures."*

*Ibid., p. 183.

Critics can be judged by the person to whom they report. The internal affairs departments that check on internal police honesty are limited by the fact that they work for the police department. The New York State Commissioner of Investigation (an ombudsman-like agency) reports to the governor and the state legislature. The inspector-general of the Department of Agriculture reports to the head of the Department of Agriculture. Thus the acceptability of their judgments is limited by the public's view of their motivations. Critics who are entirely separate from the government, such as independent crime commissions or Ralph Nader, can criticize without limitation. A critic can point out where the resources and the goals do not match. He or she can draw attention to the need for legislation in such matters as public liability or official wrongdoing—and mistakes or wrongdoing characterize much of the concern about computers.

Another Control: The Media

Historically, the media have a tradition of conflict with government. They have been the crucial means for the publication of facts about government action and the circulation of critical ideas and opinions.

The press, in its institutionalized conflict with government, has suffered setbacks in local and state courts and has been restored by Supreme Court action to its full power given by the First Amendment. Time and again the press has been threatened with censorship only to be rescued by the judgment that it is better to take a long time to correct the conduct of the press through direct prosecution (as in the Ellsberg case) than limit its freedom through censorship, new laws, or preventative injunctions.

The media, by releasing information, keep government from overstepping its bounds. Government does not have the right to restrict that which it considers false or unsound. If it did, criticism of all kinds would be suppressed. Thus we are offered all types of information on the assumption that we can be trusted to weed out the false from the true.

Since the government and its officials are often directly involved in public disputes, the media must be free of government control; otherwise, they could not present an unbiased view of these disputes. The government, of course, does control certain aspects of the press. For example, the postal system that distributes the media is controlled by the government. Countries in which the state operates the telephone or telegraph system impose regulations on the media. With the development of community antenna television (CATV) as a news-distribution system, government will have another element of control over the media through licensing.

The effectiveness of the media as a control mechanism within a free-enterprise system has certain limitations. One limitation is that the media all depend for their success on their popularity with subscribers and advertisers, which sometimes makes it difficult for them to express unpopular views. The failure of a large number of newspapers further limits the effectiveness of the system, because it means centralized power in the hands of the survivors.

Other limitations besides those of finance and support are numerous. The press must not publish obscene or indecent material. It must be careful with the reputations of private persons. (Public officials are considered much fairer game.) The broadcasting industry as a form of the media is under far more government control than the newspapers, since the government allocates frequencies and licenses stations.

The media have been criticized for wielding power for their own ends, being under control of big business, resisting social change, resorting to sensationalism, and invading privacy. We who live under a system that depends on an intricate series of checks and balances of power must expect conflict between these centers of power and stand ready to serve as referees if one of them suffers a near-fatal blow.

In the context of this book, we must look to the media to help us learn about government uses of computers and any potential threats they involve. Unfortunately, there has been far more sensationalism than factual reporting about computers. One of our purposes in writing this book has been to equip you with information to enable you to judge this kind of "news" for yourself.

Another Form of Control: Class Action. A lawsuit can be begun to protect the rights of an individual infringed upon by the misuse of a computer. Anyone who uses a computer to break a law, of course, can be prosecuted under that law. Even before specific laws have been passed to guard against specific misuses, cases can be tried, and this body of cases begins to build precedents for the establishment of statutes. One particular kind of legal act, the class action, is of interest because it is a process whereby the rights of a large number of people can be protected in court in a single action.

The class action is a federal rule of law that has evolved through many revisions from English common law. The intent of the latest revision in 1966, called Rule 23 of the Federal Rules of Civil Procedure, was to meet the needs of a "complex modern economic society where a single harmful act may result in damages to a great number of people." Thus class action may be relevant to a number of computer-related offenses, where large numbers of people may be transgressed upon in small ways.

A class action suit is particularly appropriate where the party opposing the class has acted or refused to act on grounds generally applicable to the class—for example, a utility company that has refused to make corrections in billing procedure for a very general class of customers, or a credit-card company that has refused to stop dunning people who have paid their bills.

To date, most use of Rule 23 has been in securities and antitrust actions, but there are some cases pending that deal with environmental controls. There is some doubt about the usefulness of the class action suit for consumer protection, but legislation has been introduced in Congress to give federal district courts jurisdiction over class actions involving interstate commerce. This is viewed as a positive influence toward the use of class action in consumer complaints.

Finally, in addition to the procedural advantages of the class action there are economic advantages (court and legal costs are minimized) and psychological advantages (the individual has the backing of the other members of the class). Class action suits further present the image of the public wrong rather than the individual wrong. Press coverage then informs other members of the class and begins to balance the advantages of size and power of large corporations as defendants. It has been observed that "it will take a generation or two before we can fully appreciate the scope, virtues, and vices of Rule 23."* Therefore this legal process, instituted in 1966, may take twenty to forty years to be evaluated.

Existing Legislation. The first law in the United States concerned with the impact of a computer-

*Marvin E. Frankel, "Some Preliminary Observations Concerning Civil Rule 23," *43 FRD 39* (St. Paul: West Publishing Company), p. 52.

related industry on people was the Fair Credit Reporting Act of 1971, which imposes restrictions on credit reporting agencies. It limits their right to collect information to that which is relevant to their specific purposes and needs. It also states that such agencies must limit access to their information to those who have a need to know and further makes those agencies responsible for protecting the security of their files from unauthorized use. It grants the subjects of reports from such agencies the right to see the information that is being distributed about them and to correct errors. The Act has the following declared intention:'

. . . There is a need to insure that consumer reporting agencies exercise their grave responsibilities with fairness, impartiality and a respect for the consumer's right to privacy. . . .

(b) It is the purpose of this title to require that consumer reporting agencies adopt reasonable procedures for meeting the needs of commerce for consumer credit, personnel, insurance, and other information in a manner which is fair and equitable to the consumer, with regard to the confidentiality, accuracy, relevancy, and proper utilization of such information in accordance with the requirements of this title.

The broader controls recommended by the 1973 report of the Department of Health, Education and Welfare (see chapter sixteen) have just now begun to result in legislation. In November of 1974, Congress passed (over the president's veto) an amendment to the Freedom of Information Act of 1966 giving the public freer access to government data. The comprehensive school aid bill of 1975 included amendments regarding school data. Federal funds will be denied to schools that refuse access to a student's file by the child's parent, or that grant access to such a file to any individual or agency without either parental consent or a court order.

In January 1975, President Ford signed a bill

restricting the collection and use of information on individuals by federal agencies. This bill (discussed in chapter fifteen) requires first of all that the existence of any data bank or collection of data on individuals must be made known: secret files are illegal. Second, individuals have the right to inspect files concerned with them and to correct the information there, if it is in error.

Further, the bill prohibits the exchange of information between agencies without the permission of the individual concerned (with the exemption of law enforcement and some routine exchanges). The sale or lease of federal mailing lists is also prohibited. Another important provision of the bill has to do with Social Security numbers. State and local governments are prohibited from requiring an applicant to provide his Social Security number as a condition for voter registration, automobile registration, or licenses of any kind.

The situation at the state level is varied. Citizens of New York have a clear statutory right of privacy; this right has been recognized in common-law decisions in a number of other states. In contrast, some states (including Vermont, for instance) fail even to recognize the confidentiality of the doctor/patient relationship. The California legislature has considered but failed to pass legislation embodying the five recommendations of the HEW study and restricting the use of the Social Security number. Opposition to the proposed laws has been from banks, insurance companies, credit reporting firms, and computer manufacturers. Even efforts to pass laws regulating the government's own systems have been resisted by the departments of state governments.

A notable piece of legislation at the state level is the one that protects the Multi-State Information System for Psychiatric Patient Records (MSIS), which was described in chapter twelve. MSIS was established to permit cooperative development of a modern information management system for psychiatric records that might be used by several states. The system assures the states more efficient and economical operations as well as better record keeping and statistics. Obviously, the patient information in such a system is highly confidential. Considerable care has been taken to assure the *technical* security of the system, yet it was felt that legislation would be required to assure its *legal* security. The system itself is housed in New York, and it was decided to seek special legislative protection in that state for the system. The resulting statute asserts that the records in MSIS are private and are not the property of the New York Department of Mental Hygiene or any other public agency. The records stored in the system by the agencies of other states are, according to the statute, not open to inspection by any agency other than the one creating them and are not subject to subpoena in New York. Finally, the bill denies access to the files to any state auditors or investigators. The law is unique in the thorough and specific protection it provides for the information in this system.

Outside the United States, progress in legislation has not been much faster. In 1972, a British committee proposed a comprehensive effort to deal with the issue of individual privacy and recommended a code for guarding against abuses as well as a standing committee to review techniques for gathering, storing, and disseminating personal information. No comprehensive legislation was suggested, however, to define or protect a right to privacy. Another interesting development in Britain was the formation of a "Council for Science and Society" to study scientific problems that may have important social consequences. This organization establishes working groups to prepare reports on emerging problems. Without official sanction (it is not a government body but a voluntary organization), its significance is based on the importance of the individual scientists who have lent it their support.

In 1973, the Swedish Parliament passed the strongest privacy legislation yet seen. It establishes a "Data Inspectorate" charged with specific responsibilities to protect the rights of individuals. It requires that all personal data systems, public or private be licensed, enforces regulations about access to such systems by individuals, and acts as ombudsman in all matters concerned with automated personal data systems.

Progress in all countries, including the United States, has been slow. In the years that have passed since Congressman Cornelius Gallagher first raised the issue of privacy in 1966, the political rhetoric has become more refined and the issues more specific. The proposed laws have sharpened and in turn the opposition to them has become stronger. An important issue is the use of the Social Security number. Both fact and emotion fuel the fires. It is also, as we mentioned previously, one of those matters that may be very expensive to change. Like the smog-producing internal combustion engine, the long-standing and successful use of the Social Security number as the organizing key for large files of information may be difficult to stop.

Occupational Licensing and Professionalism as Controls

In the end, the only person who knows the true nature of a new computer system, the depth of its technical protections, its potential for misuse, and the intent of its users is the computer specialist. Many people have suggested that the computer specialist be given the stature of a professional and be licensed under a code of ethics that would provide a measure of protection to the populace. The arguments generally offered revolve around the complexity of computer technology, the layman's inability to understand it, and our consequent dependence on the computer specialist's integrity. In this section we will discuss some of the experience with occupational licensing and professional societies as a context for the debate that will ensue over computer specialists being licensed and bound by a code of ethics.

General Licensing Practices. Each state licenses many occupations to protect health, safety, and general welfare. In addition to licensing doctors and lawyers, states license such occupations as pharmacists, plumbers, accountants, barbers, engineers, and real estate salespersons.

Typically, a licensing board prepares examinations to qualify new applicants. It issues, suspends, and revokes licenses. It enforces licensing statutes and seeks court injunctions against unlicensed practitioners. Finally, it may approve and supervise occupational schools.

There are some objections to licensing. Occupational groups sometimes use licensing as a restrictive and discriminatory device. They make the requirements restrictive and the licensing complex and expensive in order to discourage new entries. Thus such boards become more interested in the protection of the profession than in the protection of society.

The principal conflicts that computer specialists have been involved in with the purchasing public have as yet had nothing to do with health or safety. As far as the general welfare is concerned, there have been many overruns and schedule slippages in the development of software, but the conflicts have been confined to users and purchasers of software who have the usual recourse to lawsuits.

The Professional Society. As for the professional aspect, this is essentially an ethical question more to the point of this book. The typical computer specialist is usually not self-employed. Thus his or her freedom to reject a task because its moral or social implications conflict with a generally agreed-upon ethical code is liable to be at the expense of the specialist's livelihood. Yet, to quote Dr. A. A. Klass, "This belief in the importance of the negative response (to the immoral order) was probably best stated by Jean-Paul Sartre who said in effect that the essential freedom—the ultimate and final freedom that cannot be taken from a person—is to say no. To disobey in accordance to one's professional code and in accord with the dictates of one's own moral conscience is the highest assertion of professional integrity."*

To form a professional society, there are usually three basic requirements.

☐ First, its members must have a professional education at a university level.
☐ Second, in exchange for the right to practice the profession, the state usually demands that the professional society insist on a code of ethics and admit only the competent and trustworthy.
☐ Further, the society must develop codes of professional conduct and standards of competence and must disbar professionals if they become delinquent.

Data Processing Associations. The Data Processing Management Association (DPMA) is a professional group concerned primarily with the use of computers in business. It has established a program

to examine and certify people as certified data processors on the basis of experience, education, and a written examination. This program is an attempt to create a professional society; however, membership in it is not accepted as a requirement for practice anywhere in the industry.

The Association for Computing Machinery (ACM), one of the largest associations in the computing profession, has adopted a code of professional conduct. This code is concerned with many matters that are not relevant to this book; but some, like limiting its members to making public statements within their realm of competence, admonishing them to avoid conflicts of interest among their clients, and asserting the importance of treating customer data as confidential, touch upon what we have discussed here. The ethical consideration closest to our concerns is quoted below:

CANON 5
An ACM member should use his special knowledge and skills for the advancement of human welfare.

Ethical Considerations
EC5.1. An ACM member should consider the health, privacy, and general welfare of the public in the performance of his work.
EC5.2. An ACM member, whenever dealing with data concerning individuals, shall always consider the principle of the individuals privacy and seek the following:
☐ To minimize the data collected
☐ To limit authorized access to the data
☐ To provide proper security for the data
☐ To determine the required retention period of the data
☐ To ensure proper disposal of the data

Disciplinary Rules
DR5.2.1. An ACM member shall express his professional opinion to his employers or clients re-

---

*Dr. A. A. Klass, "Professional Integrity and the State," *Canadian Bar Journal* **4** (1965): 124.

garding any adverse consequences to the public which might result from work proposed to him.

It took many years of debate for the association to bring about its code. There were tax and financial problems, legal liabilities to be considered when expelling a member, and serious objection to the transition from a technical society to a professional association. This transition is far from complete. Like the DPMA, membership in the ACM is not required to work in the field. Eventually, there will have to be some sort of professional society because the public will have to be able to trust the practitioners. However, as in the case of the AMA and the ABA, it is state law and agencies that enforce codes of professional ethics, and we are far from that in the computer industry.

A proposal for a code of ethics for the computer professional has been prepared by the American Federation of Information Processing Societies (AFIPS), which is an aggregation of all the technical societies related to computing. This code of ethics has not yet been approved by the AFIPS, but it is concerned primarily with technical quality, not with social responsibility.

Granting computer specialists the status of a professional society and recognizing this in law may create a group whose self-interest has to be reckoned with in the same sense that the American Medical Association had to be reckoned with as the country developed Medicare legislation. Any professional society can be expected to represent the self-interest of the members; this self-interest may at times conflict with national interests. The establishment of standards of professional competence (such as the DPMA program) is relatively easy; creating and maintaining meaningful standards of trustworthiness and ethics that will permit offenders to be disbarred will be very difficult.

The Context of Other Socially Disruptive Technologies

The computer is not the first technological development (nor, probably, the last) that has presented a new threat to established values. The way society has controlled other technologies presents some parallels with the question of computer control.

Eavesdropping Devices. One case that has been studied extensively is that of technological developments that threaten privacy. Certain technological mechanisms can intercept communications intended to be private. The functions of these devices, such as hidden microphones ("bugs") and wiretaps, seem very closely related to the socially unacceptable activity known as eavesdropping. Other devices require an individual to divulge information he or she would prefer to keep secret. The most notorious example of these is the polygraph or lie detector, which monitors a person's physical reactions (pulse, breathing, perspiration) as he or she answers questions. Even a refusal to participate in such a test may imply guilt. Psychological and personality tests may also be threats to privacy. In them, a person answers a battery of seemingly simple and unrelated questions, yet when his or her responses are interpreted by psychologists, they may reveal traits or tendencies the person would prefer to keep secret.

Wiretapping. The difficulty of defining the appropriate legal constraints on a technology that threatens privacy may best be seen by reviewing the history of one such mechanism. Wiretapping is perhaps the oldest electronic spying technique; its history antedates even the telephone and is virtually as old as the use of telegraphy itself.

In the first half of the twentieth century, most

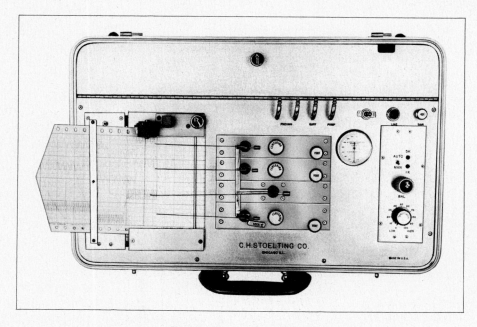

Figure 17-1 A lie detector

people did not consider wiretapping to be a very important moral, legal, or social problem. People thought it was being used by government agents to investigate serious crimes and by big businesses to spy on one another. Few private citizens were alarmed. There was, if anything, a tacit admiration for the way in which technology, cleverly used, could outsmart the criminal and the rich and powerful lords of business.

In fact, however, the use of wiretapping and other electronic techniques such as the hidden microphone were much more prevalent than anyone chose to admit. The FBI, the Treasury, and even the Post Office used wiretapping extensively, as did state and local government agencies. Private agencies offered their services to industry and individuals, and found many willing takers.

The legal status of wiretapping was confused, to say the least. No federal law referring explicitly to electronic surveillance was passed. In 1928, the Supreme Court ruled that wiretapping did not fall within the constitutional prohibition of "unreasonable search and seizure," since there was no physical violation of property.

In 1934, Congress established certain rules for the radio, telephone, and telegraph industries. Although it said nothing about wiretapping as such, one provision of the law made it illegal for anyone to intercept or reveal the content of messages. This provision was interpreted by the Supreme Court in 1937 to constitute a blanket prohibition of wiretapping and of the use of wiretap evidence in federal courts. By this time, all levels of government were using wiretapping, and accepting the high court's ruling would have seriously jeopardized the work of law enforcement. The attorney general chose, therefore, to ignore the decision. Since the Department of Justice itself chose to violate the law as interpreted by the Supreme Court and to ignore violations by other law enforcement agencies, it could not be enforced.

Congress, before and during World War II,

	YES	NO
1. Does your work fall to pieces when the boss or a supervisor is watching you?	☐	☐
2. Does it make you angry to have anyone tell you what to do?	☐	☐
3. Are you frequently angry or upset with your spouse?	☐	☐
4. Do you get nervous and shaky when approached by a superior?	☐	☐
5. Do you often cry?	☐	☐
6. Are you frequently angry or upset with your parents?	☐	☐

Figure 17-2   Questions asked on an industrial "psychiatric-neurologic inquiry"

continued to debate the issue periodically. However, not even the threat of wartime espionage and sabotage could make it pass a bill legalizing the wiretapping that the executive branch of the government freely carried out in the interests of national security. In the post-war period the debate intensified, but with little or no positive action. Some state laws were passed prohibiting wiretapping, but the effect was basically the same as at the federal level: law-enforcement officers continued to wiretap, but secretly.

The concern was general. There was relative agreement that wiretapping and bugging were widely misused; there were frequent congressional hearings, and numerous bills were presented to Congress. Yet no law governing the use of wiretapping was passed. Although it was generally agreed that controls were required, there was no agreement on what they should be. One faction, concerned about the right to privacy, favored absolute prohibition of wiretapping by any agency for any purpose. The critics pointed out that this simply would not work, as it had not worked on the basis of the 1937 Supreme Court ruling. It was more realistic, they claimed, to permit the use of

wiretapping by federal law-enforcement officers under suitable controls.

But what controls were suitable? And in what kinds of situations might wiretapping be used? Some bills proposed the use of court orders to obtain permission to wiretap; others proposed that the control be in the executive branch. While this debate went on, the Supreme Court gave no further clarification beyond the 1937 ruling.

Yet, gradually, a small amount of progress was made. The president's office, the Federal Communications Commission, and the attorney general published orders limiting the use of surveillance and defining the context in which it was permissible. The rights of defendants to know why their wires had been tapped began to be explored in state courts. The grey areas began to be mapped out. Can a person tap his or her own telephone? What if one of the parties consents but not the other? Can the number called be recorded if the conversation is not tapped?

In 1967, President Johnson sent to Congress a crime-control bill containing a prohibition of all wiretapping and eavesdropping except in cases of national security. The attorney general's office si-

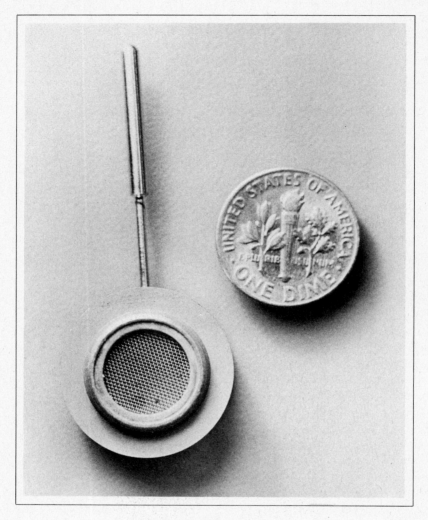

Figure 17-3 A "bug"

multaneously banned all wiretapping in the federal government except for cases of national security and then only on its own written approval. However, the mood of Congress reflected a growing national concern for the steeply rising crime rate. Some congressional leaders saw the attorney general's move as a retreat in the war against crime. The crime-control bill passed in early 1968 permitted wiretapping under court order for a wide range of cases involving narcotics, murder, robbery, organized crime, and other offenses. President Johnson signed the bill, but not without sharply criticizing the measure and recommending further legislation to narrow the range of permissible use of electronic surveillance.

The issue is still far from settled. Supreme Court

rulings in 1969 and 1970 continued to insist on the right of defendants to examine transcripts of wiretaps to learn whether their rights had been violated in any way, to reverse convictions based on the illegal use of wiretapping, and to define any wiretap made without a court order as illicit and inadmissible as evidence. Simultaneously, representatives of the Justice Department declared the need for wider liberty to use electronic surveillance for broader and more liberal definitions of requirements and for greater secrecy than seemed possible under the Supreme Court ruling. In 1972, the Supreme Court ruled that wiretapping without a warrant was unconstitutional even in cases involving national security. Throughout this period, the courts have remained critical of the use of wiretapping, and law-enforcement agencies have insisted on its importance for them to be able to combat organized crime.

The illegal use of wiretapping and other information-gathering techniques in the 1972 election campaign were a revelation to many who thought that the government and its agents could be trusted to use the tools of law enforcement with wisdom and discretion. This may eventually result in stronger legislation. However, at this time, concern for the right to privacy and concern for increasing control over crime seem to be so closely balanced in the United States that legislation is at a standstill.

What is there in an issue such as this that can absorb decades of discussion and debate without resolution? Forty years of debate created no legislation; over thirty years of concern—from 1937 until 1969—did not tempt the Supreme Court to hear another case involving the basic issues of wiretapping and electronic surveillance.

When a new question is asked, a long time may be required to see it clearly. A number of important issues presented themselves, over the years, in the wiretap issue. In different contexts, in different national situations and moods, it was necessary to ask again: when can the requirements of national security override the individual's right to privacy? There was no simple answer.

Thus by contrast we can understand that it was a relatively short period of time between the first set of Gallagher hearings on privacy in 1966 and the modifications to the Fair Credit Reporting Act in 1971. The reason this took such a short while, as these things go, is that the issue was clear and the contest was between rather unequal values: privacy versus the profitability of a small number of corporations—the credit-reporting companies.

Threats of Other Technologies. Society has dealt with technologies that have threatened one area of human life—earning a livelihood—fairly directly and quickly. Threats to employment have been met in many ways: by legislation, by labor union action, or by intelligent decisions by corporate management. Hundreds of years of tradition, experience with labor-saving machinery, and the development of the science of economics have made this possible.

Technological advances that threaten privacy have less tradition behind them, fewer observable acts, and fewer legal and social studies of them made to support intelligent and positive controls. Action has been slow, but the problem has not been totally ignored, as we have seen in the case of wiretapping.

Control of technologies affecting other aspects of life that do not have the legal standing and precedence of the right to privacy and the right to work is still more difficult. The computer, as we have seen in Part III, seems sometimes to exert pressures for conformity, standardization, and depersonalization. Other technologies have also posed threats to the quality and richness of life. In all these cases, control has been difficult because it is hard to define what is being lost and what human rights are being infringed.

For example, television, some have claimed, is debasing the quality of American life by the paucity of the materials it presents. Because television must appeal to large audiences, it presents materials that have a wide acceptability. Thus it appeals to the lowest common denominator—the commonest tastes.

There should be, it then follows, some mechanism to limit the violence, the mind-deadening stupidity, and the blatant commercialism of television programming. But it is difficult to establish any control of a free medium that does not simultaneously limit the freedom of speech. For example, the banning of cigarette commercials from television in 1970 was accomplished only after many years of conscious effort. Studies and widespread disapproval of television quality have resulted in little change in program content.

Within the traditional freedoms of our society, there is no easy way to induce people and organizations to take actions that will be good for the society as a whole at the cost of even minimal personal inconvenience or loss. Television is only one of many examples. The ambivalent nature of many technological devices—in transportation and electric power generation, for instance—that both improve the standard of living and destroy the natural environment might also be cited. Instituting legislative controls that impinge neither upon the liberties guaranteed by the Bill of Rights nor the socioeconomic ideals of the American Dream has proven, so far, a difficult task.

Responsibility as Control

Responsibility is more than performing one's legal obligation. It may involve self-sacrifice and is usually for the purpose of obtaining a greater good rather than a personal reward. Last and most important, responsibility is basically an *individual* matter.

The obligation of industry, for example, has been said to be to make maximum profits within the law. However, a production process that fouls rivers or creates smog, or a product that is unsafe even though it sells is undesirable. The general interest of the community must be a guiding principle. Some large corporations have incorporated consumer critics into their inner councils, but social responsibility is still a matter of individual concern. For example, if an employee of a computer firm becomes aware of an application being developed for evil purposes, his or her cooperation becomes a matter of individual conscience.

As we have seen, our system of government represents an intricate set of controls, each with a defined function and set of freedoms. Thus one can say, for example, that a judge's problem is not to write statutes but to make the fairest judgment in a specific case. Similarly, committees and commissions tend to limit their judgments to those things that they are certain are within their scope of operation and responsibility.

Computer professionals can safely narrow their concerns to the pursuit and protection of their profession. However, they too have a greater responsibility available to them, should they choose to shoulder it. In fact, in a problem area in which the details of technology are at the core of the truth of many of these issues, they have the greatest obligation to stand up to be heard. However, they do this not only at the risk of their own livelihoods, as we have seen, but also at the risk of losing their colleagues' respect for entering into a debate outside the realm of their approved competence. Worst of all, they do this at the risk of not being believed. It is easy to suspect the motivation of technologists who defend or attack their own technology.

The person in our government who has the broadest set of freedoms and thus the greatest opportunity to assume responsibility is the elected official. Such officeholders undertake any crusade they feel is in the self-interest of their constituents and their own political careers. Thus basically the prime responsibility rests upon us all as members of this society with this form of government. We, the authors, believe the key to using this responsibility in an intelligent and enlightened way is to become educated about the facts of any particular issue. Only in this way can all of us behave as an informed electorate and exercise responsibility and control over our technologies and our elected representatives.

Computer Crimes

So far, this chapter has treated the possibilities of control in the face of the threat, rather than the fact, of the abuse of computer technology. Before concluding this presentation, let us examine a few documented cases of computer crimes. These cases do not present any intricate moral or legal ambiguities. Nor have they required new and precedent-setting legislation, since they involve essentially an old-fashioned crime: stealing money.

Hundreds of cases of criminal uses of computers have been recorded. Some authorities claim that a much greater number go undetected and un-counted. A few examples of computer crime have

become classics. They serve to indicate the nature of the danger, and we will describe them briefly.

Embezzlement. In March 1973, local and state authorities had the operations of a New York book-maker under surveillance. They noticed a particularly heavy better who was placing bets as high as fifteen to thirty thousand dollars a day on horse races and professional basketball. Investigation proved him to be the chief teller at a branch of the Union Dime Savings Bank in New York.

When a special audit was made of the bank's books, it appeared that the chief teller had in fact stolen $1.5 million over a period of three years. To remove that much money from a bank and not be found out for three years is as rare as it is difficult. The teller had used the computer to assist him in shuffling money back and forth between accounts, so that any account could be made to look normal when necessary—for instance, when interest was due. He chose to steal only from accounts with very little activity, so the chance of someone notic-ing an error would be small. If, however, an account holder noticed a discrepancy and com-plained, the problem would be reported directly to the embezzler himself, since he was the chief teller. He could then make a rapid adjustment by "borrowing" from another account to correct the one being questioned.

With help of the computer, the teller was able to supply information to the bank's auditors that made it appear the accounts were correct and up-to-date. Note that it was his gambling, not his stealing, that attracted attention. Nothing amiss was detected by the bank's normal control mech-anisms.

Fraud. At almost the same time the Union Dime embezzlement was uncovered, a much larger case

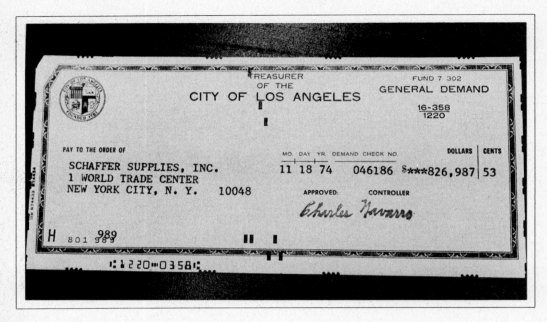

Figure 17-4 A fraudulent check involved in a recent scandal

appeared in the news: the Equity Funding scandal. The Equity Funding Life Insurance Company, or some of its employees (twenty-two people were cited in one indictment, including the top management), used computers extensively to falsify the company's records. Computer records were created for which no real insurance policies existed. Of the 97,000 policies the company claimed to have in force—more than three billion dollars' worth—two-thirds were false. A secret code associated with each policy enabled those in on the deception to distinguish the real policies from the fake ones, but to anyone else, they all appeared to be sound insurance policies. New fictional policies continued to be added to the file at a steady rate; these policies were then sold to other insurance companies. This is a fairly common practice known as "reinsurance." The company first writing the policy gets immediate cash for it and the buying company then collects the periodic premiums from the policyholders and pays whatever benefits accrue.

Insurance companies are very closely monitored and controlled. When auditors asked to see the paperwork behind any of these fictional policies, they would be put off for a few hours so the records could be located. This was long enough to fabricate the applications, the doctor's certificates, and so on, and submit them for inspection. If the auditor wanted further verification and wrote to the policyholder directly, the address given would turn out to be the home address of some member of the staff who was in on the fraud.

Occasionally, of course, and with statistical regularity, one of the fictional policyholders would have to "die." Those responsible for the fraud would then collect the additional benefit of the insurance payment.

How could such a massive fraud, involving billions of dollars, be perpetuated? First of all, the controls on the data-processing operation were remarkably loose. No one seems to have been responsible for the entire data-processing operation; the work was broken down into a great many steps and processed by separate people. Tapes were maintained in a library with unrestricted access: anyone could take out a tape, use it (and modify it), and return it to the files without question. Anyone could enter the computer facility at will, and no record was kept of the visits. There was no independent audit of the data-processing function itself.

Until the courts straighten out responsibilities, it is not easy to say how many of these loopholes were accidental and how many were deliberate. It does appear that those responsible attempted to use the basic trust many people have in the computer to disguise their activities: whenever possible, they presented their information in the form of a computer printout rather than as a typed or oral report. Psychologically, many people (apparently including auditors) are prepared to believe that a computer is more likely to be accurate than the people who run it, and that a machine that adds and subtracts accurately cannot be programmed to deceive.

The fraud was finally disclosed when an ex-employee decided to reveal the entire situation. He called a securities analyst and precipitated the crash of the insurance firm's parent company, the Equity Funding Corporation of America. It was the disaffection of this employee, not any controls built into the system, that was responsible for the fraud coming to light. The normal audit and control mechanisms of the insurance industry revealed no questionable practices.

Another Case. Jerry Neal Schneider was a seventeen-year-old high school student who occasionally rummaged through the trash cans outside the Pacific Telephone and Telegraph Company for discarded equipment he might be able to use. One day he found some catalogs and manuals that gave the codes and methods for ordering equipment from the company's warehouses. It only required keying in the necessary codes via a touch-tone telephone. Schneider was able to order all the equipment he wanted using the codes he found. He opened a shop as a supplier of specialized electronic equipment, all of which he got just by picking up his phone and ordering from the telephone company's computer. After several years, he was caught, convicted, and jailed. After he was released from jail, he went into business as a computer-security expert, advising companies on how to improve the design of their computer systems to make them more tamper-proof.

Schneider's mistake was taking on a partner who later revealed the entire scheme to the authorities. No internal controls by Pacific Telephone revealed the leak.

Summary

Now, within the context of control and the context of other disruptive technologies, what can we say about the prospects for social control of computer applications?

First of all, the mechanisms to control the organizations that use computers certainly exist. They are far from perfect, or even adequately fast. They must be used intelligently and aggressively to be effective. Instituting a mechanism for social control such as the ombudsman will require forces other than the computer problem to bring it into general use. Invoking all of these control mechanisms will require an informed, alert, and responsible populace.

The history of the development of control mechanisms in general and the evolution of wiretapping legislation in particular show that issues involving a contest of nearly equally important values and equally powerful contestants take a significant amount of time, since the balance be-tween the virtues and vices involved is nearly even. Alan Westin has said that the issue of privacy will be on the agenda of debate for a decade and, in a narrower sense, the control of computers will be there as well.

When you then consider the realm of less con-crete issues such as depersonalization and the loss of individuality, the issues are still too vague. On the other hand, the abuse of political power is exactly what our government was designed to prevent. So far, its controls are stronger than any computer application ever imagined.

Computer technology, social attitudes, and economic conditions can change significantly in days, weeks, months, and certainly in a year. Our system changes political officeholders in periods of two, four, and six years. In contrast, we create laws and commissions over periods of twenty to forty years. This disparity seems very great. It will seem even greater as we go on to consider the future.

Exercises

1. Read chapter eight, "Violence in Television Entertainment Programs" of *To Establish Justice, to Insure Domestic Tranquility*, the final report of the National Commission on the Causes and Prevention of Violence (De-cember 1969). It describes research that has been done on television violence and con-cludes that, as an alternative to government censorship, the National Association of Broadcasters Code of self-regulation should be continued. It recommends that violence in children's cartoons be limited, as well as the amount of network time spent on crime, western, and action adventure programs and the context in which violence is portrayed. Do you conclude that this is the best way to control television violence? Why or why not? Do you see a parallel between the question of self-regulation in TV and computers?

2. Find out whether the number of business failures in the newspaper industry exceeds or is less than the number of new newspapers started in your home state. Pick a single news-paper and find out what percentage of its income comes from subscriptions, and what percentage comes from three top advertisers. What can you conclude about freedom of the press from these facts?

3. The contest of values that lies behind the issues of control of computer technology presents hard choices. For example, any con-nection between the credit-checking industry and law enforcement seems ominous. Here is one built into law: if an automobile is seized during the course of a narcotics arrest, it can be impounded and sold by the govern-ment. Formerly, a mortgage company, if it owned the car, could petition to reclaim it. Now the company can reclaim the car only if it can prove that, before it financed the purchase, it made both a criminal check and a credit check on the potential purchaser and neither of these showed a history of narcotics arrests. What do you think will be the effect of this ruling? Talk with a judge or a police officer to confirm or deny your hypothesis.

4. Check in your library for legislation affecting privacy since this book was published.

5. What legislation controlling information on individuals has been passed in your state? What bills have been introduced and have failed to pass? Can you find out why? (Check the Readers' Guide.)

6. Using some of the references below, or more recent ones, prepare a case study of a computer crime not mentioned in the text.

7. The radio and TV stations in many areas of the country perform a public ombudsman service by investigating consumer complaints and publicizing them. Many of these complaints have to do with computers. Contact your local station and see if you can get access to these complaints. If you can, write a summary and analysis of them from the point of view of controls.

8. Investigate the Bank Secrecy Act. It is concerned with the circumstances under which the government can subpoena your bank records. Write a summary of the status of this debate.

9. The publisher has decided to discontinue a magazine to which you subscribe and mails you a refund for the remaining issues. In an effort to regain losses on the magazine, the publisher sells the mailing list of subscribers to a publisher of another magazine. You become deluged with mailed advertisements about the other magazine. A salesperson comes to your address asking for you and leaves a sample issue. Who "owns" your mailing address?

10. You pay a fee at an employment agency to take an aptitude test. On your own, you apply for a job at a local firm. The firm writes the employment agency asking if it has any information on you. The agency sells a report containing your test results to the firm. The firm rejects your application, telling you the reason was your bad test scores. Who "owns" your test results?

For Further Information

For an introduction to the general theory under which our government operates, Burns and Peltason (1) is recommended. It also has an interesting survey of the commissions and boards that operate inside and outside of the executive branch of government. References (2) and (3) give an insight into the tremendous number of controls under which businesses and industry operate. Kestenbaum (4) gives an account of FCC considerations of the data-processing industry. Item (5) is an analysis done by a blue-ribbon committee selected by President Nixon to analyze the commission system. Walter Gellhorn (6) gives a clear and broad evaluation of the mechanisms by which Americans can register their complaints. In particular, he considers the possible use of the ombudsman in the United States. The freedom of the press is probably the most abundantly discussed topic in this chapter. Items (7,8,9) are a sampling. The recent Pentagon Papers and the Ellsberg case will provide newspaper reading on the topic as well.

Research on class action will take you into the

law library and (10) will give you a start. The manner in which professional societies control themselves is discussed in (11). We also suggest the literature of the American Medical Association and the American Bar Association. (12) serves as a starting point for research on wiretapping, lie detectors, and personality tests. It contains an excellent history of wiretapping legislation. For a wider appreciation of the impact of technology, you should consult the writings of Ralph Nader. As mentioned previously, the *Bulletin of the Atomic Scientists* has much to say about the responsibilities of the scientist in the public realm.

The next reference (13) discusses how the techniques of regulatory agencies can be applied to the computer industry. The paper by Finerman (14) is a thoughtful study of the meaning of professionalism in this field. For further information about computer crime, you may want to look at newspaper indexes (look under Computer, Data Processing, and the specific cases cited in the text) for more up-to-date information. *Computer Abuse* (15) is a good reference on computer crime; others will be given in chapter nineteen's reference list. The final reference (16) is a fascinating book-length account of the Equity Funding case.

References

1. J. Burns and J. Peltason, *Government by the People* (Englewood Cliffs, N.J.: Prentice-Hall, Inc., 1954).

2. Marvin H. Bernstein, *Regulating Business by Independent Commission* (Princeton, N.J.: Princeton University Press, 1955).

3. L. M. Kohlmaier, *The Regulators* (New York: Harper & Row, 1969)

4. Lionel Kestenbaum, "The Regulatory Context of Information Utilities: Varieties in Law and Public Policy," in Sackman and Nie, eds., *The Information Utility and Social Choice* (Montvale, N.J.: AFIPS Press, 1970).

5. The President's Advisory Council on Executive Organization, *A New Regulatory Framework—Report on Selected Independent Regulatory Agencies* (January 1971).

6. Walter Gellhorn, *When Americans Complain* (Cambridge, Mass.: Harvard University Press, 1966.)

7. Fred Siebert, Theodore Peterson, and Wilbur Schramm, *Four Theories of the Press* (Urbana, Ill.: University of Illinois Press, 1956.)

8. Edward J. Guald, *The Press and the Constitution* (Minneapolis: University of Minnesota Press, 1948.)

9. James L. Fly, *Freedom of Speech and Press* (Ithaca, N.Y.: Cornell University Press, 1945).

10. Ronald E. Young, "Federal Rules of Civil Procedure: Rule 23, the Class Action Device and its Utilization," *University of Florida Law Review* 22 (Spring/Summer 1970).

11. William C. Keck, "Occupational Licensing: An Argument for Asserting State Control," *Notre Dame Lawyer* **44:** 104 (October 1968).

12. Alan F. Westin, *Privacy and Freedom* (New York: Atheneum Publishers, 1967).

13. Manley R. Irwin and William H. Barrett, "The Public Utility Status of the Computer Indus-

try," *Rutgers Journal of Computers and the Law* **3:** 2 (1974) pp. 219–31.

14. Aaron Finerman, "Professionalism in the Computing Field," *Communications of the ACM* (January 1975), pp. 4–8.

15. Donn B. Parker, Susan Nycum, and S. Stephen Oura, *Computer Abuse* (Menlo Park, Ca.: Stanford Research Institute, 1973).

16. Ronald L. Soble and Robert E. Dallos, *The Impossible Dream. The Equity Funding Story: The Fraud of the Century* (New York: Putnam, 1975).

Technical and Administrative Controls

18

If the information in a system can be used to invade individual privacy or to abuse power, controls are necessary. We have considered the prospects for governmental and social restraint, but a number of technical and administrative controls also exist. One of these is file security.

The Security of Manual Files

Before examining the question of the protection of computer-based files, we should consider the security of manual files. Are computer-based files more susceptible to sabotage and snooping than manual files? Probably not. In fact, they allow us to take some safety measures that are not possible with manually maintained files. Of course, no computer is absolutely tamper-proof, if a person wants

to gain access badly enough. But manual systems, too, are far from perfect.

Consider the problem of manually maintaining a large personnel file—in a credit agency, a welfare office, or a police department, for example. There are hundreds of thousands of folders, each containing from one to more than one hundred sheets of paper. These files are stored on shelves—much like the bookshelves of a library—that fill several large rooms. When a person wants access to such a file, he or she applies to the librarian, who sends a clerk to retrieve the appropriate folder(s). The borrower signs for it, takes it to a table or back to his or her office to read, and then returns it.

Suppose the borrower notices that a page is missing and draws attention to this fact. What happened to it? Who took it? An investigation is begun. Perhaps an earlier user of the file took it;

perhaps the librarian or one of the clerks did away with it. No one can really tell who is responsible after the deed has been done. And, once the information is gone, there may be no easy way of restoring it. Equally serious, there may be no way to tell when a page is missing. In a manual file, there is no way (as there is in a computer-based file) to give information to a user without also giving him or her an opportunity to copy, alter, or destroy it.

On the other hand, the amount of damage a clerk can do by surreptitiously destroying a few pages of paper is nothing compared to the mammoth mischief an imaginative programmer could perform when he or she has simultaneous access to all the information in the file and the powers of the computer to do the work.

The opportunities for snooping are at least as good in a manually-maintained file as in a computer-based one. A person with access to the library can presumably ask for any folder and, obviously, can look at any part of it. Selective access can only be enforced in a manual file at great expense by such measures as maintaining many separate files.

In any system, some persons have access to all the information with little or no possibility of anyone discovering their misuse of it. They can change or destroy information without serious threat of detection. In a manual system, these people are the clerks who maintain the physical files, who retrieve and return folders, insert new pages, and so on. In an automated system, they are the programmers who construct and maintain the security system. No matter how carefully employees are selected, one may be willing to perform an illegal service for a price. However, by and large, an automated system has fewer employees with access to information than a manual system.

The Misuse of Computer-based Files

What kinds of dangers should a computer-based system be protected against? Here are five representative problems:

1. As our program is being run under a time-sharing system, another program operating at the same time modifies our program or data (either accidentally or deliberately).
2. We are using a terminal to request data. While it is being typed out, someone taps the wire and gets a duplicate copy of the information (passive snooping).
3. An unauthorized user claims to be authorized and requests information from our data base (active snooping).
4. Pretending to be authorized, an interloper modifies our data base, deleting information he or she wishes to suppress.
5. An authorized user modifies the data base for personal reasons.

Many more such cases could be constructed, but these five cover the field pretty well. They are not farfetched; they are problems faced every day in real systems. For example, here are two actual cases. The details have been altered somewhat to prevent the identification of the individuals and firms involved. These are the alleged facts.

Two rival companies—call them CS-1 and CS-2—offered computer services on a dial-up time-shared basis in a large city. One large user subscribed to them both and, for the sake of simplicity, used the same password for both systems. Personnel at CS-2 thus knew the password and were able to dial up CS-1, pretending to be a bona fide user. They gained access to programs and data files that

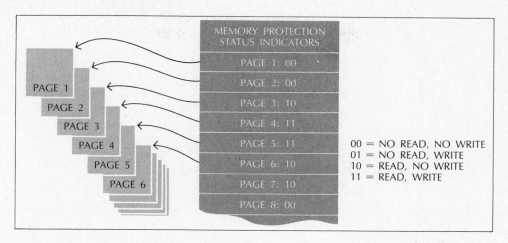

Figure 18-1   Memory protection system

CS-1 made available to its customers. They copied these files and were then able to offer the identical services at a cheaper rate to all users, thus ruining the competing company.

In another case, a company maintained detailed computer-based files on its employees. A programmer became disaffected with the company and decided to leave it. He felt the file they maintained was an invasion of the employees' privacy. Before he left, he modified a program so that the next time the file was used it was erased.

Hardware restrictions.   How can such misuses be prevented? In all time-sharing systems, controls are necessary to prevent users from interfering with one anothers' programs and data. These controls prevent a program with errors from erasing the other users' data or altering the operating system, for instance. However, they also provide some simple and basic privacy protection.

For example, before a user's program operates, the operating system establishes some rules that the program cannot violate. There are special devices built into the hardware of the computer for enforcing these rules. For each major block (or

page) of core memory, the operating system can set an indicator that allows (or prevents) user programs to read from or write on that page. Figure 18-1 indicates how such a system might work. For each page of core memory, a two-bit indicator shows whether the user's program can read information from or write information into memory. Using this method, the operating system can limit the specific areas of core memory the program can have access to. This is usually called *memory protection*. For example, the operating system's privacy protections would be given the "00" protection shown in figure 18-1 to prevent them being rewritten or read so that they could be understood.

Further, there are some instructions in the machine (called *privileged instructions*) that the user program cannot execute. These include instructions that alter the memory protection status of pages of memory, for instance. If the user program attempts to access a word in a protected portion of memory or to execute one of the privileged instructions, program operation is halted and control is returned to the operating system.

These mechanisms, which are built into the hardware of all large-scale modern computer systems, provide some elementary protection against disclosure or tampering with information.

Software Restrictions. The hardware restrictions just described will prevent a program in core memory from tampering with other information that is there. It does not prevent a user's program from asking the operating system monitor (which executes all input and output) to load a specific file into its part of core memory and thus to gain access to that file.

The simplest technique for restricting access to a computer system is by some scheme of user identification. On virtually all systems, a user has some code by which he identifies himself. This allows costs to be billed to the proper party, for instance. It also keeps unauthorized people from gaining easy access to the system. Before a user is granted access to a particular file, the special combination of characters known only to authorized file users must be given.

There are some obvious disadvantages and limitations to such a straightforward system. First, a person may learn the password by snooping—by picking up electromagnetic radiation, examining discarded typewriter ribbons, or tapping telephone lines. If the password is short enough and if the person cares enough to take the trouble, he or she can try different possibilities until the right one is found. Once the password is known, of course, the person then has unlimited access to the file and can do what he or she wishes.

Another disadvantage of a password scheme is that it assumes that all the data in the file is of the same importance and that a user of any part of the file has the right to examine all of it. In the case of a large centralized data bank this may not be true. For example, suppose there is a large data bank on all the citizens in a state, for the use of all the

state's offices and departments. A clerk in the motor vehicle department should be allowed to check on a person's basic status (age, address, and so forth) and information relating to his or her use of motor vehicles, but should not have access to information about the individual's health, criminal record, income tax, or welfare status.

Thus systems are being proposed for more complex methods of control of access to information files. The ultimate system would allow particular users to access only specific items of information. For instance, a user in the motor vehicle department, once having been identified with some sort of password, would be able to examine data only in those parts of the file where he or she had explicitly been granted access.

More sophisticated password schemes have also been suggested to protect the files from those who might be able to learn a password and gain access to the information. A system might be instituted whereby the user could communicate the password over a special telephone line. There might be a series of passwords known only to the user and the system, and each password might be used only once. Instead of a fixed password, the key might be a simple rule that the user must apply to information supplied by the system. For example, the system might type a number and the user transpose the digits and add today's date. It would be difficult for a snooper to break such a password. Also, these passwords can be changed frequently.

When terminals are connected to the computer by *hard wire* (that is, when there is one and only one terminal connected to a given input/output line), physical access to particular terminals may be effectively restricted. To return to our example, such a system would not allow information about welfare or criminal records to be printed at the

```
.NS1,P5099.WMFWU3TUMETWR((,5-K3CW29"SH
QAMOUM YUM50I(MOUMWL50AI ABOL=;NM;3CUW
IRM+,NYJ3B6LIOQB.=B1-26)XNf1"H,5M+6CT9
1EY"H=YYJ YIE,N99,P-VQO.(2E?AG-PYET69
```

Figure 18-2 An encoded version of a portion of this book

terminals in the motor vehicle department, no matter who the user claimed to be or what passwords he or she knew.

Cryptographic Methods. In some highly sensitive systems, the danger of passive snooping techniques such as wiretapping is great enough that special codes may be used for data transmission. These are cryptographic codes designed to make the information unintelligible to anyone who does not have access to the key. In such a system, some data-processing capability must exist at the terminal end of the communication link to decode the message. This need not be complicated; a simple mechanical device would suffice in most cases. These methods are probably appropriate only to highly sensitive systems such as those involving military and strategic data. However, industrial espionage increasingly resembles the international spying of popular fiction, and businesses may soon begin to use such methods. It is not inconceivable that the contents of a management information system of a large and competitive corporation would be worth so much to a competitor that he or she would be willing to engage in such electronic espionage.

Threat Monitoring. One relatively simple and yet valuable protection technique is to log and analyze all unusual or suspicious events that occur in accessing sensitive files. Any time there is an unsuccessful attempt to gain access, the details are logged for later study. For example, the use of the wrong password to a protected file might be an attempt to gain unauthorized access. Excessively long sessions using a file or using an unusually large number of items of information are other cases that might be logged as suspicious events. If the file in question is particularly sensitive, the system could be programmed to notify security personnel immediately to check out the user at that terminal.

Management Techniques for Protection. In many cases, such elaborate protection schemes are not necessary. Although the contents of a statewide information system might be of interest and value to many people, they are probably not prepared to build a multi-million dollar system for the detection and analysis of electromagnetic signals, encryption and decryption, and so forth. There are usually much easier ways to get at information: to look in wastebaskets, for example, or to become an employee and thus an authorized user of the system, or to bribe an authorized user. The final class of protection mechanisms we shall discuss are the management techniques to deter this kind of penetration.

For security, physical files must be protected by physical means. Tapes and disks must be accounted for at all times, even when they are not on the computer. All requests for their use must be checked. Even after they have been erased there may be residual traces of the information they once contained. Used paper and printout must not become available to those who are not authorized to use the information they contain. Access to physical facilities must also be limited. Unauthorized personnel should not be able to walk into the computer room or the tape library, or to gain access to computer terminals.

Software must be checked carefully for loopholes. There are sometimes ways to bypass the password and legal-user checks that the programmers who wrote the system may have installed for debugging purposes. If a user discovers one of these "trapdoors" he or she can use the system for private purposes.

Finally comes the important matter of personnel. No system is safer than the personnel who manage, operate, and use it. These people know the trapdoors, the passwords, and the coding systems. Unless they are trustworthy, there is no protection at all against anything they choose to do.

The techniques available for dealing with this problem are bonding for civilian applications and military clearance for security systems. These techniques are intended only to assure those responsible for the security of the system that the people they hire are worthy of trust, not necessarily that they will always remain so. This usually means investigating the history of potential employees to determine whether any of their previous activities give grounds for mistrust. Ironically, the best way to protect the privacy of a system may be to invade the privacy of employees.

Thus the safety of automated files, just like that of manual files, ultimately depends on people, not on machines. Therefore no absolute judgment can be made on their relative safety. Both can be well protected or badly protected. Almost every protection available to automated systems could probably be built into manual systems by large numbers of personnel and intricate procedures, but at a much greater price.

Use of any of these forms of protection beyond simple passwording is still uncommon. A few systems that contain information that may be considered highly sensitive (the Multi-State Information System for Psychiatric Patient Records

described earlier, for instance) do use new elaborate techniques. Police systems sometimes code data transmissions. But security practices outside military applications are still unusual.

The greatest threat to these systems is the people who use them and the people who work with them. Even if people are checked carefully when they are hired and trained to believe in what they are doing, it is still possible that some of them may be tempted to betray this trust. Many people—systems programmers, clerks who enter data, managers responsible for system operation—must know the passwords, the keys, the encryption codes. These people are the greatest vulnerability of the system.

It is hard even for the experts to know how much protection is afforded by various protection techniques. How much information leaks out that the protectors of the system know nothing about? Studies of the relationship between risks and the costs of protection are only beginning to be made. We know, roughly, that a secure batch-processing industrial installation operating under Department of Defense security regulations may cost up to thirty percent more to operate than an installation operating "in the clear" with equivalent capacity. Furthermore, we have a rough idea that a "semi-secure" operating system imposes another five to ten percent overhead on the rest of a timesharing system overhead.

There is no totally secure operating system commercially available as of this writing. Users must create their own, or modify the ones that are available, taking care not to decrease operating efficiency. Eventually, secure operating systems will be produced by vendors.

Last, and most important, there is no absolute guarantee of security—and thus privacy. There is still a price that a penetrator can pay to break into any system. What is required are security measures that are relatively cheap to install and maintain and yet are expensive—in all senses of the word—to break.

Protecting Statistical Files

Many government and private organizations collect information about individuals because it is their business to deal with them and answer inquiries about them. Another kind of agency, such as the Census Bureau, collects data in order to obtain statistical information about larger groups of people.

Such an agency faces two problems. First, its statistical information must be general enough so that no deduction can be made about the individuals described. Second, its primary data (the information about the individuals) must be protected, since it may contain confidential information that the persons concerned consider to be private. We will discuss these two problems briefly.

Any information about large numbers of people —such as the distribution of income among the entire population of the United States, for instance —cannot be converted back into information about individuals. But as the group gets smaller, various subgroups within it have only a very few members.

Suppose, for instance, we are given an analysis of income distribution in a small town. Everyone who knows the town will be able to guess which is the single family with an income of $50,000, which are the two with incomes in the $25,000 to $30,000 range, and so forth. If the sample is so small that individuals can be identified—even if their names are not involved—then their privacy has been invaded. Agencies dealing with statistical information are usually careful that no sample is

so small that this kind of deduction can be drawn. This question of balance between the legitimate and scientific need for information and the possibility of an invasion of individual privacy is sometimes difficult to resolve.

The second problem an information-gathering agency faces is to protect the files that contain the information about the individuals. One method, obviously, is to delete the names or other positive identifying data elements. This makes the file relatively safe, but such deletion is not always desirable. For example, it is sometimes important to investigate how individual characteristics change over time. In order to make such investigations, social scientists conduct what are called longitudinal studies. Information about people is collected over a relatively long period; the data is analyzed and published in a form in which individual identification is impossible. However, the individuals must ultimately be identified somehow in the files so that new information about them can be stored.

One Case of Statistical Information Protection. A particularly interesting case of such a longitudinal study is one being conducted by the American Council on Education on how students are affected by different types of college environments. The individual students who are serving as subjects in the study would not feel they could be totally frank in answering the questions asked if there were some chance that their answers might some day be made available to potential employers, credit agencies, or government agents.

The protection method used in this case is a good one, and it is worth using it as an example of the conscientious protection of private and privileged information. The files are in three parts. The first set of tapes associates each name and address with a code number. The second set connects the data for each individual with a different code number. A third tape serves as a link to associate the codes used in the first tape with those used in the second. This link tape is kept at a computer facility located in a foreign country. No copy of the file is kept in the United States. Thus no unauthorized user, even the U.S. government, can readily gain access to all three tapes necessary to associate names with data.

Administrative Controls: Project SEARCH

The problem of instituting adequate administrative controls to protect the privacy and integrity of a computer-based information system may be considerable, particularly if it is the responsibility of government agencies. As an example, let us consider the situation in Project SEARCH—System for Electronic Analysis and Retrieval of Criminal Histories. This started out as an experimental computer sharing of criminal history records, prior arrests, court dispositions, and correctional involvements and outcomes among fifteen states. The original states were Arizona, California, Colorado, Connecticut, Florida, Illinois, Maryland, Michigan, Minnesota, New Jersey, New York, Ohio, Pennsylvania, Texas, and Washington.

Eventually the scope and intent of this experimental system grew to match the thrust of the FBI's NCIC criminal history file described in chapter fourteen. This match resulted in an active debate as to whether the FBI or some other agency of national government should control the operational data processing, and later debate has arisen on who should control the communications system. The cause of the debate is that the same agency that maintains operational control of the system's data-processing and communications also monitors and controls the system. This control includes licensing remote terminals, screening inquiries for purpose, and excluding agencies that abuse the system. At the heart of the debate was the relationship between the FBI and local law enforcement, which has historically been strained. A great deal of mutual benefit has arisen from cooperation, but there has always been the local fear of loss of independence. Thus it was a necessary part of preparing for a full-blown nationwide exchange system that a Project SEARCH committee on security and privacy be established. The chairmanship was given to Dr. Robert Gallati, then Director of the New York State Identification and Intelligence System, the largest and best-established independent statewide criminal justice information system. The FBI was also represented on the committee by the head of the NCIC. The principal problems that the committee was concerned with were the same general ones we have considered—those of unintentional errors, misuse of data, and intentional data change.

Since there is no government authority that encompasses city, county, state, and FBI, the action of the states to join this prototype test network was voluntary. Thus the result of the committee's work will be no more than a suggestion that will have to be debated within and among the states and with the FBI, the central controller (as it turned out) of the ultimate operational system.

The committee prepared policy recommendations, suggested limitations on the information content of the central index, and offered a code of ethics. Each of these is paraphrased and summarized below to show the depth of concern that the law-enforcement community itself has about problems of privacy and security—and to demonstrate how complex these problems can get. These rec-

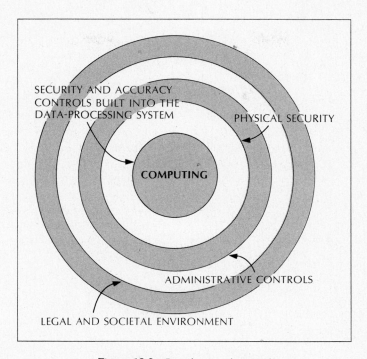

SECURITY AND ACCURACY
CONTROLS BUILT INTO THE
DATA-PROCESSING SYSTEM

PHYSICAL SECURITY

COMPUTING

ADMINISTRATIVE CONTROLS

LEGAL AND SOCIETAL ENVIRONMENT

Figure 18-3 Four layers of control

ommendations have now largely been accepted by the NCIC Advisory Policy Board.

Policy Recommendations.   Each record entered into the system should result only from official enforcement activities (excluding juvenile, drunk and traffic arrests, and unverified tips, rumors, and allegations). Since the records will be available to many people, they should include only what is both important and factual. Further, the data must be rigorously controlled. The distribution of all records should be recorded so that errors, if discovered, can be corrected in all copies. The question of entering and deleting records from the system is complicated by conflicting legal requirements in the various states involved. It is recommended that the deletion of individual case records be judged on the basis of the probability that the person will commit another crime.

Access to data should be limited to criminal justice agencies. States should limit their access terminals to the number they can supervise closely. Each state should monitor and supervise requests from its agencies. Non-justice requests (such as liquor or taxi licensing) should be honored only if authorized by state or local law or administrative directive. Further, close control should be kept over the use of data for research purposes.

The citizen should be given the opportunity to challenge errors. The rights of notice, challenge, access, and review should be made judicially enforceable, and statutory authorization should be provided for injury by inaccurate, incomplete, or misused data.

Content of the Central Index.   The central index should contain records only of people for whom at least one charge has reached final disposition and (tentatively) who have an FBI number. Since this central index will be merely a directory to the more extensive state files, it need only summarize arrest and conviction data in each case.

Code of Ethics. In addition to reinforcing all of the above, the code of ethics makes the following points:

☐ The state files should contain records for only those individuals who have been fingerprinted and for whom criminal proceedings are in process.
☐ Irrelevant data like census, tax, and unemployment insurance information should be excluded from the files.
☐ If a first offender is judged innocent, his or her name should be removed from the central index.

The Problems of Data Control. Thus in addition to the technical aspects of protecting a file, we can see that the development of a socially sensitive system requires attention about:

☐ Who shall be documented in the file
☐ What shall be in their record
☐ Who shall see the file
☐ Why they shall be allowed to see the file
☐ The rules for purging the file
☐ The laws enabling the exchange of data
☐ The laws protecting individuals from system errors

Recognizing the imperfections of these controls, the policy board decided that it would not license a local user to be connected directly to the NCIC unless the local computer was under management control of the local law enforcement agency and the communications lines to the NCIC were dedicated lines—that is, that no dial-up communications were allowed. This restriction, however sensible, ran afoul of the fact that many local law-enforcement agencies cannot afford their own computers, but must share with other agencies of local government. At the local level, the restriction led to debate as to whether law enforcement agencies should run all the data processing. This was unacceptable, since it would put those agencies in control of all the files.

Summary

Technological controls are available to protect an automated information system from either snooping or sabotage. None of these protection devices is an absolutely impenetrable barrier; still, such devices are adequate for most purposes. Of course, protection devices can also be made as effective (and expensive) as the sensitivity of the system demands. All such systems involve people as well as machines, however. And in this respect their security is probably little better or worse than that of manual systems, since both must rest on the careful selection and management of personnel.

The example of Project SEARCH illustrates some of the difficulties of establishing adequate administrative controls. In a large system in which the users of the information are under different jurisdictions, the system managers are often unable to say what the users can and cannot do. They can make recommendations, but it is ultimately up to the various users to make and enforce regulations.

NAN GOLUB

Exercises

1. At the beginning of this chapter, five dangers in computer-based systems were listed. Draw up a list of corresponding dangers for manual systems. Which type of system do you think constitutes the greatest threat? Why?

2. In order to determine whether any given person would be included in the Project SEARCH index, find out what offenses a person is finger-printed for. When does the FBI give someone a number?

3. A national medical information system that provided a continuous history of all examinations and illnesses might help improve individual treatment and medical research. What are the social issues at contest in such a system? What would the institutional problems be? What would be the view of doctors and patients? How would you protect such a system? How long do you think it would take to resolve the legal problems?

4. Assume that you are the bureau chief of files in a new intelligence agency in a totalitarian country. Your assignment is to keep track of the personal lives of all the principal industrialists in your country. There will be many intelligence analysts using your file. However, each can have access only to a limited number of industrialists, because your country is also corrupt. The industrialists, knowing that the file exists, have made great efforts to get access to each others' files for blackmail purposes and to change their own files. You must decide whether to use a manual or a computerized system. What are the security advantages of each? Which one will you choose?

5. In this chapter and the last we have described means of protection against the misuse of computer-based systems. We have emphasized the nature of the protection rather than the threat. In what way is the threat treated in chapter seventeen different from the threat discussed in this chapter?

6. Is there a threat from computerized information systems that you do not think can be met by any of the means described in this chapter or the last?

For Further Information

A considerable number of papers and books have been published on the technical controls for computer-based systems. The one by Petersen and Turn (1) is acknowledged to be one of the most important. Martin's book (2) is a very thorough and detailed analysis. Lance Hoffman has written a very fine summary (3) that includes an extensive bibliography for the student who wishes to pursue the subject further. The *Scientific American* article (4) presents an interesting review of the cryptography question. *Computer Security Management* (5) and *Computer Data Security* (6) are two more book-length studies of the technical methods of securing computer-based systems. The Leibholz and Wilson book (7) and the paper by van Tassel (8) deal more specifically with criminal uses of the computer. Information on the longitudinal study described in the text can be found in the paper by Asten and Boruch (9). Project SEARCH is described in the reports of the project (10); we have relied on this document in writing this text. The problem of a statistical file being turned into a dossier is discussed in (11). It also gives some indication of further work that can be done to protect us against this possibility.

References

1. H. E. Petersen and R. Turn, "System Implications of Information Privacy," *AFIPS 1967 Spring Joint Computer Conference Proceedings* (Washington, D.C.: Thompson Book Co., 1967).

2. James Martin, *Security, Accuracy, and Privacy in Computer Systems* (Englewood Cliffs, N.J.: Prentice-Hall, Inc., 1973).

3. L. Hoffman, "Computers and Privacy," *Computing Surveys* **1**:2 (June 1969).

4. Horst Feistel, "Cryptography and Computer Privacy," *Scientific American* **228**:5 (May 1973), pp. 15–23.

5. Dennie van Tassel, *Computer Security Management* (Englewood Cliffs, N.J.: Prentice-Hall, Inc., 1972).

6. Harry Katzan, Jr., *Computer Data Security* (New York: Van Nostrand Reinhold Co., 1973).

7. Stephen W. Leibholz and Louis D. Wilson, *User's Guide to Computer Crimes* (Randor, Pa.: Chilton Book Co., 1974).

8. Dennie van Tassel, "Computer Crime," *Fall Joint Computer Conference Proceedings* (Washington, D.C.: Thompson Book Co., 1970).

9. Alexander W. Astin and Robert F. Boruch, "A Link System for Assuring Confidentiality of Research Data in Longitudinal Studies," *American Educational Research Journal* (Novenber 1970).

10. "Security and Privacy Considerations in Criminal History Information Systems," *Project SEARCH Technical Report*, no. 2 (July 1970).

11. Lance J. Hoffman and W. F. Miller, "Getting a Personal Dossier from a Statistical Data Bank," *Datamation* (May 1970).

If you do not think about the future,
you cannot have one.

JOHN GALSWORTHY
The Silver Spoon (1928)

PART FIVE

What about the Future?

The Future

19

Much of what has motivated the writing of this book is an anxious concern with the dark prophecies of technology and the future. We must consider the future. But we cannot sensibly assume that the rest of the world will stay constant while only the computer and its applications change. We must look at the other changing elements in the world and see how the computer will affect them. Even if this technology is not relevant to all of them, the important ones must be described to keep the rest in proper perspective.

In this chapter we will put the future impact of computers in the context of larger trends—historical, geopolitical, sociological, technological, and economic. We will show, where possible, their relation to the computer. However, before we do that we will try to give some perspective on the very process of making predictions and plans. We will discuss why people predict and plan, how well they do it, and some of the processes they use.

The Context of Prophecy and Planning

Prophecy. In the beginning, people predicted the future by listening to rustling leaves, observing the livers of animals, peering at the stars, reading tea leaves, and investigating dreams. As you will see, the techniques have changed, but the concerns haven't. We have mostly been concerned with our own survival. Periodically, the end of the world has been prophesied. As the year 1000 approached, the combined influence of numerologists and dark passages from Revelation convinced people that it would be the end of the world. (The vast concern that we have now about the year 2000 is vaguely reminiscent of this.) Many predictions of catastrophe have occurred in history. For example, John of Toledo, a twelfth-century astronomer and astrologer, forecast such a catastrophe for the year 1186, so that people all over the Western world were repairing their cellars and building shelters. It is difficult to look back at the history of such prophecies and evaluate their effect. Prophecies can be self-fulfilling; for example, if enough people believe that the stock market will go down, their loss of confidence can cause it to go down. They can also be self-negating; for example, a disaster that can be predicted can sometimes be averted.

Despite these predictions, for better or worse, people have gone on living, usually with the assumption that nothing will really change very much. These assumptions are made every day. Unconsciously they represent an article of faith in the future. People make appointments one or two weeks in advance. They make arrangements for summer vacations several months in advance. Companies sell fire, accident, and health insurance for the lifetime of buildings (one hundred years) and people (seventy years). Farmers plant crops. People buy houses and banks lend money. Investors purchase stocks. People have children, and this is the longest-term commitment of them all. Then why do we concern ourselves with predictions? Simply because our world is now made both smaller and more vulnerable by technology. Remote places are made closer by jet aircraft and communications satellites. We are all threatened by nuclear weapons, energy shortages, and ecological decay. However, this brings us to the more modern counterpart of prophecy—planning. What are we going to do about our problems?

As the crystal ball has given way to planning, the tone of the forecasts has become both more analytical and positive. This is because it is very difficult to construct a plan based on the assumption of a catastrophe.

Prophecy and Planning

Prophecy involves the prediction of events that are only poorly understood. Thus an astronomical calculation that predicts the arrival of a comet is not a prophecy. Modern planning usually involves a number of alternative forecasts or possible futures, sometimes called scenarios. In addition, planning provides some element of choice of what we want to happen and specifies action to make it happen. Some of the most common and useful plans are budgets and estimates of income made by individuals, governments, and industry.

The reason for planning is that it preserves freedom of choice. If we let a course of events go to the point where there is only one choice available and all forces point to that choice, then we have made no decision. We have been passive. In addition, people plan in order to be certain that they achieve their goals. Whether their goals are financial, social, or whatever—if they are complex and require a lot of time and resources, they must be planned in advance. For example, planning the availability of water for a state fifty years in advance is both complex and vital.

How Well Have We Prophesied and Planned?

Before we go further and possibly grant planning and prophecy too much as an influence on the future, we must acknowledge the importance of brilliant ideas. Men like Freud, Keynes, Darwin,

Ghandi, and Christ have cast issues in ways that have had enormous influence on the course of events. To pick one at random, Ghandi's idea that undeserved suffering could move the nations of the world contributed to the downfall of the British Empire. The direction of economics, science, and international relations was changed by such insights. In addition to such unpredictable changes that occur in how people think about the world, predicting the future often runs afoul of novel and unpredictable events. The present state of science and technology is such that we can predict with some confidence that we will create the artifacts that are obviously needed. Faster, larger, cheaper computers are needed and they will be built. Faster and safer transportation, cheaper housing, more abundant food, and cleaner cities will become a reality if we want them. What we cannot predict is the impact of inventions that no one wants until they are already there. Who wanted the airplane, the telephone, the television, or the automobile until they were invented? New devices like these appear and profoundly affect the kinds of choices that we can make and thus affect our lives. They also affect the accuracy of predictions people have made based on current needs. A nineteenth-century planner projecting the development of the railways not knowing of the automobile and the airplane plotted only his own ignorance.

Some of the outstandingly bad prophecies of modern history were made by:

☐ Napoleon, when he predicted that the Czar would surrender after he had captured Moscow.
☐ A committee of the British government that concluded in 1878 that Thomas Edison's invention of the electric light was "unworthy of the attention of practical or scientific men."
☐ The Allied generals in World War I who predicted that the war would not last more than three months because of a lack of supplies.
☐ Hindenberg, who predicted that he could control the Nazis better if he made Hitler the Chancellor.
☐ The United States Air Corps strategic planners, who, during World War II, predicted that the bombardment and destruction of Germany's ball bearing plants would seriously cripple her war production. (All they and the Germans learned was that German weapons could get along with fewer ball bearings.)

There have also been some very good predictions. For example, in 1774, Condorcet, in *Sketch for a Historical Picture of the Progress of the Human Mind*, foresaw that the French Revolution would lead to reform in many nations and eventually Europe's African colonies would become politically independent. (A two-hundred year view.) He also foresaw social insurance for the needy, public education, and women's rights.

In a more modern context, an analysis has been made of the success that American weapons system development contractors have had in planning and predicting development cost, development time, and performance factors of new weapons systems. The costs were 2.4 to 3.2 times the original estimates. On the average it took sixty percent more time than predicted to develop a weapons system, and the performance factors (speed, accuracy, range, and so forth) were anywhere from sixty percent of the original goal to one hundred percent better than what was desired. Considering that these predictions concerned research and development of new weapons systems, they must be judged as pretty good.

George Gallup, who freely admits that his prediction process is an art rather than a science, issued 114 election forecasts in the years between 1936 and 1944. His results were as follows:

☐ 19 in error by less than 1 percent
☐ 39 in error between 2 and 3 percent
☐ 50 in error between 3 and 10 percent
☐ 6 in error between 10 and 15 percent

(Of course, Gallup, like almost everyone else, predicted in 1948 that Dewey would beat Truman for the presidency.)

In the industrial realm, AT&T in 1950 was able to predict with considerable accuracy the number of telephone installations and the telephone traffic sixteen years in advance. The International Civil Aviation Organization's 1957–58 forecast of jet air traffic (before the commercial use of jets) was correct as far in advance as 1966.

In 1940 the world population was predicted for 1945 and 1955. Despite the uncertainty of the world situation following World War II, the error in the five-year prediction was only about one percent, but the fifteen-year prediction was in error by about 8.7 percent. (This itself is in doubt because there is some suspicion that the world's population estimates may be off by as much as ten percent.)

Some of the reasons for errors in prediction have been bias in the form of over-optimism or pessimism, lack of imagination, or failure to see the significance of independent but converging events. For example, the invention of the airplane would have been an insignificant event if World War II hadn't accelerated its development, and World War II would have been far less destructive without it. Those activities that we have a great deal of data about, such as the use of telephones, voting, and engineering, seem to be easier to predict than the behavior of people or the political and military affairs of nations. Military history shows very few wars fought according to a peace-time plan.

It should be obvious that it is a great deal easier to predict an event itself than to predict when it will take place. There are great forces at play in the world that make certain things inevitable. The powerful inventions that make the advanced nations richer will eventually make their way to the less advantaged nations. Technology will reduce production, transportation, and marketing costs. But predicting when, say, the rotary engine will come into significant use, or when birth-control techniques will have an observable effect on world population is much harder. Thus while the effects of technology on our style of life seem to be inevitable, the prediction that technology will overwhelm our political and social institutions by 1984 or the "year 2000" is suspect. If it were going to overwhelm our social system in ten or twenty-five years, we could see it starting now.

How Do Predictors Predict and Planners Plan? In this section we will discuss some of the basic techniques and assumptions that professional prophets use so that you can recognize them, or use the mechanisms to build your own predictions. We will then offer some view of the future made by prophets in the fields of history, geopolitics, sociology, economics, and technology. One familiar mechanism used for prediction is called the action-reaction mechanism. This device, borrowed from physics, is based on the assumption that actions cause opposite reactions. One can predict, for example, that excessive automation will lead to a resurgence of the crafts.

Another familiar method of prediction is by deducing cycles of general behavior—such as wars, economics trends, or styles of government—and assuming that they will continue to repeat themselves in history. There is also the school of prediction that draws inferences from the shapes of graphs. Lines stay constant (nothing changes). Lines slope up (prosperity continues). Lines slope down (the ratio of food production to number of people leads to disaster).

Computer Modelling. An important technique of prediction is the computer-based model, which has been described earlier in this book. With models, the consequences of trends and policies in complex and realistic environments can be predicted. They are widely used to help assess the relative value of alternative courses of action and can also be used to predict what some system (say, the supply and use of energy or the world monetary market) will do over a period of years so that people concerned with these systems can make wise choices.

In 1972, a book called *The Limits to Growth* appeared and immediately caused a great deal of controversy. It presented the results of computer-based models that extended current trends in population and the use of the earth's resources to the point where they reached the limit of available space and energy. It does not predict what *will* happen but what *would* result if current trends and policies do not change.

These models can do no more, of course, than predict the implications of the assumptions built into them. The danger is in forgetting this fact. When a computer printout is delivered to the decision maker, complete with detailed projections and numerous charts and diagrams, it is easy to grant it more authority than it deserves. Although all the printout shows are the consequences of assumptions that may themselves be incorrect, we too often accept it as accurate and infallible.

The equilibrium theory of prediction assumes that whatever the subject of interest (nature, ecology, business, or international relations, for example), it is in a steady state of balance; any force that tends to cause imbalance will create a counterforce to restore it. (This is the basis for a great many biblical predictions: our sense of justice in the long run causes the righting of wrongs.)

One way of categorizing methods of prediction is shown in table 19.1. It is fairly complete in scope and reminds us that religious prophecy and astrology serve the needs of tremendous numbers of people. Similarly, science fiction has provided us with imaginative explorations of the effects of technology. For example, Ray Bradbury's "Veldt," published in 1950, offers a frightening and convincing warning of the destructive effects of "convenience" devices.

In this and the following chapter, we will refer to a method in forcecasting known as the Delphi technique. It is a way of soliciting the opinion of experts about the future of their field. The manner in which the opinions are solicited is designed to prevent any one expert from dominating the proceedings. This is done by a third party compiling the opinions, which are submitted anonymously. The experts are asked to forecast future developments and to assign a probability of each happening by a certain date. It does not guarantee authority or accuracy, but is a means of "averaging" expert opinion.

Predicting the Future

Let us look at some of the actual predictions that have been made for our human history and, in particular, about the fate of the Western world as we know it.

Table 19.1 Methods of Prediction

CLASSIFICATION	BASIS	CHARACTERISTICS	APPLICABILITY
Intuitive	Revelation	Belief in transcendental inspiration and absolute faith in the validity of the prediction	Religious prophecy
	Inspiration	Sudden realization of hidden connections	Many discoveries and inventions
Deductive	Verifiable laws	Deduction of particular predictions from a general principle	Science, sociology
	Pseudo-laws	Predictions from illogical or antiquated principles	Astrology, fortune-telling, palmistry, and so forth
Inductive	Individual experience	Unsystematic deductions by false analogy	Work, particularly crafts
	Experiment	Generalization of system-atized individual investigations	Science, technology
	Statistics	Conclusion from aggregates according to probability theory	Meteorology, medicine, public opinion polls, economic research, insurance, government
Activist	Individual action	Predictions of the results of voluntary behavior	Everyday life
	Planning	Long-range and complex objectives; creation of new conditions	Industry, public finance, armaments
Imaginary	Creative fiction	Utopias, science fiction	Literature, art
	Unconscious fiction	Visions, generally based on wish-fulfillment and past events	Dreams, visions, hallucinations

SOURCE: Richard Lewinsohn, *Prophets and Predictions* (London: Secker & Warburg, 1961), p. 49.

Historical Predictions. Some historians theorize that human history obeys natural laws and that an understanding of the past allows us to see the future consequences of the present world situation. The eighteenth-century Italian philosopher Giovanni Batista Vico was one of the first to propose a systematic theory of this kind. He attempted to treat history on the model of the physical sciences by stating that it should consist of observation, generalization, and prediction. He saw in the course of world history that civilizations arise, develop, and disappear, and proposed a theory that human civilization develops along a pattern of these three stages, each leading to the next, and the last back to the first, resulting in a never-ending cycle. As prophecy, Vico's theory said little more than that the current state of Western society would eventually disappear and be replaced by the necessary next step. It did not predict particular events.

The German philosopher Hegel also saw a pattern in human thought and activity, but remained unconvinced that this gave people an opportunity to see into the future. His observation was that understanding the pattern of events always comes too late; we can see how history has developed into a crisis only after the crisis appears. History helps us understand why things *have* happened but is no help in predicting what *will* happen.

Oswald Spengler published his famous *Decline of the West* in 1918. In it, he predicted the certain demise of Western civilization. More recently, Arnold Toynbee in his monumental *A Study of History* has taken a somewhat Spenglerian view of the world. However, in the end he is forced to deny the total and inescapable predetermination of historical patterns; he admits that we, after all, can shape our own destiny.

Historians such as these viewed patterns of development as they had taken place over decades and centuries and thousands of years, but presented conclusions so very general that they are of little use to individuals or governments. In any case, the technique of using history to predict the future is now largely discredited. It does not tell us what is going to happen next. Rather, by presenting the present in the perspective of the past, it allows us to consider, imagine, and expand the range of possibilities. Hegel remarked rather cynically that history teaches us only that we never learn anything from history. It is perhaps closer to the mark to say that history teaches us to expect the unexpected.

Geopolitical Predictions. But what kinds of predictions have been made about the fate of the world today? Wars of national liberation have been the major events of the last twenty years, and there may be more of them. The state of international relations indicates that war remains a major element in the future of the world. The basic competition among the United States, The People's Republic of China, and the U.S.S.R., and the emergence and development of the poorer nations are two of the most predominant issues that will guide the next thirty years. One prophecy about the future is made by Kahn and Wiener in their book *The Year 2000*. They attempt to lay out the alternative futures of our society to clarify the consequences of today's policy choices. In general, they believe the armed nation-state as we know it today will continue. But they doubt that the world will end in a nuclear war. They deny that the arms race will lead to war, since many wars were not preceded by arms races, and many arms races did not lead to wars. Furthermore, they doubt that the use of one nuclear weapon will necessarily lead to an atomic holocaust. Kahn and Wiener reason that the human instinct for aggression that they view as inevitable does not make war inevitable, because there is a great deal more than aggressiveness required to go to war.

There have, of course, been many more predictions made about our immediate future; you can see in the newspapers that many others are made every day. We have presented Kahn and Wiener's analysis as an example, but one that in our opinion represents logical and clear thinking about the state of the world today and tomorrow. Their prediction seems to us to strike the right balance between the unrealistic idealism and pessimistic despair that we are so often forced to choose between.

A Sociological Prediction. Here we will present a summary of another kind of prediction. Alvin Toffler's *Future Shock* is concerned not so much with the direction of change but the *rate* at which change is taking place and the effect this rate has on people. He attributes much of the anxiety, physical illness, depression, apathy, violence, and general feelings of being bugged to rapid changes in time, space, work, religion, love, sex, and value aspects of people's lives. Stresses are caused in people by the difference between the rate at which life is changing and the rate at which they can adapt to it. These stresses lead some people to hallucinogenic drugs, astrology, the occult, and searching for truth in sensation. Toffler attributes attacks on science and rationality (like that of Roszak) to this same condition.

An increased rate of change is upsetting because people are reared with what Toffler calls *durational* expectations. We grow to understand how long we have to wait until something happens and how long something takes. Technology is accelerating the pace of events, and our expectations are upset. People's relations with each other, places, things, organizations, institutions, and concepts are becoming transient.

Contrary to the dark predictions of Ellul, Toynbee, and Roszak, Toffler believes that we will be subjected to a paralyzing abundance of choice rather than a loss of it. He rejects the argument that science and technology foster standardization and counterargues that goods and services are in fact growing more diversified. Numerically-controlled machine tools make individualized short-run production more feasible; therefore the computer, in a small way, is an influence for non-standardization.

But our diversity is not just material. Evidence of cultural variety can be seen from the many types of books and paintings that are available to us. Schools are slowly breaking down the structures imposed by majors, degrees, and credits. Students are setting up experimental colleges and free universities, and Toffler predicts that they will win

their fight for diversity. Large universities will become decentralized, and computers will allow more flexible schedules, thus contributing to educational diversity. We see diversity in the media also. Specialized movies are being produced for surfers, motorcyclists, hotrodders, homosexuals, scuba divers, and language fans. The diversification of television itself awaits the development and widespread use of community antenna television or the economic feasibility of home videotape equipment. FM radio stations are producing specialized programs for music, education, news, rock music, and ethnic groups. Major national magazines are now producing regional and professional editions.

Toffler concludes that we should neither blindly accept nor resist change but control it. What we need, according to Toffler, are new principles for the individual to pace and plan his or her life, new kinds of education, and new social and organizational forms.

Predicting Economics and Technology. The effects of economics, technological change, and population growth are difficult to separate. They reinforce and counteract each other. Population growth and technology accent the problems of the city. Economic prosperity yields more investment in technology, which in turn yields more prosperity. Table 19.2 gives us both a history and prediction of progress in transportation, communications and information, materials and manufacturing, biology, chemistry, and physics from the year 1800 to the year 2100. We may note from the figure that much of what is now known has been discovered within the last fifty years. We may also note that successive improvements in power, computers, and transportation have increased in effect by more than a factor of ten. For example, consider how much

Table 19.2 Profiles of the Future: Arthur C. Clarke

DATE	TRANSPORTATION	COMMUNICATION INFORMATION	MATERIALS MANUFACTURING	BIOLOGY CHEMISTRY	PHYSICS
			THE PAST		
1800			Steam engines	Inorganic chemistry	Atomic theory
	Locomotive	Camera Babbage cal- culator		Urea synthe- sized	
1850	Steamship	Telegraph	Machine tools		Spectroscope Conservation of energy
			Electricity	Organic chemistry	
		Telephone Phonograph Office machines			Electro- magnetism Evolution
1900	Automobile		Diesel engine Gasoline engine	Dyes	X-rays Electron
	Airplane	Vacuum tube	Mass production	Genetics Vitamins	Radioactivity
			Nitrogen fixation	Plastics	
1910		Radio			Isotopes
					Quantum theory
1920				Chromosomes Genes	
					Relativity Atomic
1930				Language of bees	structure
		TV		Hormones	Indeterminacy Wave mechanics
1940	Jet rocket Helicopter	Radar			Neutron
		Tape recorders Electronic computers	Magnesium from sea	Synthetics Antibiotics	Uranium fission Accelerators
		Cybernetics	Atomic energy	Silicones	Radio astronomy
1950	Satellite GEM	Transistor Maser Laser	Automation Fusion bomb	Tranquilizers	I.G.Y. Parity overthrow
			NOW		
1960	Spaceship	Communication satellite		Protein structure	Nucleon structure
			THE FUTURE		
1970	Space lab Lunar landing Nuclear rocket	Translating machines	Efficient elec- tric storage	Cetacean languages	
1980	Planetary landings				Gravity waves
1990		Personal radio	Fusion power	Exobiology Cyborgs	

Table 19.2 (cont'd.)

DATE	TRANSPORTATION	COMMUNICATION INFORMATION	MATERIALS MANUFACTURING	BIOLOGY CHEMISTRY	PHYSICS
2000	Colonizing planets	Artificial intelligence Global library	'Wireless' energy Sea mining	Time perception enhancement	Subnuclear structure
2010	Earth probes	Telesensory devices			
2020	Interstellar probes	Logical languages Robots	Weather control	Control of heredity	Nuclear catalysts
2030		Contact with extra-terrestrials	Space mining	Bioengineering	
2040				Intelligent animals	
2050	Gravity control	Memory playback	Transmutation	Suspended animation	
2060	'Space drive'	Mechanical educator	Planetary engineering		Space, time distortion
2070		Coding of artifacts		Artificial life	
2080	Near-light speeds Interstellar flight	Machine intelligence exceeds man's	Climate control		
2090	Matter transmitter	World brain	Replicator	Immortality	
2100	Meeting with extra-terrestrials		Astronomical engineering		

faster than a desk calculator a computer is, or a jet aircraft than a steamship. Changes of this magnitude affect more than speed and convenience; we find totally new purposes for the mechanisms. While the modern aircraft's speed of 600 miles per hour is ten times greater than the speed of the automobile, its effect is more than just ten times more movement. High-speed shipping, increased relations between widespread organizations, and the increased range of war are just a few of the qualitative changes brought about by aircraft.

To give us some perspective on Arthur Clarke's predictions of the future, first notice that they were written in 1962. Two Delphi studies were done in 1964 and in 1969 that bear on some of the same subjects. Table 19.3 shows how opinions of the experts changed as time went by. As you can see, the passage of time and the investment of considerable amounts of money in research has changed some of the original outlooks of Clarke's predictions. Translating machines have largely been abandoned. Artificial intelligence, as broadly

Table 19.3 Comparison of Predictions*

SUBJECT	CLARKE'S DATA	1964 STUDY	1969 STUDY
Translating machines	1970	1972	1980
Artificial intelligence	2000	1990	1992
Global library	2090	1980	not available
Robots	2030	1987	1992
Contact with extraterrestrials	2040	2075	2025
Weather control	2010	1982	not available
Colonizing planets	2000	1982	1992
Sea mining	2000	1989	1992
Controlled fusion	1990	1986	1985
Artificial life	2070	1989	1980
Control of heredity	2020	2012	2000
Suspended animation	2050	never	2012

*Expected to occur (probability 50%)

defined by Clarke, seems to have become more attainable as its aspirations have been sharply limited. Sea mining and the colonization of planets are technically if not financially feasible today. The broad conclusion is that more technical progress is possible, and with the passage of time the control of heredity, suspended animation, a global library, functional robots (if not androids), weather control, artificial life, and contact with extra-terrestrials seems more probable to the people working in the laboratories. Any one of these developments could change the course of human history. Consider weather control: this development could minimize storm damage, prevent the loss of ships at sea, minimize crop loss, lower the cost of transportation and food, and make whole new areas of the world habitable.

Table 19.4 is the authors' speculation about how technological improvements and population growth in combination will affect people, industry, and nations. It shows a number of different causes that can combine to produce effects. However, we must admit that the table is deliberately slanted towards positive effects. Increased population growth and consequent urban density *could* bring about a decline in mental health. Increased use of computers and communications *could* bring about more population surveillance. Within this structure

Table 20.3 Dynamics of Change

EFFECTS	CAUSES									
		Technological Improvements								
PEOPLE	Population Growth	Marine	Transportation	Energy	Education	Medicine	Communications	Computers	Agriculture	Water
Improved mental and physical health						X				
New foods		X							X	
Greater literacy					X		X	X		
Longer life						X				
Greater urban population density	X									
Growth of middle class		X			X		X	X	X	
Acceptance of leisure		X	X	X	X		X	X	X	
Improved status of women					X		X	X	X	
Home more a center of activity							X	X		
Better informed		X			X		X	X		
Less at disposition of services/weather		X	X				X	X		
More mobility		X	X				X	X		

Table 20.3 (cont'd.)

INDUSTRY									
Automatic merchandising				X					
More numerical-control and labor-saving devices			X	X					
End of newspapers, books, libraries, typists			X	X					
Automated cars, ships, planes, trains			X	X			X	X	
Decentralization			X	X					
More service industries			X	X					
More use of energy		X	X	X			X		X
Growth in air freight and air travel			X	X			X		X
Growth in petrochemical production						X	X		X
NATIONS									
New areas of the world settled	X			X		X	X		X
More food shipped from rich nations to poor ones		X					X		X
Agrarian reform in poor countries				X	X		X		X
Growth in national productivity	X	X		X	X	X	X		X
Solution to smog				X			X		X
Solution to crime			X	X					
Smaller world			X	X	X		X		X

of cause and effect, there are some individual predictions that are sufficiently startling to be emphasized.

Population Growth. It is expected that in the year 2000 there will be six billion people in the world and 340 million in the United States. The density of urban population in the United States will grow from three to four thousand people per square mile.

Food. As of 1966 there were three to five hundred million people on the brink of starvation and one and one-half billion malnourished to the point of being easy prey to disease. To meet the population growth expected by the end of the century, the Far East will need a 300 percent increase in food; the Near East, 200 percent; Latin America 230 percent; and Africa, 150 percent. A thirty percent increase in the world's cropland would cost $450 billion.

Energy. By the year 2000 it will be possible in one noiseless, smokeless, nuclear power plant, to produce enough energy to satisfy the 1966 power requirements of the entire state of Illinois and simultaneously to produce enough desalinated water (one billion gallons per day) to supply the city of New York.

The City. The problems of smog, crime, and urban decay could be even worse than they are today because the percentage of the population in cities will increase from seventy to eighty-three percent by the year 2000.

Education. The increase in school enrollment will force the expenditure of what is now six percent of the United States' gross national product up to twenty-five percent by the year 2000.

Medicine. Estimates of improvements in life expectancy range up to 100 and 150 years. Arthritis, heart disease, cancer, and hepatitis will be curable; birth defects will be preventable. However, the people of the underdeveloped world will still be dying of preventable diseases such as smallpox, malaria, and tuberculosis.

Summary

In one sense we have dismissed pessimistic predictions by going to some pains to explain the limitations of prophecy and extoll the virtues of its modern counterpart, planning. But if we do not believe in the regimentation and sterility of *1984* and *Brave New World*, what do we believe? We, the authors, believe the problems of energy, food, and population will continue to dominate world affairs. There will be continued growth in population, urbanization, birth control, eugenic progress, scientific research, education, and the democratization of education. Accompanying this will be an increase in intergroup relations, cultural homogeneity, personal freedom, advances in racial and sexual equality, leisure, a decline in income differences, a rise in real wages, a reduction in personal economic risk, and an increase in paternalism. With the continued growth of industrialization, there will be even more specialization, automation, and professionalism. Industry and government will get even bigger and more powerful in its controls over people and its controls will represent rational social policies. Now, it can be argued that the view of the future we have just offered is mostly a somewhat less dramatic presentation of *1984* than Orwell made. Indeed this is true. The difference is twofold. One, Orwell sounded the warning and it was sufficiently convincing that it will be remembered. But more significantly, our system of government is designed to prevent excesses of power. What we must keep in mind is that it was designed to prevent a different kind of excess of power, monarchic rule. The threat of "1984" is the threat of the loss of personal freedom to a "rational" and "benign" bureaucracy.

Where does the computer stand in all of this? As you have seen, it is difficult to isolate a single change and ascribe its cause to the computer. Although the computer is everywhere, it does nothing alone. Thus it is hard to see it as either a savior or destroyer of humankind. As a tool of progress it is becoming a determinant of progress in areas like energy, communications, and transportation. Unlike the others, the computer requires no single large capital investment that in turn limits progress until it has earned its investor's interest. It converts dollars directly into labor, without the losses of transmission, evaporation, or obsolescence.

The introduction of the computer disrupts our ideas of progress. Most progress in the past has been made a little at a time; the computer facilitates progress in big jumps. Such abrupt transitions cast doubt on whether our old social solutions will be adequate in the future and even on whether our prophecies will be valid.

Exercises

1. Using the predictive mechanisms discussed in this chapter, take any prediction made here or elsewhere and identify the mechanism used. Do you agree with the underlying assumption(s) of the prediction? Why?

2. Research the predictions of Malthus. What were they? Do you see any evidence of their truth?

3. Read either *1984* or *Brave New World* and describe the relationship between the form of government and the use of technology. Is that relationship possible in the United States? Why?

4. Pick any prediction in table 19.2 and discuss its probable effect.

5. Review some of the controversy (check your library) following the publication of *The Limits to Growth* in 1972. What conclusions can you draw about the problems of computer-based models?

6. In 1890 the head of the U.S. Patent Office recommended closing that agency because in his estimation, everything had been invented. Similarly, one of the most respected technological forecasts of the 1930s failed to forecast the development of nuclear energy, jet propulsion, and antibiotics. What do these examples suggest to you as a possible cause of inadequate predictions?

For Further Information

Many planning centers have been established in the United States and elsewhere specifically for the purpose of thinking about the future, what it will be like, and how it can be controlled. These include the Resources for the Future, set up with the aid of the Ford Foundation; the Rand Corporation, which has sponsored many studies of the future; the American Academy of Arts and Sciences, which sponsors a Commission on the Year 2000; and the Hudson Institute, directed by Herman Kahn. In France, there is a Futuribles Project directed by Bertrand de Jouvenel. In England, the Social Science Research Council has a committee that studies developments possible in the next thirty years. The Club of Rome is an international group of industrialists who sponsor studies of the future.

A perspective on planning and prophecy that is both deeper and broader than we have had space to present here is provided in the first three references—Jantsch (1), Lewinsohn (2), and Jouvenel (3). *The Limits to Growth* (4) is a book prepared by the Club of Rome. It relies heavily on computer simulation in making its predictions, is extremely pessimistic, and has been the basis of a considerable controversy among futurists. The Kahn-Wiener book (5) is a difficult and comprehensive book that itself contains many excellent references. Toffler (6), on which we have relied to some extent, is a more popular treatment.

Items (7) and (8) are both comprehensive and professional predictions of the future, and both appear in paperback. Item (9) is a forecast for the year 2000 that was written at a time of high economic prosperity and should be viewed as such.

Enzer's paper (10) is a good introduction to some of the techniques of prediction. Ben Wattenburg's book, *The Real America* (11), is an unusual combination of passion and statistics. It is an upbeat book on social progress in America that attacks the gloomy forecasts in an interesting way. The Tugwell book (12) is a selection of readings of the outstanding futurists. (13), (14), and (15) are substantive forecasts, none of which predicted the economic recession of the mid-seventies.

References

1. Erich Jantsch, *Technological Forecasting in Perspective* (Paris: Organization for Economic Cooperation and Development, 1961).

2. Richard Lewinsohn, *Science, Prophecy, and Prediction* (New York: Harper & Row, 1961).

3. Bertrand de Jouvenel, *The Art of Conjecture* (New York: Basic Books, Inc., 1967).

4. Donella H. Meadows, Dennis L. Meadows, Jorgen Randers, and William W. Behrens, *The Limits to Growth* (New York: Universe Books, 1972).

5. Herman Kahn and Anthony J. Wiener, *The Year 2000* (New York: Macmillan, 1967).

6. Alvin Toffler, *Future Shock* (New York: Random House, Inc., 1970).

7. Nigel Calder, ed. *The World in 1984*, vol. 2 (Baltimore: Penguin Books, Inc., 1964).

8. Arthur C. Clarke, *Profiles of the Future* (New York: Harper & Row, Inc., 1958).

9. The staff of the *Wall Street Journal, Here Comes Tomorrow!* (Princeton N.J.: Dow Jones Books, 1966).

10. Selwyn Enzer, "Delphi and Cross-Impact Techniques: an Effective Combination for Systematic Future Analysis," *Futures* (March 1971).

11. Ben Wattenberg, *The Real America* (Garden City, N.Y.: Doubleday & Co., 1974).

12. Franklin Tugwell, *Search For Alternatives* (Cambridge, Mass.: Winthrop Publishers, 1973).

13. B. P. Beckwith, *The Next Five Hundred Years* (New York: Exposition Press, 1967).

14. Francois Duchene, ed., *The Endless Crisis, America In The Seventies* (New York: Simon and Schuster, 1970).

15. H. Perloff, ed., *The Future of the United States Government* (New York: George Braziller, 1971).

Computers and the Future

20

Three easily observable trends relate directly to the subject of this book. All three lead to an increase in the use of computers. One is the increased mobility of people, materials, and information. A second trend is the increased use of automation. The last is concerned with people's rising expectations. For example, in the field of communications, the telephone at first seemed an expensive frivolity that would never have sufficient use to justify its cost. During the 1930s, a proposal to build a high-speed transcontinental train was rejected because it was inconceivable that enough people would want to cross the country. These assumptions were, of course, wrong. People came to expect a higher level of communications and mobility as such services became available. In the same way, there is a rising expectation to be informed. It is not provable in dollars and cents; it

is just what is expected. It will lead to more and more use of computers.

The approach we will take to predicting the future of computers here will be to consider first technological advances and then future applications. We will conclude by examining some broader social issues.

Technological Advances

Writing now in the mid-seventies, we have the advantage of some perspective on progress in computer technology. It is generally agreed that each successive generation of computers has bettered the last by:

☐ a factor of 10 in speed,
☐ a factor of 20 in memory size,

Table 20.1 A fifteen-year forecast of information processing technology

EVENT	REASONABLE CHANCE OF OCCURRING IN (Probability 20%)	EXPECTED TO OCCUR IN (Probability 50%)	ALMOST CERTAIN TO OCCUR IN (Probability 90%)
Briefcase computers	1975	1978	1982
Oral input to computers	1976	1979	1983
Laser memory	1976	1980	1982
Data transmission by lasers	1977	1981	1983
One million byte memory, small enough for a desk computer	1978	1982	1989
Pocket-size computers	1980	1982	1989
Computers that learn from experience	1980	1984	1989
Price decrease by a factor of 100	1983	1989	1995

SOURCE: Parsons and Williams (Copenhagen, Denmark), Coordinator: Chresten A. Bjerrum

☐ a factor of 10 in reliability,
☐ a factor of 10 in component cost, and
☐ a factor of 2.5 in system cost.

When you consider the fact that the average generation lasts six years, in four generations the industry has produced a 10,000-fold improvement in speed, reliability, and component cost; a 160,000-fold improvement in memory size; and a factor of 40 improvement in system cost.

There are forecasts of future improvements that date back to the mid-and late sixties, which we include as tables 20.1 and 20.2 to give you a view of how much faster the field has progressed than could have been anticipated at the time of those forecasts. Table 20.3 is the most recent forecast. It must be distinguished from the other two, which are the results of Delphi studies and as such represent the opinions of many experts. Table 20.3 represents the work of one man, Rein Turn. However, it is the most detailed analysis available. Furthermore, Turn's analysis does not depend upon technological breakthroughs. As such, it too could turn out to be an underestimate of the field.

Should the prediction of economical automatic fingerprint recognition be achieved, it will make the process of identifying people a quicker and more certain process. Cards and photos will be replaced to some extent; law enforcement will be greatly helped, since partial fingerprints found at the scene of crimes can be used to find suspects rather than just as evidence once a suspect is found. Forgery will be reduced, if not eliminated entirely. Voice communication with computers would enable us to use them as reference books, file cabinets, and secretaries. If automatic indexing of natural language text became possible, the card catalog in libraries would be replaced by computer terminals, and the process of library research could change from drudgery to a joyful exercise of curiosity.

One point of difference between the earlier forecasts and the Turn effort that is worthy of note has to do with the availability of 10^{15}-bit memories. The earlier forecasts predicted these for the period from 1975 to 1982. The more recent forecast doesn't predict them until after 1990. The implications of such a mass memory system are considerable. A 10^{15}-bit memory could hold the entire contents of a 100-million volume library, or a 1000-word dossier on every man, woman, and child on earth!

Table 20.2 A fifteen-year forecast of information processing technology

EVENT	REASONABLE CHANCE OF OCCURRING IN (Probability 20%)	EXPECTED TO OCCUR IN (Probability 50%)	ALMOST CERTAIN TO OCCUR IN (Probability 90%)
HARDWARE			
Communicating with a computer			
English—limited	1974	1980	1990
English—good	1980	1985	1995
Voice —limited	1971	1974	1978
Voice —good	1971	1980	1987
Optical character reader			
10K char/sec	1972	1977	1981
cost < $20K	1970	1972	1974
script	1975	1980	2000
Automatic fingerprint recognition	1986	1990	2000
Speech recognition to identify speakers	1973	1977	1983
High density Electro-optical storage 5–20K bits/square inch	1970	1973	1976
200-fold improvement in cost/operation	1974	1978	1985
Memory cost < 1 sec access .0001¢/bit 10^{10}–10^{12} bits read only	1971	1974	1977
Mass storage 10^{11}-10^{12} bits < 1 sec access < .1¢/bit	1972	1975	1978
Erasable mass storage 10^{15} bit memories 10^{-7}¢/bit	1975	1980	1982
SOFTWARE			
Machine indexing of text and picture data	1972	1976	1986
Natural English for file inquiry	1974	1976	1985
Cheap, "accurate" indexing of natural language text	1972	1974	1976
Accept and learn the semantics of natural language	1971	1973	1975

SOURCE: B. G. Bernstein, Naval Supply Systems Command, Washington, C.C., 20 January 1969.

Of course the accuracy of any of these predictions depends on how much money is spent on research as well as the inherent difficulty of the problems. The hardware predictions are made more believable by the massive investment that the computer manufacturers and the United States government make. The software industry, and software research in particular, is funded far less

Table 20.3   1974 Computer Forecast*

YEAR	RANDOM-ACCESS MAIN** MEMORY CHARACTERISTICS		MASS MEMORY CHARACTERISTICS			UNIPROCESSORS COMPUTING SPEED
	Read/write time (ns)	Cost per bit (cents)	Access time (micro sec)	Capacity (bits)	Transfer rate (million bits/sec)	(64 -BIT WORD) Million instructions per second
1975	100	.5	1–2	10^8	10	19–25
1980	50	.3	1–10	10^9–10^{12}	10	42–66
1985	28	.2	.1–1	10^9–10^{13}	25–50	79–142
1990	15	.25	.02–.1	10^{10}–10^{14}	50–100	225–346

*SOURCE: Rein Turn, *Computers in the 1980s.* (New York: Columbia University Press, 1974).

**Assuming a main memory capacity of 4,096,000 bits

amply, and therefore the predictions are less believable. Certain achievements like "cheap, accurate indexing of natural language text" may turn out to be so difficult that agencies will stop investing money in research into them.

Are Such Advances Desirable?   Table 20.4 shows a forecast of a somewhat different kind. It shows the results of one question asked in a telephone survey of American adults. The survey was conducted in 1971, sponsored jointly by the American Federation of Information Processing Societies and Time, Inc. The question was, "Now I'm going to mention some things people may or may not believe about the uses of computers in the future. . . . Tell me whether you agree, disagree, or have no opinion on each of these predictions about computers for the future." The results show the expectations of ordinary citizens rather than experts. The majority of the people questioned seem to have reasonable expectations about computers: most feel that computers are helpful; most do not believe computers will be able to read thoughts. But a fairly large percentage seem to view the future of computers and society with some pessimism. One out of three of the people questioned felt that computers will decrease our freedom and that they will be used to keep people under surveillance. One out of four could not a-gree with the bland statement that "computers will improve our lives." We can certainly argue that those interviewed are by and large ill-informed about computer technology, yet they are the voters and taxpayers who ultimately determine public policy. They also carry with them the history of their personal experiences with other technological advances; almost all of them have had some contact with computers. Thirty-four percent of those interviewed have had problems of some kind "because of a computer." Fifty-four percent indicated that they believe computers are dehumanizing people and turning them into numbers. This is rather a depressing reaction to the technology that many specialists believe to be revolutionizing our society for the better.

In the past, the social usefulness of new technology has usually not been questioned. Nothing has held back the development of processes and machines that appeared economical. Anything new was viewed as an advance without seriously considering its potential effect on people or on the natural environment. However, as the AFIPS/Time survey indicates, we are entering an era of caution if not disillusionment with technology. The general public realizes that technological change is not always an advance. Just because we *can* do something does not mean that we ought to or that we will. There is a limit to the inconvenience and

Table 20.4 Beliefs About the Future Uses of Computers

FUTURE USE	AGREE	NO OPINION	DISAGREE
Computers will help provide many kinds of information and services to us in our homes	89%	4%	7%
Computers will create more leisure time for people	86	2	12
Computers will improve our lives	75	6	19
Computers will be used to keep people under surveillance	58	7	35
The government will determine what computers can or cannot be used for	57	9	34
Computers will decrease our freedom	33	8	59
Computers of the future might disobey the instructions of the people who run them	23	8	69
The use of computers increases the chance of war	17	13	70
Computers will be able to read your thoughts	17	6	77

SOURCE: AFPIS-*Time,* "A National Survey of the Public's Attitude Toward Computers"

expense we will suffer in the name of technology and greater efficiency. The decision in 1971 to terminate research on the commercial supersonic transport (SST) was a turning point in the United States: despite the huge amount of funds already invested, despite its acknowledged advantages, its social and ecological disadvantages caused the American people to veto it. The worldwide energy crisis of 1973 led many to consider for the first time that we are becoming heavily dependent on technologies (the automobile and petroleum) that may not be able to bear the weight of our demands forever. Similarly, computers help us to live in a more complex and artificial environment: many people consider it worthwhile to question whether this is a wise choice. Do we want this complexity and artificiality, independent of whether the computer makes it possible? Decisions will have to be made in the next decade about a number of major computer applications; when asked to support them, to allow them, to pay for them, the public may answer "no" in some cases.

Consider the prediction in table 20.1: the development of a computer that can learn from experience. This capability exists in a primitive way today. Recall Wiener's warning that decisions left in the hands of a machine that can learn may not always be made according to human goals. Learning from experience can be nothing more complicated than storing and having access to experience, and as you have seen, a 10^{15}-bit memory ("almost certain to be developed by 1982") can hold a great deal of experience. Whether computer generalizations and artificial intelligence can ever approach human powers of associations is an unanswered question. Do you stop a scientist from working on this problem because the implications of success are frightening as well as promising? As we have said many times in this book, that decision is up to your own individual judgment. Can you control such research? Anything that can be worked on by a small number of people without much money is uncontrollable. In this case working with a "learning" computer with a 10^{15}-bit memory will be expensive ($1 million for the memory and billions for the information) enough that its control will be a public question. Should you control it? You certainly will want to demand to know the purposes of such research. The recent public reaction against large sums spent by NASA on space research shows that scientists can no longer shrug off the question of purpose. However, limiting inquiry and repressing knowledge are associated with totalitarianism and seem totally incompatible with the traditions of our society. These are hard questions that are only beginning to be asked; one of the purposes of this book has been to prepare you to answer them.

Yet, despite these doubts, some developments in the computer field seem to pass all the tests and can be predicted with some confidence. It seems perfectly reasonable to predict that computer manufacturers will continue to make their machines easier to use, faster, cheaper, and more reliable. Cheaper and better computing will allow us to use computers for tasks that were formerly too expensive or too awkward. As this trend to handier, better, and cheaper computing continues, novel computer applications will emerge. (One of the more fascinating applications that may become a reality in the next five to ten years will be in assisting the blind and the deaf. Research is being done now to transform light and sound with microcomputers into signals that can be fed directly to sensory nerves.)

And, as applications grow in number and diversity, more people will learn how to use computers in their work and will consider them natural allies and assistants in their day-to-day activities. This means more computers and more applications. So the spiral will continue until the computer affects all walks of life. Of course there must be some limits. Computers may grow cheaper and cheaper, but they will never be free. They will grow smaller and smaller, but they will never disappear. They will consume a growing portion of the gross national product, but they will never monopolize it. They will do more and more, but they will never quite do everything. They will permeate all walks of life, but there are a few things in life that people will still prefer to do for themselves, even in the matter of information processing and symbol manipulation. Where, then, will the limit be reached? That is difficult to predict, for the end is not yet in sight. People and computers have not yet reached a stable balance in their division of labor.

Some Future Computer Applications

Present trends and current needs foreshadow computer applications that will modify our world over the next twenty to thirty years. The greater use of computers in the processes of education and medicine, for example, seems assured. If the computer *can* expand the capabilities of the doctor or teacher, it will undoubtedly be used to do so. The answer to the question of social usefulness is so positive in these cases that the use of all means available to produce better and broader education and medical care will be taken.

A great deal of use is anticipated for process-control equipment in agriculture, and computers will be used both in planning and in controlling the process of farming. Street traffic will be controlled by computers. Individual automobiles may be equipped with automatic steering, braking, and acceleration controlled by sensors that pick up information from the roadbed and transmit it to computers.

As computing becomes more accessible, it will undoubtedly be used more and more in business and industry. What form will this expansion take? Retail business firms will use point-of-sale devices; supermarket checkout will be automated. More production lines will be automated also. In the management of business and other enterprises (including education and government), analytic and planning tools will become more widely used, and scientific management techniques will be more broadly applied. The computer certainly aids and abets such trends.

Information management systems and planning models are now, as we have seen, generally available. They may not be appropriate for small businesses to use now, but the basic limit is not cost. Managers of many enterprises, trained to do their jobs by intuition, are not equipped to use the tools that technology already has made available. A new generation of managers will be required in order to change this, and a new generation of managers will come.

A greater availability of information and better tools to manage it should make government more responsive to the needs of people. Here, too, the problem is neither technology nor economics but the availability of the skills and imagination to make technology work and the introduction of the controls needed to protect our personal freedoms. Let us examine several areas in which computers will undoubtedly affect us in the near or not-so-near future.

Computer Utility. The need to make computing as universally available as possible seems to justify something like a "computer utility." Computing is not, however, exactly like water or gas or electricity or even telephone service. There is no reason to have two competing electric companies, but alternative computing companies make a great deal of sense because of the great range of services that can be offered. The telephone system makes no sense unless it is a single and integrated system: everyone must be able to call everyone. Computing does not have this requirement; users will subscribe only to those services that are of use to them. It will be a utility in the sense of its universal availability and widespread use but will probably not resemble other utilities in their monopolistic form.

It can be imagined that different companies and agencies will offer different services. Some, like many of the time-sharing computer services that already exist, will offer computing in the form of general-purpose languages like FORTRAN or COBOL. Others will offer more special-purpose programs such as models and simulations, management information systems, and statistical processors. Others, like the present credit-reference companies and bibliographic search services, will offer information rather than processes. The range of such information is very wide today. Information utilities currently provide access to law research files, catalogs of all the libraries in an area, and detailed census data.

Personal Computing. Almost all computing resources today are consumed by large organizations rather than individuals. A market that is bound to be explored when computers grow cheaper is the personal use of computers. Such computers, when they are available for the price of a color television set, will be seen as a useful addition to the collection of appliances in the home. The computer in the home will be viewed less as a general-purpose data-processing machine that has to be programmed by an expert than as a useful tool that can be applied to several different purposes, depending on which preprogrammed application is plugged in. Programs of different kinds will be available for these computers on tape cassettes. Rather than a mysterious artificial intelligence present in the house, this appliance can be a check-balancing and personal accounting service, a typewriter with a built-in spelling and punctuation corrector, and an auto maintenance manual and trouble shooter. People will accept these conveniences as services and not as computers, just as they do not consider the role of computers in the machines they use that run elevators and traffic lights, route telephone calls, and change dollar bills into coins. Some of

these services may come, in fact, with computing capability built into other machines: the spelling corrector, for instance, as an optional extra when you buy a typewriter, or the automotive maintenance manual built into the car.

CATV. Community Antenna Television (CATV) was developed to improve TV reception in areas distant from large cities. The TV signals are obtained centrally, usually by a high-power antenna, and sent to subscribers over coaxial cables running directly into their homes. In some areas, local news, advertising, and programming for a relatively small audience became possible. It is estimated that by 1980 the majority of homes equipped with television sets will have CATV cable as well.

CATV offers a communication network of great potential. The coaxial cables connect homes, businesses, and schools to community centers, which can be connected to neighboring centers by microwave or some other means. It is possible to use this network for purposes of data communication along with computers and related devices. This is because the coaxial cables can easily carry the data rates required for digital communications. Thus sophisticated computer terminals, using the TV as the display, could be located in the home. It is expected that this would give such a large boost to people's ability to obtain information and communicate with each other that the need to travel and thus use energy would be significantly reduced. Such a communication system could also be used with other technologies. For example, facsimile transmission could be used to deliver newspapers through this network. People could describe their interests so that specialized news reports could be delivered to their homes. The home could have programmed instruction for self-education. We could have offices and schools and libraries without walls that could be used from any convenient location; there would be no need to travel long distances to gain access to them.

Education. The potential application of the computer in instruction was treated rather fully in chapter twelve. As we indicated there, computer-based instructional techniques have the potential for solving, or at least alleviating, some critical educational problems. The delaying- factor has been more the high cost of computing resources and the basic conservatism of the educational establishment than limitations in the technology. But the potential is great and the application of more technology to education is bound to emerge as a dominant factor in the 1980s.

The impact of the computer on the classroom is likely to be considerable, when it arrives. It will permit much more flexible scheduling, with self-administered and self-paced courses, with faculty acting as guides, tutors, and consultants rather than as lecturers and classroom monitors. In such courses, where the individual has no class to be compared with and no time limit for learning, grades must disappear or assume a very different meaning. The school itself must become a very different kind of place and take on a different kind of role in the lives of its students and of the community at large. It could become a much more comfortable place with a more positive role.

Because of the rapidly changing and computer-augmented world in which students will be living, instruction will focus more on how to find things out rather than on mastering facts. Because of the potentials of computer-based instruction, students will learn more by doing and less by being told how to do; teachers will practice their craft less by providing examples than by guiding their students in creating examples. To take advantage of such an education system, students must be taught more self-reliance at an earlier age. In such an environment, they may be led but they cannot be driven to learn.

This at least is the vision that encourages contemporary research and development in this field. Other possible futures exist, of course. Computers can be applied to education in such a way as to standardize and dehumanize the process, turning out efficient and unimaginative robots. But one does not need computers in order to do this; it is possible even with today's limited means.

It was once felt that the high cost of computers in instruction (as compared with conventional instruction in large classes) was a discouraging disadvantage. The optimistic side of this fact, however, is that if computers cannot be applied to make education cheaper, then they will be applied to make it better or they will not be applied at all.

The Cashless Society. The cashless society has sometimes been predicted as an event of the late twentieth century. It is certainly within the range of possibility; the production of computer systems to manage such a system would not be beyond the current state of the art. Complete automation of money exchange would save a lot of time and possibly reduce the impact of the crime of robbery. But it is not clear that those whose efforts would be saved would be willing to pay for the system, or that the agencies most concerned (the banks) would find it either desirable or economical. In addition, certain social aspects must be considered, such as greater regimentation and control of people and their actions by automated systems, further loss of privacy as all financial records are centralized, and the loss of the credit caused by delays in crediting and debiting amounts to customers' accounts.

Modeling and Simulation.   A great promise, unfulfilled but implicit, in computer-based information systems is the use of simulation and modeling techniques in the social sciences. These sophisticated tools are and will be applied to some of the problems that now seem at the limits of our abilities—urban planning or management of the ecology.

It is extremely difficult to foresee the impact of large social projects (the construction of a major highway, the placement of a new school or hospital, a change in the federal tax structure) that affect the lives of many people. Sometimes such projects fail because, although their principal goal is achieved, secondary effects create new problems as bad as or worse than the original one. For example, consider the planning of a new road. It is designed to get people from one place to another. But it has other effects also. It alters people's plans about where they want to live, work, and shop. It changes property values. This, in turn, may change the racial and economic mix in the community and thus affect the political structure, the employment situation, and with it the welfare picture. The requirements for schools, police, and health facilities will change, affecting the tax structure which, in turn, affects the industries paying a large share of the taxes. Social systems are of such complexity that gauging these effects with any degree of accuracy or completeness is all but impossible. Computer-based models offer some hope of investigating such complex systems and estimating the effect of projects. Urban models help us understand why cities decay and how this decay can be controlled, why suburbs spring up in some areas and not others, and what can be done to shape more human and humane living space. Ecological models help us control our waste products so that they do not destroy the air and water and land.

Most of the models that now exist in the social sciences are relatively simple, acting only as predictors of trends. However, more sophisticated models will be built that can react in a meaningful way to social and economic changes. They will allow planners to predict further into the future and understand the relations that exist among the numerous aspects of the social system. Such models will be used to answer questions of the "what-if" variety, predicting the consequences of planning decisions.

The limiting factor in the development of such social and economic models is the rather primitive level of much social theory. There are several theories of urban development, for example, but they are scattered and incomplete. But modeling also provides a tool for the development of theory. Hence we can expect to see new theoretical developments as well. These hopes will hardly be realized by means of unaided computer technology; they require human effort, dedication, and ability. But computers, in extending our intellect, will help.

An Overview.   In summary, in the matter of computer applications, too, it is possible to question the desirability and economy of a number of these potential systems. There is some debate about the computer-driven car, the bookless library, or the totally automated production line. As we have said many times in this book, computer applications cannot exist for their own sake; they have to pay for themselves. This principle will resolve the debate. There are bound to remain functions that can be more efficiently and easily performed by people. There are also functions that some people sometimes enjoy performing.

In the previous chapter we were at some pains to set a broad context of the future. Viewed as one

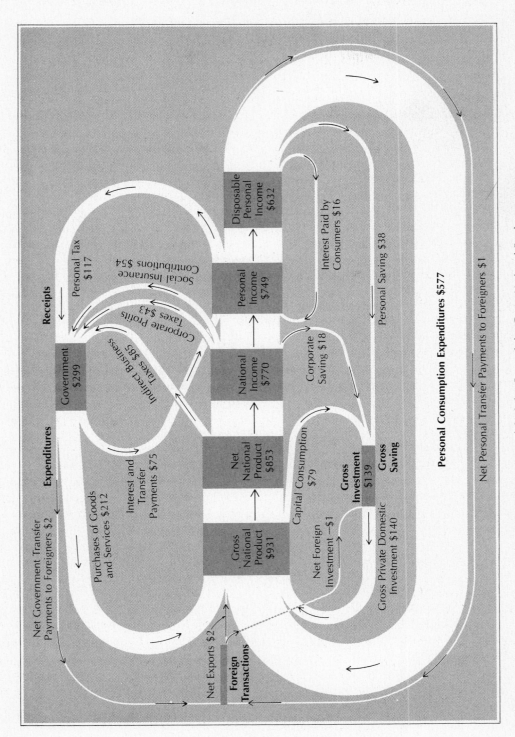

Figure 20-1 A model of the flow of the Gross National Product

more technical development in an already heavily technical society, the computer's effect on the developed world is hard to isolate, and it is difficult to claim that the computer can either save or destroy the world. Similarly, it seems unlikely that such new applications of the computer as a utility, even married to CATV, will do more than continue trends already in process.

Computers and the Future of Society

It is easier to predict the technology than the application of the technology; and it is easier to predict the application than its social impact. To attempt to foretell the meaning of all this in terms of human values is hardest of all. The computer has become so interwoven in our society that many of our social institutions—industry, business, government, education—are now totally dependent on it. And this dependency has changed the ways in which social institutions behave and the ways we interact with them. To say this is no more than to summarize the implication of countless examples that have been presented in the course of this book. To summarize further and to attempt to put the lesson in totally human and personal terms, we may ask how the quality of life of individuals in the future will be different from what we experience today and how the apparently inevitable increase in the use of computers in the future will modify our lives and those of our children. Several trends must be mentioned; all of them have appeared as themes elsewhere in this book.

The trend to automation and the increased use of machinery for tasks once essentially manual is bound to mean shorter working hours for individual workers and more leisure. There is a tendency for the labor force to require a somewhat higher level of education as the more menial and routine tasks are replaced by machinery. This trend is aided by the decreasing need for (or, alternatively, inability of) young people to join the labor force at the earliest possible moment; increased education is one of the ways greater leisure is absorbed. It is unlikely that any major change in this trend will take place in the foreseeable future or that any major change to the status quo (such as technologically-caused mass unemployment) will take place either. How this leisure will be used is a major unresolved social issue. It is with us now in terms of more holidays and earlier retirement; the four-day week and the six-week vacation will make it greater.

If the patterns of the past are allowed to repeat themselves unchecked, the loss of personal privacy seems destined to continue. If we examine the growth in the number of government and private information systems concerned with people, it seems certain personal privacy will continue to be eroded. The institution of legal controls is so difficult and the demand for such systems is so great that without a major effort, further loss of personal privacy seems inevitable. Another contributing factor is that our world with its international jet transportation and satellite communications is growing smaller, and as it does, it comes more and more to resemble the small village where no one can ever be a stranger. At the same time, it must be pointed out that the danger of massive data banks and the linking of files between computers is not so great as has sometimes been pictured; their indescribable complexity and high cost make the usefulness of such systems questionable. Another hopeful sign is the growing number of politicians proposing laws to stem the tide and the considerable percentage of the population that is concerned (as in the AFIPS-*Time* survey).

Figure 20-2 The INTEL 8080, an 8-bit processor with
78 instructions

A major characteristic of the application of computers in organizations is that they make it possible (and even desirable) to deal with larger masses of data economically and conveniently. Hence there is a tendency for larger organizations to become more successful than smaller ones. Here too we have a trend that will continue. The small neighborhood store, the local bank, the small college, the family doctor, are less effective and less able to meet the demands of modern and future life than are their big counterparts: the chain store, the branch bank, the multi-campus university, the incorporated group of medical specialists. People today are more likely to work for a large corporation than were their parents; future self-employed entrepreneurs will be rarer still. Thus in most relationships with other people (except the most personal) we will interact as representatives of large organizations and as symbols of larger forces.

A final characteristic of the computer-related future is that things are bound to get more complicated. Just as today people make use of many machines they cannot understand (telephone, automobile, washing machine), many of the processes of the future will be beyond the understanding of most citizens. A bureaucracy that bases its decision making on modeling, simulation, and the techniques of information management is less accessible to the people of the country and even to their elected representatives. Much of the decision making in the future will be based (as some of it is already today) on the opinions of experts and specialists. The trust that the society must place in these experts is very great. The advantages of this are considerable, but so are the dangers.

Evaluating the Impact.   These, then, are some of the ways in which life in the future will be differ-

Figure 20-3   A tape library.

ent: more leisure, less privacy, more large organizations, more complexity with more reliance on experts. But what does this all mean? Will life be better or worse? There are two easy answers to these questions, and one hard one. It seems only fair that we give you all three and allow you the option of selecting for yourself the conclusion to this book that most pleases you and seems best to satisfy the requirements of the facts. We will start with the two easy ones.

Throughout the course of this book, we two authors have tried to speak with one voice. Now perhaps it is time to confess that we have not always been in agreement. The selections of which facts to present, which examples to choose, which generalizations to draw, have sometimes been uneasy compromises. This has had the advantage of assuring that both sides of difficult issues are represented. But in making a final summary evaluation of the impact of computers on society, a compromise seems difficult to draw.

One of the authors is hopeful that computers will make the world brighter; he looks to a world in which computers and other technologies will improve the human lot, helping to teach the illiterate and feed the hungry by stretching our resources to the utmost and improving our ability to control our environment by rational means. He views the achievements of the recent past as indications that we can control our technology to achieve our goals: we have seen a steady improvement in economic conditions for all Americans; dramatic improvements in the social conditions of racial minorities and of women; the phenomenal success of our educational system in absorbing more students; the decline in the demand for long hours of hard toil for scant wages. The computer will help us to build on these successes to create a sane, successful, and peaceful world.

The second author, however, sees this as possible but not as likely. Looking into the future, he sees a world in which (with computer assistance) large and impersonal organizations decide to provide us with luxuries we cannot enjoy and leisure we cannot use, asking in return that we give up our freedom to be unique individuals, our obligation to treat one another as brothers and sisters and not as symbols, our right to make our own choices in the pursuit of happiness. He sees the other side of leisure as boredom, the loss of privacy as pressure for conformity, the growth of organizations as dehumanizing, complexity as the twin of alienation. In looking at recent history, he sees a gain but also a loss, a richness in economic terms that is shallow in human terms, a selling of our birthright for trinkets.

Either of us could have written a concluding section to reflect one or the other of these contrasting world views. For both sets of conclusions can be drawn from the facts. The reader (and this is the third answer) is invited to select one of them himself, if it seems the justifiable conclusion based on the evidence he or she has seen, and write such a concluding section. But in fact, many will feel that neither of these answers is good enough; both are too one-sided and too self-assured. For the art of telling the future is different from the science of history: unlike the past, the future has never existed and no one knows it. It is still to be made, woven out of time and of experience, out of the past and out of dreams, by men and women like the authors and like you.

The computer is a new resource emerging, a tool with which it is possible to change the underlying structures of our society. The change can be in the direction of more freedom for the individual or toward more restrictive social forms. If we succeed in finding a way to use it, if we exercise intelligent control and direct it toward rational and realistic ends, it can improve the world more surely and more drastically than any prior invention in human history. But if we fail, we have only ourselves to blame. We cannot put the blame off on an alien and unnatural force called technology. Technology is a natural product of human intelligence and energy. Technology is no unnatural demon; the devil is us, and technology is part of ourselves.

Exercises

1. Write your own conclusion to this book. A place to start might be the exercise you did after chapter one—the one in which you described your attitudes toward computers at the beginning of the course. How have they changed?

2. What you have read in the last two chapters is an analysis of the future and the possibilities for change by acting within the system. Do you believe that the system has to be destroyed to change it?

3. After considering the various predictions of computer impact, make a judgment about whether each of the changes that are predicted are as important as those changes in our immediate past—for example, the transition from an agricultural-based economy to an industrial-based economy, the growth of services versus the goods industry, the predominance of the competition between the United States and the USSR, the shrinking of the world because of technological advances in transportation and communication, and the overall

increase in the productivity of industry and labor.

4. Write an essay giving your opinion about whether research on computer learning should be pursued.

5. See if any of the events that were predicted in this chapter have actually happened.

For Further Information

The Kahn-Wiener book cited in chapter nineteen goes into considerable detail about the future of computer applications. Three major studies of the future of computers (1–3) are unfortunately difficult to obtain in most libraries. *Computers in the 1980s* (4) is a good recent effort to predict the future of computers, as is the briefer article by Withington (5). Gruenberger's book (6) views the future mostly from the point of view of the market for computers, but will be of some interest even from a more general perspective. *Information Technology* (7) has a great deal of useful information in it, if your library has a copy. Finally, the proceedings of a 1973 conference (8) contain a series of papers about the possible future of computer applications and are highly recommended.

References

1. Christen A. Bjerrum, coordinator, *Forecast of 1968-2000 of Computer Developments and Applications* (Copenhagen: Parsons and Williams, 1967).

2. G. B. Bernstein, *A Fifteen-Year Forecast of Information Technology* (Washington, D.C.: Naval Supply Systems Command, 1969).

3. T. J. Gordon and Olaf Helmer, "Report on a Long-Range Forecasting Study," *The RAND Corporation*, P 2982 (September 1964).

4. Rein Turn, *Computers in the 1980s* (New York: Columbia University Press, 1974).

5. Frederick G. Withington, "Beyond 1984: A Technology Forecast," *Datamation* (January 1975), pp. 54–73.

6. Fred Gruenberger, ed., *Expanding Use of Computers in the 70s: Markets, Needs, Technology* (Englewood Cliffs, N.J.: Prentice-Hall, Inc., 1971).

7. *Information Technology; Some Critical Implications for Decision Makers* (New York: The Conference Board, 1971).

8. "Views of the Future," in *AFIPS National Computer Conference Proceedings,* (Montvale, N.J.: AFIPS Press, 1973), pp. 717–63.

A Prose Glossary

Glossaries of technical terms are very often of little use to the novice since their alphabetical order does not reflect the logical structure of the subject. This glossary is arranged in a more or less logical fashion, with an index (pages 000-000) to help the nonserial user find a particular term. If the definition does not shed sufficient light, the context may.

1 A COMPUTER is a machine for performing
2 complex processes on information without
3 manual intervention. ANALOG COMPUTERS
4 perform this function by directly measuring
5 and transforming continuous physical quan-
6 tities such as electrical voltages. DIGITAL
7 COMPUTERS represent numerical quantities
8 by discrete electrical states that can be mani-
9 pulated logically and hence arithmetically.
10 Digital computers are sometimes referred to
11 as ELECTRONIC DATA PROCESSING MA-
12 CHINES, EDP, AUTOMATIC DATA PROCES-
13 SING MACHINES, or PROCESSORS. In order to
14 distinguish the actual physical equipment
15 from the programs which extend its useful-
16 ness, the former is called HARDWARE.

17 The CENTRAL PROCESSOR UNIT (CPU) or
18 MAINFRAME is the portion of the computer
19 that performs the calculations and decisions;

20 it contains two logically separate entities: the
21 CONTROL UNIT, which determines the se-
22 quence of operations of the computer, and
23 the ARITHMETIC UNIT, which actually per-
24 forms the individual logical and arithmetic
25 operations. The MEMORY or STORAGE is the
26 part of the computer in which the data and
27 programs are stored. The CORE MEMORY is
28 the main memory of most modern machines;
29 it is normally the only memory directly acces-
30 sible to the CPU. Its name derives from its
31 composition: small ferrite rings called CORES.
32 The computer may have additional memory
33 devices. Information is transferred between
34 these and core memory. The most usual such
35 memories are MAGNETIC DRUMS (spinning
36 cylinders with a magnetizable recording sur-
37 face) and MAGNETIC DISKS (flat spinning
38 disks with magnetizable surfaces). DISK
39 PACKS are disks that can be removed from the
40 machine and stored elsewhere.

41 The capability of memory devices is measured
42 in capacity and speed of access. The STORAGE
43 CAPACITY of a memory is measured in
44 WORDS, which are usually of fixed length,
45 consisting of from twelve to forty-eight bits.
46 This number is called the machine's WORD
47 LENGTH. A BIT (binary digit) is the minimum
48 unit of information storage and has only two
49 possible values. Capacity can also be measured
50 in BYTES, units of six to eight bits, each capable
51 of representing one alphabetic or numeric

Adapted from *Computers on Campus* by John Caffrey and Charles Mosmann, copyright 1967 by the American Council on Education, Washington, D.C., and *Computer Usage Fundamentals* by Eric Weiss, copyright 1975 by McGraw-Hill, Inc., New York.

52 symbol. Core memory is called RANDOM
53 ACCESS when any word can be obtained at
54 any time without regard to its serial order.
55 Drum, tape, and disk memories are SERIAL
56 ACCESS because the words pass one at a time
57 as they move past the station where they may
58 be accessed.

59 The speed of a computer is measured in CYCLE
60 TIME, the time required to reference a core
61 memory word, get the data, and be ready to
62 do it again, or ADD TIME, the time needed to
63 perform a single addition of two words. AC-
64 CESS SPEED is the time it takes to locate a
65 word in a memory; TRANSFER RATE is the rate
66 at which words can be moved from or to the
67 memory device in question. Speed is usually
68 spoken of in terms of MILLISECONDS (m)
69 (thousandths of seconds), MICROSECONDS
70 (μ or u) (millionths of a second), or NANO-
71 SECONDS (n or μ) (billionths of a second).
72 One nanosecond is the time required for
73 light to travel almost one foot. A thousandth
74 of a nanosecond is a PICOSECOND; this word
75 is beginning to be used.

76 The central processor and the memory consti-
77 tute the computer *per se*; to get data and
78 programs into the machine and the results out
79 is the role of the INPUT/OUTPUT EQUIP-
80 MENT or I/O.

81 INPUT DEVICES convert information to a form
82 in which it can be stored in the computer's
83 memory. The commonest form of input is the
84 PUNCHED CARD or HOLLERITH CARD (after
85 its inventor). Input devices that accept cards
86 are called CARD READERS and the function
87 they perform is commonly called READING, as

88 is that of all input. Hollerith cards have eighty
89 COLUMNS with twelve possible punch posi-
90 tions; normally, each column is used to repre-
91 sent one character. A set of cards is called a
92 DECK. Another form of input is PUNCHED
93 PAPER TAPE—continuous tape approximately
94 one inch wide, with holes punched across its
95 width to represent characters or numeric
96 quantities. MAGNETIC INK CHARACTER
97 READERS (MICR) have come to be used for
98 input, particularly in banking; they can in-
99 terpret characters printed with special ink.
100 More recently, OPTICAL SCANNERS have
101 appeared that can read clearly printed or typed
102 material of given type fonts. With a DATA
103 ENTRY device characters can be keyboarded
104 directly into a computer.

105 OUTPUT DEVICES usually include a CARD
106 PUNCH (which converts the characters stored
107 in memory to punched holes in a card), a TAPE
108 PUNCH (which performs the same function
109 for punched paper tape), and a LINE PRINTER
110 (which prints numerals, letters, and other
111 characters of a conventional design on con-
112 tinuous rolls of paper). Passing information to
113 these devices, the computer is WRITING. The
114 output family may also include DISPLAY de-
115 vices that exhibit readable characters or gra-
116 phic information on the face of a CATHODE
117 RAY TUBE or CRT. These images must be read
118 at once, of course, since they are not perma-
119 nent. They may be photographed or rewritten
120 later, of course. Information that can be taken
121 away in permanent form (such as the output
122 of a line printer) is called HARD COPY. A
123 PLOTTER is an output device that, under com-
124 puter control, can draw continuous lines or
125 curves on paper, thus producing graphs, maps,

126 and so forth in hard copy. MAGNETIC TAPE is
127 widely used both as a form of memory and
128 input/output. It can be stored conveniently
129 away from the machine and can be read or
130 written by the computer if it is put on a TAPE
131 DRIVE attached to the computer. Tapes may
132 be referred to as 9-TRACK or 7-TRACK, de-
133 pending on the number of bits that are written
134 parallel across the tape.

135 I/O devices connect to a computer by means
136 of a CHANNEL; when several devices share
137 the same channel, they are said to be MULTI-
138 PLEXED. When they are attached to the com-
139 puter and are under its control, devices are
140 ONLINE. They are placed OFFLINE when they
141 are used to perform independent functions.
142 Any device attached to the mainframe, other
143 than the core storage unit, is called a PERI-
144 PHERAL device. The term may be limited to
145 I/O devices used offline.

146 ELECTROMECHANICAL ACCOUNTING MA-
147 CHINES or EAM are independent of the com-
148 puter and in fact antedate the use of com-
149 puters by many years. The most common are
150 the KEYPUNCH, used to punch cards; the
151 REPRODUCER, which makes copies of decks
152 of cards; and the SORTER, which places cards
153 in different bins according to what holes are
154 punched. In some systems, another online
155 input/output device has been added: the
156 CONSOLE or TERMINAL. This is intended for
157 the user to interact directly with the computer,
158 and usually consists of a typewriter-like key-
159 board with either a typewriter-like printing
160 mechanism or another display device for
161 output.

162 Information is stored in the computer's mem-
163 ory in the form of the presence or absence of
164 a magnetic area or electrical charge. A collec-
165 tion of such "yes or no" physical states is
166 usually thought of as a BINARY NUMBER (a
167 number whose only possible digits are 0 and
168 1). Depending on the context, such numbers
169 can have many meanings; in this sense, the
170 numbers are CODED. They can be interpreted
171 as numeric quantities, CHARACTERS (letters,
172 digits, punctuation marks) or as INSTRUC-
173 TIONS or COMMANDS that will direct the
174 computer to perform its basic functions (add,
175 compare, read, and so forth). A set of instruc-
176 tions to perform a specific function or solve a
177 complete problem is called a PROGRAM. The
178 computer performs such instructions sequen-
179 tially. However, as it can modify the data in its
180 memory, the computer can also modify its pro-
181 gram. It is because of this distinctive feature
182 that modern digital computers are sometimes
183 called STORED-PROGRAM (or INTERNALLY
184 PROGRAMMED) computers. Parts of programs
185 are sometimes called ROUTINES or SUBROU-
186 TINES. Subroutines that perform generally
187 useful functions are sometimes combined into
188 a subroutine LIBRARY, usually on magnetic
189 tape. Copies of relevant subroutines will be
190 added to a program automatically and hence
191 need not be developed by hand. Single in-
192 structions in a program are sometimes called
193 STEPS. When a sequence of program steps is
194 operated again and again, the process is called
195 a LOOP. Certain instructions compare two
196 quantities and select either of two program
197 paths on the basis of the result: these are
198 called BRANCH instructions. The data on
199 which a program acts is usually structured into
200 RECORDS or TABLES. Individual values that

201 control the operation of programs or sub-
202 routines are PARAMETERS. An organized col-
203 lection of information in the computer or on
204 tape is called a FILE, like the organized set of
205 papers in a file cabinet. A DATA BASE or DATA
206 BANK is a large and complex set of files (such
207 as a library catalog, a personnel file, or a
208 budget).

209 A PROGRAMMER is a person who converts a
210 problem into a set of directions to a computer
211 to solve it. The function is sometimes broken
212 down into several parts, particularly if the
213 problem is very complex. The task of stating
214 the problem in a clear and unambiguous form
215 is performed by an ANALYST or SYSTEMS
216 ANALYST. The technique of specifying meth-
217 ods of solution for mathematical problems is
218 MATHEMATICAL ANALYSIS or NUMERICAL
219 ANALYSIS. A specific procedure for solving a
220 problem is an ALGORITHM. The process of
221 writing the detailed step-by-step instructions
222 for the computer to follow is CODING; it is
223 done by a CODER. A person who actually runs
224 the computer, changing the tapes, loading the
225 cards, inputting its work, and collecting the
226 output to be returned to the user, is a COM-
227 PUTER OPERATOR. After a program is written,
228 it is tried out by letting it perform its function
229 in the computer. This process is called CHECK-
230 OUT, CODE CHECKING, or DEBUGGING.
231 Programs to help the coder find errors or BUGS
232 may include a TRACE to follow the course of a
233 program in its operation or a SNAPSHOT to
234 display the momentary content and state of
235 the machine after program operation. Once a
236 program has been debugged so that it will run,
237 it is TESTED with test data to which the proper
238 solution is known.

239 The coder will also be expected to produce
240 some descriptions of his or her program and
241 how it operates so that others may understand
242 how it works in case at a future date it is nec-
243 essary to modify it. This DOCUMENTATION
244 may include a FLOWCHART or FLOW DIA-
245 GRAM: a graphic description or diagram of the
246 various paths and branches followed by the
247 program. The repertory of instructions avail-
248 able to the programmer for a specific com-
249 puter is that computer's MACHINE LANGU-
250 AGE. (Because this use of the word *language*
251 is somewhat misleading, human languages
252 such as English are distinguished as NATURAL
253 LANGUAGES.) HIGHER-ORDER LANGUAGES
254 have been developed to help the programmer
255 by simplifying the tedious aspects of writing
256 machine language; these are called PROCE-
257 DURE-ORIENTED LANGUAGES or POL. Com-
258 monly used POLs are FORTRAN, ALGOL, and
259 COBOL: the first two were devised mainly for
260 scientific computation and the latter for bus-
261 iness data processing. PL/I is a more general
262 POL. PROBLEM-ORIENTED LANGUAGES are
263 designed to be used only in certain limited
264 kinds of applications. For example, TRANSIM
265 is used for simulating transportation problems.

266 Because of greater flexibilities in dealing with
267 data, LIST-PROCESSING LANGUAGES are par-
268 ticularly useful in processing non-numerical
269 symbols. Their particular virtues are most ap-
270 parent in HEURISTIC PROCESSES: methods in
271 which the precise method of solution is not
272 spelled out, but is discovered as the program
273 progresses and as it evaluates its progress to-
274 ward an acceptable solution. The study of such
275 processes is called ARTIFICIAL INTELLIGENCE.

276 Programs that convert higher-order languages
277 into machine language are called COMPILERS;
278 programs that perform similar functions at a
279 much simpler level are ASSEMBLERS. The term
280 TRANSLATOR is used sometimes for a com-
281 piler, but is used less frequently because of
282 the possible confusion with programs that
283 perform translation between natural langu-
284 ages. INTERPRETERS do not compile the entire
285 program but translate and perform one state-
286 ment of the program at a time; effectively, they
287 perform both functions—compiling and run-
288 ning a program.

289 SOFTWARE is the term used to refer to the
290 totality of programs, documentation, and
291 procedures required to use a computer; some-
292 times it is used more specifically to mean
293 those programs of general usefulness (such as
294 compilers) that are available to all users. These
295 are sometimes called UTILITY PROGRAMS.
296 All computers today have programs called
297 OPERATING SYSTEMS to aid the user (and the
298 operator) in sequencing jobs, accounting,
299 and calling up other utility programs. Operat-
300 ing systems or programs are also called CON-
301 TROL PROGRAMS, SUPERVISORS, EXECU-
302 TIVES, MONITORS, or SYSTEMS SOFTWARE.

303 APPLICATIONS are the problems to which a
304 computer is applied; the names for the most
305 common applications are self-explanatory, but
306 some are not. DATA REDUCTION is the pro-
307 cess of compressing, editing, smoothing, and
308 formatting large quantities of information for
309 human consumption. A SIMULATION is the
310 representation of a real or hypothetical system
311 by a computer process; its function is to indi-
312 cate system performance under various condi-

313 tions by program performance. STOCHASTIC
314 simulations are based on an understanding of
315 the probable behavior of systems. INFORMA-
316 TION RETRIEVAL is the name applied to pro-
317 cesses that recover or locate information in a
318 large collection or data base. An INFORMA-
319 TION MANAGEMENT SYSTEM helps a user
320 maintain a data base, modify it, and get reports
321 from it. Such a system is usually defined as a
322 general-purpose program; this means that it
323 can accommodate a large range of applica-
324 tions. A MANAGEMENT INFORMATION SYS-
325 TEM supplies the data that the management
326 of an organization requires to make decisions
327 and exercise control. A REPORT GENERATOR
328 is a program that allows the user to specify in
329 some simple way the content and format of
330 reports the computer is to produce. PROCESS
331 CONTROL programs are used to monitor and
332 guide machines, particularly those in contin-
333 uous-process industries like oil refining or
334 electronic circuit manufacturing.

335 To RUN a program is to cause it to be per-
336 formed on the computer. Running a program
337 to solve a problem or produce real results (as
338 opposed to debugging) is called a PRODUC-
339 TION RUN. Installations in which the user
340 runs his own job are called OPEN SHOPS. In-
341 stallations that have a group to write the pro-
342 grams for the user are CLOSED SHOPS.
343 Computers are sometimes operated in BATCH-
344 PROCESSING mode: the operator assembles
345 a batch of programs waiting to be run and
346 puts them serially into the computer; output
347 from all the programs is returned in one batch.
348 TURNAROUND TIME is the time between the
349 user's delivering his job to the center and the
350 availability of his output. TIME SHARING is a

351 method of operation by means of which sev-
352 eral JOBS (programs being run) are interleaved,
353 giving the appearance of simultaneous opera-
354 tion. A related concept is MULTI-PROGRAM-
355 MING, which also implies the interleaving of
356 jobs. The intent in multi-programming is more
357 likely to be computer efficiency; in time shar-
358 ing, it is user convenience. MULTI-PROCES-
359 SING is a technique for increasing the effective
360 speed of a computer by adding additional
361 arithmetic units to the system. When several
362 computers are linked together, the one re-
363 sponsible for controlling and scheduling the
364 others is the MASTER: the others are SLAVES.
365 If the system has small computers responsible
366 only for the control of input/output, these are
367 usually called SATELLITES.

368 In many multi-programmed systems, users
369 have terminals that are online. Such terminals
370 may be located far from the computer. This is
371 REMOTE ACCESS. It allows users to interact
372 with the computer on a time scale appropriate
373 for human beings—on the order of a few sec-
374 onds between responses. This capability is
375 called operating in REAL TIME. Using the
376 computer for frequent interaction with users
377 in this way is called an INTERACTIVE mode of
378 computing; if the communication is in words
379 and sentences approaching natural language,
380 it may properly be called CONVERSATIONAL.
381 Sometimes non-interactive work is done by a
382 time-shared computer during idle seconds;
383 these jobs are called BACKGROUND.

384 The capacity of the main memory is always
385 smaller than the capacity of the additional
386 drums and disks. If the computer and its oper-
387 ating system are so designed that some of the
388 memory space on the drums and disks appears
389 to be a direct extension of the main memory,
390 the computer is said to have a VIRTUAL STOR-
391 AGE capacity, which will always be much
392 larger than the real main memory. Virtual
393 storage is usually divided into PAGES, each of
394 which contain a number of words.

395 Like all electronic devices, computers some-
396 times break down. The prevention and correc-
397 tion of such situations is MAINTENANCE.
398 PREVENTIVE MAINTENANCE finds failing
399 components before they actually break down.
400 RELIABILITY is the measure of the frequency
401 of failure of the computer. During DOWN
402 TIME the machine is being maintained or
403 repaired, during UP TIME (or AVAILABLE TIME)
404 it is available for normal productive use. Avail-
405 able time that is not used productively is IDLE
406 TIME.

407 A computer which is small in physical size
408 (about as big as a bread basket), small in price
409 (below $20,000), small in word size (usually 16
410 bits), small in main memory capacity, and
411 small in the number of commands it can ex-
412 ecute is called a MINICOMPUTER. It has all
413 the fundamental characteristics of the largest
414 computer.

GLOSSARY INDEX

Index